INFANTS TODDLERS & PRESCHOOLERS

The Best Resources To Help You Parent

D1709862

A Resource Pathways Guidebook

Seattle, Washington

Editors: Julie Soto, M.S.
Managing Editor:
Lisle Steelsmith, M.A.
Associate Editors and Researchers:
Lillias Bever, Rebecca Bilbao,
Pamela Mauseth, Susan Woodward
Book Design and Production:
Sandra Harner and Kelly Rush
Laing Communications Inc., Redmond, Washington
Printing: Hignell Book Printing, Winnipeg, Manitoba, Canada

Published by Resource Pathways, Inc.
22525 S.E. 64th Place, Suite 253
Issaquah, WA 98027

Publisher's Cataloging-in-Publication

Infants, toddlers, & preschoolers : the best resources to
help you parent / Julie Soto, editor. -- 1st ed.
p. cm. -- (LifeCycles series)
Includes bibliographical references and indexes.
ISBN: 0-9653424-8-4

1. Child care--Bibliography.   2. Parenting--
Bibliography.   I. Soto, Julie.   II. Resource Pathways
(Firm)   III. Title: Infants, toddlers, and preschoolers

Z7164.C5I64 1998   016.649'12
                            QBI98-578

Printed in Canada.

CONTENTS

III. The Single Best Resource For Selected Topics
(This section is arranged by AGE GROUP; within Age Group, by SUBJECT) **65**

INTRODUCTION

THE FINE ART OF PARENTING

"Life affords no greater responsibility, no greater privilege, than the raising of the next generation"

—C. Everett Koop

Those tiny hands and solemn stares, those cries and smiles that tug at your heart . . . these are signals that you have become a parent. But what does it really mean to "become a parent"? In basic terms, it means you have taken on the task of caring for and raising a child to become a contributing member of adult society. It also means that you have embarked on a journey whose destination is not clearly defined; you'll experience days full of new challenges and insights, ending with nights of wonderment and, on occasion, exhaustion.

In many ways, parenting today is characterized by the same challenges and solutions parents have always faced. Nonetheless, parenting today is dramatically different than it was just a generation ago. For example, new research in infant and child development emphasizes the importance of effective parenting in the first three years. These findings, along with new "methods" to handle various parenting situations, require that new decisions be made by new parents. This new body of knowledge, coupled with societal changes, lifestyle trends, and the evolving roles of men and women, mean that some issues facing new families are more complex than they've ever been before.

With close to 75% of men and women returning to work shortly after the birth of their baby, new parents are concerned whether or not their baby's caretaker is truly qualified to offer their child quality care. Working parents need information and advice to help them make informed decisions on care for their baby or child in their absence. Additionally, trying to juggle careers and home life can create anxiety for working parents. This is compounded by guilt they impose on themselves or that others impose on them for placing their child in someone else's care.

On the other hand, some parents choose to take a leave of absence from their job or career and stay home to be the primary caretaker of their child. Not only are family finances impacted, but responsibilities shift for each parent, and confusion can set in as new roles are defined. Stay-at-home parents, too, need information, support, and ideas to make this transition easier and help them use available time and money effectively.

With time at a premium and budgets constrained, parents today want to make wise choices, whether it be the furniture they buy to outfit their nursery, the childcare provider they hire to care for their baby or child, or the way they structure their "spare time" with their child. But no matter what their circumstances are, whether one parent is staying at home with the children or both parents are working, one thing remains constant: parents want the best information available. In short, they want answers to their questions and they want practical, concise guidance that can be digested quickly.

Whether you find yourself with a great support system or you find yourself searching for someone to help you as you parent, resources are available to suit your needs! Our purpose in creating this guidebook is to help you find your way to those resources that can answer your questions and concerns. This guidebook will identify resources that:

- Help you **care for** your child from their birth up to their fifth birthday, and that:

  - Inform you about breastfeeding and children's nutritional needs

  - Help you sort through various approaches to dealing with baby and children's sleep habits and crying

  - Detail necessary equipment and supplies for your baby and child

  - Provide support and encouragement for those who are parenting twins or multiples

  - Present available child care options

- Help you become better informed on how infants, toddlers, and preschoolers **develop**, and that:

  - Explain expectations for babies and children that are age-appropriate

  - Offer advice on how to develop effective discipline philosophies and strategies to deal with children's behavior, whether it be with adults, other children, or siblings

  - Provide age-appropriate activities for your baby or child

  - Offer comparisons of various preschool philosophies and settings

  - Assist you when your child differs markedly from the "norm" and needs special guidance or assistance

- Help you find resources that focus on **parent-to-parent connections** to assist you with your questions, concerns, and need for support

HOW THIS BOOK IS ORGANIZED

During the course of our ongoing research, we've identified the best resources to use to understand the different challenges involved with parenting a young child. We've grouped our recommendations together in **Section II** of this guidebook: "Infants, Toddlers, and Preschoolers: The Best Resources To Help You Parent." Use this section to identify those resources which are best suited to help you understand and manage aspects of parenting that relate to your family's specific needs. We always recommend several resources for each subject area, so you'll have the freedom to choose resources that are convenient for you to find and that meet your specific requirements.

For those who want to focus on the single best resource for **specific age groups** (Infants, Toddlers, Preschoolers, or All Ages) and topics related to that age group, we've grouped a number of outstanding resources together in **Section III**: "The Single Best Resource For Selected Topics." Use this section to find the single best resources that highlight specific age-related topics for each age group. We would encourage you to peruse the recommendations we make in Section II, as well.

Finally, in **Section IV** we've provided a complete listing of all the resources we've reviewed, in a section titled "Resource Reviews." In this section, we've arranged our full-page reviews by subject, so that those who might be interested in a particular subject can review **all** the resources we've found on that subject. Within each subject, these reviews are ranked by Overall Star Rating (1–4 Stars), so that the best resources are always listed first.

We've also provided a variety of indexes, which list all the resources reviewed in this guidebook alphabetically by title, author, publisher, subject, age group, and media type, so that those who might be interested in one resource they've heard about can easily find our full-page review of that particular resource.

At the end of this guidebook, we've also provided a helpful listing of support organizations and other groups you may want to contact for more information.

CONVENTIONS USED

Throughout this guidebook, we've defined important terms as follows:

- **"Infants"** refers to children from birth to the age when they begin walking (about one year of age)

- **"Toddlers"** refers to children from the time they are walking (about one year of age) to age three

- **"Preschoolers"** refers to children from age 3 to age 5 at which time they typically enter into a formal school setting (kindergarten, etc.)

- "Parent" or "parents" refers to biological parents, stepparents, adoptive parents, foster parents, or any other guardians responsible for the care and safety of a child

- "Caregiver" refers to those who provide care for a child during the parents' absence

- "Educator" refers to those who are involved with children in various learning programs

Additionally, picture icons are provided on each full-page resource review to designate the age level to which the resource's information applies. When age classifications overlap within a resource, multiple icons are supplied to illustrate all age groups that are discussed. For example, a resource that discusses both infant and toddler activities will have both an infant icon and a toddler icon presented. Picture icons used are as follows:

 =Infant    =Toddler   =Preschooler

We know you're trying to learn and absorb everything you can about parenting, while trying to raise your child at the same time! Remember, **you aren't alone.** Try to find comfort in knowing that other new parents, too, are doing the best they can to raise a wonderful child they can be proud of. Good luck to you and may your reading prove rewarding!

"Children are our most valuable natural resource"
—Herbert Clark Hoover

MEET RESOURCE PATHWAYS

In this Information Age, we all want to take advantage of the many sources of information available to help us make important decisions or deal with major events we experience. Unfortunately, we don't always know where to find these sources of information. Often, we don't know very much about their quality, value, or relevance. In addition, we often don't know much about the issues we're facing, and as a result don't really know where to begin our learning process.

Resource Pathways' guidebooks solve the problem of "information overload" faced by those who want to learn about a topic of critical importance in their life. Those interested in doing such research typically:

- Don't know what resources are available, particularly those outside traditional print media.

- Don't know where to find most of those resources, particularly since most bookstores stock only a limited selection.

- Can't assess the quality or focus of those resources before spending time and money first finding, then evaluating, and perhaps buying them.

- Don't understand which resources will be particularly useful for each dimension of a multi-dimensional issue. For each aspect of the challenge we're trying to deal with, certain resources will be very helpful, while others may be completely worthless.

This guidebook will help you overcome these hurdles. In this guidebook, you will find that:

- Virtually all available quality resources are reviewed, including those from "high-technology" media like the Internet or CD-ROMs.

- We make a reasoned judgment about the quality of each resource, and decide whether or not a resource should be recommended (roughly 1 in 4 are recommended).

- We define and explain the different issues typically encountered in easy-to-read chapter introductions, and classify each resource we review according to its primary focus.

- Where to buy or how to access each resource is provided, including ISBN numbers for obscure print media, direct order numbers for publishers, and URL "addresses" for sites on the Internet's World Wide Web.

After you have used this guidebook to learn which sources of information are best suited to you, you can then acquire or access those resources knowing that your time and money will be well spent.

Our Quality Standards

Those who turn to Resource Pathways guidebooks find the best sources of information on critical issues having an important impact on their lives. To ensure that we merit the trust placed in our recommendations, we've developed a proven set of quality standards:

- We are independent from the publishers of products we review; we do not accept advertising or compensation of any kind from those companies.

- We employ Editors and Advisory Councils of independent professionals with many years of experience in each subject area we cover. These professionals help ensure that we are kept abreast of developments in the field, and that our evaluations meet their standards for accuracy and relevance.

- We review new products and editions as they become available, so that our guidebooks include the most up-to-date information about products available in various media. We revisit websites on the Internet and the online services frequently, to keep up with changes in those offerings as they are introduced.

We put a great deal of time and effort into reviewing and evaluating each resource carefully. Here's what that process includes:

- Printed Guidebooks: For these resources, we read the book from cover to cover, identify the particular focus taken by each author, and make a judgment about how the book's contents could be best applied. Our judgment about the relative quality of each source is based upon useful content, readability, organization, depth, and style. We make every effort to ensure that the latest editions of books are reviewed, and that no out-of-print resources are included.

- Internet Websites & Online Services: We review websites and online services that have any significant amount of original material related to the subject. Our reviews include judgments about the site's graphic and navigation design, as well as the usefulness of material provided relative to that available in other media. We revisit sites frequently to stay abreast of changes and improvements.

- CD-ROM & Software: We carefully review each facet of each CD, including all branches and multimedia options, and thoroughly test software applications available on disk. Our reviews include judgments about the "cost/benefit" of multimedia additions, as well as the usefulness of the content provided relative to the same offering in other media by the same publisher. We note technical problems in loading or using programs provided.

Because our mission is to help you find your way through this "forest" of information, we also provide you with our recommendations on which resources are best to help you each step of the way (roughly 25% of the resources we review are recommended). Our recommendations are based upon our judgment of value, not only relative to alternatives in the same media, but against **all** available resources regardless of media.

INFANTS, TODDLERS & PRESCHOOLERS: THE BEST RESOURCES TO HELP YOU PARENT

II

INTRODUCTION

This section provides you with our recommendations for resources that will be particularly helpful to you as you raise your child throughout infancy, toddlerhood, and their preschool years. During the process of creating this guidebook, we've classified the resources we've encountered into **four subject areas**, starting with resources focused on taking care of your baby and child, and ending with those resources that provide a useful overview of many of the issues involved with becoming a parent and raising a child. Within two of these four subject areas, we've further classified resources we've reviewed into "sub-categories" that should help you find exactly the right resource for specific concerns or questions. These resources will help you understand what you need to know, whether it be how to soothe baby's cries and help them sleep, how to find appropriate child care, how to toilet train your toddler, ways to find a perfect preschool for your four year old, or activities to share with your child on rainy days.

Each subject area also includes our introduction to the subject and an explanation of its importance to parenting and your child's development, along with details and possible issues involved in each sub-category. For each of the four subject areas and multiple sub-categories, our editors and researchers have picked several resources as "recommended," roughly 25% (1 in 4) of those resources we've reviewed. In making these recommendations, we have attempted to err on the side of providing too many choices rather than too few. In some cases, we have recommended additional resources to broaden representation from different media. Take some time to read the full descriptions and evaluations for each recommended resource carefully; we're certain that you will discover the right resources to best serve your needs.

We also provide several other "views" of the resources we've reviewed. First, in Section III, we provide our recommendations for the single best resource dealing with the same four subjects and sub-categories but organized by **age groups**—infants, toddlers, preschoolers, and all ages. In this way, a parent of a toddler may find the single best resource on a specific age-related topic, such as "Behavior and Discipline."

In Section IV, you'll find full-page reviews of all the resources we've reviewed. These are arranged by subject area and sub-categories as listed in the Table of Contents, then in rank order by their Overall Rating (from 1–4 stars). Finally, in Section V we've provided a number of helpful indexes, with all resources listed by title, author, publisher, principal subject, specific age group, and media. Here, you can find listings of **all** the resources we've reviewed, including those that we haven't recommended in Sections II and III.

PUBLISHER'S NOTE:

In our reviews of websites, we include the current "address" of the website home page or specific page within a website, to facilitate direct access on the Internet. The Internet's World Wide Web is, of course, dynamic; this means that many website/page "addresses" change over time. If you find that an address is outdated, the recommended solution is simple; just delete the last expression within the address and hit the "Enter" or "Return" key again. Here's an example:

http://www.sourcepath.com/cguide/bookorder.html

If this is an outdated address, try this instead:

http://www.sourcepath.com/cguide

This will simply point your browser to a file "further up" in the website's file directory. In most cases, you can follow this procedure until you find yourself at the website's home page (indicated by the phrase ending in ".com" or ".edu" or ".gov", etc.). Usually, you can then find your way back to the specific information (or page) that you were interested in.

RECOMMENDED RESOURCES

I.

CARE

"How can they send us home from the hospital without an owners' manual?" New parents are naturally concerned they won't know how to take care of this new member of their family. They get countless "words of wisdom" from others trying to help. In trying to solve this mystery, parents may venture into a bookstore or a library in search of that elusive complete "how-to manual" only to be overwhelmed at the number of resources available. Where do parents start?

The good news is that there are lots of "owners' manuals" out there, waiting for someone to "drive" them home and be "parked" next to a parent's reading chair. The bad news is that many of them barely meet parents' needs, or fail to answer their questions in a concise and readily digested manner. Recommendations on child care seem to be constantly changing and come from all directions—the medical community, researchers and educators, politicians, and one's own parents.

Prospective parents may find it hard to understand why taking care of a new baby should be so difficult. But as soon as their newborn starts crying, parents generally start panicking, and the louder the cry, the stronger the panic: "What do we do now? Are we doing something wrong?" New and prospective parents are hungry for answers to such questions as:

- How do I choose a pediatrician? How will I know when to call?

- If I'm going to return to work, I will need to find a caregiver; what are my options? How do I make the right choice?

- Should I breastfeed my baby or use a bottle? How will I know if my baby is getting enough nourishment?

- What things do I need to have for my baby? What furniture, what equipment, what clothing, what toys work best?

- My baby is crying! What's wrong? Is she sick, hurt, hungry, too hot, too cold?

- Is my baby sleeping too much, or perhaps too little?

- How and when do I bathe my new baby?

- How do I hold him or her? Is there such thing as holding a baby too much?

Parents of older babies and young children also have concerns, but their concerns differ. They focus more on their child's daily habits—eating, sleeping, hygiene, dental care—along with whether or not their child is "normal" in terms of their physical development. As their child begins to explore his or her environment, parents also worry about poisons and

I. Care

injuries. They want easily accessed information on how to take care of minor cuts and scrapes, along with how to handle major emergency situations.

Taking care of children requires that we understand the choices to be made in a wide variety of issues. These issues typically involve decisions often made during one's pregnancy, or shortly after childbirth:

- Breastfeeding

- Choosing a Caregiver

- Taking Care of Twins and Multiples

- Equipment and Supplies

Other decisions are often made after parents and their newborn get settled in, or after baby grows older and approaches school age; these issues typically include the following:

- Crying and Soothing

- Nutrition and Eating

- Sleeping

In the paragraphs below, you'll be introduced to some of the issues you'll encounter in each of these areas. Following this introduction, you'll find our recommendations for resources that can help parents deal with these (and other) issues.

Breastfeeding

Recent scientific studies and findings emphasize the benefits involved with breastfeeding a baby and child. Some studies suggest that infants who have been breastfed have less chance of developing allergies, cancer, and other serious illnesses later on in life; others suggest that breastfeeding may even be good for a baby's brain development, their interpersonal relationships, and their ability to comfort others and themselves. Breastfeeding satisfies a baby's inherent need to suck for comfort and security, and contributes to a gentle introduction into their new world.

Some women may have already decided while they were pregnant that they are going to breastfeed their baby. Others may be unsure whether or not they want to nurse their baby, or how long they will do it. Many prospective mothers want to nurse their infants but also know they will be returning to their jobs. Finally, how does a father fit into the picture? Without information to support him, a father may feel left out of the bond growing between mother and baby. It is imperative that fathers understand

1. Care

the nature and benefits of breastfeeding and how their support for a mother's decision to breastfeed is important.

The resources that we recommend can help you decide whether or not breastfeeding will be right for you. We've included a number of resources that will answer your questions from "How do I get started breastfeeding my baby?" to "How do I wean my child?" Many are written by lactation consultants specializing in breastfeeding. Many of these resources address special situations, such as returning to work while your baby is still young and breastfeeding, breastfeeding an adopted baby, how to breastfeed while your baby is in intensive care or if she or he has a handicap, how to nurse a toddler, and even how to breastfeed twins! These resources offer the support and information new fathers and mothers need to make breastfeeding a positive experience for the whole family.

Choosing A Caregiver

Many parents have concluded they will be needing childcare at some point, while others may still be weighing this decision as they research their choices. Options for parents to choose from can range from one-on-one care in a parent's home, to a facility that houses children from infancy to school-age. If parents wish to have in-home care, they can hire a nanny, a student from another country (commonly known as an "Au Pair"), or solicit help from a parent or relative. Parents who wish a home-like setting (but not necessarily their own home) may consider a family home center in which children of varying ages are cared for by one or more childcare workers. Another option is, of course, childcare centers that are set up as a business, employing both trained and untrained staff. Finally, some employers address parents' needs for childcare and include a workplace childcare center for their employees' children, sometimes subsidized by the organization.

Regardless of which choice parents eventually make, there are a number of issues to keep in mind during their decision process. As parents search for quality care, the resources we recommend will help parents weigh the pros and cons of the various childcare situations and settings that are available. These resources offer application forms, ideas for interview questions, forms for screening applicants, tips on how to conduct criminal record checks, tax information, descriptions of your responsibilities as an employer, agreements and contracts, and more. They also offer advice and support to help parents and children through this transition. Be sure to read the full-page review of any resource you select to be sure it covers all the facets of this decision that pertain to your family's needs.

Taking Care Of Twins And Multiples

Whether it's a surprise to parents or not, the prospects of caring for more than one baby is a challenge many parents are not prepared to deal with. While the impact on a family that results from introducing one baby into their life is amazing, bringing home two or more babies will make for more complications. As twins or multiples get older, the challenges and joys parents face are understandably different than parents with one child. For example, parents of toddlers must figure out strategies to deal with their children's explorations when each goes off in a different direction. They might also be facing the how-tos of toilet training two children at the same time. The natural rivalry that twins or multiples may exhibit may also pose new concerns for parents. Disciplining two of the same age and developmental level can also present a challenge to parents.

Fortunately, we have found several resources that address these concerns and other questions parents may have. These resources are usually written from the authors' firsthand experiences with twins or multiples and/or incorporate other parents' feedback and advice. Having twins or multiples can be a challenge, but using the resources we recommend should ease the process for you and help you master this challenge.

Equipment & Supplies

Many parents are faced with tight budgets, yet innumerable equipment and supplies are suggested by well-meaning friends. Which ones are really necessary, which ones will last, and for how long? If parents have ventured into the baby supply section of any store, they may find their choices overwhelming. Fortunately, there are resources available to help you make some sound decisions. We've listed some resources that can not only tell you what you REALLY need but also compare one manufacturer's product with another. Some offer advice on how to find items for free or for a relatively inexpensive price. Some resources also include information about relative safety, pricing information, and manufacturer contact information.

Check out a few of our recommendations. Whether you are shopping for your new baby, a friend's shower present, or your future grandchild, chances are these resources will save you money.

Crying & Soothing

"Why does my baby keep crying? What's wrong?" It's rare to find a baby that doesn't cry, because instinctively babies know that is their primary way of communicating their needs. This distress signal is designed by nature so that parents can't ignore it. Responding to a baby's cries, figuring out what they need, and finding ways to soothe them can be a tiresome yet rewarding proposition. Babies cry for many reasons, and their cries have definite meanings (pain, needs changing, bored, hungry, and so on). And then there's "colic," for which scientists and doctors have yet to find a definitive cause. Babies with colic typically cry continually for more than three hours a day on more than three days within a week. Colic often begins a few weeks after birth and continues until the baby is about three months old. Knowing these bouts of crying will end at some juncture, however, doesn't help alleviate parents' frustrations and exhaustion. "What can we do to help our baby (and us) through this?"

Fortunately, several resources we recommend focus on the baby's primary means of communicating, their cries. These resources explain the importance of responding to a baby's cries, along with what the different cries sound like and what they mean. You will find tips on how to survive a "colic phase" that makes your baby miserable and fussy. If you are breastfeeding, many of these resources offer nursing tips that can help if your baby is fussy at the breast. These resources also briefly address the disadvantages and advantages of several "sleep trainers" that believe in a step-by-step process of letting babies cry themselves to sleep (for more in-depth information on the subject of nighttime waking/crying, look to other recommended resources in the section following entitled "Sleeping").

Nutrition & Eating

"When do I start my baby on solids?" Surprisingly, this simple question has become a hot topic. In the past, it was suggested that babies would sleep better at night if they were fed solids as soon as possible. However, recent studies have shown that this may not be the case. Experts now suggest that, because of babies' immature digestive systems, parents should delay starting their baby on solids until they are 4–6 months old and certain readiness signs begin to appear, such as interest in what parents are eating, attempts to grab others' food, lessening of the tongue-thrust reaction (whereby food is projected back out), and more. Starting as late as possible helps combat certain food allergies and digestive problems, some suggest.

Once parents begin to give their baby solids, they can choose between manufactured baby food and homemade. Recently, nutritionists have publicized the extent to which manufactured baby foods contain additives and fillers, and conversely stressed the ease by which parents can make and store their own more nutritive food. To address this need, authors with backgrounds in cooking have compiled baby food recipes along with basic nutritional needs of babies, tips on how to prepare food, and ways to make and store larger quantities. Other authors have followed suit and explored recipes to get toddlers and preschoolers (often known for their discriminating or "picky" eating habits) to try healthy snacks, main courses, desserts, and more.

Cookbooks involve a personal adventure since not everyone's tastes are the same. We've tried to recommend those resources that offer recipes that not only use fairly common household ingredients but are also nutritious for growing bodies and are easily prepared. After all, feeding your child is important, but spending all day on a recipe as likely to be met with a "yum" as it is with a "yuck" may not be a good idea!

Sleeping

"Should I let my baby cry it out or should I pick her up and help her go back to sleep?" Who would have thought that the gentle act of helping a child go to sleep would create such controversy? "Sleep trainers" suggest that babies' cries (or children's) be ignored for progressive periods of time each night, with the parents responding only after the timer goes off; this way, a baby will learn to soothe themselves. This approach has been rejected by those who believe in responding to all of baby's cries, simply because a baby needs to know that their needs are important and that their parents are there to help them. Sleep trainers stress that these "attached" parents will keep their child dependent and wear themselves out unnecessarily by constantly responding to baby's cries. To this, "attachment parenting" proponents reply that a baby IS dependent and adults need to change their sleep habits temporarily instead of insisting babies and children do so prematurely. One camp says that it won't do babies any harm to cry by themselves, while the other camp says that babies will learn that when they cry, it doesn't matter. To add to this confusion, other child experts argue the advantages of the "family bed" or "shared sleep" whereby parents and baby (or child) share the same bed with one another. To judge any method, parents need to look closely at the method's basis in objective research, and assess how well the method supports their own beliefs.

We've recommended those resources that we believe are backed by solid research and reflect undisputed facts about the developmental stages of babies and young children. Be sure to read the full one-page review of any resource we recommend to ensure it will meet your needs and answer specific questions you may have.

All-Inclusive

During the course of our research, we've reviewed "all-inclusive" resources designed to help new parents survive those first few days, weeks, months, and years as they learn to take care of their new baby and child. These resources detail a child's general development along with suggestions of how parents can promote those milestones in growth. The "how-tos" of caring for, cleaning, diapering, and feeding a newborn are explained, as well as the basics for how to deal with a child's illnesses, hygiene, comforting, sleep issues, feeding decisions, and more. Information is given on how to take care of a baby from the minute they are born until they reach school age. Parents will find tips on how to deal with anxious moments, along with how to decide when to enlist the help of their baby's doctor.

1. Care

Our recommendations for all-inclusive guides include those resources whose recommendations are up-to-date, those which include numerous how-to photographs or illustrations, and those who present an objective parenting style so parents can decide important issues for themselves. Any one of these recommended guides will be a worthwhile companion to any new mother or father as they struggle to learn the fine art of parenting. Although all-inclusive guides do a tremendous service by presenting much information in one convenient package, they often cannot offer in-depth information in any one area. Whenever you find you need help in a specific area, check out the recommendations we have made for these specific topics.

To help focus your search for answers, we've divided our recommendations into these eight categories:

Think of parenting in terms of traveling a long distance by car. As you're driving, you will encounter advertising and conflicting information, quick decisions to be made, and destinations that change. But, with the best "owners' manuals" and a couple of detailed maps by your side, you can develop the confidence and skills to take care of any adjustments and emergencies along the way. Although being a parent is the most difficult job you will ever have, your journey is one whose destinations will bring you smiles, laughter, and joy.

I. Care

Recommended Resources—Breastfeeding

Title:	**Breastfeeding Your Baby**
Overall Rating:	★★★★
Media Type:	Print
Author/Editor:	Sheila Kitzinger
Short Description:	Believing that breastfeeding involves a combination of your feelings about your baby and your body along with the technical how-tos, this book strives to offer information on everything women need to know about breastfeeding. Suggestions, advice, and numerous color or black and white photographs help illustrate techniques and address problems. Also discussed are issues centered around family dynamics, returning to work, and more.

■ **Read The Full Review Of This Resource On Page 101.**

Title:	**Mothering Your Nursing Toddler**
Overall Rating:	★★★★
Media Type:	Print
Author/Editor:	Norma Jane Bumgarner
Short Description:	Believing that nursing plays a great role in a child's ability to grow up, Bumgarner focuses on the breastfeeding relationship in terms of the child's developmental needs. Advice and information is given on the "whys" of breastfeeding (for mother and for child), the "hows" of nursing (marital concerns, night nursing, mother's health, etc.), the changing dynamics of the breastfeeding relationship (to age 4+), and various ways to approach weaning.

■ **Read The Full Review Of This Resource On Page 102.**

Title:	**Nursing Mother, Working Mother**
Subtitle:	The Essential Guide For Breastfeeding And Staying Close To Your Baby After You Return To Work
Overall Rating:	★★★★
Media Type:	Print
Author/Editor:	Gale Pryor
Short Description:	Extending a section of her other book, *Nursing Your Baby*, Pryor discusses how to combine work and breastfeeding. Within its 184 pages, this seven chapter book highlights the whys and hows of breastfeeding along with a plea to change workplace attitudes toward motherhood. Three chapters specifically focus on the transition from new motherhood to work including maternity leave, getting ready (supplies, finding care, etc.), and returning.

■ **Read The Full Review Of This Resource On Page 103.**

I. Care

Title:	**Momness Center**
Subtitle:	The Place For Information And Inspiration For Moms And Moms-To-Be
Overall Rating:	★★★
Media Type:	Internet
Short Description:	This site, developed by a manufacturer of baby formula, offers you information on breastfeeding, descriptions of the changes a woman goes through during her pregnancy (in journal format), how the fetus develops until birth, how pregnancy affects a woman's body (skin, hair, nails), and more. Breastfeeding information includes rationale, positions, how to breastfeed and return to work, and more.

■ **Read The Full Review Of This Resource On Page 107.**

Recommended Resources—Choosing A Caregiver

Title:	**Child Care That Works**
Subtitle:	A Parent's Guide To Finding Quality Child Care
Overall Rating:	★★★★
Media Type:	Print
Author/Editor:	Eva Cochran and Mon Cochran
Short Description:	How to find quality child care is the focus of this 355 page book. The six parts of this guide deal separately with the various options that are available, the possible emotional reactions children and parents may have to child care, ways to build a partnership with a caregiver, how much to pay, and how to become an advocate for quality care. Checklists, forms, and organization contact information are given in the appendices.

■ **Read The Full Review Of This Resource On Page 116.**

Title:	**Complete Nanny Guide (The)**
Subtitle:	Solutions To Parents' Questions About Hiring And Keeping An In-Home Caregiver
Overall Rating:	★★★★
Media Type:	Print
Author/Editor:	Cora Hilton Thomas
Short Description:	This book contains information on finding and choosing appropriate in-home care. Chapter topics in this 154 guide include finding the right person, costs, interviewing, screening, keeping a nanny, filing government forms, using a placement agency, and more. One chapter focuses on finding care for children that have special needs. Appendices contain numerous forms and checklists (criminal background release forms, tax and government forms, etc.).

■ **Read The Full Review Of This Resource On Page 117.**

I. Care

Recommended Resources—Care For Twins & Multiples

Title:	**Mothering Twins (Print/Novotny)**
Subtitle:	Having, Raising, And Loving Babies Who Arrive In Groups
Overall Rating:	★★★
Media Type:	Print
Author/Editor:	Pamela Patrick Novotny

Short Description:

■ **Read The Full Review Of This Resource On Page 126.**

The author strives to offer "an upbeat, practical guide to raising and loving babies that arrive in groups of two or more." This 324 page book contains medical, psychological, and sociological findings on all aspects of caring for two or more children simultaneously. Chapter topics include: the logistics of caring for multiples after birth, to their first year, and beyond; mothercare; family adjustments; premature births; and more.

Recommended Resources—Equipment & Supplies

Title:	**Baby Bargains**
Overall Rating:	★★★★
Media Type:	Print
Author/Editor:	Denise Fields and Alan Fields

Short Description:

■ **Read The Full Review Of This Resource On Page 129.**

This book seeks to answer the big question—"Can we afford a baby?" It is a 333 page guide full of suggestions and contacts for how to save money on nursery furniture, clothing, toys, equipment, carseats, strollers, and much more. Reviews are given on name brand items along with a rating system (four stars). Information is independent of manufacturer input and is based upon the authors' experiences and the parents they interviewed.

1. Care

Recommended Resources—Crying & Soothing

Title:	**Crying Baby, Sleepless Nights**
Overall Rating:	★★★★
Media Type:	Print
Author/Editor:	Sandy Jones

Short Description

■ **Read The Full Review Of This Resource On Page 133.**

The meanings behind an infant's cries and the importance of a parent's response are outlined in this 162 page book written by an authority on crying babies. Various techniques are presented for each of 16 different cries along with coping tips for parents. The author debunks the myth of babies sleeping through the night including current researchers' sleep-training methods. Colic is addressed along with ways for parents to handle it.

Title:	**Fussy Baby (The)**
Subtitle:	How To Bring Out The Best In Your High-Need Child
Overall Rating:	★★★★
Media Type:	Print
Author/Editor:	William Sears, M.D.

Short Description

■ **Read The Full Review Of This Resource On Page 134.**

"A fussy baby can bring out the best and the worst in a parent. This book is designed to bring out the best," states Sears in his introduction. Within this 192 page book, you'll find explanations of why babies fuss, what you can do to soothe them, how to discipline the high need child, and more. The book's premise is based upon a parenting style where babies and caregivers best form a secure relationship by being very connected to each other's cues.

Recommended Resources—Nutrition & Eating

Title:	**Healthy Baby Meal Planner (The)**
Subtitle:	Mom-Tested, Child-Approved Recipes For Your Baby And Toddler
Overall Rating:	★★★★
Media Type:	Print
Author/Editor:	Annabel Karmel

Short Description

■ **Read The Full Review Of This Resource On Page 136.**

This book is intended for parents who want "their babies and toddlers to eat well and enjoy their food," with fresh food, low animal fat, and low salt or sugars. Recipes are broken down into the following age groups: four to six months, six to nine months, nine to twelve months, and toddlers. Seven-day meal planning guides are also included for each age group. An index cross-references ingredients to other recipes containing that ingredient.

I. Care

Title:	**Small Helpings**
Subtitle:	A Complete Guide To Feeding Babies, Toddlers And Young Children
Overall Rating:	★★★★
Media Type:	Print
Author/Editor:	Annabel Karmel
Short Description:	This book contains over 120 easy, quick recipes using fresh, natural ingredients. Included are recipes for babies, toddlers, and small children with emphasis placed on cooking for the whole family. Recipes cover occasions and meals (healthy snacks, "fast foods," lunch boxes, parties, etc.) and many can be frozen for a ready meal. Nutritional advice is given with the intent that a pattern of healthy eating can be established for young children.

■ **Read The Full Review Of This Resource On Page 137.**

Title:	**Baby Let's Eat**
Overall Rating:	★★★
Media Type:	Print
Author/Editor:	Rena Coyle with Patricia Messing
Short Description:	Within this 128 page book, parents will find nutritional information and recipes for babies and toddlers. Nutritional basics, suggested daily servings and serving sizes for children ages 1 to 3 years, food preparation methods, and more are provided. The recipes are divided by ages for children 6 to 12 months, 12 to 18 months, 18 to 24 months, and 24 to 36 months. A weekly meal planning chart is given for each age group along with 20–25 recipes.

■ **Read The Full Review Of This Resource On Page 138.**

Title:	**Sugar-Free Toddlers**
Subtitle:	Over 100 Recipes Plus Sugar Ratings For Store-Bought Foods
Overall Rating:	★★★
Media Type:	Print
Author/Editor:	Susan Watson
Short Description:	This 170 page book offers over 100 recipes for toddlers. All recipes exclude refined sugars and flours and are high in nutritional value. Information on introducing new foods is given as well as freezing techniques, ingredient substitutions, and more. Evaluation charts are provided for store-bought foods listing calories, type of sweetener used, a toddler rating, and comments. Although these are sugar-free recipes, they are not for children with diabetes.

■ **Read The Full Review Of This Resource On Page 141.**

1. Care

Recommended Resources—Sleeping

Title:	**Family Bed (The)**
Subtitle:	An Age Old Concept In Child Rearing
Overall Rating:	★★★
Media Type:	Print
Author/Editor:	Tine Thevenin

Short Description:

■ **Read The Full Review Of This Resource On Page 147.**

This book explores the concept of shared family sleep. It explores the historical, psychological, and cultural dimensions of a practice that has been in use since the "dawn of time," but which has fallen by the wayside in the last 150 years. Using persuasive arguments and first-person accounts of real families who share sleep, the author builds a case for the practical and psychological benefits of "the family bed."

Title:	**Nighttime Parenting**
Subtitle:	How To Get Your Baby And Child To Sleep
Overall Rating:	★★★
Media Type:	Print
Author/Editor:	William Sears, M.D.

Short Description:

■ **Read The Full Review Of This Resource On Page 148.**

Sears wrote this guide to answer the question, "Should I let my child cry it out at night, or console my crying child?" Using research findings and the results from a questionnaire given to patients, Sears addresses this question within the book's 17 chapters. Topics focus on: baby vs. adult sleep, where baby should sleep, night-waking, sleep disorders, SIDS, demands of the high need child, and more.

I. Care

Recommended Resources—All Inclusive

Title:	**Babysense**
Subtitle:	A Practical And Supportive Guide To Baby Care
Overall Rating:	★★★★
Media Type:	Print
Author/Editor:	Frances Wells Burck
Short Description:	In its 2nd edition, this baby care guide was conceived by a first-time mother who felt that other mothers could benefit from a book combining emotional support with practical know-how. Drawing on mothers' responses to a questionnaire, this book combines anecdotes and advice for everything from dealing with the transition into motherhood to nutrition and feeding, and to other matters of everyday care for the first year of your baby's life.

■ Read The Full Review Of This Resource On Page 153.

Title:	**Your Pregnancy, Your Newborn**
Subtitle:	The Complete Guide For Expectant And New Mothers
Overall Rating:	★★★★
Media Type:	CD-ROM
Short Description:	Developed by the editors of *PARENTING* magazine, this CD-ROM focuses on pregnancy topics and a newborn baby's needs. Pregnancy issues include how to plan for pregnancy, a month-by-month description of pregnancy, and labor & delivery. Discussions about a newborn's care focus on the first few weeks and "Life With Baby." Advice is given on how to adapt to the changes, how to take care of a baby, and how to seek childcare.

■ Read The Full Review Of This Resource On Page 154.

Title:	**You And Your Newborn Baby**
Subtitle:	A Guide To The First Months After Birth
Overall Rating:	★★★★
Media Type:	Print
Author/Editor:	Linda Todd, M.P.H.
Short Description:	This 134 page book answers many of the practical questions parents have about the first months after a baby is born. i.e. questions both about themselves and their baby. Secondly, it explores the emotional adjustment parents make as they incorporate a baby into their lives and encourages them to build their own support networks.

■ Read The Full Review Of This Resource On Page 155.

2.

GROWTH AND LEARNING

"They grow up so fast!" One moment a baby is crying indiscriminately, the next they need consoling about their "owie." A baby awkwardly grabs at the mobile in their crib; before you know it, they're steering their tricycle in circles round the park. Childhood is but a fleeting period compared to a lifetime, but their experiences and interactions during these formative years will have effects lasting the rest of their lives.

Child development experts place great importance on the first three years of a child's life. This period offers opportunities to substantially impact a young child's future abilities, skills, attitudes, personality, social interactions with others, their way of looking at the world, and their self-esteem. The latest research shows that the quality of care and variety of experiences given to a child during the first three years contributes substantially to their brain development. Neglecting a child's needs and their inherent quest for answers to make sense of their world may have irreversible effects. How do parents begin to fulfill this overwhelming responsibility? Their first step is to gain an understanding of their child's development process.

Child Development

Most parents understand well-known developmental milestones such as "they'll be walking at one, talking at two." Although children's rates of development vary from one child to the next, each child does follow a certain progression **physically**; that is, they progress from lying down to rolling over, sitting up, pulling up to stand, standing, walking, running, climbing, and so on. Their fine motor skills (eye-hand coordination) progress from seeing a confusing field of objects, to seeing one desired object and intentionally trying to grasp it with their whole hand. From there, babies progress to finger control as they develop their "pincer grasp" and begin to manipulate smaller objects. Eventually, young children will be able to coordinate all of these efforts as they learn to cut with scissors, write their own name, and pick up bugs.

However, some parents, preoccupied with their child's physical development, fail to realize that their child develops in other ways at the same time. For example, children's **language** development follows another sequence. It starts with a baby's cry that communicates his or her needs, and progresses to smaller units of sound (babbling). Then one word utterances begin to take shape, and so on, until children are speaking sentences that adults can fully comprehend.

In addition, children's **emotional** patterns of responding to situations and others are being developed and refined from birth: "Should I be fearful of this new situation or should I be confident? Is it okay to be mad, sad, or frustrated? If I do something naughty, do my mommy and daddy still love me? What kind of things do I do that make people like me?"

2. Growth And Learning

During this crucial period of time, children's **cognitive** abilities are also developing by leaps and bounds. Children are quickly forming, adapting, and refining concepts in their brain to make sense of their environment. They work toward distinguishing the differences between similar things—"is this a cat or a dog?" They work toward understanding the relationship between things and how these things are organized in their world—"a cat and a dog are both animals." And children actively work toward understanding cause-and-effect relationships and figuring out how things work . . . much to our chagrin when we find something other than a videotape in the VCR.

Children also develop socially, going from a "me-centered" universe to an "us-centered" universe. Their first interactions concentrate on how to get their needs met with their parent or caregiver. Then, as they play with others, they continue to develop their social interaction skills. Initially, children may play in the same vicinity as other children but not actually participate with them (parallel play). Eventually, children actively engage in fantasy play and games with their peers—"you be the mommy, I'll be the baby." As they experience more social interactions, children better understand appropriate ways of responding to friends, adults, and strangers.

Development, however, does not happen in a vacuum, as both scientific research and common sense would dictate. The impact parents and caregivers have on a child's development has been demonstrated over and over again through positive and negative examples. A child's growth and learning in their first five years, when properly guided by parents and caregivers, will afford any child the best possible start in life.

In the pages that follow, we have selected recommended resources that offer parents an excellent background in child development. Some of these resources focus on a specific age group's development, while others focus on the entire period from birth to five years of age. Be sure to read the full-page review of any recommended resource, to be sure it will be the best resource to address your family's specific needs and questions.

By knowing what is developmentally appropriate and inappropriate at any given stage or age, adults will have a better grasp on how to address specific situations such as discipline, sibling relationships, and toilet training to name a few. Once a child's general development is understood, parents can also choose activities that can capitalize on their child's skills and interests rather than frustrating or boring their child. This knowledge can then be projected into the child's "formal learning environment" as parents seek to determine which preschool program best fits the needs of their child and their parenting approach.

Beyond those resources we've identified as essential to building a solid understanding of child development, we have also recommended resources in this section to assist parents as they tackle other important parenting issues, including the following:

2. Growth And Learning

- Behavior & Discipline
- Sibling Relationships
- Toilet Training
- Age-Appropriate Activities
- Choosing A Preschool
- Special Circumstances

Behavior & Discipline

"How can I get my child to behave?" As a child struggles with their growing drive for independence and autonomy, they invariably test their limits, as well as parents' patience and resolve. But discipline is not about control, at least not parent-control. As one researcher pointed out, "Where did we ever get the crazy idea that in order to make children do better, first we have to make them feel worse?" Children will naturally make mistakes, sometimes by accident, sometimes intentionally. The long-term goal of discipline is not to make children pay for their mistakes. It is not an opportunity to show who is the boss and in charge. The long-range goals of discipline should be **independence** (to make one's own informed decisions), **responsibility** (for one's actions), and **self-control** (to learn by one's efforts). Most child development experts believe that discipline should be another arena for parents to teach children how to make good decisions, live with consequences, and problem-solve.

In our research, we found that the resources we reviewed typically fall somewhere along the continuum of three different parenting styles (authoritarian, permissive, democratic), each of which approach discipline differently. Some offer a style that places the parent in complete command: the child is told to behave "because I said so." Others place the child in complete control: the parents say "do what you want because we love you." The resources we have found that embody long-range goals of discipline, however, treat children's mistakes not as punitive opportunities but as a shared learning process. Children learn that there are natural and logical consequences to their choices; they learn that if they make a mistake, they must then figure out a way to solve their problem. In this approach, parents are not placed in an adversarial role but are considered "facilitators" of this process. The child's behavior doesn't place parents and child at odds with each other, but simply extends the learning relationship to other contexts.

The excellent resources we have recommended in this section differentiate between developmental issues and intentional actions: for example, a toddler's natural curiosity to play with an "off-limits" object versus a preschooler's act of intentionally grabbing something to gain attention. These resources will ease parents' frustrations as they are offered strategies, tips, and constructive advice about handling discipline problems such as hitting playmates, not picking up toys, not getting ready for bedtime, and more.

2. Growth And Learning

Sibling Relationships

As parents introduce a new baby or child into the family, new questions arise. Methods for helping children adjust to their new brother or sister vary from one child to the next and from one age group to the next. Parents wonder when they should start this adaptation process. They wonder how they'll be able to handle the stress, how they should delegate responsibility for solving sibling problems, and how they can keep their sanity intact as concerns arise. Resources we recommend in this section address these issues, and other questions including:

- What is the recommended age spacing between siblings?

- When should the older child meet the new sibling: at birth, later at the hospital, or when the new baby comes home?

- When siblings vie for parents' attention, should parents step in, back off, or expect the older child to behave most responsibly?

- How can parents win the "fairness" game?

- If an older sibling is ready for preschool or childcare at this time, will separation from the home with a new baby be a positive experience or contribute to the older child's sense of displacement?

Whether children must face having to share their parents with other children through birth, remarriage, adoption, or foster care, excellent resources exist to offer great insights to help ease this adjustment for children and parents.

Toilet Training

This is a parenting issue that continues to be controversial. Some experts claim that toilet training should begin before a child turns one, while others claim that training should definitely be finished before children enter the challenges of the "terrible twos," when they begin to demand that parents relinquish control. Most child development experts, however, believe that toilet training, or what is now considered by some to be "toilet learning," should begin when children have reached certain readiness milestones, such as being aware of the elimination process and expressing it in words ("potty," "wet," etc.). Other readiness signs include disliking wet or soiled diapers, staying dry for several hours, waking up dry after a nap, being anxious to please parents, being able to pull their clothes off quickly, and of course, asking to use the toilet!

While some toilet teaching/learning methods insist that children can learn to use the toilet early, this is considered by critics to be a battle that parents will not win, and which may negatively impact a child's self-esteem and need for independence. Unfortunately, many parents feel pressured to get their child toilet-trained before their child is ready. This is partly due to past practices and partly due to the inability or unwillingness of some preschools or childcare centers to accept a diapered child into the facility's program.

Once again, if parents are properly equipped with the developmental information they need to understand their child's growth and learning, they will be best able to make informed decisions about this important rite of passage in their child's life. The resources we have included here discuss readiness signs, the equipment needed, how to ease your child into the process, how and when to reward your child, how to deal with accidents, how to toilet train your child at night, how to deal with bedwetting, and more.

Age-Appropriate Activities

Nothing is more fun than finding an activity to do with a child . . . unless that activity frustrates them, bores them to tears, or involves too much preparation. Knowing the progression of a child's development will better serve parents as they work toward finding age-appropriate activities to do with their child. Since children are working at different skills at different ages, activities that would be done with an infant will naturally be different than activities that will be done with a preschooler. Some will overlap. Much of it involves trial and error.

Infants respond well to activities that promote touching, bonding, soothing, and security. Toddlers, on the other hand, want to impact and control their environment. Activities might include things that can be manipulated, taken apart, and put together. Preschoolers crave imaginative play. They engage in role-play and imaginative play with their peers, taking turns being the important people in their daily lives or characters from books or movies.

If activities are introduced at a time when children are not developmentally ready, either the child will get frustrated and give up, or the parent will wonder why they bothered to begin with. It is important to extend one's knowledge of child development to include the variety of activity resources that exist. We have recommended some excellent resources that will not only stimulate your child but also motivate you to try other activities. Many of these recommended resources include various subjects, involve simple or inexpensive materials, concentrate on a given skill or concept (eye-hand coordination), and include ways to extend the activity if it was a success. Most important, these activities are open-ended, focusing on the process and not the product; there are no right or wrong ways for the child to participate. This leads to success and the wonderful feeling of mastery.

2. Growth And Learning

Choosing A Preschool

Finding that perfect match between a preschool and a parenting style can be either a painful process or an exciting one. As parents explore this new avenue for their child's growing independence and self-sufficiency, they may feel overwhelmed at what they discover. The various programs to choose from either subscribe to one expert's theory of child development (Waldorf, Montessori, Piagetian), or offer a more generalized approach combining various philosophies. Programs vary in their intent: some stress academics and kindergarten preparedness, while others focus on children's need for play and learning by discovery. What programs are best for three and four year olds? That is a question every parent needs to answer based upon their individual parenting approach and their child's developmental level.

Some experts discuss the merits of children working at their own individual pace, while others stress the importance of working cooperatively with others. Some authorities believe that children should be given an advanced start on academics and can be taught to read at an early age, while others state that this contributes to "educational burn-out" when the child gets into school. The resources we have selected illustrate the pros and cons of the various programs that are available. What to look for, what to ask, how to help your child make the transition to school, and how to maintain good communications between teacher and parent are all topics addressed by these resources.

Special Circumstances

Understanding the course of "normal" child development need not preclude an understanding of what is not "normal." Parents may find themselves facing different concerns at different times; for example, as some parents struggle with a challenging or strong-willed child, they may become aware that their child exhibits certain behaviors that "normal" discipline advice does not address. Other parents may worry that their child has learning disabilities or physical development delays. Some parents may notice that their child's emotional and social development seem to have reached a crisis point as their child becomes excessively angry, withdrawn, or depressed. And many parents must help their child struggle through the effects of divorce, separation, or loss of a loved one while others must deal with their child's reactions to abuse.

In this section, we've included several excellent resources that offer parents comfort, information, and constructive suggestions on how to tackle these difficult situations. Many resources offer a combined approach that take into account the effects of heredity, parenting style, and environment as the basis of many "disorders." These supportive resources will reassure and enlighten parents and caregivers about the symptoms of specific childhood disorders and present the latest information on appropriate treatments. Some of the following childhood disorders are included within these resources: ADHD, learning disabilities, childhood depression, social phobia/shyness, generalized anxiety disorder, enuresis/bedwetting, Tourette syndrome, eating disorders, schizophrenia, conduct disorder, autism, fetal alcohol syndrome/effect, and others. As always, be sure to read the full one-page review of any resource to be sure that it will meet your family's specific needs.

All-Inclusive

In this section, we have included some additional resources that focus on how children generally grow and learn. These resources may not include all of the topics mentioned above, and they may not necessarily go into the specific "how-tos" of subjects like toilet training. But they can, however, offer parents a wonderful overview of how an infant develops into a young child and how parents can make that a positive experience for all. Use these resources to gain an understanding of the various developmental changes and learning that your child will undergo. As your parenting skills and style develop alongside your child, an all-inclusive guide can not only help answer your general questions but help you appreciate the magnitude of this adventure. All-inclusive guides, by their very nature, are useful in presenting the big picture but usually don't offer in-depth information in any one area. Whenever you find you need help in a specific area, check other recommendations we have made for topics we've identified.

As in the previous section, we've divided our resource recommendations into several categories to help focus your search for answers:

Remember, parenting is an adventure! Although the scenery continues to change along the way, the trip should be one that brings forth mutual learning, understanding, comfort, enjoyment, and memories to cherish and share.

2. Growth And Learning

Recommended Resources—Child Development

Title:	**Touchpoints**
Subtitle:	Your Child's Emotional And Behavioral Development
Overall Rating:	★★★★
Media Type:	Print
Author/Editor:	T. Berry Brazelton, M.D.

Short Description:

■ **Read The Full Review Of This Resource On Page 162.**

Whereas most books focus on the physical development of a child, this book seeks to provide parents with an understanding of the emotional and behavioral development of the child as well. Broken up into three parts, this book addresses "touchpoints" (those predictable times that occur before a surge of rapid growth), challenges, and allies in a child's development.

Title:	**Touchpoints, Volume 2**
Subtitle:	The First Month Through The First Year
Overall Rating:	★★★★
Media Type:	Videotape

Short Description:

■ **Read The Full Review Of This Resource On Page 163.**

Brazelton's 45 minute videotape focuses on the emotional, cognitive, and motor development of babies from one month to 15 months. Five different families are showcased along with their frustrations, concerns, and joys. More than fifteen "touchpoints" are illustrated and explained sequentially through the tape. Touchpoints are, as Brazelton defines them, "periods of time that precede a rapid growth in learning for both child and parent."

Title:	**Emotional Life Of The Toddler (The)**
Overall Rating:	★★★★
Media Type:	Print
Author/Editor:	Alicia F. Lieberman

Short Description:

■ **Read The Full Review Of This Resource On Page 164.**

Written by a senior psychologist with a background in mother-child attachments, this 244 page book focuses on understanding how a toddler "thinks, feels, and responds to the challenges of growing up, and how parents can help them meet these challenges with greater self-confidence and joy." Chapter topics include the parent-toddler relationship, the variety of temperaments, toddler anxieties, and the impact of divorce and childcare.

2. Growth And Learning

Title:	**Know Your Child**
Subtitle:	An Authoritative Guide For Today's Parents
Overall Rating:	★★★★
Media Type:	Print
Author/Editor:	Stella Chess and Alexander Thomas
Short Description:	This resource focuses on child development in terms of the research based on children's temperament. Based upon the authors' extensive experience, this 397 guide highlights children's early developmental stages and aims to provide parents with answers to their most often asked questions. Parents are shown how to avoid some of the pitfalls of parenting by comparing their own expectations and attitudes with their child's temperament.

■ **Read The Full Review Of This Resource On Page 165.**

Title:	**Baby Steps**
Subtitle:	The "Whys" Of Your Child's Behavior In the First Two Years
Overall Rating:	★★★
Media Type:	Print
Author/Editor:	Claire B. Kopp, Ph.D. with Donna L. Bean
Short Description:	This guide takes parents through their child's first two years noting various developmental changes—motor, visual, language, cognitive, social, self-concepts, and emotions. This book aims to help parents understand their child's behavior patterns by offering information, suggestions, and advice based on the author's 30 years of professional and personal experiences. Summary charts are provided for each age group and for the entire two years.

■ **Read The Full Review Of This Resource On Page 168.**

Title:	**Infants And Mothers**
Subtitle:	Differences In Development
Overall Rating:	★★★
Media Type:	Print
Author/Editor:	T. Berry Brazelton, M.D.
Short Description:	The infant's individuality is highlighted in this 300 page book. It traces the baby's inner drives as he constantly tries to control his environment. Brazelton's goal is to improve a new parent's sense of competence and enjoyment in the role of being a parent, so they can pass these feelings on to the new baby. This is done by reviewing, month-by -month to one year, the development of three different baby styles—average, quiet, and active.

■ **Read The Full Review Of This Resource On Page 169.**

2. Growth And Learning

Title:	**Your Four-Year-Old**
Subtitle:	Wild And Wonderful
Overall Rating:	★★★
Media Type:	Print
Author/Editor:	Louise Bates Ames, Ph.D. and Frances L. Ilg, M.D.
Short Description: ■ **Read The Full Review Of This Resource On Page 170.**	The fourth in a series of ten books, this 150 page, 9 chapter resource focuses on the development of the four year old. Topics include: general characteristics of a 4 year old preschooler, their interactions with other children, techniques for dealing with their "wilder ways," major "accomplishments and abilities," advice for planning a four year old's birthday party, typical daily routines, and more. A Q & A segment concludes the book.

Title:	**Your Three-Year-Old**
Subtitle:	Friend Or Enemy
Overall Rating:	★★★
Media Type:	Print
Author/Editor:	Louise Bates Ames, Ph.D. and Frances L. Ilg, M.D.
Short Description: ■ **Read The Full Review Of This Resource On Page 171.**	The third book in a series of ten, this 167 page resource focuses on the development of the three year old. Based on studies of the Gesell Institute, topics include: characteristics of three year olds, their interactions with other children, techniques for dealing with their behavior, their major "accomplishments and abilities," how to plan a successful birthday party, dealing with typical daily routines, and more. A Q & A segment concludes the book.

Title:	**Your Two-Year-Old**
Subtitle:	12 To 24 Months
Overall Rating:	★★★
Media Type:	Print
Author/Editor:	Louise Bates Ames, Ph.D. and Frances L. Ilg, M.D.
Short Description: ■ **Read The Full Review Of This Resource On Page 172.**	As the second in a series of ten books, this one outlines the toddler's development and behavior from 2 to 3 years old. This 148 page resource discusses general characteristics of toddlers, their social interactions with others, techniques for handling their behavior, major "accomplishments and abilities," typical daily routines, the "mental life" of toddlers, individual differences, and more. A Q & A segment offers "stories from real life."

2. Growth And Learning

Recommended Resources—Behavior & Discipline

Title:	**Stop Struggling With Your Child**
Overall Rating:	★★★★
Media Type:	Videotape
Short Description:	Developed by the authors of a book by the same title, this 30 minute video focuses on ways to minimize family power struggles and maximize a child's self-esteem. The authors suggest that if parents change their own behavior, then children will change theirs. The four-steps of this method have been developed so children can be given opportunities to become cooperative, to practice problem-solving, and to take responsibility for themselves.

■ **Read The Full Review Of This Resource On Page 189.**

Title:	**Avoiding Power Struggles With Kids**
Overall Rating:	★★★★
Media Type:	Audiotape
Author/Editor:	Jim Fay and Foster W. Cline, M.D.
Short Description:	Based on the authors' book *Parenting with Love and Logic*, this 65 minute audiotape focuses on the "Science of Control" and how parents can avoid power struggles with their children. The authors believe that the more control parents give away, the more control they will have. A four-step procedure is illustrated with specific examples of how to use "thinking words," offer choices, and allow children to live with the consequences of their choices.

■ **Read The Full Review Of This Resource On Page 190.**

Title:	**Parenting With Love And Logic (Print)**
Subtitle:	Teaching Children Responsibility
Overall Rating:	★★★★
Media Type:	Print
Author/Editor:	Foster Cline, M.D. and Jim Fay
Short Description:	This book offers "pearls" to parents on how to raise children who are self-confident, motivated, and ready for the real world. The love and logic approach teaches children responsibility and how to solve their own problems. Parents are encouraged to allow their children to make choices and live with the logical consequences in this approach. Ways to help children deal with their mistakes and accomplishments are included.

■ **Read The Full Review Of This Resource On Page 191.**

2. Growth And Learning

Title:	**Positive Discipline (Print)**
Subtitle:	Revised Edition
Overall Rating:	★★★★
Media Type:	Print
Author/Editor:	Jane Nelsen, Ed.D.
Short Description:	This 258 page resource emphasizes firmness with dignity, kindness, and respect. Based on the beliefs of Adler and Dreikurs, positive discipline concepts include: treat mistakes as opportunities to learn, seek solutions to problems together as a family (rather than blame), believe that children do better when they feel better, the "significant seven" of successful people ("I am capable," etc.), children listen when they feel listened to, and more.

■ **Read The Full Review Of This Resource On Page 192.**

Title:	**Raising A Thinking Child**
Subtitle:	Help Your Young Child To Resolve Everyday Conflicts And Get Along With Others—The "I Can Problem Solve" Program
Overall Rating:	★★★★
Media Type:	Print
Author/Editor:	Myrna B. Shure, Ph.D. with Theresa Foy DiGeronimo, M.Ed.
Short Description:	This book centers on helping your child become a thinking, feeling individual. Based on 25 years of research and evaluation, this book encourages parents to raise socially adjusted, self-confident children utilizing the ICPS (I Can Problem Solve) approach. Through this program, children are encouraged to learn how to think, not what to think or do. Sample dialogues, techniques, activities, and games are included within this 210 page guide.

■ **Read The Full Review Of This Resource On Page 193.**

Title:	**Change Your Child's Behavior By Changing Yours**
Subtitle:	13 New Tricks To Get Kids To Cooperate
Overall Rating:	★★★
Media Type:	Print
Author/Editor:	Barbara Chernofsky, M.S. and Diane Gage
Short Description:	This guide is a "how-to manual" for parents who "have few precious moments to read, don't want to be preached to, and want encouragement" for their efforts on their children's behalf. Using a light-hearted approach, this book's goals are twofold: to teach parents how to change their child's behavior by modifying their own behavior, and to help parents understand that most inappropriate behaviors are developmentally appropriate.

■ **Read The Full Review Of This Resource On Page 194.**

2. Growth And Learning

Title:	**Discipline Book (The)**
Subtitle:	Everything You Need To Know To Have A Better-Behaved Child—From Birth To Age Ten
Overall Rating:	★★★
Media Type:	Print
Author/Editor:	William Sears, M.D., and Martha Sears, R.N.
Short Description:	With a focus on preventing behavior problems as well as managing them when they arise, this book offers parents philosophical and practical advice on discipline issues. The three parts of this 19 chapter book focus on how to promote desirable behavior, correct undesirable behavior, and internally equip children so they will "make right choices" in their adult life.

■ **Read The Full Review Of This Resource On Page 195.**

Title:	**Parenting With Love And Logic (Audiotape)**
Subtitle:	Teaching Children Responsibility
Overall Rating:	★★★
Media Type:	Audiotape
Author/Editor:	Foster Cline, M.D. and Jim Fay
Short Description:	This 3 1/2 hour long audiotape offers "pearls" to parents on how to raise children who are self-confident, motivated, and ready for the real world. The love and logic approach teaches children responsibility and how to solve their own problems. Children are encouraged to make choices and live with the logical consequences in this approach. Ways for parents to help children deal with their mistakes and accomplishments are included.

■ **Read The Full Review Of This Resource On Page 196.**

Title:	**Positive Discipline A–Z**
Subtitle:	1001 Solutions To Everyday Parenting Problems
Overall Rating:	★★★
Media Type:	Print
Author/Editor:	Jane Nelsen, Ed.D., Lynn Lott, M.A., M.F.C.C., and H. Stephen Glenn
Short Description:	This book offers 1000+ suggestions and advice to help parents solve problem behavior, while also helping children "feel good about themselves, gain self-confidence and self-discipline, learn responsibility, and develop problem-solving skills." Topics addressed within this 354 page book include basic parenting "tools" (family meetings, follow-through, etc.), solutions to problems using positive discipline, and short tips to avoid common problems.

■ **Read The Full Review Of This Resource On Page 197.**

2. Growth And Learning

Recommended Resources—Sibling Relationships

Title:	**Those Baby Blues**
Subtitle:	A Parent's Guide To Helping Your Child Adjust To The New Baby
Overall Rating:	★★★★
Media Type:	Videotape
Short Description:	Combining family stories, footage of interactions between siblings, and professional advice, this 30 minute videotape focuses on sibling rivalry. Discussions include changes in behavior, throwing tantrums, aggression, hidden hostility, regression, "nothing's wrong," depression, and withdrawal. Advice is given for how to handle each reaction along with tips on understanding the child's behavior. A complimentary video for siblings is also provided.

■ **Read The Full Review Of This Resource On Page 222.**

Title:	**Loving Each One Best**
Subtitle:	A Caring And Practical Approach To Raising Siblings
Overall Rating:	★★★★
Media Type:	Print
Author/Editor:	Nancy Samalin with Catherine Whitney
Short Description:	This guide offers information, advice, and a discussion of the feelings parents and children have when new siblings enter into the family. Introducing a new sibling into a family, relieving parental stress, helping fathers become equal parenting partners, and what children think about having a new brother or sister are some of the topics discussed within this 210-page resource. Numerous parent-child dialogues are also included throughout.

■ **Read The Full Review Of This Resource On Page 223.**

Title:	**Siblings Without Rivalry**
Subtitle:	How To Help Your Children Live Together So You Can Live Too
Overall Rating:	★★★★
Media Type:	Print
Author/Editor:	Adele Faber and Elaine Mazlish
Short Description:	The authors' updated edition about sibling rivalry strives to show how skillful adult intervention and interaction may help curb impending sibling confrontations and conflicts. The focus of this resource is to help parents understand the feelings of their children by first understanding their own. Based on the author's own experiences and a questionnaire they devised, this guide offers solutions to parents trying to solve this most common problem.

■ **Read The Full Review Of This Resource On Page 224.**

2. Growth And Learning

Recommended Resources—Toilet Training

Title:	**Mommy I Have To Go Potty!**
Subtitle:	A Parent's Guide To Toilet Training
Overall Rating:	★★★★
Media Type:	Print
Author/Editor:	Jan Faull, M.Ed.
Short Description:	This guide offers a step-by-step approach to toilet training your child from diapers to dry nights. The author offers her "simple, common-sense approach" to teach parents such things as how to tell if their child is really ready to toilet train, how to deal with accidents, why it's OK to return to diapers temporarily, and tips to make toilet training fun for kids. Numerous parental anecdotes are given to introduce sections along with bulleted tips.

■ **Read The Full Review Of This Resource On Page 231.**

Title:	**Toilet Training**
Subtitle:	A Practical Guide To Daytime And Nighttime Training
Overall Rating:	★★★
Media Type:	Print
Author/Editor:	Vicki Lansky
Short Description:	This resource offers information on toilet training your preschooler. Within its 107 pages, parents will find discussions on whether or not their child is ready, toilet training equipment, how to begin training, opinions from child development experts (Brazelton, Leach, and more), how to work with an uncooperative child, and more. A list of contacts for supplies is given along with lists of children's books, videos, games, and more.

■ **Read The Full Review Of This Resource On Page 232.**

2. Growth And Learning

Recommended Resources—Age-Appropriate Activities

Title:	**Baby Games**
Subtitle:	The Joyful Guide To Child's Play From Birth To Three Years
Overall Rating:	★★★★
Media Type:	Print
Author/Editor:	Elaine Martin

Short Description:

■ Read The Full Review Of This Resource On Page 239.

The book suggests that playing with your baby creates special bonds of love, communication, and caring that will last a lifetime. Divided by age groupings (birth to age 3) and by activity types (music, art, kitchen, etc.), this guidebook focuses on open-ended creative activities. As a child develops from infant to toddler to preschooler, this resource aims "to create a magical childhood" through its rhymes, songs, finger plays, games, and more.

Title:	**Great Explorations**
Subtitle:	100 Creative Play Ideas For Parents And Preschoolers From Playspace At The Children's Museum Boston
Overall Rating:	★★★★
Media Type:	Print
Author/Editor:	Amy Nolan

Short Description:

■ Read The Full Review Of This Resource On Page 240.

This 245 page activity guide was developed by the manager of Playspace (part of the Children's Museum in Boston). Offering 100 of the center's favorite art, science, music, cooking, and dramatic play experiences, this resource focuses on a discovery-based approach to learning. Each activity is explained in a two-page spread with a list of materials, length of time needed, recommended ages, directions, enhanced skill, and ways to extend it.

Title:	**Preschool Art**
Subtitle:	It's The Process, Not The Product
Overall Rating:	★★★★
Media Type:	Print
Author/Editor:	MaryAnn Kohl

Short Description:

■ Read The Full Review Of This Resource On Page 241.

This book has over 200 process-oriented art projects for children ages 3 to 5. Using materials commonly found in the home, children can create open-ended art experiences. Arranged by the "Basics" (art ideas for any time of year) and by the seasons, each activity includes a list of materials needed, how to do the activity, possible variations, a line drawing of the process, and more. Indexes divide activities by project, materials, and art medium.

2. Growth And Learning

Title:	**300 Three Minute Games**
Subtitle:	Quick And Easy Activities For 2–5 Year Olds
Overall Rating:	★★★★
Media Type:	Print
Author/Editor:	Jackie Silberg
Short Description:	This 191 page book offers 300 games involving minimal preparation, and many of which include rhymes, poems, or songs. Activities are grouped within 14 categories such as animal games, bath games, book games, outside games, storytelling games, "stuck inside" games, stuffed animal games, and more. Step-by-step directions are included for each with an occasional black line drawing. An index lists all activities alphabetically by name.

■ **Read The Full Review Of This Resource On Page 242.**

Title:	**365 Outdoor Activities You Can Do With Your Child**
Overall Rating:	★★★★
Media Type:	Print
Author/Editor:	Steve Bennett and Ruth Bennett
Short Description:	Offering 365 outdoor activities to encourage "quality family time," this compact 430 page book is an extension of one of the authors' other books. Grouped alphabetically (and by category), activities are divided into 25 categories including: backyard fun, beach activities, environmental activities, gardening, imagination games, natural science, old-fashioned games, sports, seasonal activities, toys and gadgets, and more.

■ **Read The Full Review Of This Resource On Page 243.**

Title:	**365 TV-Free Activities**
Subtitle:	You Can Do With Your Child
Overall Rating:	★★★★
Media Type:	Print
Author/Editor:	Steve Bennett and Ruth Bennett
Short Description:	Offering 365 activities to wean children from TV watching, this compact 425 page book is designed for "the family that plays together." Grouped alphabetically (and by category), activities are divided into 16 categories including: arts and crafts, food stuff, math and numbers, recycled household materials, science, words and language, toymaking, and more. Each activity is covered on one page with a list of materials, instructions, and safety tips.

■ **Read The Full Review Of This Resource On Page 244.**

2. Growth And Learning

Title:	**Active Learning For Infants**
Overall Rating:	★★★★
Media Type:	Print
Author/Editor:	Debby Cryer, Thelma Harms, and Beth Bourland
Short Description:	This guidebook, developed at a child development center in Chapel Hill, North Carolina, was tested in 17 daycare centers and is the first book in the "Active Learning Series." With over 300 activities for newborns to 12 month old infants, this book contains a complete planning guide for educators, and activities for babies that promote listening and talking, physical development, creativity, and learning about the world around them.

■ **Read The Full Review Of This Resource On Page 245.**

Title:	**Read-Aloud Handbook (The)**
Overall Rating:	★★★★
Media Type:	Print
Author/Editor:	Jim Trelease
Short Description:	Now in its fourth edition, this 387 page book is two books in one. The first half includes information on when, why, and how to read aloud to your child along with updated statistics, current research, and new anecdotes. The second half encompasses the "Treasury of Read-Alouds" (200+ pages) listing books by type (wordless, picture, etc.); each annotation includes cross-references to books by the same author and books of the same theme.

■ **Read The Full Review Of This Resource On Page 246.**

Title:	**Play, Learn, & Grow**
Subtitle:	An Annotated Guide To The Best Books And Materials For Very Young Children
Overall Rating:	★★★
Media Type:	Print
Author/Editor:	James L. Thomas
Short Description:	This 439 page guide offers an annotated list of children's books and other media (not games or toys) for use with children under the age of 5. Over 5,000 print and non-print titles were evaluated in compiling this list and the criteria is included. A "developmental portrait" for infants to five years old is included along with an essay concerning literacy. Five indexes access entries by name, subject, age & category, age & purchase priority, and format.

■ **Read The Full Review Of This Resource On Page 248.**

2. Growth And Learning

Recommended Resources—Choosing A Preschool

Title:	**Smart Start**
Subtitle:	The Parents' Complete Guide To Preschool Education
Overall Rating:	★★★★
Media Type:	Print
Author/Editor:	Marian Edelman Borden
Short Description:	This step-by-step 222 page guide provides information on various preschool program philosophies along with suggested guidelines to use when making a choice and ways to make the transition successful. Checklists and highlighted tips are provided throughout. Additional advice is given for parents of children with handicapping conditions, families with children in daycare who wish to include preschool in their child's day, and more.

■ **Read The Full Review Of This Resource On Page 272.**

Recommended Resources—Special Circumstances

Title:	**Helping Children Cope With Separation And Loss**
Overall Rating:	★★★★
Media Type:	Print
Author/Editor:	Claudia Jewett Jarratt
Short Description:	Written by a respected child and family therapist, this 232-page book serves as a guide for parents, therapists, and other caregivers who wish to help children move through the stages of grief and loss. Ways of identifying and dealing with children's grief reactions are found here, as well as creative methods to help children give voice to their feelings at all stages of the grief process.

■ **Read The Full Review Of This Resource On Page 276.**

Title:	**It's Nobody's Fault**
Subtitle:	New Hope And Help For Difficult Children
Overall Rating:	★★★★
Media Type:	Print
Author/Editor:	Harold S. Koplewicz, M.D.
Short Description:	This 303 page guide focuses on the genetic make-up of brain disorders, their symptoms, their causes, and how to treat them. The author highlights 13 "no-fault brain disorders" that are biologically caused and not a reflection of what the parents have done. Disorders profiled include: ADHD, obsessive compulsive disorder, separation anxiety, social phobia, eating disorders, bedwetting, tourette syndrome, depressive disorder, autism, and more.

■ **Read The Full Review Of This Resource On Page 277.**

2. Growth And Learning

Title:	**Learning Disabilities: A To Z**
Subtitle:	A Parent's Complete Guide To Learning Disabilities From Preschool To Adulthood
Overall Rating:	★★★★
Media Type:	Print
Author/Editor:	Corinne Smith, Ph.D. and Lisa Strick
Short Description: ■ **Read The Full Review Of This Resource On Page 278.**	The three parts of this 407 page book describe the symptoms, causes, and treatments of learning disabilities. The types of learning disabilities that are highlighted include ADHD, visual perception disabilities, language processing disabilities, and fine motor disabilities. Suggestions are offered throughout in terms of how to help a child with learning disabilities succeed in school, at home, and in transitioning on their own.

Title:	**Parenting The Strong-Willed Child**
Subtitle:	The Clinically Proven Five-Week Program For Parents Of Two- To Six-Year-Olds
Overall Rating:	★★★★
Media Type:	Print
Author/Editor:	Rex Forehand, Ph.D. and Nicholas Long, Ph.D.
Short Description: ■ **Read The Full Review Of This Resource On Page 279.**	This book focuses on a program to help parents of strong-willed children find positive and manageable solutions to their children's difficult behavior. The four parts of this 256 page book highlight factors that cause and contribute to strong-willed behavior, techniques of the authors' five-week program, how to develop a positive environment in the family and home, and how to deal with specific behavior problems (temper tantrums, aggression, etc.).

Title:	**Lonely, Sad And Angry**
Subtitle:	A Parent's Guide To Depression In Children And Adolescents
Overall Rating:	★★★★
Media Type:	Print
Author/Editor:	Barbara D. Ingersoll, Ph.D. and Sam Goldstein, Ph.D.
Short Description: ■ **Read The Full Review Of This Resource On Page 280.**	Written by clinical psychologists, this 225 page book describes symptoms, causes, and types of treatment for depressive disorders in children and adolescents. Related emotional and behavioral problems are discussed in addition (anxiety disorders, conduct disorder, ADHD, oppositional defiant disorder, learning disabilities). Separate chapters offer advice on how families and teachers can cope. Another chapter focuses on suicidal behavior.

2. Growth And Learning

Title:	**When You Worry About The Child You Love**
Subtitle:	Emotional And Learning Problems In Children
Overall Rating:	★★★★
Media Type:	Print
Author/Editor:	Edward Hallowell, M.D.
Short Description:	Developed by a "therapeutic optimist," this 280 page book offers a balanced approach of nature and nurture in dealing with childhood problems. Conditions associated with the states of anger, sadness, fear, and confusion are highlighted along with some less common childhood problems. Specific examples of over 30 treatable emotional and/or learning problems are provided. A chapter is included that discusses medications.

■ **Read The Full Review Of This Resource On Page 281.**

Recommended Resources—All-Inclusive

Title:	**Parenting Young Children**
Subtitle:	Systematic Training For Effective Parenting Of Children Under Six
Overall Rating:	★★★★
Media Type:	Print
Author/Editor:	Don Dinkmeyer, Sr., Gary D. McKay, James S. Dinkmeyer, Don Dinkmeyer, Jr., and Joyce L. McKay
Short Description:	This guidebook, based upon a parenting program called STEP—Systematic Training for Effective Parenting—aims to help parents' confidence in working with children from birth to six years of age. It is founded on using a "consistent, positive, and democratic approach." Areas covered include: children's development, behavior, discipline, self-esteem, listening and talking to children, teaching cooperation, and social and emotional development.

■ **Read The Full Review Of This Resource On Page 285.**

2. Growth And Learning

Title:	**Preschool Years (The)**
Subtitle:	Family Strategies That Work—From Experts And Parents
Overall Rating:	★★★★
Media Type:	Print
Author/Editor:	Ellen Galinsky and Judy David
Short Description:	This 504 page guide on topics associated with preschoolers combine parents' most frequently questions, solutions from parents and "experts" (T. Berry Brazelton, Benjamin Spock, Bruno Bettleheim, etc.), and "successful strategies" from 300+ interviewed parents. Topics discussed include: discipline, learning routines, daycare, preschool, work and family life, emotions, and more.

■ **Read The Full Review Of This Resource On Page 286.**

Title:	**Sesame Street Parents**
Overall Rating:	★★★★
Media Type:	Internet
Short Description:	Developed by Children's Television Workshop (CTW), host of the TV show "Sesame Street," this site offers information and tips primarily for parents of preschoolers. Options at their homepage include: activities, behavior & discipline, child development, education, family & community, health & safety, and product reviews. A discussion forum is also available along with email contact to CTW's contributing consultants.

■ **Read The Full Review Of This Resource On Page 287.**

3.

PARENT-TO-PARENT ADVICE & FORUMS

In the past, parents' access to advice on parenting young children was limited. They generally had the choice of raising their children by listening to the experts of that time or following the advice provided by their own parents. Resources that were available to parents often had more of an instructional tone to them. Parents were "told what to do" and usually given few, if any, alternatives for many parenting situations. Parenting methods that "strayed from the norm" were viewed with suspicion.

But today, new parents find themselves barraged by well-meaning advice from others, whether it be their own parents, friends, pediatricians or other caregivers, childcare providers, or whomever else they meet as they go about their daily activities. Just as new parents get a handle on one aspect of parenting, another opinion comes along to disrupt their new-found confidence. In frustration, they may then turn to the "experts." But even the experts can't always agree. Being forced to evaluate the relative quality of all this advice and information can cause consternation at a time when new parents just want to simplify their rapidly changing lifestyle.

Advice from an older generation may add more confusion, since new parents face issues that their parents typically did not have to deal with. Many decisions, foreign to their own parents, now need to be made **before** a baby is born. For example: "Will one of us take family leave; will the mother return to work after maternity leave; will the father stay home; can quality affordable childcare be found; is breastfeeding an option?" As their baby grows older, new parents face issues that were considered routine in their parents' time, but are now considered controversial by some: "Should our baby sleep in our room, our bed, or should we teach our baby to sleep in their own crib? Should we pick up baby every time she cries or let her "cry it out"? Should we use spanking as a discipline tool or should we use time-out? Should our preschooler be taught basic academic skills or be allowed to just play?" Parents search for guidance but don't know where to turn for immediate answers.

Eventually, many parents realize that the best advice comes from the real experts: **other parents** who have asked the same questions and faced similar decisions. Being able to discuss options and weigh alternatives with others can help alleviate parenting stress. Other parents who have dealt with the same problems or who have tried various parenting "strategies" can be one of the best resources to give new parents the support and help they hunger for.

Many current parenting resources place greater importance on the value of direct experience in learning to be a good parent. Parents' input is solicited, incorporated into methodology, and practical advice is tendered to answer parents' most pressing questions. Many of the new childhood education experts now rely on a combined approach of observational research, field-tested methods, and parental contributions. Our

3. Parent-To-Parent Advice & Forums

recommendations favor those resources that illustrate this more balanced approach to parenting information and advice.

Additionally, with the advent of modern technology, numerous Internet websites and online services have sprung up to address new parents' needs to converse with others. Here, parents can ask questions, reply to others' concerns, or simply just chat about any parenting topic. And, most important, they can "get together" **any** time, day or night. If parents are awake for their baby's feeding during the night, they can get "online" and find another parent out there who can offer them the support and reassurance they need.

In the pages that follow, we've recommended a number of resources to help support you as you make parenting decisions and feel more confident in your role as a new mother or new father. You'll find the best resources to help you understand how other parents have solved various problems, from dealing with scrapes and bumps to how to make toilet training successful (and fun), to how to adapt to motherhood and fatherhood.

We've also recommend several Internet websites that cater to new parents' needs. Parent forums are available to help parents read others' point of view on a variety of topics, offer their own opinions, and simply feel more connected and part of the "real world." Most of these sites contain chat rooms where parents can have "live" conversations with others at any time, night or day.

Take some time to carefully select the best resources for your family's specific needs. Be sure to read the one-page review of any resource of interest, so you will fully understand its content, focus, style, and quality before you purchase or acquire that resource. You'll find that support and advice from others is readily available to help you make confident decisions on every facet of parenting.

3. Parent-To-Parent Advice & Forums

Recommended Resources

Title:	**Family.Com**
Subtitle:	Disney.Com
Overall Rating:	★★★★
Media Type:	Internet
Short Description:	Developed with Disney, this website offers customized searches of parenting information based upon drop-down lists (about 15 subtopics) and specified age ranges (birth on up). Options at their homepage include searches under the headings of "Activities," "Education," "Food," "Parenting," "Boards," and more. Future plans include an interactive "Chat" segment.

■ **Read The Full Review Of This Resource On Page 321.**

Title:	**Father's Almanac (The)**
Subtitle:	Revised
Overall Rating:	★★★★
Media Type:	Print
Author/Editor:	S. Adams Sullivan
Short Description:	Revised from its original publication in 1980, this edition notes how fathers' roles have changed. This 391 page book's intent is to encourage "involved fatherhood." Chapter topics include: pregnancy/childbirth; baby care; fathers' jobs; family issues; "providing;" daily care; outings and special events; teaching and discipline; learning, playing, and working with kids; and photographing, videotaping, etc.

■ **Read The Full Review Of This Resource On Page 293.**

Title:	**Practical Parenting Tips**
Subtitle:	Over 1,500 Helpful Hints For The First Five Years
Overall Rating:	★★★★
Media Type:	Print
Author/Editor:	Vicki Lansky
Short Description:	This guide contains a collection of practical hints for parents. Topics discussed include new baby care, child care "basics," hygiene and health, childproofing and safety, parenting "challenges" (manners, tantrums, rivalry, etc.), family relationships (traditions, relatives, etc.), traveling, and playtime ideas (seasonal fun, arts and crafts, etc.). The 1,500+ tips were accumulated from the author's parenting columns and contacts with other parents.

■ **Read The Full Review Of This Resource On Page 294.**

3. Parent-To-Parent Advice & Forums

Title:	**The Year After Childbirth**
Subtitle:	Surviving And Enjoying The First Year Of Motherhood
Overall Rating:	★★★★
Media Type:	Print
Author/Editor:	Sheila Kitzinger
Short Description:	The focus of this book is on the woman's experience of becoming a mother during the first year after birth. Information is provided to help her get back in shape and to understand the physical, emotional, and identity issues involved. Many chapters include highlighted self-help inserts of what to do for each of the topics covered. Colorful inserts, illustrations and diagrams are included, as well as a glossary of terms and referrals.

■ **Read The Full Review Of This Resource On Page 295.**

Title:	**Parent Soup**
Subtitle:	An iVillage Community
Overall Rating:	★★★★
Media Type:	Internet
Short Description:	At this website, you can participate in live chats, get involved in discussion groups, read articles from pregnancy through the teen years, get listings of baby names, and more. As part of the "Parent Soup community," you can post announcements, ask for advice, get other parents' opinions on any topic, read relaxation tips, etc. Six experts are available to answer questions (10 per week) on various topics, and past Q & As can also be browsed.

■ **Read The Full Review Of This Resource On Page 327.**

Title:	**Parenting An Only Child**
Subtitle:	The Joys And Challenges Of Raising Your One And Only
Overall Rating:	★★★★
Media Type:	Print
Author/Editor:	Susan Newman
Short Description:	Divided into three parts and 12 chapters, this 239 page guide focuses on the needs of only children and their parents. Myths are debunked, advice tendered on raising only children, and suggestions given on dealing with others' demands and questions. Compiled from over 200 people's input, quotes and anecdotal stories are offered to support "threesome" families' decisions not to have additional children. Also provided are quotes from only children.

■ **Read The Full Review Of This Resource On Page 296.**

3. Parent-To-Parent Advice & Forums

Title:	**Traits Of A Healthy Family**
Subtitle:	Fifteen Traits Commonly Found In Healthy Families By Those Who Work With Them
Overall Rating:	★★★★
Media Type:	Print
Author/Editor:	Dolores Curran
Short Description: ■ **Read The Full Review Of This Resource On Page 297.**	Based upon results from the author's survey of 551 professionals, this 322 page book explores family traits and strengths. Fifteen qualities that are most often found in healthy families are highlighted along with ways that families can work to develop and incorporate them into their personal lives.

Title:	**Baby Maneuvers**
Overall Rating:	★★★★
Media Type:	Print
Author/Editor:	Ericka Lutz
Short Description: ■ **Read The Full Review Of This Resource On Page 298.**	Presented by a veteran traveler turned parent, this 224 page guide aims to encourage parents to do excursions with their child by supplying parents with factual information to make the process easier. Topics include dealing with: bodily functions, eating out, day trips, various types of travel, what to pack in a day pack, various types of vacation lodgings, outdoor adventures, traveling alone with a child, work travel with a baby, and overseas travel.

Title:	**ParentsPlace**
Subtitle:	An iVillage Community
Overall Rating:	★★★★
Media Type:	Internet
Short Description: ■ **Read The Full Review Of This Resource On Page 299.**	Believing that "parents are the best resource for other parents in the adventure of child-rearing," this site hosts the following: reading rooms featuring professional "experts" (doctor, dentist, nutritionist, preschool teacher, and more), chat topics (20+ with numerous subtopics), daily special events, bulletin boards, activities, reading lists, recipes, and more. Their target audience ranges from pregnancy through childhood, teens, and into adulthood.

3. Parent-To-Parent Advice & Forums

Title:	**CyberMom Dot Com**
Subtitle:	A Home On The Net For Moms With Modems
Overall Rating:	★★★
Media Type:	Internet
Short Description:	Created by a husband-and-wife team, this site states that "our casa es su casa." Eight "rooms" offer access to gardening tips, relationship issues, politics, health/ beauty advice, and more. Parenting topics can be found in The Study (working at home, working on the Internet, day care issues), The Family Room (costume ideas, Walt Disney World tips), The Kitchen (recipes, organizing tips), and The Playroom (a chat forum on 10 parenting topics).

■ **Read The Full Review Of This Resource On Page 300.**

Title:	**Keys To Becoming A Father**
Overall Rating:	★★★
Media Type:	Print
Author/Editor:	William Sears, M.D.
Short Description:	This book offers support for and addresses concerns of fathers as they take on new roles with their children. The book is divided into 36 "Keys" which include narratives on topics (2–3 pages each). Topics include: fathering tips with newborns, fussy babies, juggling career and parenthood, being a single father, playing with and disciplining your child, and more. Sears, a father of 8, describes mistakes, revelations, and joys he personally has experienced.

■ **Read The Full Review Of This Resource On Page 301.**

4.

GAINING AN OVERVIEW: ALL-INCLUSIVE

Watching a newborn baby gaze with wonder at his or her parents' face for the first time, and watching new parents smile and coo in return, illustrates the wonder and joy of becoming a parent. It's hard to imagine that in just a few short years, that same baby will become the star player on the softball team, or the waltzing flower in the ballet recital, or the child at the dinner table who talks about what homework they must do that night and what they learned at school that day. Parenting decisions will evolve from "How do I take care of him?" to "How do I teach him to take care of himself?" A parent's concern will also evolve, from "How do I hold her?" to "How do I let her go?" Those first few days, weeks, and months of a baby's life are intensified by the worries, joys, and trial-and-error involved with becoming a parent. Learning on the job, minute by minute and day by day, results in pride and exhilaration as well as concern and exhaustion.

As daunting as this process of learning may seem, any new parent will attest to the fact that there are plenty of answers available: **everyone's** answers! From the moment their child is born, advice begins pouring in. How do new, inexperienced parents drink from this well of information and separate the good tips from the not-so-good tips? In search of answers, parents may turn to the bookstore's vast array of parenting resources only to discover yet another question: "How do we choose the best resource to guide us as we guide our child?"

The heart of parenting **is** guidance—each child guides their parents and each parent guides their child. Parents are constantly observing how other adults and children respond to each other and in the process reject some approaches while embracing others. During these observations, parents compare their child to others' children. Through it all, parents ask themselves: "Is our child developing correctly? Are we doing things right?"

Every child is unique and every child's growth pattern and responses will vary even within the same family. Their development relies on the interplay of various factors, including their biological heredity, their social environment, and their experiences within the family. What works for one child will not always work for another. The learning curve never remains constant but continues to change. "What do we do now?"

Keeping all these issues and questions in mind, parents need a resource that can become their "24 hour companion" to explain what to expect as their child grows, inform them of their available choices, and assuage their worries. Most of all, parents need reassurance that they **are** doing their best and **are** doing a great job. They need a resource that will educate them about options, possibilities, and consequences. In other words, parents need an "all-inclusive" manual or resource. But what type of information should be present to make this resource a worthwhile investment of time and money?

4. Gaining An Overview: All-Inclusive

As we developed this guidebook, we looked for resources that would offer parents a full perspective of child development, children's growth and learning issues, and basic child care. Since effective parenting often does not rely on one authority's opinion, all-inclusive resources should strive to remain objective, allowing parents to understand other parenting styles while developing and refining their own. Most new parents will most likely combine elements of their own personality, beliefs, and experiences to create an environment that works best for them and their child.

We have identified some of the best all-inclusive resources available in the following pages. These resources will address topics ranging from how to diaper your newborn to how to prepare your five year old for kindergarten. You'll find advice and information on how to take care of your baby and young child through illnesses, injuries, and emergencies, along with how to nurture their development with activities, experiences, and appropriate parental responses. Please take the time to carefully read our full-page review of each recommended resource, so that you can choose those that are best for you.

Parenting offers rewards, gifts, and riches that absolutely nothing else in life can bring. Becoming a parent allows you to experience the magic of being the center of your child's universe, revisit your own childhood again through the eyes of your own child, and discover your world in new and glorious ways.

4. Gaining An Overview: All-Inclusive

Recommended Resources

Title:	**Baby Basics (Videotape)**
Subtitle:	The Complete Video Guide For New And Expectant Parents
Overall Rating:	★★★★
Media Type:	Videotape
Short Description:	Divided into eight "chapters," this 110 minute videotape focuses on the care and development of newborns and infants. Topics discussed include: the newborn's appearances, postpartum care of the mother, the adjustment during the first days at home, daily care (bathing, diapering, dressing, and more), feeding (breastfeeding, bottlefeeding), health and safety, babies' cries, sleep patterns, and infants' growth and development.

■ **Read The Full Review Of This Resource On Page 316.**

Title:	**Baby Book (The)**
Subtitle:	Everything You Need To Know About Your Baby—From Birth To Age Two
Overall Rating:	★★★★
Media Type:	Print
Author/Editor:	William Sears, M.D. & Martha Sears, R.N.
Short Description:	As parents of 8 and pediatric specialists, this husband and wife team present a parenting philosophy believed to promote "connected" parents and children. They call this philosophy "attachment parenting;" it lays the foundation for the rest of their 689 page book. Various topics are included such as: baby-care basics, infant feeding and nutrition, "contemporary parenting," infant development and behavior, and keeping your baby safe and healthy.

■ **Read The Full Review Of This Resource On Page 317.**

Title:	**Becoming The Parent You Want To Be**
Subtitle:	A Sourcebook Of Strategies For The First Five Years
Overall Rating:	★★★★
Media Type:	Print
Author/Editor:	Laura Davis and Janis Keyser
Short Description:	This book uses 9 parenting principles to provide parents with the building blocks they need "for the parenting journey." These principles include: developing a vision, learning about children, cultivating a spirit of optimism, teaching children to feel safe and good about their world, and more. The 28 chapters include tips about dealing with crying, separation, childcare, friendships, discipline and behavior, and more.

■ **Read The Full Review Of This Resource On Page 318.**

4. Gaining An Overview: All-Inclusive

Title:	**Caring For Your Baby And Young Child**
Subtitle:	Birth To Age 5
Overall Rating:	★★★★
Media Type:	Print
Author/Editor:	Steven P. Shelov, M.D., F.A.A.P.
Short Description:	*Caring for Your Baby and Child* covers the first five years of a child's life. Part One addresses how to prepare for a new baby, including equipment, infant care, feeding, etc. A month-by-month guide follows and includes what to expect and how to care for your baby up to their fifth birthday. Part Two is a medical reference guide, with an alphabetical coverage of emergencies, illnesses, behavior, disabilities, family issues, and more.

■ **Read The Full Review Of This Resource On Page 319.**

Title:	**Complete Baby And Child Care**
Overall Rating:	★★★★
Media Type:	Print
Author/Editor:	Miriam Stoppard, M.D.
Short Description:	This comprehensive guide covers aspects of taking care of a child and understanding their growth (physical, speech and language, and mental development). 500+ color photographs and drawings accompany explanations within this 352 reference guide. Each topic is separated into four age groups (young baby, older baby, toddler, and preschool child) with color-coded bands given to access key information for each gender and age group.

■ **Read The Full Review Of This Resource On Page 320.**

Title:	**Family.Com**
Subtitle:	Disney.Com
Overall Rating:	★★★★
Media Type:	Internet
Short Description:	Developed with Disney, this website offers customized searches of parenting information based upon drop-down lists (about 15 subtopics) and specified age ranges (birth on up). Options at their homepage include searches under the headings of "Activities," "Education," "Food," "Parenting," "Boards," and more. Future plans include an interactive "Chat" segment.

■ **Read The Full Review Of This Resource On Page 321.**

4. Gaining An Overview: All-Inclusive

Title:	**Father's Almanac (The)**
Subtitle:	Revised
Overall Rating:	★★★★
Media Type:	Print
Author/Editor:	S. Adams Sullivan
Short Description:	Revised from its original publication in 1980, this edition notes how fathers' roles have changed. This 391 page book's intent is to encourage "involved fatherhood." Chapter topics include: pregnancy/childbirth; baby care; fathers' jobs; family issues; "providing;" daily care; outings and special events; teaching and discipline; learning, playing, and working with kids; and photographing, videotaping, etc.

■ **Read The Full Review Of This Resource On Page 293.**

Title:	**I Am Your Child (CD-ROM)**
Subtitle:	The First Three Years Last Forever
Overall Rating:	★★★★
Media Type:	CD-ROM
Short Description:	Supporting a national campaign "to make early childhood development a top priority for our nation," this CD-ROM correlates the latest findings in brain research to the first three years of a child's development. Ten guidelines for raising children are offered, along with brain research data, details about child development from prenatal to age three, questions from parents, answers and insight from "top experts" (Brazelton, Koop, etc.), and more.

■ **Read The Full Review Of This Resource On Page 322.**

Title:	**I Am Your Child (Internet)**
Overall Rating:	★★★★
Media Type:	Internet
Short Description:	Supporting a national campaign "to make early childhood development a top priority for our nation," this website correlates the latest findings in brain research to the first three years of a child's development. Ten guidelines for raising children are offered, along with brain research data, details about child development from prenatal to age three, questions, answers, and insight from "top experts" (Brazelton, Koop, etc.), and more.

■ **Read The Full Review Of This Resource On Page 323.**

4. Gaining An Overview: All-Inclusive

Title:	**I Am Your Child (Videotape)**
Subtitle:	The First Years Last Forever
Overall Rating:	★★★★
Media Type:	Videotape
Short Description:	This video (about 30 minutes) correlates the latest findings in brain research to the first three years of a child's development. Guidelines for infant and child care are offered, along with current brain research data, details about child development from prenatal to age three, questions, answers, and insight from "top experts" (Brazelton, Koop, etc.), and more.

■ **Read The Full Review Of This Resource On Page 324.**

Title:	**Portable Pediatrician For Parents (The)**
Overall Rating:	★★★★
Media Type:	Print
Author/Editor:	Laura Walther Nathanson, M.D., FAAP
Short Description:	Reflecting recommendations from professional organizations and child development researchers, this 502 page guide offers descriptions of a child's physical and behavioral development from birth to five years of age. Topics include: narrative descriptions of each age, separation issues, limits, health and illness, developmental milestones, "windows of opportunity," and more. Other sections focus on illness, injury, pediatric opinions, etc.

■ **Read The Full Review Of This Resource On Page 325.**

Title:	**Practical Parenting Tips**
Subtitle:	Over 1,500 Helpful Hints For The First Five Years
Overall Rating:	★★★★
Media Type:	Print
Author/Editor:	Vicki Lansky
Short Description:	This guide contains a collection of practical hints for parents. Topics discussed include new baby care, child care "basics," hygiene and health, childproofing and safety, parenting "challenges" (manners, tantrums, rivalry, etc.), family relationships (traditions, relatives, etc.), traveling, and playtime ideas (seasonal fun, arts and crafts, etc.). The 1,500+ tips were accumulated from the author's parenting columns and contacts with other parents.

■ **Read The Full Review Of This Resource On Page 294.**

4. Gaining An Overview: All-Inclusive

Title:	**What To Expect The Toddler Years**
Overall Rating:	★★★★
Media Type:	Print
Author/Editor:	Arlene Eisenberg, Heidi E. Murkoff, Sandee E. Hathaway, B.S.N
Short Description:	This guidebook is an all-inclusive reference for the parents of toddlers. Within its 900 pages, parents will find information on self-esteem; emotional, physical, and social development; discipline; and eccentric behaviors. The first of four parts in this guide includes chapters that focus separately on each month of development from thirteen months to 36 months.

■ **Read The Full Review Of This Resource On Page 326.**

Title:	**Parent Soup**
Subtitle:	An iVillage Community
Overall Rating:	★★★★
Media Type:	Internet
Short Description:	At this website, you can participate in live chats, get involved in discussion groups, read articles from pregnancy through the teen years, get listings of baby names, and more. As part of the "Parent Soup community," you can post announcements, ask for advice, get other parents' opinions on any topic, read relaxation tips, etc. Six experts are available to answer questions (10 per week) on various topics, and past Q & As can also be browsed.

■ **Read The Full Review Of This Resource On Page 327.**

Title:	**Your Baby & Child**
Subtitle:	From Birth To Age Five
Overall Rating:	★★★★
Media Type:	Print
Author/Editor:	Penelope Leach
Short Description:	Encompassing "the latest research and thinking" today, this book, in its third revision, offers information on child development, learning, and parenting styles. Five progressive stages of development are highlighted, from a newborn's birth to a child's fifth birthday. This 559-page guide explains the developmental changes occurring within a child through what they do, what they experience, and what they feel. Parent Q & As are also given.

■ **Read The Full Review Of This Resource On Page 328.**

4. Gaining An Overview: All-Inclusive

Title:	**Keys To Becoming A Father**
Overall Rating:	★★★
Media Type:	Print
Author/Editor:	William Sears, M.D.
Short Description:	This book offers support for and addresses concerns of fathers as they take on new roles with their children. The book is divided into 36 "Keys" which include narratives on topics (2–3 pages each). Topics include: fathering tips with newborns, fussy babies, juggling career and parenthood, being a single father, playing with and disciplining your child, and more. Sears, a father of 8, describes mistakes, revelations, and joys he personally has experienced.

■ **Read The Full Review Of This Resource On Page 301.**

Title:	**What Every Baby Knows**
Overall Rating:	★★★
Media Type:	Print
Author/Editor:	T. Berry Brazelton, M.D.
Short Description:	This is a book about five families and how they raise their children. Dr. Brazelton follows their distinct family histories, addresses issues that arise, and supplies detailed follow-up visits of their varying lifestyles and philosophies. This guide strives to answer questions most asked by parents about day-to-day issues as well as advice for tackling and identifying universal family problems.

■ **Read The Full Review Of This Resource On Page 331.**

THE SINGLE BEST RESOURCE FOR SELECTED TOPICS

III

INTRODUCTION

We've made recommendations for the best resources for various **subjects** and their subtopics in the previous section (Section II—"Infants, Toddlers, and Preschoolers: The Best Resources To Help You Parent") of this guidebook. As we've developed this guidebook, however, we've realized that many parents will want to access resources not solely on the basis of subject matter, but also by **age group**. For example, a parent may be in search of resources that answer questions such as: "What resources explain how my baby develops?" "What kinds of activities can I do with my toddler?" "What resources offer behavior methods I can use with my **preschooler**?"

In this section, then, we've identified resources that we feel are the **single best choice** we've found for each age group (Infants, Toddlers, Preschoolers, and All Ages). We've arranged these recommendations by age-specific topic when appropriate. Resources focused on more general topics (toilet training, choosing child care, etc.) may be appropriate to **all ages;** if parents cannot locate a topic of interest within a specific age range, we suggest they review the resource recommendations found under the heading "All Ages."

Many of the resources we recommend in this section are also recommended in the previous section, Section II; this duplication exists because "single best" resources are always included in the group of resources we recommend by subject. We also wanted to ensure that parents who search this directory from the standpoint of the age of their child will discover many of the same excellent resources we've recommended in the subject-oriented Section II.

While you'll find this list of outstanding resources helpful in every case, most parents will benefit from using more than one resource for each question or concern of importance. Be sure to read the complete, one-page review of any recommended resource, to help ensure that you gain a full understanding of its content, focus, style, and quality before you purchase or acquire that resource.

If parents wish to review additional recommended resources on any given topic, they can also refer to Section II, noting the age groups identified for each recommended resource (see the "age graphic" included on each full-page review) and selecting those relevant to their needs.

=Infant   =Toddler   =Preschooler

The recommended resources that follow refer to printed guidebooks unless otherwise noted.

1. INFANTS

In this section, we've included those resources we feel are the **single best** focusing on topics applicable for **infants,** typically from birth to their first birthday. These resources will offer you a full range of insights and information on the same topics offered in Section II, but are selected on the basis of those resources that address topics that concern parents of infants.

The resources recommended for those parenting **infants** include the following topics:

If a topic of interest to you is not included on this list, please check additional topics included in **"Single Best Resources For: All Ages (Infants To Preschoolers),"** the final chapter in this section.

1. Infants: Care

Overview Of Infant Care

Title:	**Babysense**
Subtitle:	A Practical And Supportive Guide To Baby Care
Overall Rating:	★★★★
Media Type:	Print
Author/Editor:	Frances Wells Burck

Short Description:

In its 2nd edition, this baby care guide was conceived by a first-time mother who felt that other mothers could benefit from a book combining emotional support with practical know-how. Drawing on mothers' responses to a questionnaire, this book combines anecdotes and advice for everything from dealing with the transition into motherhood to nutrition and feeding, and to other matters of everyday care for the first year of your baby's life.

■ **Read The Full Review Of This Resource On Page 153.**

Understanding And Soothing Babies' Cries

Title:	**Crying Baby, Sleepless Nights**
Overall Rating:	★★★★
Media Type:	Print
Author/Editor:	Sandy Jones

Short Description:

The meanings behind an infant's cries and the importance of a parent's response are outlined in this 162 page book written by an authority on crying babies. Various techniques are presented for each of 16 different cries along with coping tips for parents. The author debunks the myth of babies sleeping through the night including current researchers' sleep-training methods. Colic is addressed along with ways for parents to handle it.

■ **Read The Full Review Of This Resource On Page 133.**

Internet Website That Offers Breastfeeding Information

Title:	**Momness Center**
Overall Rating:	The Place For Information And Inspiration For Moms And Moms-To-Be
Media Type:	★★★
Author/Editor:	Internet

Short Description:

This site, developed by a manufacturer of baby formula, offers you information on breastfeeding, descriptions of the changes a woman goes through during her pregnancy (in journal format), how the fetus develops until birth, how pregnancy affects a woman's body (skin, hair, nails), and more. Breastfeeding information includes rationale, positions, how to breastfeed and return to work, and more.

■ **Read The Full Review Of This Resource On Page 107.**

1. Infants: Care

Nutritional Information And Baby Food Recipes

Title:	**Healthy Baby Meal Planner (The)**
Subtitle:	Mom-tested, Child-approved Recipes For Your Baby And Toddler
Overall Rating:	★★★★
Media Type:	Print
Author/Editor:	Annabel Karmel
Short Description:	This book is intended for parents who want "their babies and toddlers to eat well and enjoy their food," with fresh food, low animal fat, and low salt or sugars. Recipes are broken down into the following age groups: four to six months, six to nine months, nine to twelve months, and toddlers. Seven-day meal planning guides are also included for each age group. An index cross-references ingredients to other recipes containing that ingredient.

■ **Read The Full Review Of This Resource On Page 136.**

Equipment And Supplies For Infants

Title:	**Baby Bargains**
Overall Rating:	★★★★
Media Type:	Print
Author/Editor:	Denise Fields and Alan Fields
Short Description:	This book seeks to answer the big question—"Can we afford a baby?" It is a 333 page guide full of suggestions and contacts for how to save money on nursery furniture, clothing, toys, equipment, carseats, strollers, and much more. Reviews are given on name brand items along with a rating system (four stars). Information is independent of manufacturer input and is based upon the authors' experiences and the parents they interviewed.

■ **Read The Full Review Of This Resource On Page 129.**

CD-ROM Focusing On Infants' Care And Development

Title:	**Your Pregnancy, Your Newborn**
Subtitle:	The Complete Guide For Expectant And New Mothers
Overall Rating:	★★★★
Media Type:	CD-ROM
Short Description:	Developed by the editors of PARENTING magazine, this CD-ROM focuses on pregnancy topics and a newborn baby's needs. Pregnancy issues include how to plan for pregnancy, a month-by-month description of pregnancy, and labor & delivery. Discussions about a newborn's care focus on the first few weeks and "Life With Baby." Advice is given on how to adapt to the changes, how to take care of a baby, and how to seek childcare.

■ **Read The Full Review Of This Resource On Page 154.**

1. Infants: Care

Continuing Breastfeeding Upon Returning To Work

Title:	**Nursing Mother, Working Mother**
Subtitle:	The Essential Guide For Breastfeeding And Staying Close To Your Baby After You Return To Work
Overall Rating:	★★★★
Media Type:	Print
Author/Editor:	Gale Pryor
Short Description:	Extending a section of her other book, Nursing Your Baby, Pryor discusses how to combine work and breastfeeding. Within its 184 pages, this seven chapter book highlights the whys and hows of breastfeeding along with a plea to change workplace attitudes toward motherhood. Three chapters specifically focus on the transition from new motherhood to work including maternity leave, getting ready (supplies, finding care, etc.), and returning.

■ **Read The Full Review Of This Resource On Page 103.**

Breastfeeding Information

Title:	**Breastfeeding Your Baby**
Overall Rating:	★★★★
Media Type:	Print
Author/Editor:	Sheila Kitzinger
Short Description:	Believing that breastfeeding involves a combination of your feelings about your baby and your body along with the technical how-tos, this book strives to offer information on everything women need to know about breastfeeding. Suggestions, advice, and numerous color or black and white photographs help illustrate techniques and address problems. Also discussed are issues centered around family dynamics, returning to work, and more.

■ **Read The Full Review Of This Resource On Page 101.**

1. Infants: Growth & Learning

Videotape Focusing On Infant Development

Title:	**Touchpoints, Volume 2**
Subtitle:	The First Month Through The First Year
Overall Rating:	★★★★
Media Type:	Videotape
Short Description:	Brazelton's 45 minute videotape focuses on the emotional, cognitive, and motor development of babies from one month to 15 months. Five different families are showcased along with their frustrations, concerns, and joys. More than fifteen "touchpoints" are illustrated and explained sequentially through the tape. Touchpoints are, as Brazelton defines them, "periods of time that precede a rapid growth in learning for both child and parent."

■ **Read The Full Review Of This Resource On Page 163.**

Guide To Infant Development

Title:	**Touchpoints**
Subtitle:	Your Child's Emotional And Behavioral Development
Overall Rating:	★★★★
Media Type:	Print
Author/Editor:	T. Berry Brazelton, M.D.
Short Description:	Whereas most books focus on the physical development of a child, this book seeks to provide parents with an understanding of the emotional and behavioral development of the child as well. Broken up into three parts, this book addresses "touchpoints" (those predictable times that occur before a surge of rapid growth), challenges, and allies in a child's development.

■ **Read The Full Review Of This Resource On Page 162.**

Activities To Do With Infants

Title:	**Active Learning For Infants**
Overall Rating:	★★★★
Media Type:	Print
Author/Editor:	Debby Cryer, Thelma Harms, and Beth Bourland
Short Description:	This guidebook, developed at a child development center in Chapel Hill, North Carolina, was tested in 17 daycare centers and is the first book in the "Active Learning Series." With over 300 activities for newborns to 12 month old infants, this book contains a complete planning guide for educators, and activities for babies that promote listening and talking, physical development, creativity, and learning about the world around them.

■ **Read The Full Review Of This Resource On Page 245.**

**I. Infants:
Parent-To-Parent
Advice & Forums**

Guide For New Moms Adjusting To Motherhood

Title:	**The Year After Childbirth**
Subtitle:	Surviving And Enjoying The First Year Of Motherhood
Overall Rating:	★★★★
Media Type:	Print
Author/Editor:	Sheila Kitzinger

Short Description:

■ **Read The Full Review Of This Resource On Page 295.**

The focus of this book is on the woman's experience of becoming a mother during the first year after birth. Information is provided to help her get back in shape and to understand the physical, emotional, and identity issues involved. Many chapters include highlighted self-help inserts of what to do for each of the topics covered. Colorful inserts, illustrations and diagrams are included, as well as a glossary of terms and referrals.

**1. Infants: Gaining
An Overview:
All-Inclusive**

Guide To Infants' Care And Development

Title: **Baby Book (The)**

Subtitle: Everything You Need To Know About Your Baby—From Birth To Age Two

Overall Rating: ★★★★

Media Type: Print

Author/Editor: William Sears, M.D. & Martha Sears, R.N.

Short Description:

■ **Read The Full Review Of This Resource On Page 317.**

As parents of 8 and pediatric specialists, this husband and wife team present a parenting philosophy believed to promote "connected" parents and children. They call this philosophy "attachment parenting;" it lays the foundation for the rest of their 689 page book. Various topics are included such as: baby-care basics, infant feeding and nutrition, "contemporary parenting," infant development and behavior, and keeping your baby safe and healthy.

CD-ROM Focusing On Infants' Care And Development

Title: **I Am Your Child (CD-ROM)**

Subtitle: The First Three Years Last Forever

Overall Rating: ★★★★

Media Type: CD-ROM

Short Description:

■ **Read The Full Review Of This Resource On Page 322.**

Supporting a national campaign "to make early childhood development a top priority for our nation," this CD-ROM correlates the latest findings in brain research to the first three years of a child's development. Ten guidelines for raising children are offered, along with brain research data, details about child development from prenatal to age three, questions from parents, answers and insight from "top experts" (Brazelton, Koop, etc.), and more.

Internet Website Focusing On Infants' Care And Development

Title: **I Am Your Child (Internet)**

Overall Rating: ★★★★

Media Type: Internet

Short Description:

■ **Read The Full Review Of This Resource On Page 323.**

Supporting a national campaign "to make early childhood development a top priority for our nation," this website correlates the latest findings in brain research to the first three years of a child's development. Ten guidelines for raising children are offered, along with brain research data, details about child development from prenatal to age three, questions, answers, and insight from "top experts" (Brazelton, Koop, etc.), and more.

**1. Infants: Gaining
An Overview:
All-Inclusive**

Videotape Focusing On Infants' Care And Development

Title:	**Baby Basics (Videotape)**
Subtitle:	The Complete Video Guide For New And Expectant Parents
Overall Rating:	★★★★
Media Type:	Videotape

Short Description:

■ **Read The Full Review Of
This Resource On Page 316.**

Divided into eight "chapters," this 110 minute videotape focuses on the care and development of newborns and infants. Topics discussed include: the newborn's appearances, postpartum care of the mother, the adjustment during the first days at home, daily care (bathing, diapering, dressing, and more), feeding (breastfeeding, bottlefeeding), health and safety, babies' cries, sleep patterns, and infants' growth and development.

4. TODDLERS

In this section, we've included those resources we feel are the **single best** focusing on topics applicable for **toddlers,** typically from their first birthday (or when they begin walking) to their preschool years (about age 3). These resources will offer you a full range of insights and information on the same topics offered in Section II, but are selected on the basis of those resources that address topics that concern parents of toddlers.

The resources recommended for those parenting **toddlers** include the following topics:

If a topic of interest to you is not included on this list, please check additional topics included in **"Single Best Resources For: All Ages (Infants To Preschoolers),"** the final chapter in this section.

2. Toddlers: Care

Breastfeeding Support And Information

Title:	**Mothering Your Nursing Toddler**
Overall Rating:	★★★★
Media Type:	Print
Author/Editor:	Norma Jane Bumgarner
Short Description:	Believing that nursing plays a great role in a child's ability to grow up, Bumgarner focuses on the breastfeeding relationship in terms of the child's developmental needs. Advice and information is given on the "whys" of breastfeeding (for mother and for child), the "hows" of nursing (marital concerns, night nursing, mother's health, etc.), the changing dynamics of the breastfeeding relationship (to age 4+), and various ways to approach weaning.

■ **Read The Full Review Of This Resource On Page 102.**

Nutritional Information And Recipes For Toddlers

Title:	**Baby Let's Eat**
Overall Rating:	★★★
Media Type:	Print
Author/Editor:	Rena Coyle with Patricia Messing
Short Description:	Within this 128 page book, parents will find nutritional information and recipes for babies and toddlers. Nutritional basics, suggested daily servings and serving sizes for children ages 1 to 3 years, food preparation methods, and more are provided. The recipes are divided by ages for children 6 to 12 months, 12 to 18 months, 18 to 24 months, and 24 to 36 months. A weekly meal planning chart is given for each age group along with 20–25 recipes.

■ **Read The Full Review Of This Resource On Page 138.**

2. Toddlers: Growth & Learning

Activities To Do With Toddlers

Title:	**Baby Games**
Subtitle:	The Joyful Guide To Child's Play From Birth To Three Years
Overall Rating:	★★★★
Media Type:	Print
Author/Editor:	Elaine Martin
Short Description:	The book suggests that playing with your baby creates special bonds of love, communication, and caring that will last a lifetime. Divided by age groupings (birth to age 3) and by activity types (music, art, kitchen, etc.), this guidebook focuses on open-ended creative activities. As a child develops from infant to toddler to preschooler, this resource aims "to create a magical childhood" through its rhymes, songs, finger plays, games, and more.

■ **Read The Full Review Of This Resource On Page 239.**

Understanding Strong-Willed Children

Title:	**Parenting The Strong-Willed Child**
Subtitle:	The Clinically Proven Five-Week Program For Parents Of Two- To Six-Year-Olds
Overall Rating:	★★★★
Media Type:	Print
Author/Editor:	Rex Forehand, Ph.D. and Nicholas Long, Ph.D.
Short Description:	This book focuses on a program to help parents of strong-willed children find positive and manageable solutions to their children's difficult behavior. The four parts of this 256 page book highlight factors that cause and contribute to strong-willed behavior, techniques of the authors' five-week program, how to develop a positive environment in the family and home, and how to deal with specific behavior problems (temper tantrums, aggression, etc.).

■ **Read The Full Review Of This Resource On Page 279.**

Guide To Toddler Development

Title:	**Emotional Life Of The Toddler (The)**
Overall Rating:	★★★★
Media Type:	Print
Author/Editor:	Alicia F. Lieberman
Short Description:	Written by a senior psychologist with a background in mother-child attachments, this 244 page book focuses on understanding how a toddler "thinks, feels, and responds to the challenges of growing up, and how parents can help them meet these challenges with greater self-confidence and joy." Chapter topics include the parent-toddler relationship, the variety of temperaments, toddler anxieties, and the impact of divorce and childcare.

■ **Read The Full Review Of This Resource On Page 164.**

2. Toddlers: Gaining An Overview: All Inclusive

Guide To Toddlers' Care And Development

Title:	**What To Expect The Toddler Years**
Overall Rating:	★★★★
Media Type:	Print
Author/Editor:	Arlene Eisenberg, Heidi E. Murkoff, Sandee E. Hathaway, B.S.N

Short Description:

■ **Read The Full Review Of This Resource On Page 326.**

This guidebook is an all-inclusive reference for the parents of toddlers. Within its 900 pages, parents will find information on self-esteem; emotional, physical, and social development; discipline; and eccentric behaviors. The first of four parts in this guide includes chapters that focus separately on each month of development from thirteen months to 36 months.

3.

PRESCHOOLERS

In this section, we've included those resources we feel are the **single best** focusing on topics applicable for **preschoolers,** typically from their third birthday to age 5 when they typically enter into a formal education program such as kindergarten. These resources will offer you a full range of insights and information on the same topics offered in Section II, but are selected on the basis of those resources that address topics that concern parents of preschoolers.

The resources recommended for those parenting **preschoolers** include the following topics:

Growth & Learning 83

Understanding preschoolers' behavior and appropriate ways to discipline
Internet website focusing on preschoolers' growth and development
Overview of preschoolers' growth and development
Art activites to do with preschoolers
Activities to do with preschoolers
Selecting an appropriate preschool
Dealing with learning disabilities

If a topic of interest to you is not included on this list, please check additional topics included in **"Single Best Resources For: All Ages (Infants To Preschoolers),"** the final chapter in this section.

3. Preschoolers:
Growth & Learning

Understanding Preschoolers' Behavior And Appropriate Ways To Discipline

Title:	**Positive Discipline For Preschoolers**
Subtitle:	For Their Early Years—Raising Children Who Are Responsible, Respectful And Resourceful
Overall Rating:	★★★
Media Type:	Print
Author/Editor:	Jane Nelsen, Ed.D., Cheryl Erwin, and Roslyn Duffy
Short Description:	This 320 page book offers "practical solutions" for parents and teachers of young children in the areas of positive discipline, temperament, and personality. Other topics include teaching independence, developing logical consequences for actions, and encouraging positive behavior.

■ **Read The Full Review Of This Resource On Page 200.**

Internet Website Focusing On Preschoolers' Growth And Development

Title:	Sesame Street Parents
Overall Rating:	★★★★
Media Type:	Internet
Short Description:	Developed by Children's Television Workshop (CTW), host of the TV show "Sesame Street," this site offers information and tips primarily for parents of preschoolers. Options at their homepage include: activities, behavior & discipline, child development, education, family & community, health & safety, and product reviews. A discussion forum is also available along with email contact to CTW's contributing consultants.

■ **Read The Full Review Of This Resource On Page 287.**

Overview Of Preschoolers' Growth And Development

Title:	**Preschool Years (The)**
Subtitle:	Family Strategies That Work—From Experts And Parents
Overall Rating:	★★★★
Media Type:	Print
Author/Editor:	Ellen Galinsky and Judy David
Short Description:	This 504 page guide on topics associated with preschoolers combine parents' most frequently questions, solutions from parents and "experts" (T. Berry Brazelton, Benjamin Spock, Bruno Bettleheim, etc.), and "successful strategies" from 300+ interviewed parents. Topics discussed include: discipline, learning routines, daycare, preschool, work and family life, emotions, and more.

■ **Read The Full Review Of This Resource On Page 286.**

**3. Preschoolers:
Growth & Learning**

Art Activities To Do With Preschoolers

Title:	**Preschool Art**
Subtitle:	It's The Process, Not The Product
Overall Rating:	★★★★
Media Type:	Print
Author/Editor:	MaryAnn Kohl
Short Description:	This book has over 200 process-oriented art projects for children ages 3 to 5. Using materials commonly found in the home, children can create open-ended art experiences. Arranged by the "Basics" (art ideas for any time of year) and by the seasons, each activity includes a list of materials needed, how to do the activity, possible variations, a line drawing of the process, and more. Indexes divide activities by project, materials, and art medium.

■ **Read The Full Review Of This Resource On Page 241.**

Activities To Do With Preschoolers

Title:	**365 TV-Free Activities**
Subtitle:	You Can Do With Your Child
Overall Rating:	★★★★
Media Type:	Print
Author/Editor:	Steve Bennett and Ruth Bennett
Short Description:	Offering 365 activities to wean children from TV watching, this compact 425 page book is designed for "the family that plays together." Grouped alphabetically (and by category), activities are divided into 16 categories including: arts and crafts, food stuff, math and numbers, recycled household materials, science, words and language, toymaking, and more. Each activity is covered on one page with a list of materials, instructions, and safety tips.

■ **Read The Full Review Of This Resource On Page 244.**

**3. Preschoolers:
Growth & Learning**

Selecting An Appropriate Preschool

Title:	**Smart Start**
Subtitle:	The Parents' Complete Guide To Preschool Education
Overall Rating:	★★★★
Media Type:	Print
Author/Editor:	Marian Edelman Borden
Short Description:	This step-by-step 222 page guide provides information on various preschool program philosophies along with suggested guidelines to use when making a choice and ways to make the transition successful. Checklists and highlighted tips are provided throughout. Additional advice is given for parents of children with handicapping conditions, families with children in daycare who wish to include preschool in their child's day, and more.

■ **Read The Full Review Of
This Resource On Page 272.**

Dealing With Learning Disabilities

Title:	**Learning Disabilities: A To Z**
Subtitle:	A Parent's Complete Guide To Learning Disabilities From Preschool To Adulthood
Overall Rating:	★★★★
Media Type:	Print
Author/Editor:	Corinne Smith, Ph.D. and Lisa Strick
Short Description:	The three parts of this 407 page book describe the symptoms, causes, and treatments of learning disabilities. The types of learning disabilities that are highlighted include ADHD, visual perception disabilities, language processing disabilities, and fine motor disabilities. Suggestions are offered throughout in terms of how to help a child with learning disabilities succeed in school, at home, and in transitioning on their own.

■ **Read The Full Review Of
This Resource On Page 278.**

4. ALL AGES

In this section, we've included those resources we feel are the **single best** focusing on topics applicable for **all ages** of young children, from infancy through the preschool years. These resources will offer you a full range of insights and information on the same topics offered in Section II, but are selected on the basis of those resources that address all age groups of children we've researched.

The resources recommended for those parenting children of **all ages** include the following topics:

4. All Ages: Care

Choosing A Nanny

Title:	**Complete Nanny Guide (The)**
Subtitle:	Solutions To Parents' Questions About Hiring And Keeping An In-Home Caregiver
Overall Rating:	★★★★
Media Type:	Print
Author/Editor:	Cora Hilton Thomas
Short Description:	This book contains information on finding and choosing appropriate in-home care. Chapter topics in this 154 guide include finding the right person, costs, interviewing, screening, keeping a nanny, filing government forms, using a placement agency, and more. One chapter focuses on finding care for children that have special needs. Appendices contain numerous forms and checklists (criminal background release forms, tax and government forms, etc.).

■ **Read The Full Review Of This Resource On Page 117.**

Taking Care Of Twins And Multiples

Title:	**Mothering Twins (Print/Novotny)**
Subtitle:	Having, Raising, And Loving Babies Who Arrive In Groups
Overall Rating:	★★★
Media Type:	Print
Author/Editor:	Pamela Patrick Novotny
Short Description:	The author strives to offer "an upbeat, practical guide to raising and loving babies that arrive in groups of two or more." This 324 page book contains medical, psychological, and sociological findings on all aspects of caring for two or more children simultaneously. Chapter topics include: the logistics of caring for multiples after birth, to their first year, and beyond; mothercare; family adjustments; premature births; and more.

■ **Read The Full Review Of This Resource On Page 126.**

4. All Ages: Care

Nutritional Information And Recipes

Title:	**Small Helpings**
Subtitle:	A Complete Guide To Feeding Babies, Toddlers And Young Children
Overall Rating:	★★★★
Media Type:	Print
Author/Editor:	Annabel Karmel

Short Description:

■ **Read The Full Review Of This Resource On Page 137.**

This book contains over 120 easy, quick recipes using fresh, natural ingredients. Included are recipes for babies, toddlers, and small children with emphasis placed on cooking for the whole family. Recipes cover occasions and meals (healthy snacks, "fast foods," lunch boxes, parties, etc.) and many can be frozen for a ready meal. Nutritional advice is given with the intent that a pattern of healthy eating can be established for young children.

Selecting Child Care

Title:	**Child Care That Works**
Subtitle:	A Parent's Guide To Finding Quality Child Care
Overall Rating:	★★★★
Media Type:	Print
Author/Editor:	Eva Cochran and Mon Cochran

Short Description:

■ **Read The Full Review Of This Resource On Page 116.**

How to find quality child care is the focus of this 355 page book. The six parts of this guide deal separately with the various options that are available, the possible emotional reactions children and parents may have to child care, ways to build a partnership with a caregiver, how much to pay, and how to become an advocate for quality care. Checklists, forms, and organization contact information are given in the appendices.

4. All Ages: Growth & Learning

Overview Of Young Children's Growth And Development

Title:	**Parenting Young Children**
Subtitle:	Systematic Training For Effective Parenting Of Children Under Six
Overall Rating:	★★★★
Media Type:	Print
Author/Editor:	Don Dinkmeyer, Sr., Gary D. McKay, James S. Dinkmeyer, Don Dinkmeyer, Jr., and Joyce L. McKay
Short Description:	This guidebook, based upon a parenting program called STEP—Systematic Training for Effective Parenting—aims to help parents' confidence in working with children from birth to six years of age. It is founded on using a "consistent, positive, and democratic approach." Areas covered include: children's development, behavior, discipline, self-esteem, listening and talking to children, teaching cooperation, and social and emotional development.

■ **Read The Full Review Of This Resource On Page 285.**

Guide To Toilet Training/Learning

Title:	**Mommy I Have To Go Potty!**
Subtitle:	A Parent's Guide To Toilet Training
Overall Rating:	★★★★
Media Type:	Print
Author/Editor:	Jan Faull, M.Ed.
Short Description:	This guide offers a step-by-step approach to toilet training your child from diapers to dry nights. The author offers her "simple, common-sense approach" to teach parents such things as how to tell if their child is really ready to toilet train, how to deal with accidents, why it's OK to return to diapers temporarily, and tips to make toilet training fun for kids. Numerous parental anecdotes are given to introduce sections along with bulleted tips.

■ **Read The Full Review Of This Resource On Page 231.**

4. All Ages: Growth & Learning

Guide To Understanding The Dynamics Of Sibling Relationships

Title:	**Loving Each One Best**
Subtitle:	A Caring And Practical Approach To Raising Siblings
Overall Rating:	★★★★
Media Type:	Print
Author/Editor:	Nancy Samalin with Catherine Whitney
Short Description:	This guide offers information, advice, and a discussion of the feelings parents and children have when new siblings enter into the family. Introducing a new sibling into a family, relieving parental stress, helping fathers become equal parenting partners, and what children think about having a new brother or sister are some of the topics discussed within this 210-page resource. Numerous parent-child dialogues are also included throughout.

■ **Read The Full Review Of This Resource On Page 223.**

Videotape Offering Advice About Sibling Relationships

Title:	**Those Baby Blues**
Subtitle:	A Parent's Guide To Helping Your Child Adjust To The New Baby
Overall Rating:	★★★★
Media Type:	Videotape
Short Description:	Combining family stories, footage of interactions between siblings, and professional advice, this 30 minute videotape focuses on sibling rivalry. Discussions include changes in behavior, throwing tantrums, aggression, hidden hostility, regression, "nothing's wrong," depression, and withdrawal. Advice is given for how to handle each reaction along with tips on understanding the child's behavior. A complimentary video for siblings is also provided.

■ **Read The Full Review Of This Resource On Page 222.**

Videotape Focusing On Children's Behavior And Discipline Strategies

Title:	**Stop Struggling With Your Child**
Overall Rating:	★★★★
Media Type:	Videotape
Short Description:	Developed by the authors of a book by the same title, this 30 minute video focuses on ways to minimize family power struggles and maximize a child's self-esteem. The authors suggest that if parents change their own behavior, then children will change theirs. The four-steps of this method have been developed so children can be given opportunities to become cooperative, to practice problem-solving, and to take responsibility for themselves.

■ **Read The Full Review Of This Resource On Page 189.**

4. All Ages: Growth & Learning

Books To Share With Young Children

Title: **Read-Aloud Handbook (The)**

Overall Rating: ★★★★

Media Type: Print

Author/Editor: Jim Trelease

Short Description:

■ **Read The Full Review Of This Resource On Page 246.**

Now in its fourth edition, this 387 page book is two books in one. The first half includes information on when, why, and how to read aloud to your child along with updated statistics, current research, and new anecdotes. The second half encompasses the "Treasury of Read-Alouds" (200+ pages) listing books by type (wordless, picture, etc.); each annotation includes cross-references to books by the same author and books of the same theme.

Understanding Behavior And Appropriate Ways To Discipline

Title: **Positive Discipline (Print)**

Subtitle: Revised Edition

Overall Rating: ★★★★

Media Type: Print

Author/Editor: Jane Nelsen, Ed.D.

Short Description:

■ **Read The Full Review Of This Resource On Page 192.**

This 258 page resource emphasizes firmness with dignity, kindness, and respect. Based on the beliefs of Adler and Dreikurs, positive discipline concepts include: treat mistakes as opportunities to learn, seek solutions to problems together as a family (rather than blame), believe that children do better when they feel better, the "significant seven" of successful people ("I am capable," etc.), children listen when they feel listened to, and more.

Understanding How Children Deal With Grief And Loss

Title: **Helping Children Cope With Separation And Loss**

Overall Rating: ★★★★

Media Type: Print

Author/Editor: Claudia Jewett Jarratt

Short Description:

■ **Read The Full Review Of This Resource On Page 276.**

Written by a respected child and family therapist, this 232-page book serves as a guide for parents, therapists, and other caregivers who wish to help children move through the stages of grief and loss. Ways of identifying and dealing with children's grief reactions are found here, as well as creative methods to help children give voice to their feelings at all stages of the grief process.

4. All Ages: Growth & Learning

Activities To Do With Young Children

Title:	**Great Explorations**
Subtitle:	100 Creative Play Ideas For Parents And Preschoolers From Playspace At The Children's Museum Boston
Overall Rating:	★★★★
Media Type:	Print
Author/Editor:	Amy Nolan
Short Description:	This 245 page activity guide was developed by the manager of Playspace (part of the Children's Museum in Boston). Offering 100 of the center's favorite art, science, music, cooking, and dramatic play experiences, this resource focuses on a discovery-based approach to learning. Each activity is explained in a two-page spread with a list of materials, length of time needed, recommended ages, directions, enhanced skill, and ways to extend it.

■ **Read The Full Review Of This Resource On Page 240.**

Understanding And Treatment Of Brain Disorders

Title:	**It's Nobody's Fault**
Subtitle:	New Hope And Help For Difficult Children
Overall Rating:	★★★★
Media Type:	Print
Author/Editor:	Harold S. Koplewicz, M.D.
Short Description:	This 303 page guide focuses on the genetic make-up of brain disorders, their symptoms, their causes, and how to treat them. The author highlights 13 "no-fault brain disorders" that are biologically caused and not a reflection of what the parents have done. Disorders profiled include: ADHD, obsessive compulsive disorder, separation anxiety, social phobia, eating disorders, bedwetting, tourette syndrome, depressive disorder, autism, and more.

■ **Read The Full Review Of This Resource On Page 277.**

4. All Ages: Growth & Learning

Understanding And Treatment For Childhood Depression

Title:	**Lonely, Sad And Angry**
Subtitle:	A Parent's Guide To Depression In Children And Adolescents
Overall Rating:	★★★★
Media Type:	Print
Author/Editor:	Barbara D. Ingersoll, Ph.D. and Sam Goldstein, Ph.D.
Short Description:	Written by clinical psychologists, this 225 page book describes symptoms, causes, and types of treatment for depressive disorders in children and adolescents. Related emotional and behavioral problems are discussed in addition (anxiety disorders, conduct disorder, ADHD, oppositional defiant disorder, learning disabilities). Separate chapters offer advice on how families and teachers can cope. Another chapter focuses on suicidal behavior.

■ **Read The Full Review Of This Resource On Page 280.**

Understanding And Treatment Of Children's Emotional And Learning Problems

Title:	**When You Worry About The Child You Love**
Subtitle:	Emotional And Learning Problems In Children
Overall Rating:	★★★★
Media Type:	Print
Author/Editor:	Edward Hallowell, M.D.
Short Description:	Developed by a "therapeutic optimist," this 280 page book offers a balanced approach of nature and nurture in dealing with childhood problems. Conditions associated with the states of anger, sadness, fear, and confusion are highlighted along with some less common childhood problems. Specific examples of over 30 treatable emotional and /or learning problems are provided. A chapter is included that discusses medications.

■ **Read The Full Review Of This Resource On Page 281.**

4. All Ages: Growth & Learning

Audiotape Focusing On Children's Behavior And Ways To Avoid Power Struggles

Title:	**Avoiding Power Struggles With Kids**
Overall Rating:	★★★★
Media Type:	Audiotape
Author/Editor:	Jim Fay and Foster W. Cline, M.D.
Short Description:	Based on the authors' book *Parenting with Love and Logic*, this 65 minute audiotape focuses on the "Science of Control" and how parents can avoid power struggles with their children. The authors believe that the more control parents give away, the more control they will have. A four-step procedure is illustrated with specific examples of how to use "thinking words," offer choices, and allow children to live with the consequences of their choices.

■ **Read The Full Review Of This Resource On Page 190.**

Understanding Children's Temperament

Title:	**Know Your Child**
Subtitle:	An Authoritative Guide For Today's Parents
Overall Rating:	★★★★
Media Type:	Print
Author/Editor:	Stella Chess and Alexander Thomas
Short Description:	This resource focuses on child development in terms of the research based on children's temperament. Based upon the authors' extensive experience, this 397 guide highlights children's early developmental stages and aims to provide parents with answers to their most often asked questions. Parents are shown how to avoid some of the pitfalls of parenting by comparing their own expectations and attitudes with their child's temperament.

■ **Read The Full Review Of This Resource On Page 165.**

4. All Ages: Parent-To-Parent Advice & Forums

Advice From Other Parents To New Parents

Title: **Practical Parenting Tips**

Subtitle: Over 1,500 Helpful Hints For The First Five Years

Overall Rating: ★★★★

Media Type: Print

Author/Editor: Vicki Lansky

Short Description: This guide contains a collection of practical hints for parents. Topics discussed include new baby care, child care "basics," hygiene and health, childproofing and safety, parenting "challenges" (manners, tantrums, rivalry, etc.), family relationships (traditions, relatives, etc.), traveling, and playtime ideas (seasonal fun, arts and crafts, etc.). The 1,500+ tips were accumulated from the author's parenting columns and contacts with other parents.

■ **Read The Full Review Of This Resource On Page 294.**

Guide For New Dads Adjusting To Fatherhood

Title: **Father's Almanac (The)**

Overall Rating: ★★★★

Media Type: Print

Author/Editor: S. Adams Sullivan

Short Description: Revised from its original publication in 1980, this edition notes how fathers' roles have changed. This 391 page book's intent is to encourage "involved fatherhood." Chapter topics include: pregnancy/childbirth; baby care; fathers' jobs; family issues; "providing;" daily care; outings and special events; teaching and discipline; learning, playing, and working with kids; and photographing, videotaping, etc.

■ **Read The Full Review Of This Resource On Page 293.**

4. All Ages: Gaining An Overview: All-Inclusive

Dealing With Sleep Issues

Title:	**Nighttime Parenting**
Subtitle:	How To Get Your Baby And Child To Sleep
Overall Rating:	★★★
Media Type:	Print
Author/Editor:	William Sears, M.D.

Short Description:

■ **Read The Full Review Of This Resource On Page 148.**

Sears wrote this guide to answer the question, "Should I let my child cry it out at night, or console my crying child?" Using research findings and the results from a questionnaire given to patients, Sears addresses this question within the book's 17 chapters. Topics focus on: baby vs. adult sleep, where baby should sleep, night-waking, sleep disorders, SIDS, demands of the high need child, and more.

Internet Website Focusing On Young Children's Care And Development

Title:	**Family.Com**
Subtitle:	Disney.Com
Overall Rating:	★★★★
Media Type:	Internet

Short Description:

■ **Read The Full Review Of This Resource On Page 321.**

Developed with Disney, this website offers customized searches of parenting information based upon drop-down lists (about 15 subtopics) and specified age ranges (birth on up). Options at their homepage include searches under the headings of "Activities," "Education," "Food," "Parenting," "Boards," and more. Future plans include an interactive "Chat" segment.

**4. All Ages: Gaining
An Overview:
All-Inclusive**

Guide To Young Children's Care And Development

Title:	**Caring For Your Baby And Young Child**
Subtitle:	Birth To Age 5
Overall Rating:	★★★★
Media Type:	Print
Author/Editor:	Steven P. Shelov, M.D., F.A.A.P.

Short Description:

■ **Read The Full Review Of
This Resource On Page 319.**

Caring for Your Baby and Child covers the first five years of a child's life. Part One addresses how to prepare for a new baby, including equipment, infant care, feeding, etc. A month-by-month guide follows and includes what to expect and how to care for your baby up to their fifth birthday. Part Two is a medical reference guide, with an alphabetical coverage of emergencies, illnesses, behavior, disabilities, family issues, and more.

RESOURCE
REVIEWS

INTRODUCTION

In this section you'll find our full-page reviews of **all** the resources we've encountered in our research on the best information available on the subject of parenting infants, toddlers, and preschoolers. These reviews are organized by subject, within each subject by overall "Star" rating (1–4 Stars), and alphabetically within overall rating.

Print Resources: Some of these books are hundreds of pages long; some just dozens of pages. We work hard to ensure that we've reviewed the latest edition of books. The edition date included in each review shows when the most recent edition was published or the latest copyright date shown in the liner notes. We don't review books that are no longer in print or not readily available from bookstores, since we want our recommendations to be readily available to those who want to acquire them.

Internet Websites: These reviews include Internet websites we've been able to find that are focused on various subjects related to parenting young children. Our criteria for selecting a website for review include these requirements:

- A substantial portion of its content must be focused on the subject we're researching; our review evaluates **this** content, not necessarily the site as a whole (for those sites that have more broadly defined coverage).

- It must be substantially complete, not substantially under construction.

- Commercial sites that have products or services for sale to visitors are reviewed, provided they also contain some relevant, free content.

- We generally don't review sites which have as their primary focus simply providing links to other sites, particularly since most of those linked sites will be included in our reviews.

Commercial Online Services: These reviews include forums or special interest areas containing proprietary or sponsored content focused on parenting young children; we provide "Keywords" used to directly access these pages (when available). Content offered by the commercial online services through linked websites are generally reviewed in the Internet section.

Videotape & Audiotape Resources: These reviews include videotape and audiotape products that are focused on various subjects related to parenting young children.

Care: Breastfeeding

BREASTFEEDING YOUR BABY

 Best Resource For:
Breastfeeding information

 Recommended For:
Care

Description:

There are eight major sections in this 160 page book. The first section outlines the benefits of breastfeeding, how pregnancy can change your breast shape, and problem-solving tips for various breast types (large, small, inverted nipple, breast surgery). The second section discusses the first days of breastfeeding including topics such as nursing positions, latching on, sucking rhythms, nursing at night, and clothing suggestions for mother and baby. The physiological process of breastfeeding is addressed in the next section along with suggestions on how to take care of yourself to ensure a good milk supply, and more. Section Four offers help for possible problems, such as engorgement, sore and cracked nipples, mastitis, and other deterrents to nursing. The next four sections highlight: learning about your baby's needs (the sleepy baby, the excited baby, etc.), the baby with special needs (jaundice, handicaps, etc.), the family's dynamics (baby, siblings, parents), and "security and adventure" (older baby, sex, traveling, weaning, and returning to work). A reference section, support organization contact information, and an index are given.

Evaluation:

This is clearly a beautiful, well-written book. Numerous color and black and white photographs are provided on virtually every page with clear, concise captions that fully explain and illustrate each topic. Step-by-step instructions, bulleted notations, and bold subheadings also add to this book's ease of use. This guide does an excellent job of covering all aspects of breastfeeding in a progressive, matter-of-fact format. Not just concerned with the basics and how-tos, this resource also covers other issues, such as time management, what to do if you are thinking of giving up breastfeeding, how to deal with babies with special needs, how to nurse the older baby, and more. Topics are presented knowledgeably, with constant reassurance and advice on the most frequently encountered aspects of breastfeeding. Additional resources will be needed to support nursing mothers planning to return to work; minimal advice is given here. But for those women who want a companion to support them in their decision to breastfeed, this is the book that will guide them each step of the way.

Where To Find/Buy:

Bookstores and libraries.

Overall Rating
★★★★
Complete, supportive & affirming guide sure to be a companion to every nursing mother

Design, Ease Of Use
★★★★
A guide with style; user friendly and intelligently formatted; numerous color photos

1–4 Stars; N/R = Not Rated

Media Type:
Print

Price:
$20.00

Principal Subject:
Care

Age Group:
Infants & Toddlers (0–3)

ISBN:
0679724338

Edition Reviewed:
(6th) 1997

Publisher:
Dorling Kindersley (Alfred A. Knopf/Random House)

Author/Editor:
Sheila Kitzinger

About The Author:
(From Cover Notes)
Sheila Kitzinger, a childbirth educator, has written over 16 books on pregnancy, birth, and childcare.

★★★★

Overall Rating
★★★★
Compassionate, supportive advice for those who breastfeed beyond baby's first year

Design, Ease Of Use
★★★
A detailed table of contents would help; subchapter headings good; easily read

I–4 Stars; N/R = Not Rated

Media Type:
Print

Price:
$8.95

Principal Subject:
Care

Age Group:
Toddlers (1–3)

ISBN:
0912500123

Edition Reviewed:
1982

Publisher:
La Leche League International

Author/Editor:
Norma Jane Bumgarner

About The Author:
(From Cover Notes)
Bumgarner has been very active in La Leche League for 14 years and is a frequent contributor to La Leche League publications and a speaker at LLLI conferences. She has three sons and a daughter, three of which nursed well past their first birthdays.

MOTHERING YOUR NURSING TODDLER

Best Resource For:
Breastfeeding support and information

Recommended For:
Care

Description:

Bumgarner believes that "young children need the calming and reassuring effects of sucking . . . (and) the very best place for this sucking to take place is in mother's arms, at her breast, where it is entirely natural and complete." She further states that the ensuing suckling plays an enormous part in a child's ability to mature and grow up without the need for alternatives (pacifiers, thumbs, blankets, etc.) that are difficult to rid from the child's life. Her book describes the continued breastfeeding relationship between mother and child, focusing on the child's development and their consequent natural desire to wean once their sucking need has been met. This 208 page book is divided into four parts. Part I discusses the "whys" of nursing your toddler from the perspectives of both mother and child. Part II then offers the "hows" of nursing with advice on marriage, night nursing, mother's health, and more. Part III highlights a toddler's development year by year (age 4+) and their accompanying nursing needs. Various ways to approach weaning are offered in Part IV (natural, time-honored/time-worn, etc.).

Evaluation:

This is the bible for those mother-child relationships that have consciously or unconsciously decided to continue breastfeeding past their child's first birthday. At this point in time, many mothers often get discouraged, have little or no support, and often become misinformed about the nature of breastfeeding. These are the mothers who will benefit most from reading this book. Bumgarner does an excellent job of shedding light on why nursing is not only beneficial for a child's development but can also help foster the independence that child is seeking. Mothers will learn that breastfeeding is not just for nourishment, but helps satisfy a child's basic needs while the child learns to satisfy these needs himself. When nursing mothers doubt that weaning will ever occur, Bumgarner offers support, guidance, and reassurance to help mothers focus on the positive aspects of their relationship with their child while they breastfeed. No other book addresses these concerns quite succinctly, or with complete compassion and honesty. This is a must-have for those beginning to nurse or those continuing to nurse their child.

Where To Find/Buy:

Bookstores and libraries.

NURSING MOTHER, WORKING MOTHER
The Essential Guide For Breastfeeding And Staying Close To Your Baby After You Return To Work

 Best Resource For:
Continuing breastfeeding upon returning to work

 Recommended For:
Care

Description:

This 184 page book extends a section of the author's book, *Nursing Your Baby*. Divided into seven chapters, this guide focuses on the needs of the woman who wishes to continue breastfeeding when she returns to work. Pryor's preface and Chapter 1 offer a treatise on the importance of forming an attached relationship between baby and mother; beliefs of current society are challenged here (encouraging the baby to be "independent," i.e., letting baby cry it out, sleep separately, not room-in after birth, etc.). She then details why breastfeeding is important for both mother and baby along with "breastfeeding basics." The next three chapters are dedicated to enjoying maternity leave and adjusting to baby, getting ready to go back to work (getting necessary supplies/ equipment, reconnecting with coworkers, finding care), and returning to work (dealing with fatigue, pumping and storing milk at work, business travel, baby's illness, and more). Chapter 7 is a plea to help change negative attitudes in the workplace concerning motherhood. Resources, a sample proposal for a pumping space at work, and an index are given.

Evaluation:

If read from cover to cover, this guide offers working women answers to just about every breastfeeding question they can think of, except how to choose childcare. Parents will need to look to other resources for that information. Sometimes distracting, but always interesting, are Pryor's strong opinions, mostly backed by research. The message she threads throughout the book is that women need to take more initiative about their role in the workplace as they tackle new motherhood. She believes that women and children suffer because women feel they must ignore motherhood while working and vice versa. To that end, she has included numerous strategies and offers welcome tips for those who choose to go back to work and continue breastfeeding. The chapter on "Your Return to the Outside World" is especially useful offering advice from how to deal with leakage at work, to taking baby on business trips, to what to do when baby gets sick. No other guide is available that focuses solely on this subject. Every prospective mother who plans to breastfeed and eventually return to work needs to read this resource before her child is born.

Where To Find/Buy:

Bookstores and libraries.

Overall Rating
★★★★
Full explanations of how to continue breastfeeding upon returning to work

Design, Ease Of Use
★★
More details in table of contents would help; flows well but must be read cover to cover

1–4 Stars; N/R = Not Rated

Media Type:
Print

Price:
$9.95

Principal Subject:
Care

Age Group:
Infants (0–1)

ISBN:
1558321179

Edition Reviewed:
1997

Publisher:
The Harvard Common Press

Author/Editor:
Gale Pryor

About The Author:
(From Cover Notes)
Pryor, a graduate of Cornell University, is the co-author with her mother, Karen, of the highly respected *Nursing Your Baby*. She lives outside of Boston with her husband and her two children, both of whom she breastfed while working full-time.

★★★★

Overall Rating
★★★★
Great tips on integrating breastfeeding into your life, including working moms

Design, Ease Of Use
★★
Small type, rather dense style; more illustrations would help breastfeeding discussion

1–4 Stars; N/R = Not Rated

Media Type:
Print

Price:
$6.99

Principal Subject:
Care

Age Group:
Infants (0–1)

ISBN:
0671745484

Edition Reviewed:
3rd (1991)

Publisher:
Simon & Schuster (Pocket Books)

Author/Editor:
Karen Pryor and Gale Pryor

About The Author:
(From Cover Notes)
Karen Pryor is a writer and a biologist specializing in behavior and learning. Her daughter, Gale Pryor, is a freelance writer and collaborated on this while nursing her own first child and working full-time.

NURSING YOUR BABY

Description:

Written by a mother-daughter writing team, this 416 page book's 3rd edition includes updated information "reflecting changes since the sixties." Part 1 discusses the facts behind human lactation. Included in this part are descriptions of how the breasts function, how the baby functions (body and behavior), the positive benefits of human milk, how breastfeeding strengthens the mother-baby bond, and the "politics of breastfeeding" (lack of support, the marketing of formula to medical professionals, etc.). In part 2, a "mother-to-mother, month-by-month practical guide" is provided for breastfeeding newborns to toddlers. You'll find tips on selecting a hospital and doctor (obstetrician, pediatrician) that support breastfeeding. You'll find suggestions on first and subsequent nursings including positioning, relaxation tips, dealing with home stresses, and problem-solving; "confidence builders" are also included for dealing with others' criticisms. The final two chapters focus on breastfeeding for working mothers (24 pages) and nursing an older baby. An appendix lists sources of breastfeeding information and supplies.

Evaluation:

The only complaint we find with this resource on breastfeeding is the way the information is presented. The table of contents at times is vague, the headings within the chapters impersonal, the writing style dense, the type compact, and not enough illustrations (we counted 6 total). But, if you're ambitious and can wade through it, this is a great book on breastfeeding at a great price. Especially useful are the week-to-week and then month-by-month advice that reflect the changes you and your baby go through. No other book addresses the evolution of the breastfeeding relationship quite so thoroughly. We also appreciated the effort that went into the section for "The Working Mother: How Breastfeeding Can Help." Practical input such as getting yourself and your baby ready to go back to work (from four weeks onward), how to express, pump, and store milk, realistic points to consider (fatigue, stress, leaking, etc.), and more are highlighted. The book's strong supportive dialog, its discussion of how breastfeeding changes as your baby develops, and its suggestions for working mothers makes this book a first choice for women considering breastfeeding.

Where To Find/Buy:

Bookstores and libraries.

BESTFEEDING
Getting Breastfeeding Right For You

Description:

This guide to breastfeeding, accompanied by photos and drawings, presents the "mechanics" of breastfeeding and cultural and emotional issues. The authors state that "breastfeeding is not always easy for women who live in societies where it is hidden, and we don't get a chance to learn how to do it." Thus, this book focuses on convincing mothers that breastfeeding is really "bestfeeding," and gives ways to overcome cultural/social resistance and emotional/physical obstacles. The first part offers a rationale for breastfeeding. The next three parts deal with: becoming familiar with positioning, posture, support, and latching on; learning to express and store breast milk, diet; what to do for babies with special needs; how to deal with too much or little milk flow, sore nipples, and fussy/dissatisfied babies. Cultural factors are discussed, including a look at harmful "modern myths." Closing sections include case studies of women with specific problems, and a "storyboard" detailing the basics of breastfeeding in English and Spanish with drawings. Also included are lists of other resources (groups, books) offering help and support.

Evaluation:

If you are considering or have chosen to breastfeed, this is one of many good resources to help you. This book includes a strong message about the importance and superiority of breastfeeding, and it will help women overcome many of the problems that arise when they make the effort to breastfeed their babies. It focuses on the mechanics of positioning (of both mother and baby) which is often the real source of a myriad of problems from sore nipples to too much or little milk flow to a fussy baby. Invaluable illustrations and photos show correct and incorrect positions, and how a baby should properly latch on to the breast. This book also focuses on the emotional aspects of breastfeeding since successful breastfeeding depends on a relaxed, confident mother as well. Overall this is an excellent guide for mothers who plan to breastfeed.

Where To Find/Buy:

Bookstores and libraries, or order direct by calling 1-800-841-BOOK.

Overall Rating
★★★
A sensitive, instructive guide to successful breastfeeding

Design, Ease Of Use
★★★★
Well written, with numerous and very helpful photos and drawings

1–4 Stars; N/R = Not Rated

Media Type:
Print

Price:
$14.95

Principal Subject:
Care

Age Group:
Infants (0–1)

ISBN:
0890875715

Edition Reviewed:
1990

Publisher:
Celestial Arts Publishing

Author/Editor:
Mary Renfrew, Chloe Fisher, and Suzanne Arms

About The Author:
(From Cover Notes)
Renfrew is a midwife who earned a doctorate for her research in breastfeeding. Fisher has over 30 years' experience as a community midwife. Arms has been a teacher, mother, and photographer, as well as an author of other books on women, childbirth, and adoption. Maggie Conroy is an artist and illustrator, with experience also as an art therapist.

Overall Rating
★★★
An informed guide to diet and nutrition for nursing mothers, with healthy recipes

Design, Ease Of Use
★★★★
Well laid-out, easy to work through

1–4 Stars; N/R = Not Rated

Media Type:
Print

Price:
$11.00

Principal Subject:
Care

Age Group:
Infants (0–1)

ISBN:
0679733558

Edition Reviewed:
1992

Publisher:
Villard Books (Random House)

Author/Editor:
Eileen Behan, R.D.

About The Author:
(From Cover Notes)
Eileen Behan, R.D., is a member of the American Dietetic Association, a registered dietitian, and a mother of two. She is the author of another book on child nutrition, and works currently as a nutrition consultant for individual families.

EAT WELL, LOSE WEIGHT WHILE BREASTFEEDING
The Complete Nutrition Book For Nursing Mothers . . .

Description:

Drawing from her experience as a dietitian and as a mother, the author wrote this book to help other mothers learn about healthy ways to eat and lose weight as they breastfeed. The first chapter discusses the benefits of breastfeeding for infants. Chapters 2–4 describe how a mother's body makes milk, and the specific foods, vitamins, and minerals her body needs. Safe, healthy weight loss and caloric requirements for lactating mothers are discussed next. A simple and safe meal plan for losing weight is included in chapter 6, including a one week sample menu for breastfeeding mothers. Chapter 7 discusses the benefits of exercise, as well as suggestions about safe conditioning. The next two chapters focus on real and mythical dangers in the foods you eat (spicy food, caffeine, alcohol, etc.) and complications (allergies, colic, lactose intolerance, vegetarian diets, anemia, high blood pressure, etc.). Chapter 10 consists of healthy, easy recipes for breakfast, lunch, dinner, and dessert. The last chapter includes answers to common questions that breastfeeding mothers may have.

Evaluation:

Diet and nutrition are significant concerns during a woman's pregnancy. However, few books focus on the months after birth when a breastfeeding mother either has difficulty losing weight or is concerned about eating well for her baby's sake. As the author points out, it is important for mothers to focus first and foremost on themselves and their babies, remembering that weight loss is not as important as "a safe and satisfying nursing experience." However, as many mothers find that the weight isn't coming off while they are breastfeeding, the simple suggestions in this book should help them slim down safely. Newer information is included about foods traditionally not recommended for nursing mothers either because the foods were found to be distasteful or dangerous as it passed into the breastmilk and consequently to the baby. For example, new studies show that garlic may actually make breastmilk more flavorful to babies; on the other hand, studies have found that foil-wrapped wines may be a source of lead. The recipes included are healthful and easy to prepare—something useful for busy health-conscious nursing mothers.

Where To Find/Buy:
Bookstores and libraries.

MOMNESS CENTER
The Place For Information And Inspiration For Moms And Moms-To-Be

Best Resource For:
Internet website that offers breastfeeding information

Recommended For:
Care

Description:

Brought to you by a formula manufacturer, this site's homepage directs you to five options: "Baby Care," "Chronicle of a New Mom," "As Your Baby Grows," "Beautiful Mom . . . and Mom-to-be," and "Baby 1-2-3." In "Baby Care," you'll find four subtopics: breastfeeding, weaning & supplementing, managing diarrhea, and daycare. The breastfeeding contents include rationale, techniques, expressing and storing your milk, how to breastfeed and return to work, and more. Numerous illustrations are used throughout. How to choose a daycare, how to breastfeed or use formula, etc. are the focus of the daycare section. "Chronicle of a New Mom" presents, in journal format, a first person narrative of the thoughts and physical changes of a pregnant woman from first month of pregnancy to about 2 months after her child is born; each month's entry is about 2 pages in length. The month to month development of a baby in utero is detailed in "As Your Baby Grows." "Beautiful Mom . . ." explains physical changes of a mom-to-be (skin, hair, nails, body); wardrobe tips are offered. "Baby 1-2-3" focuses on Q & A's, site links, Enfamil Formula, etc.

Evaluation:

One would expect that a site sponsored by manufacturers of baby formula would concentrate their efforts on promoting their product. Not so here. The wealth of information given about breastfeeding is certainly one of the best sources—if not the best—compared to other websites. Most sites will offer the rationale, the support organizations, and a little tidbit on how to breastfeed and return to work. But here one finds that information plus detailed pictures and explanations on various breastfeeding positions, how to manage work and breastfeeding, and more. Moms returning to work will appreciate the depth of info given in the "Daycare for Your Baby" subtopic. The chronicle is concise, enjoyable to read, feels personal, and yet it contains useful information directed at both the mother-to-be and her baby. Other segments of this site are fairly average, containing some basics but little more. More illustrations would have been helpful especially within "As Your Baby Grows." But if the visitor to this site is fairly certain she will be breastfeeding, she should check out this site.

Where To Find/Buy:

On the Internet at the URL: http://www.womenslink.com/momness.

Internet URL:

http://www.womenslink.com/momness

Overall Rating
★★★
Outstanding details of the how-tos of breastfeeding

Design, Ease Of Use
★★★★
Easily navigated, excellent illustrations where given

1–4 Stars; N/R = Not Rated

Media Type:
Internet

Principal Subject:
Care

Age Group:
Infants (0–1)

Overall Rating
★★★

An experienced, relaxed and personal support resource for breastfeeding

Design, Ease Of Use
★★★

Clear, easy to read; inserts are poorly positioned and occasionally confusing

1–4 Stars; N/R = Not Rated

Media Type:
Print

Price:
$10.00

Principal Subject:
Care

Age Group:
Infants (0–1)

ISBN:
0671749633

Edition Reviewed:
1993

Publisher:
Pocket Books (Simon & Schuster)

Author/Editor:
Janis Graham

About The Author:
(From Cover Notes)
Janis Graham is the author of *Your Pregnancy Companion*. She also writes articles on health and fitness that have been published by *Family Circle*, *Self*, *McCall's* and *Working Mother*.

BREASTFEEDING SECRETS & SOLUTIONS
Fast, Reliable Answers To The Questions Mothers Really Ask

Description:

This 211 page book takes the experienced mother approach to provide a modern woman's perspective on the issues and challenges a first-time mother will encounter when choosing to breastfeed her baby. Common questions that occur during pregnancy are fielded first, then each successive stage is addressed, from how to hold the baby for comfort and healthy posture, to how to prevent soreness, diet and nutrition information, milk supply concerns, and food allergies. The later chapters of the book deal with related issues, including those of a working mother maintaining a breastfeeding schedule, concerns about food supplements, and solid foods and weaning. The author also summarizes family and behavioral issues that can occur with older babies and second children. The author cites resources such as the American Association of Pediatrics, La Leche League International and the International Childbirth Education Association. Additional resources are listed for women with special needs such as mothers of multiples, mothers of babies with Down Syndrome, cleft lips and/or palates, and mothers of adopted babies.

Evaluation:

This is a useful book on preparing to breastfeed, and is supportive of the practice regardless of lifestyle. The writing style is clear, relaxed, and personal. Information is presented informally and made relevant by a light intermingling of personal experience. The author is a mother herself (still in the process of nursing her second child), which gives the book an informed, balanced and experienced perspective. She avoids sermonizing and assists mothers with choosing the best course through the maze of "Dos & Don'ts" that are offered by well-meaning relatives, friends, and conservative medical professionals. Of use to the first-time mother in particular, the book is still useful during additional breastfeeding experiences due to its insightful and informative approach to the problems, issues and concerns that can arise from differences between one child and the next. To the woman who is not surrounded by other mothers who can share their experience, this book will be a welcome companion.

Where To Find/Buy:

Bookstores and libraries.

MILK, MONEY, AND MADNESS
The Culture And Politics Of Breastfeeding

Description:

The aim of this book, written by a science writer and a former advisor to UNICEF and WHO, is to "bring alive the history, the culture, the biology, and the politics of breastfeeding so women can appreciate the contribution of breastfeeding to the survival of our species." As the authors state, this is not a how-to book but rather a why-to book. They also do not intend the book to be a "tirade" against formula but instead to balance the scales, "to make informed choice a reality." Within the 256 pages of this 3 section, 6 chapter book, you'll be exposed to breastfeeding beliefs and practices around the world past and present, a comparison of breastmilk with formula/artificial feeding, and the relationships between formula manufacturers/promoters, politics, and economics throughout the years. Seven appendices offer the following information: organizations working to promote breastfeeding, reading and resource lists, infant formula recalls (1982–1994), boycott information (Nestle and American Home Products), breastfeeding legislation (as of June 1995), and more.

Evaluation:

Not for the faint-of-heart, this book doesn't mince words. Intimidating at first due to the amount of information, data, and historical accounts contained within, this book nonetheless packs a powerful punch you can't avoid. The authors' expose of formula manufacturers' tactics to push their products upon the medical profession, arguments used to convince lower economic groups and developing countries to not breastfeed, and the rates of infant mortality, especially in the U.S., as a result will leave you angry. Although pregnant women, unsure of whether or not they should breastfeed, will be better able to make informed decisions after reading this book, breastfeeding mothers will also find it useful as they deal with criticism for continuing to breastfeed after society's "approved" nursing period. We recommend this book primarily for professionals and hospitals who are bombarded with enticing freebies from formula manufacturers, yet must struggle to offer an unbiased opinion to new or prospective mothers. You'll be frightened but you'll become enlightened.

Where To Find/Buy:

Bookstores and libraries.

Overall Rating
★★★
Excellent "why-to"—best for medical professionals & those who need supportive data

Design, Ease Of Use
★★★
Table of contents lists all chapter contents, good graphics, reads much like a textbook

1–4 Stars; N/R = Not Rated

Media Type:
Print

Price:
$26.95

Principal Subject:
Care

Age Group:
Infants (0–1)

ISBN:
0897894073

Edition Reviewed:
1995

Publisher:
Bergin & Garvey

Author/Editor:
Naomi Baumslag, M.D., M.P.H. and Dia L. Michels

About The Author:
(From Cover Notes)
Baumslag is Clinical Professor of Pediatrics at Georgetown University Medical School in Washington, D.C. and president of the Women's International Public Health Network (Bethesda, MD). Michels is a science writer. Both are published authors and frequent lecturers.

Overall Rating
★★★
Terrific for the beginning nurser, may be intimidating for the unsure mother-to-be

Design, Ease Of Use
★★
Table of contents dense; each chapter lists contents separately on chapter cover page

1–4 Stars; N/R = Not Rated

Media Type:
Print

Price:
$11.95

Principal Subject:
Care

Age Group:
Infants (0–1)

ISBN:
1558321055

Edition Reviewed:
3rd (1995)

Publisher:
Harvard Common Press

Author/Editor:
Kathleen Huggins, R.N., M.S.

About The Author:
(From Cover Notes)
Huggins has been a maternity and newborn nurse and is founder of a breastfeeding clinic and telephone counseling service.

NURSING MOTHER'S COMPANION (THE)

Description:
Huggins, a maternity and newborn nurse and founder of a breastfeeding clinic, has written this book "to provide mothers with a practical guide for easy reference throughout the nursing period." The seven chapters of her 240 page guide focus on breastfeeding and deal with the following topics: preparation during pregnancy, the first week, special mothers (mothers with diabetes/epilepsy/herpes/thyroid conditions, nursing after breast surgery, nursing an adopted baby, and more), and special babies (premature, twins, birth defect, etc.); four chapters specifically focus on baby's needs the first two months, from two to six months, and needs of the older baby and toddler. Following each of these special chapters are "survival guides." The cover page of each of these guides lists its contents. These sections are intended to be a "quick yet thorough reference for almost any problem you or your baby may encounter. . . ." The end of the book includes three appendices listing resources for nursing mothers, charts to determine baby's milk needs during the first six weeks, and a listing of drugs and whether or not they are safe while breastfeeding your baby.

Evaluation:
Mothers-to-be and nursing mothers will find this reference guide useful, practical and up-to-date. Of special interest are the sections on dealing with "special mothers" and "special babies"—situations not often covered in many breastfeeding guides. Also of use are the survival guides, helpful for busy mothers who need suggestions quickly. The appendices of resources and drug effects is something every hospital should give mothers upon their departure. Chapters focusing on nursing the older baby and toddler offer many reassurances in dealing with disapproval from others. The only unnecessary item is the appendix for determining the baby's milk needs. Breast milk can only be measured if it's expressed into a bottle. Since bottles are not suggested until AFTER six weeks (due to nipple confusion), this section seems unclear. The chapters focusing on preparing during pregnancy and breastfeeding the first week are good, and old advice about breast preparation is dispelled—"nipple 'toughening' maneuvers . . . brisk rubbing," etc. This is a helpful and recommended resource.

Where To Find/Buy:
Bookstores and libraries.

WOMANLY ART OF BREASTFEEDING (THE)
La Leche League International

Description:

The Womanly Art of Breastfeeding is an acknowledgment of the 9,000+ active Leaders in the U.S., Canada, and 43 other countries who contributed to this work. This 446 page book begins with "Planning to Breastfeed" with a chapter each focusing on the "whys" of breastfeeding, the "hows" of planning before birth, and ways to gather support networks. Part 2, "The Early Months," covers ways to adapt to breastfeeding, stating that it is 10 percent technique and 90 percent attitude. Many basic issues on child and mother care are addressed, like latching-on, engorgement, the family bed, breastfeeding in public, and more. Part 3 discusses issues related to "Going Back to Work," and part 4 addresses "Life as a Family" with tips on how fathers can get involved, how to manage home duties, other children, etc. Part 5, "As Your Baby Grows," addresses solid food, weaning, and discipline as "loving guidance." Part 6 discusses "special situations" (C-sections, multiple births, premature babies, etc.) and how to breastfeed. Part 7 highlights advantages of "why breast is best" and Part 8 commemorates LLL's 35th anniversary.

Evaluation:

This book contains useful information and is touted as the "bible of breast feeding." Although this revised edition includes updated information about the benefits of breastfeeding, some extension of the section for working mothers would enhance the book. The sixteen pages that are included on how to juggle breastfeeding and working seems far too light a treatment of the topic. The reality for most women is that they do return to work; more logistical tips, information on their rights on the job, resources that are available, and information on skills that could help combine work and breastfeeding would be useful. For the first-time mother all the anecdotes may provide the support she needs; to others they distract from the facts buried in the text. But, for most women with busy lives this book will seem to drag on and on. There are other resources on the market which address the same issues in a more succinct fashion.

Where To Find/Buy:

Bookstores and libraries.

Overall Rating
★★★
A great deal of information, much of it conveyed through anecdotes

Design, Ease Of Use
★★
Clear, well-illustrated, and organized; anecdotal sidebars distract from text

---

1–4 Stars; N/R = Not Rated

Media Type:
Print

Price:
$13.95

Principal Subject:
Care

Age Group:
Infants (0–1)

ISBN:
0452266238

Edition Reviewed:
5th (1991)

Publisher:
Penguin Books USA (Plume)

Author/Editor:
La Leche League International

About The Author:
(From Cover Notes)
La Leche League International started 35 years ago when seven women, committed to breastfeeding at a time when most babies were bottlefed, met to provide information and encouragement to breastfeeding mothers. Currently there are 3000+ groups worldwide.

Overall Rating
★★
Stirs up the issue and will prompt some to affect a change in our culture's attitude

Design, Ease Of Use
★★
Straightforward navigation, information is minimal; graphics would be an added asset

1–4 Stars; N/R = Not Rated

Media Type:
Internet

Principal Subject:
Care

Age Group:
Infants (0–1)

BREASTFEEDING ADVOCACY PAGE (THE)

Description:

The homepage of this website begins with a Renoir painting depicting a mother breastfeeding her infant. The page continues with its focus on our cultural taboos on breastfeeding. Links to a book excerpt dealing with our "deeply-imbedded cultural misunderstanding" and laws protecting public breastfeeding can be found here. This website is organized into two main sections, "Advocacy" and "Help With Breastfeeding." Subtopics found under the first part, "Advocacy," deal with the importance of breastfeeding, why breastfeeding rates are so low, how to support breastfeeding either as an individual or through organizations, and more. Mothers can find links and contact information if they need help with breastfeeding using the second part of this website. Additionally, expecting parents can read "ten things . . . (they) need to know about breastfeeding" along with tips on how to return to work and continue breastfeeding. A sample letter to an employer explaining the need to have a private, clean area for mothers to pump is offered for your use here; rationale and solutions are included.

Evaluation:

The main message you'll get from this website is that breastfeeding is not only the best thing one can do for one's child and oneself, but that there are support systems available to make it easier. What is not available are the "how-tos" or "what-to-do-ifs." That information must be found through contacting a lactation consultant or one of the organizations this site is linked to. The articles detailing our culture's prejudice against breastfeeding may be useful in arousing some mothers and fathers to take action. Perhaps if our society could take on different perspectives and attitudes toward breastfeeding, more websites could be made available offering breastfeeding mothers more support and guidance. The only feature lacking in this website are graphics to soften the text's edges. Surely there are more classic paintings that could add to the spirit and flavor of the site.

Where To Find/Buy:

On the Internet at the URL: http://www.clark.net/pub/activist/bfpage/ bfpage.html.

Internet URL:

http://www.clark.net/pub/activist/bfpage/bfpage.html

BREASTFEEDING PAGE (THE)

Description:

Six options are presented at The Breastfeeding Page's homepage. "Breastfeeding Information" offers you links to organizations, articles, resources, and book abstracts dealing with the benefits, the how-tos, and the problems associated with breastfeeding; a list of organizations is also provided. A second option—"Breastfeeding Discussion"—gives you three links that explore the world of breastfeeders. "Attachment Parenting" offers brief explanations of this parenting style along with links to sites focusing on the family bed, home birth, midwifery, etc. How to become a breastfeeding advocate and information about current breastfeeding issues are detailed in linked sites at "Breastfeeding Issues." Lists and links of items related to breastfeeding (pumps, pillows, clothing patterns, fashions, magazines, and more) are supplied in "Books and Businesses." The last option—"Women On The Web"—summarizes 12 websites sponsored by women that focus on their various careers and interests, ranging from pregnancy, breastfeeding, and parenting to crafts, gardening, and more.

Evaluation:

Some linked sites are rated at this website and some include summaries. However, few of them will be of significant help to busy breastfeeding mothers. On the flip side, many of the linked sites' titles give a picture of what is available there. The best links at this site are those mentioned in "Books and Businesses." Here the visitor can find comprehensive resources to help get started breastfeeding or to continue doing so in comfort. Also, the user will appreciate the help she can glean from links found in "Breastfeeding Information" ("Problems"), especially if she is looking for information relative to a specific case, e.g. tandem nursing, adoptive nursing, etc. This site, then, is a start but its user will then need better resources to really help with the whys, the how-tos, and problem-solving tips regarding breastfeeding.

Where To Find/Buy:

On the Internet at the URL: http://www.islandnet.com/~bedford/brstfeed.html.

Internet URL:

http://www.islandnet.com/~bedford/brstfeed.html

Overall Rating
★★
Consists mostly of links and lists, this site concentrates on various breastfeeders' needs

Design, Ease Of Use
★★
Confusing navigation at times due to inexact link descriptions; resource list a plus

1–4 Stars; N/R = Not Rated

Media Type:
Internet

Principal Subject:
Care

Age Group:
Infants (0–1)

Overall Rating
★★
Good information, but a strong commercial tone promoting their products

Design, Ease Of Use
★★
Well-organized site layout

1–4 Stars; N/R = Not Rated

Media Type:
Internet

Principal Subject:
Care

Age Group:
Infants (0–1)

Publisher:
Medela, Inc.

BREASTFEEDING SOLUTIONS (AND MEDELA, INC.)

Description:

Medela "has been providing superior-quality breastpumps and breastfeeding accessories to nursing mothers" since 1979. Their homepage features: the benefits of breastfeeding, how to breastfeed, choosing a breastpump, common problems and solutions, and how to combine working and breastfeeding; a list of their products, prices, and where they can be purchased is also available here. "How To Breastfeed" offers an article written by Dr. William Sears and Martha Sears, R.N., detailing techniques and positions with color photographs. Information about collecting, storing, and freezing milk is also given along with how to use various breastpumps. "Problems and Solutions" offers remedies for various breastfeeding problems (breast engorgement, breast infections, sore nipples, flat/inverted nipples, and more). "Working and Breastfeeding" focuses on creating employer awareness of your needs and desires, selecting a caregiver who supports your desire to breastfeed, and helpful hints for combining work and breastfeeding. Medela's product lists include breastpump systems, accessories, and resource materials (videotapes, books, etc.).

Evaluation:

Good basic information can be found here to get a mother through most problems or questions she'll encounter with breastfeeding. However, some will get annoyed at the constant thread of commercialism apparent at this site to buy Medela products. While the information is pertinent and ample to get her through the difficulties of breastfeeding, she will find the product promotion intrusive (for example, on "How to Breastfeed," you get the message "to help make breastfeeding an easy and pleasant process, Medela offers a variety of resources to give you expert instruction and helpful information."). On the other hand, if she already uses and/or likes Medela products and/or she can ignore the "propaganda," she will obtain good information here on breastfeeding.

Where To Find/Buy:

On the Internet at the URL: http://www.medela.com/.

Internet URL:

http://www.medela.com/

LA LECHE LEAGUE INTERNATIONAL

Description:

La Leche League International (LLLI), "an international, nonprofit, nonsectarian organization dedicated to providing education, information, support, and encouragement to women who want to breastfeed," offers many features at their homepage. Pertinent to new moms' needs are the topics of "Breastfeeding Information from LLLI Periodicals," "Frequently Asked Questions about Breastfeeding," and "Breastfeeding Help Form." LLLI's periodicals contain selected breastfeeding topics including 90+ articles dealing with subjects such as "Breastfeeding Multiple Babies and Tandem Breastfeeding," "Common Breastfeeding Concerns," "Working and Breastfeeding," and more. Each subject area lists how many articles can be found within it; each article typically includes about 1/2 page of information. Answers to "Frequently Asked Questions" are found within general topic headings (varying from newborn needs to special situations—adopted baby, tandem nursing, etc.). Mother-to-mother breastfeeding support is available through LLLI's online help form; answers to questions will be sent via email "within one week."

Evaluation:

La Leche League's reputation and proactive stance in the breastfeeding arena are well-known. One will visit this site, then, with great expectations that this is **the** site for all there is to know about breastfeeding. Those expectations will be dashed—only the bare minimum of information is offered on any one subject. New moms may find their questions answered within the "FAQ" section, although this area lacks the graphics necessary to illustrate key points; for example, in answering the question of how to position a baby at your breast, it is difficult to translate words into actions without visual aids. A chat room or discussion forum would be helpful for moms who can't get to a La Leche League meeting for support—hopefully a future expansion will address those needs The online help forum is useful unless one needs immediate advice from someone other than another mom. In summary, La Leche League meetings generally are excellent sites for obtaining information on breastfeeding; their website is not, and one needs to check other sites for information and help.

Where To Find/Buy:

On the Internet at the URL: http://www.lalecheleague.org/.

Internet URL:

http://www.lalecheleague.org/

Overall Rating

★

Disappointingly meager information from a well-respected breastfeeding advocacy

Design, Ease Of Use

★★

Well-organized, topical headings make access easy; no graphics, no illustrations

---

1–4 Stars; N/R = Not Rated

Media Type:
Internet

Principal Subject:
Care

Age Group:
Infants (0–1)

Publisher:
La Leche League International

Care: Choosing A Caregiver

★★★★

Overall Rating
★★★★
Presents a reassuring but informative study of the various child care options

Design, Ease Of Use
★★★
Needs bolder headings, there's a tendency to get lost; excellent checklists & forms given

1–4 Stars; N/R = Not Rated

Media Type:
Print

Price:
$14.00

Principal Subject:
Care

Age Group:
All Ages (0–5)

ISBN:
0395822874

Edition Reviewed:
1997

Publisher:
Houghton Mifflin

Author/Editor:
Eva Cochran and Mon Cochran

About The Author:
(From Cover Notes)
Mon Cochran is a member of the governing board of NAEYC and was a professor of early child development and family studies at Cornell University for 25 years. Eva Cochran is a former director of the Day Care and Child Development Council in New York.

CHILD CARE THAT WORKS
A Parent's Guide To Finding Quality Child Care

Best Resource For:
Selecting child care

Recommended For:
Care

Description:

Divided into 6 parts with 19 chapters, this 355 page book highlights various options and considerations to "help you locate and organize child care arrangements that satisfy you and support the healthy development of your child during your absence." Part 1 offers an overview of the available options using several examples to illustrate the look and feel of quality care. Six chapters are included in Part 2 and deal separately with various types of care (family and group family child care, center care, part-day programs, care in your home, school-age child care, and "creative alternatives"), how to find them, and what to look for. Possible emotional reactions to child care, both from the standpoint of the child and the parent, are illustrated in Part 3. Part 4 outlines various ways to build a partnership with a caregiver and Part 5 focuses on how much to pay for a caregiver's services as well as tax information. In Part 6, the authors invite readers to become advocates and work toward improving child care conditions. Appendices (9) are provided including organization and referral agency contacts, checklists and child care forms, and more.

Evaluation:

The strength in this book lies in its continual thread of support for those parents who must choose child care for their children. Unlike many books on this topic, it combines an emotional and informational approach when discussing the various choices available. In terms of the emotional side, it refutes the myths parents generate internally when they must place their child in the care of others and their feelings of guilt and anxiety in doing so. Also, many of the other resources on this subject mention, but don't devote much effort to, the importance of building a partnership with a caregiver. This one does a nice job of this. Careproviders get equal time here; although parents may complain about the high rate for quality care, the effects of low compensation for a careprovider's services unfairly leads them to a lower quality of life. The sample forms this resource provides are also a plus. Parents looking for a book on quality care will find this to be a quality book.

Where To Find/Buy:

Bookstores and libraries.

COMPLETE NANNY GUIDE (THE)
Solutions To Parents' Questions About Hiring And Keeping An In-Home Caregiver

 Best Resource For:
Choosing a nanny

 Recommended For:
Care

Description:

This 154 page guide, written by the founder of a child care agency, seeks to help parents find and keep a reliable nanny. It provides "all the information you need to hire in-home help and will save you the labor and cost of enlisting a child care placement agency." The book contains 12 chapters. Subjects discussed include in-home care vs. daycare; finding the right kind of person; costs; conducting interviews and screening applicants; keeping a nanny; filing taxes, Social Security, and payroll programs; using a placement agency; and current laws. In addition, chapter 11 deals with finding a nanny for children with special needs. There are seven appendices. These contain a listing of U.S. nanny training schools, sample employment applications, checklists for screening applicants, a criminal background release form, tax and government forms, and more. A listing of childcare placement agencies and services in the United States is also given. There is no index.

Evaluation:

This is a well researched book with good, sound, up-to-date information. The author's experiences from owning a placement agency adds strength to this book. She offers a detailed outline of the standard procedures a nanny placement agency uses when screening household help for families. Her suggestions on securing and keeping a nanny along with her presentation of hard facts and laws on hiring in-home help makes this book credible. Questions are answered succinctly in a progressive, logical manner. Additional sources of information for parents are noted where appropriate in each chapter. Using this book as a guide, parents will be able to successfully sort out the best way to obtain childcare for their specific family's needs. Unique to this resource is the wealth of forms provided by the author. This affords parents the opportunity to familiarize themselves with these forms before beginning the hiring process. Parents looking to add a nanny to their family will find this guide to be very informative and necessary.

Where To Find/Buy:

Bookstores and libraries.

Overall Rating
★★★★
Good information presented in a step-by-step format w/ many helpful employee forms

Design, Ease Of Use
★★★
Descriptive chapter titles, an index would also help; blocks of highlighted text useful

1–4 Stars; N/R = Not Rated

Media Type:
Print

Price:
$10.00

Principal Subject:
Care

Age Group:
All Ages (0–5)

ISBN:
0380782286

Edition Reviewed:
1995

Publisher:
Avon Books (Hearst Corporation)

Author/Editor:
Cora Hilton Thomas

About The Author:
(From Cover Notes)
Cora Hilton Thomas is the founder and owner of Mother's Helpmates, a childcare placement agency. The mother of three, she lives and works in Brandon, Florida.

Overall Rating
★★★

A true resource to guide busy parents; comprehensive and complete

Design, Ease Of Use
★★

Smooth, progressive flow; numerous worksheets to focus parents; no index provided

1–4 Stars; N/R = Not Rated

Media Type:
Print

Price:
$9.95

Principal Subject:
Care

Age Group:
All Ages (0–5)

ISBN:
0963557572

Edition Reviewed:
1994

Publisher:
André & Lanier

Author/Editor:
Elaine S. Pelletier

About The Author:
(From Cover Notes)
Elaine S. Pelletier is a business professional, wife, and mother of two children.

HOW TO HIRE A NANNY
A Complete Step By Step Guide For Parents

Description:

This step-by-step 96 page guidebook presents a progressive plan to hiring a nanny. The table of contents includes six sections. Section one discusses how to define the job or the nanny's role. This also includes fundamental issues (safety, health, discipline, etc.) as well as specific tasks (housekeeping, cleanup, etc.) and responsibilities (meals, bathing, etc.); worksheets are included. Section two involves costs. Salary vs. hourly wages, benefits, and filing state and federal employer tax forms are just some of the topics addressed. "Finding the Right Nanny," in section three, highlights the pros and cons of using an agency, how to interview, network, extend an offer, and more. Sections 4 and 5 focus on the management issue of having a nanny and the changes in family priorities, respectively. Self-explanatory examples are included throughout the book, such as examples of phone interviews, reference interviews, employment applications, and writing a classified advertisement. There is no index.

Evaluation:

Logically ordered and concise, this reference offers an easy-to-follow plan for parents interested in hiring a nanny. Clearly written and appropriately detailed, this book guides you through the process of searching for, interviewing, hiring, and keeping a nanny. It also offers input on responsibilities your nanny will undoubtedly do, and how to understand current tax and employee regulations without feeling overwhelmed; a useful table is provided of "what to do" and "when to do it." Parents will find that this succinct resource provides a summary list of required activities so that finding the right nanny will be a relatively pain-free experience. For serious but busy parents, this book will be a big timesaver, arming them with all of the right tools to help in their decision. Although there is no index, the table of contents aptly serves as a competent compass to help parents find answers to their specific questions. This book is a handy resource and well worth the buy.

Where To Find/Buy:

Bookstores and libraries.

ARE OUR KIDS ALL RIGHT?
Answers To The Tough Questions About Child Care Today

Description:

This 372-page guide consists of two main parts with ten chapters. Part One offers results from various research studies. Topics discussed include: the problems associated with the various types of childcare available, the day care debate (day care vs. mother care, day care and behavior problems, etc.), parental attachment, the realities of parental/family leave, and how a parent's work life affects the lives of their children. Part Two—"Growing Children: A Practical Guide"—focuses on childcare and how it affects babies' development, how to choose the right care for children, how to meet the needs of young children, and what to consider when seeking care for school-age children; interview questions and problem checklists are also given. Each chapter concludes with a summary of the material presented. A "Notes" section is included offering a chapter-by-chapter cross-reference. A 14-page bibliography is included along with an index.

Evaluation:

This guide exposes the many pitfalls of our current childcare system and attempts to allay parental fears by offering answers to their questions based on research studies. This book neatly cites child development research and examines several issues that are controversial depending on one's point of view—the correlation between how much parents work and its effect on their children, the effect of childcare on children at various ages, and the correlation of good/bad childcare and school/life performance. The book concludes with pointedly making the statement that the present system of childcare in America today is abominable and change should be a priority. While a rather depressing dissertation, this interesting book should prove useful in opening adults' eyes for the betterment of our children. While not easy reading and not well-organized, this guide should be reviewed by all parents facing the childcare situation before they give birth to their child.

Where To Find/Buy:

Bookstores and libraries.

Overall Rating
★★★
Informative resource coupling research studies with suggestions on finding quality care

Design, Ease Of Use
★
Broad, non-specific table of contents; not easily read or cross-referenced

1–4 Stars; N/R = Not Rated

Media Type:
Print

Price:
$19.95

Principal Subject:
Care

Age Group:
All Ages (0–5)

ISBN:
1560793341

Edition Reviewed:
1994

Publisher:
Peterson's

Author/Editor:
Susan B. Dynerman

About The Author:
(From Cover Notes)
Susan B. Dynerman, a journalist and speech writer, has previously worked in corporate communications as an executive. She and her husband live in Washington, D.C. with their two sons.

Overall Rating
★★
Good practical advice outlining the advantages and disadvantages of various options

Design, Ease Of Use
★★
Topics easy to find but not detailed in table of contents; some tables might need updating

1–4 Stars; N/R = Not Rated

Media Type:
Print

Price:
$24.95

Principal Subject:
Care

Age Group:
All Ages (0–5)

ISBN:
0816022321

Edition Reviewed:
1991

Publisher:
Facts On File

Author/Editor:
Sonja Flating

About The Author:
(From Cover Notes)
Sonja Flating, a child care consultant, is a member of the Child Care Coalition in Sacramento, CA. This coalition is an organization that studies child care and works with real estate developers in incorporating child care into their master planning.

CHILD CARE
A Parent's Guide

Description:
There are seven chapters in this 173 page book focusing on finding "the best child care." Chapter 1 offers the author's early childhood memories along with a "Self-Test" the results of which are to be used by parents as they narrow down their childcare choices. Chapters 2 and 3 offer suggestions on how to find the appropriate childcare for children based on their age and needs. Chapters 4 and 5 discuss in-home care and family day care centers. Also provided are interview questions and ways to make the transition. Alternatives to childcare are addressed in Chapter 7. Chapters 8, 9, 10, and 11 offer an "action plan" for finding childcare (a step-by-step check-off list), an overview of employer-sponsored childcare options, ways to cope with guilt, and the long-term consequences of child care. A resource listing, day care center regulations by state, and an index complete the book. There are many sample charts, question and answer examples, and a bibliography for each chapter.

Evaluation:
This guide offers practical advice on finding and evaluating a nanny, a day care center, or an in-home care provider. Using a personal approach, the author provides basic suggestions and alternatives for parents looking for quality childcare. "Homework" assignments, given at the end of some chapters, help parents to discover needs specific to their own child's personalities. Good information is provided within this resource including things to look for in a care facility, questions to ask prospective caregivers, and a list of emergency instructions. This guide presents both the advantages and disadvantages of the various programs based on children's age and development needs. The book is weak, however, at helping children make the transition; one paragraph is devoted to this purpose whereas a chapter is devoted to the parents' transition. Well-written and easy to understand, this is a good first approach book for families considering day care for their children. Other resources will answer more in-depth questions.

Where To Find/Buy:
Bookstores and libraries.

CHILD CARE CHOICES
Balancing The Needs Of Children, Families, And Society

Description:

Written by the architect of the Head Start program and a specialist in child and family policy issues, this 271 page book observes the childcare situation from a society's viewpoint. It explores the economic issues of childcare as well as the quality of care given and the obligations of a democratic society to provide families with "real choices" for raising responsible children. This text contains ten chapters. Chapters 1 and 2 examine the childcare system with information on working mothers, a child's environment, and the various types of childcare available. Chapters 3–7 focus on ways to meet a family's childcare needs and how to find quality care for infants, toddlers, school-age children, and children with special needs. Chapter 8 addresses how companies are tackling the childcare issue. Chapter 9 outlines a unified system of childcare for the 21st century. Chapter 10 details a child allowance trust fund to create childcare options for families of infants and toddlers. There is an extensive reference section, followed by an author index and a subject index.

Evaluation:

Although this book delves deeply into the challenges and solutions of our current day childcare system, many new insights and ideas have come to pass since this book was copyrighted. This text is not about how to find and keep good childcare help. It is about understanding the system, so that society can offer parents good supportive childcare choices that best suits their family's needs and parenting goals. This book does a great job in gathering all of the information about the childcare system and what it will take to change the system to address the issues most worrisome to parents of today. The book offers well-presented proposals for revamping our present system to improve the quality and quantity of day care services. These proposals are aimed at the educational system, the corporate environment, the family, and the child and health care systems (specifically social security). This resource is more of a treatise for policy changes than a "how-to" guide; parents will need to compare present-day policies of the childcare system, however, to determine the accurateness of this text.

Where To Find/Buy:

Bookstores and libraries.

Overall Rating
★★
Treatise on the crisis in the childcare system with proposals for societal changes

Design, Ease Of Use
★★
Heavy textbook style; author and subject index, with an adequate table of contents

1–4 Stars; N/R = Not Rated

Media Type:
Print

Price:
$27.95

Principal Subject:
Care

Age Group:
All Ages (0–5)

ISBN:
0029358213

Edition Reviewed:
1991

Publisher:
The Free Press (Macmillan)

Author/Editor:
Edward F. Zigler and Mary E. Lang

About The Author:
(From Cover Notes)
Zigler, designer of the Head Start Program, Sterling Professor of Psychology and Director of the Bush Center in Child Development and Social Policy at Yale University, has earned many awards for his contributions. Lang specializes in child and family policy issues.

Overall Rating

★

Addresses the many ways of returning to work, but light treatment of childcare options

Design, Ease Of Use

★★★

Bulleted and blocks of highlights; great parent quotes; light on forms, checklists, etc.

1–4 Stars; N/R = Not Rated

Media Type:
Print

Price:
$12.95

Principal Subject:
Care

Age Group:
All Ages (0–5)

ISBN:
1555611265

Edition Reviewed:
1997

Publisher:
Fisher Books

Author/Editor:
Teresa Wilson

About The Author:
(From Cover Notes)
Wilson, a postnatal counselor for the National Childbirth Trust (NCT), has written about pregnancy and early childhood issues, and has been a full-time, stay-at-home mother, worked part time, and worked full time.

YOUR BABY & YOUR WORK
Balancing Your Life

Description:

The author of this 180 page guide states that her aim is to "reflect the many ways of working that now exist and the kinds of childcare you can choose." Including numerous quotes from working parents, the book is divided into 11 chapters with a conclusion, list of resources, and an index. The author explores issues such as why women return to work, how they feel about returning, how they balance their work and home life, how mothers and fathers juggle their roles as a family, and more. Six chapters discuss the various types of childcare available—family daycare homes, preschools, workplace childcare centers, nannies, au pairs, informal childcare (neighbors, friends, relatives), after-school options, and other support care (postpartum doulas, mother's helper). Each chapter lists the benefits derived from that kind of care, the problems, how to find quality care, and more. Also presented are viewpoints from the childcare providers about the benefits and problems for each of these childcare options. The final chapter focuses on how mothers can continue to breastfeed when they return to work.

Evaluation:

Parents using this book will get great advice on how to assuage their feelings of guilt about returning to work but they will get less direct advice on how to get childcare. The author includes numerous parent anecdotes to illustrate her points, the main one being that being a working parent is a challenge, a balancing act in which women and men work to resolve all their family's needs while enjoying a role in the workplace. Wilson states that if parents understand all of their options for both work-related and child-related issues, then they can strike this balance more successfully, hence the reason for this book. The issues related to returning to work are treated in-depth here, but less so are the issues related to childcare. Parents will get an overview of each option but nothing in detail. Interview questions, for example, are given for hiring a nanny, but none for the other available options. Many other resources include various checklists, forms for checking references, forms for applicants, etc. that help busy parents stay organized and prepared. Parents can use this resource to assuage feelings of guilt but they may well want to use other resources for finding quality childcare.

Where To Find/Buy:

Bookstores and libraries.

WORKING AND CARING

Description:

Dr. Brazelton, in the beginning of this book, describes the conflicts working mothers face when torn between their beliefs in women's rights to experience the satisfaction of working, and their love and intense attachment to their babies. Here, he tries to address a woman's feeling of being split apart and ways to heal them. This is done by pointing out that the ambivalence a woman feels toward returning to her job generates new energy as she discovers new abilities. The big questions are when to return to work, how to share the care, and how to handle the development hurdles of normal childhood when caring for children is not your only job—issues that confront all parents, whatever their circumstances. By following the lives of three families (working professionals, a single parent, and a couple in which the father must be away for long stretches of time) through the first year of their new baby's life, he illustrates the challenges these families faced, and how these families managed to adjust. The center of his advice is to save some energy at the end of the day for the family's physical and emotional needs.

Evaluation:

In this book, Brazelton does a credible job of emphasizing that it is not just women's dilemma about how to combine work and home life. "The problem in a working family is that no one is there all the time to care for the children." To reflect men's changing roles in terms of fathering, men also need to take steps to further their nurturing abilities, says the author. The main problems of this book center on its presentation. It tends to ramble between the narratives on the families and Brazelton's interjected, sometimes distracting, comments. The type used in printing this book is also a negative, i.e. its too small for easy reading, leaving one feeling cramped. Also, the book needs to be updated regarding the facts and statistics quoted concerning working parents. And so, while this book is filled with experienced insights on the issues involved with returning to work after having a baby, there are other better books on the market today.

Where To Find/Buy:

Bookstores and libraries.

Overall Rating

★

Too outdated to be of much use to busy parents trying to combine work and home life

Design, Ease Of Use

★★

Difficult to read, unclear on helpful solutions, rambling text

---

1–4 Stars; N/R = Not Rated

Media Type:
Print

Price:
$13.00

Principal Subject:
Care

Age Group:
All Ages (0–5)

ISBN:
0201632713

Edition Reviewed:
2nd (1985)

Publisher:
Addison-Wesley Publishing (Merloyd Lawrence)

Author/Editor:
T. Berry Brazelton, M.D.

About The Author:
(From Cover Notes)
T. Berry Brazelton, M.D. is Associate Professor of Pediatrics at Harvard Medical School and Chief of the Child Development Unit at the Boston Children's Hospital Medical Center. Dr. Brazelton is considered a leading authority on child development.

Overall Rating
★
Short, elementary, and concise information on how to find good childcare

Design, Ease Of Use
★
Resource contains no index; relies heavily on marginal table of contents

1–4 Stars; N/R = Not Rated

Media Type:
Print

Price:
$9.95

Principal Subject:
Care

Age Group:
All Ages (0–5)

ISBN:
1895292573

Edition Reviewed:
1995

Publisher:
Childcare Publications

Author/Editor:
Faye D. Campeau

About The Author:
(From Cover Notes)
Faye D. Campeau has personal and professional experience, both as a parent, caregiver, and an owner/operator of a childcare referral service.

CHILDCARE KIT
How To Recruit, Screen And Monitor Baby-Sitters And Caregivers

Description:

This larger-sized 63 page book contains three major sections. The section following the Introduction contains information to help parents create their own personal childcare kit, definitions of some terms, and current childcare prices. The next section focuses on "outside-the-home childcare" and discusses safety inspections, how to check a caregiver's references, some suggested questions to ask potential prospects, and more. The rest of the guide deals with childcare in the home including topics of how to find care whether for baby-sitting, full-time, or occasional care. Examples of interview questions, applications, reference check forms, checklists, agreements, and an orientation list for the home are given. Also provided are forms for daily schedules, safety expectations (outside play, infant and toddler equipment, etc.), medical release info, discipline statements, allergy/special diet information, and more Black and white line drawings are repeated throughout this resource. There is no index.

Evaluation:

This book, based on the author's personal experience as owner of a daycare operation and referral business, offers numerous generic forms that parents may find useful, but it provides little value in helping parents decide upon a caregiver. Overall, the guide seems hurried and incomplete. The redundancy and often misplaced clip-art style art is distracting at times—why is there a picture of a fire fighter in the section concerning observation of a daycare? These drawings could have been omitted. Many of the sample questions are droll and uninspiring— "What are your interests and/or hobbies?" "How will you entertain my children while I am absent?"—perhaps resulting in an uninspiring caretaker. Other books offer similar forms with more homework done in their development. The content contained in this resource is very basic and hardly worth the price. Parents should look to other resources with better scope, more depth, and thorough content to help them make this important decision.

Where To Find/Buy:

Bookstores and libraries, or order direct from Childcare Publications, 49 Evergreen Estates, Sudbury, Ontario, Canada P3G 1B3.

GOOD NANNY BOOK (THE)
How To Find, Hire, And Keep The Perfect Nanny For Your Child

Description:

How to find, hire, and keep a nanny for your child is explained in this 276 page, 8 chapter book. Chapter 1 focuses on whether or not a nanny is needed. Chapter 2—"Visualizing a Nanny from Heaven"—discusses realistic expectations. Chapters 3 and 4 offer suggestions on how to find a nanny and how to select a nanny, respectively. How to prescreen applicants, interview them, check their references, devise an application, and more are highlighted. Chapter 5 presents an array of nannies from "heaven" and "hell"; various scenarios are illustrated along with questions to use to match a nanny's personalities with your family's needs. Chapters 6, 7, and 8 give information on setting up your home for a nanny, managing an employee, and living with a nanny. The Epilogue includes testimonials from parents and children on the good nannies in their lives, and from nannies who speak about their jobs. Three appendices offer a list of in-home childcare definitions, a sample work agreement, and childrearing tips. There is no index.

Evaluation:

Most of this book is about the author's own experiences with nannies. At first glance, much of the book seems to offer sound advice and suggestions. But, the parent anecdotes, while interesting, are often a bit overdone and lengthy, perhaps used to fill in space to pad the book's real content. Although these real life situations lend an interesting point of view, the book still tends to be the author's biased singular opinion in many cases, often with far too much negativity. Her judgements about good and bad nannies are somewhat harsh and prejudicial ("Make sure if you hire a Queen Bee that she gets her own phone and is financially responsible for it."); these suppositions are not always based on performance, but rather personality types. This resource would have fared better moving in a positive direction with the subject matter. Focusing on strategies to find a good nanny and letting the "down" side go, would have been a better approach. There are other, better, resources.

Where To Find/Buy:

Bookstores and libraries.

Overall Rating
★
Too much negative element to help you approach this process positively

Design, Ease Of Use
★
What? No index? You'll need help to find your way through this one

---

1–4 Stars; N/R = Not Rated

Media Type:
Print

Price:
$12.00

Principal Subject:
Care

Age Group:
All Ages (0–5)

ISBN:
0425151336

Edition Reviewed:
1996

Publisher:
Berkley Books (Berkley Publishing Group)

Author/Editor:
P. Michele Raffin

About The Author:
(From Cover Notes)
P. Michele Raffin is the coauthor of a previous book and has four children.

Care: For Twins & Multiples

Overall Rating
★★★
This resource offers fundamental information with a positive approach

Design, Ease Of Use
★★★★
Sidebar tips, numerous black and white photos; extensive resource and bibliography section

1–4 Stars; N/R = Not Rated

Media Type:
Print

Price:
$16.00

Principal Subject:
Care

Age Group:
All Ages (0–5)

ISBN:
0517880717

Edition Reviewed:
2nd (1994)

Publisher:
Crown Trade Paperbacks
(Crown Books)

Author/Editor:
Pamela Patrick Novotny

About The Author:
(From Cover Notes)
Pamela Patrick Novotny is a journalist whose work has appeared in many magazines and newspapers. She currently teaches writing at the University of Colorado. She is the parent of five children, two of which are twins.

MOTHERING TWINS (Novotny)
Having, Raising, And Loving Babies Who Arrive In Groups

 Best Resource For:
Taking care of twins and multiples

 Recommended For:
Care

Description:

The author states that this 324 page resource grew out of her belief that "twinship is a gift: to parents who can learn they are far more capable that they ever dreamed. . . ." There are 12 chapters in this parenting guide. Chapter 1 explains how multiple births occur, while Chapter 2 discusses how parents can understand and take care of themselves and their babies after birth. Chapters 3 and 4 offer the "how-tos and whys" of feeding, and developing attitudes and routines through the first year. The next four chapters include information on mothercare, family adjustments, going back to work, and language ability. Developing a sense of identity is the focus of Chapter 9. A quick-reference list is offered in chapter 10. Chapter 11 deals with premature births and chapter 12 offers tips on how to deal with more than two babies. A reader questionnaire, a list of resources, a bibliography, and an index complete the book. Sidebar tips are given in bold, along with numerous black and white photographs throughout.

Evaluation:

This book strives to offer a realistic and positive outlook to parents of multiples. This guide, taking a look at the most "recent research," shows parents options they may not have considered in raising their children. Myths about having multiples are dispelled throughout this resource helping parents cope with the advice and comments of others. The book is meant to be used as a "browse through" to fetch useful ideas when parents don't really have time to sit down and read. The index is extensive allowing for easy access to specific topics. There is an incredible 8 page bibliography, and the "Resources" section lists: useful organizations for parents of multiples; information sources for childbirth, infant and new mother care; parent and marriage support groups; baby equipment; and additional periodicals and publications. While this guide does not spend too much energy on any one topic, it does a good job of touching on the important primary issues, mainly parenting twins. As a quick reference, this book is a good deal.

Where To Find/Buy:

Bookstores and libraries.

MOTHERING TWINS (Albi)
From Hearing The News To Beyond The Terrible Twos

Description:
This guide's 15 chapters focus on having and caring for twins. Chapter 1's highlights begin with parents' revelation when they find out they are carrying twins and continues with what to expect. Chapter 2 through 4 take parents through the birthing experience including information on what to expect and focusing on the possibility of having premature twins. Chapters 6 through 9 show parents how to establish a support system, locate childcare, and help older siblings adjust. Chapters 11 and 12 speak to the "couple relationship" and how to find time to regenerate oneself. Chapters 5, 10, 13, and 14 discuss the development of twins from the first six months through preschool. Chapter 15 is dedicated to the father's perspective of life with twins. An epilogue of the authors' final thoughts and reflections follows this final chapter. A resource directory is given supplying contact information for organizations, support groups, and more. A suggested reading list and a 9 page index are also provided.

Evaluation:
Offering a variety of personal narratives and "it worked for me" solutions, this 414 page guide is a unique approach to the caring for twins. Emphasizing individuality and adaptability, the authors seek to encourage mothers to develop their own parenting approach based on what's best for themselves and their children. This is a wonderful book full of insight and practical tips. A special chapter is chapter 15: five fathers of twins (the authors' husbands) give their touching and sensitive perspectives on what it's like to have twins. Parents of twins will find this to be a well-written guide—relaxed, but comprehensive. Neither dictating nor forcing solutions, the authors merely express suggestions and advice from their own experiences. Parents of twins will find this very thoughtful book to be both interesting and informative from all five points of view. This resource has managed to cover a lot of ground, while being careful not to omit the essentials.

Where To Find/Buy:
Bookstores and libraries.

Overall Rating
★★★
Unique approach invites parents to develop their own style while relaying others' tips

Design, Ease Of Use
★★★
Use the table of contents and index to guide you; could use bolder headings and graphics

1–4 Stars; N/R = Not Rated

Media Type:
Print

Price:
$14.00

Principal Subject:
Care

Age Group:
Infants & Toddlers (0–3)

ISBN:
067172357X

Edition Reviewed:
1993

Publisher:
Fireside (Simon & Schuster)

Author/Editor:
Linda Albi, Deborah Johnson, Debra Catlin, Donna Florien Deurloo, and Sheryll Greatwood

About The Author:
(From Cover Notes)
Linda Albi, Deborah Johnson, Debra Catlin, Donna Florien Deurloo, and Sheryll Greatwood are mothers of twins and members of the same support group.

Overall Rating
★★
Lots of info and resources given to cover topics of pregnancy through early child care

Design, Ease Of Use
★★★★
Numerous quotes from families of multiples; detailed table of contents and index

1–4 Stars; N/R = Not Rated

Media Type:
Print

Price:
$12.00

Principal Subject:
Care

Age Group:
All Ages (0–5)

ISBN:
0688116426

Edition Reviewed:
1994

Publisher:
Hearst Books (William Morrow)

Author/Editor:
Betty Rothbart, M.S.W.

About The Author:
(From Cover Notes)
Betty Rothbart is a psychiatric social worker. She is currently a science and health writer, educator, and trainer of teachers for the New York City Board of Education. She is also an adjunct professor at the Bank Street College of Education.

MOTHERING TWINS (Rothbart)
From Pregnancy Through Childhood, A Guide For Parents Of Twins, Triplets, Or More

Description:
This guidebook is divided into four sections. The first section is about pregnancy and includes such topics as the delivery, planning for your multiples' births, premature babies and coping with the loss of a child. Section Two's focus is on "Life with Multiples," dealing with the parent partnership and expectations, naming your babies, breastfeeding, and the logistics of caring for multiples. It also includes advice on how to select a pediatrician and helping siblings to adjust. Section Three offers advice on enlisting help and support, finding babysitters, and a discussion of Mothers of Twins Clubs and a listing of other resources. The final section speaks to the parenting challenges and joys. One-on-one time, overcoming favoritism, bonding, handling stress, and making comparisons are just a few of the subtopics in this section. The appendices include a glossary of terms, additional resources, a bibliography, and a listing of books for children about twins and triplets. An index is also included.

Evaluation:
Using quotes from interviews with the family of multiples, this 383-page book offers advice and suggestions on raising twins, triplets, and more. A large section of the book deals, in general, with the birthing/delivery aspect, followed by broad-based blanketed advice on what parents might expect life to be with multiples. One valuable section in Part Two is "Multiple Feats: The Logistics of Caring for Multiples." Some of the subtopics in this section include how to bath babies; deal with mealtime, scheduling and routines; toilet training; and record keeping. "Parenting Challenges and Joys," Section Four, contains good material (handling stress, giving equal love, avoiding typecasting, etc.), but otherwise seems a rather random array of issues. The resource section includes periodicals, organizations, and mail-order buying information for parents of multiples. There are, however, more comprehensive books on multiples than this one.

Where To Find/Buy:
Bookstores and libraries.

Care: Equipment & Supplies

BABY BARGAINS
Secrets To Saving 20% To 50% . . .

 Best Resource For:
Equipment and supplies for infants

 Recommended For:
Care

Description:

This 9" x 4-1/4" resource contains 333 pages of information on how to find bargains as parents prepare for a new baby. There are twelve chapters in this book's second edition. Chapter 1 discusses how a baby will monetarily change your life. Chapters 2, 3 and 4 contain information on nursery necessities (furniture, bedding, layette). Chapter 5 includes information on maternity/nursing clothes and equipment for feeding baby. Chapter 6 addresses things around the house: baby monitors, toys, bath, food, high chairs, swings, and more. Chapter 7 discusses car seats, strollers, and carriers. Chapter 8 suggests ways for affordable baby proofing. Chapters 9, 10, and 11 offer the "best gifts for baby," "etcetera" (books, Internet websites, and choosing child care), and lists of mail-order catalogs grouped by subject matter with contact information. In Chapter 12, the authors compare typical savings parents can attain if they use the book's suggestions. Child product sources and safety requirements of Canada are included in the appendix.

Evaluation:

This revised second edition includes more brand name reviews, e-mail suggestions from readers, an added section on playpens, baby bottles, formula, and money-saving advice. All of the information and prices have been updated. Overwhelmed at first, parents will need to take some time because this resource covers a great many items. The reviews in the book are based upon the authors' experiences and those of parents interviewed. Reviews of selected manufacturers are rated on a star system from a Four Star rating ("Excellent—our top pick!") down to a One Star rating ("Poor—yuck! could stand some major improvement"). There is no advertising in the book, crediting the authors' intent to not accept money to "buy" favorable reviews, thus also insuring objectivity. Helpful "Smart Shopper Tips," "Wastes of Money," "Money Saving Secrets," and more are included throughout the book. Parents willing to do a bit of homework will find this resource offers the best bargains for anything their baby will need.

Where To Find/Buy:

Bookstores and libraries, or order direct by calling (303) 442-8792 or 1-800-888-0385.

Overall Rating
★★★★
Lots of helpful tips and useful information "guaranteed" to save parents at least $250

Design, Ease Of Use
★★★★
Intimidating at first but a 13 page index & a detailed table of contents make access easy

1–4 Stars; N/R = Not Rated

Media Type:
Print

Price:
$13.95

Principal Subject:
Care

Age Group:
Infants (0–1)

ISBN:
1889392006

Edition Reviewed:
2nd (1998)

Publisher:
Windsor Peak Press

Author/Editor:
Denise Fields and Alan Fields

About The Author:
(From Cover Notes)
Denise and Alan Fields are consumer advocates who have been featured on *Oprah*, *The Today Show*, *Good Morning America*, and *Dateline NBC*. Their previous books include *Bridal Bargains*, *The Bridal Gown Guide* and *Your New House*.

Overall Rating
★★★★
An expert assessment of the most (and least) necessary baby products

Design, Ease Of Use
★★★★
Succinct, highly usable, with helpful page "tabs"; appendices offer contact info, etc.

1–4 Stars; N/R = Not Rated

Media Type:
Print

Price:
$9.95

Principal Subject:
Care

Age Group:
Infants (0–1)

ISBN:
0440507847

Edition Reviewed:
1997

Publisher:
Dell Publishing (Bantam Doubleday Dell)

Author/Editor:
Ari Lipper and Joanna Lipper

About The Author:
(From Cover Notes)
Ari Lipper manages Albee's, a baby products store in New York City, where he and his wife, Joanna, also live.

BABY STUFF
A No-Nonsense Shopping Guide For Every Parent's Lifestyle

Description:

The author introduces his 215 page guide to baby products by stating that, "reading this book should give you a good understanding of the products that are out there, how they work, which ones are necessities, and which ones are best for you to consider based on your lifestyle." Drawing on his familiarity with baby-related items, Lipper gives a run-down of "must haves" (necessities), "might wants" (items to consider based on your budget), and "totally optional" products (frills). The products are divided into 6 main subject areas: the Nursery, the Layette, Carriages and Strollers, Getting Around, Food, and Safety, easily located by both a table of contents and page tabs. Each section describes the products, rates them, tells how long your baby may need them, what their "borrowability" is (and advice in case you do borrow an item), safety issues, and how to fit them into your budget (brand names, prices, where to buy). Also included are sections on where to shop to get the best value, borrowing tips, and nannies. Three appendices give timetables for products, brand names and prices, and a list of manufacturers' telephone numbers.

Evaluation:

In the buying fever that often arrives even before baby does, parents hoping to purchase the best possible products for their baby find themselves unprepared for the expense and overwhelming array of baby items all of which tout themselves as "necessities." Ari and Joanna Lipper's book should prove to be a steady and expert guide to the world of baby products. Its no-nonsense evaluations of each baby item allow parents to purchase the necessities (the crib, diaper pail, clothing, thermometer, stroller, car seat, high chair, etc.), weigh and consider desirable items (bassinet, changing table, baby monitor, portable crib, etc.), and take a look at the "frills" (comforter, pram, jogging stroller, hip carrier/backpack, etc.). There is help here for every parent's budget: well-made, reasonably priced items are recommended and some pricier items are justly critiqued ("A crib is a crib. No matter if you pay $200 or $600. . ."). In this age of consumerism, this book will save parents time, money, and frustration while showing them how to purchase the best products for their baby.

Where To Find/Buy:

Bookstores and libraries.

BABY BASICS (Print)
A Guide For New Parents

Description:

To quote: "It's common knowledge that babies cost a bundle. That's . . . what this book is all about—keeping the bundle from becoming the national debt by simplifying baby care." This is a guide to the practicalities of baby care. The 15 chapters of this 295 page book focus on identifying one's options, ways to save family money, and understanding health and safety issues for such areas as medical care, health insurance, traveling with baby, and babyproofing one's home. Other chapters focus on other investments such as choosing maternity clothes, buying nursery furniture, selecting baby clothes, diapers, and toys. Additional tips are offered in areas such as feeding the baby, choosing child care, weighing decisions about returning to work, and investing in one's future (financial matters). Each chapter introduces its topic which is accompanied by a "necessity checklist" of things to do/buy, and includes tips on safe use, what to consider when buying an item, smart shopping tips, and "budget helpers," as well as a list of further reading, catalog resources, support groups and organizations, and more.

Evaluation:

The author provides a rather eclectic array of topics related to baby care in her book, all of which seem to revolve around issues of decision-making, finance and budgeting, and safety. Reading through this book should give one a grasp of many of the practical aspects involving raising a baby. What it lacks is overall coherence. Is this book about safety or budgeting or health/nutrition? At times the book makes up for this lack of coherence with a good chapter, e.g. "Baby's Basic Wardrobe," a chapter which provides in-depth information about buying clothing a few sizes ahead to save money as your baby grows, safety tips such as avoiding drawstrings and arm/leg bands, laundry tips, etc. Also useful are the chapters on travel safety, babyproofing your home, and childcare. But other chapters, such as those on feeding and health, really include only the basics and do not offer the depth of advice that other resources do. Overall this book might best be used to introduce some practical concerns and identify those that need to be researched further with the help of other resources.

Where To Find/Buy:

Bookstores and libraries, or order direct by calling 1-800-338-2232.

Overall Rating
★★
A generally useful list of practical and monetary concerns during your baby's first year

Design, Ease Of Use
★★
Eclectic gathering of topics with some uneven treatment; "necessity checklist" a plus

1–4 Stars; N/R = Not Rated

Media Type:
Print

Price:
$12.95

Principal Subject:
Care

Age Group:
Infants (0–1)

ISBN:
1565610903

Edition Reviewed:
1997

Publisher:
Chronimed Publishing

Author/Editor:
Anne K. Blocker, R.D.

About The Author:
(From Cover Notes)
The author has taught prenatal nutrition and counseled on gestational diabetes, maternal nutrition, infant feeding, and breastfeeding for over 10 years. She is also the mother of three children.

Overall Rating
★★
Offers products that meet authors' or Consumers Union's safety standards

Design, Ease Of Use
★
Listing information is too small and lacks overall ratings; listing criteria unclear

1–4 Stars; N/R = Not Rated

Media Type:
Print

Price:
$14.95

Principal Subject:
Care

Age Group:
Infants (0–1)

ISBN:
0890438544

Edition Reviewed:
5th (1996)

Publisher:
Consumer Reports Books

Author/Editor:
Sandy Jones and Werner Freitag

About The Author:
(From Cover Notes)
Sandy Jones is a well-known expert on baby products and safety, and is the author of many books and articles for parents. Werner Freitag is a project leader at Consumers Union, where he has worked for over 30 years. He has helped draft baby product safety standards.

GUIDE TO BABY PRODUCTS
Buy The Best For Your Baby

Description:

This 326 page guidebook is targeted to all consumers of baby products. Beginning with the statement that there is no guaranteed safety for a product made for children, the book then looks at the range of products currently sold in American markets and the availability of safety information on each product. Not all products are rated, but ratings are included when available. Topics covered include: backpacks/soft carriers, various infant beds, bathing accessories, bottlefeeding equipment, breastfeeding accessories, changing tables, child safety seats, clothing and footwear, baby foods, gates, hazard reduction/childproofing products, high chairs/booster seats, infant seats, monitors, nursery decor/accessories, playpens, strollers, swings, toilet-learning aids, toys, and walkers. Information is arranged alphabetically and with occasional photographs. Each section begins with information and advice on what to look for, rules on how to use some products, and a list of recalled products. Items selected for testing were based on information obtained from manufacturers. Manufacturers' contact information and an index are included.

Evaluation:

Though the book is subtitled "Buy the Best for Your Baby," too little information was provided in most cases for a "best" evaluation. The introduction was somewhat disorganized and illogical. Is the assumption here that the consumer wants to buy the safest product for the least money? Or is safety the primary rating factor? Information on how products are rated and who is responsible for the rating should be presented more clearly—did the same parents who tested the products also rate them? The product listings contain maker and model, description, design info, and special features, but often there is no safety rating specific to that product, making evaluation difficult. It is unclear as to whether omission from these lists means the products were found unsafe or simply not supplied by the manufacturer. The text in these listings is small and hard to read. Photographs would be an added plus but there are too few to really be helpful. There is certainly a need for books like this one to facilitate consumers wading through the overwhelming mass of baby products, but this one falls short.

Where To Find/Buy:

Bookstores and libraries.

CRYING BABY, SLEEPLESS NIGHTS

 Best Resource For:
Understanding and soothing babies' cries

 Recommended For:
Care

Description:

Written by a "recognized authority on crying babies," this 162 page book details the meaning and importance of a baby's cries. The first of 11 chapters explains "Baby Crying Basics," including a quick reference chart listing different types of cries (16), descriptions, and what to do. Chapter 2 follows with techniques for dealing with a baby's cries (motions, sounds, touch, etc.). Chapters 3 and 5 debunk the myths of babies sleeping through the night; included is evidence that contradicts those researchers who insist that babies should be trained to sleep using various behavior mod techniques. How to successful feed your baby is the topic of Chapter 4 with the focus on breastfeeding. Descriptions of possible causes of colic and ways to help a baby with colic are highlighted in Chapters 6 and 7. The effects of various diseases and drugs on a baby are presented in Chapter 8 along with advice on how to find a good match between you and a doctor for your baby. Chapter 9 deals with crying in older babies and toddlers. The book finishes with tips for parents on handling stress in Chapters 10 and 11.

Evaluation:

Sleepless nights, a crying baby—these are things that either bring out the best or worst in a parent. In an era of parenting in which babies are being trained at an early age to "cry it out," Chapters 3 and 5 are especially enlightening. Sleep trainers who insist that the baby's cries should not interrupt the parents' sleep offer, as the author suggests, "seductive promises" that can easily convince them to buy into their methodology. A reading of these chapters, however, can only leave them cautious about "magic cures" which not only cause them to override the baby's normal communication signals but also shame them into believing that they are being manipulated by the baby. On the contrary, this book offers insights as to why the baby **needs** to cry and why the parental role is to heed that cry. And it does so in a way filled with support and helpful techniques which can only be reassuring and comforting to any sleep-starved parent.

Where To Find/Buy:

Bookstores and libraries.

 ★★★★

Overall Rating
★★★★
Parent support and insight based on studies of thousands of infants

Design, Ease Of Use
★★★★
Checklists, quick reference charts to summarize points, parental anecdotes in margins

1–4 Stars; N/R = Not Rated

Media Type:
Print

Price:
$10.95

Principal Subject:
Care

Age Group:
Infants (0–1)

ISBN:
1558320458

Edition Reviewed:
2nd (1992)

Publisher:
Harvard Common Press

Author/Editor:
Sandy Jones

About The Author:
(From Cover Notes)
Sandy Jones, a recognized authority on crying babies, has written six books and has published numerous articles in major magazines.

★★★★

Overall Rating
★★★★
Comforting explanations of why babies are colicky; tips for how to soothe them

Design, Ease Of Use
★★★
Well-organized table of contents with subheadings; small dense text due to book's size

1–4 Stars; N/R = Not Rated

Media Type:
Print

Price:
$5.99

Principal Subject:
Care

Age Group:
Infants (0–1)

ISBN:
0451163273

Edition Reviewed:
1989

Publisher:
Penguin Books (Signet Books)

Author/Editor:
William Sears, M.D.

About The Author:
(From Cover Notes)
Sears, "one of America's most renowned pediatricians," has been in practice for 20 years and authored 10 books. Currently, he's a clinical assistant professor of pediatrics at USC School of Medicine.

FUSSY BABY (THE)
How To Bring Out The Best In Your High-Need Child

 Recommended For:
Care

Description:
A fussy baby can bring out the best and the worst in a parent. This book is designed to bring out the best," says Sears in his introduction. Various words are used to describe fussy babies throughout this 192 page book—colicky, fussy, high need. The underlying premise of this book, along with Sears' other books, is attachment parenting. The first two chapters of this 14 chapter guide highlight characteristics of high need babies along with explanations as to why they fuss. The next seven chapters focus on taking care of your baby. Topics focus on the early weeks of baby care, a detailed chapter on baby's cries, possible reasons for babies being colicky, and soothing, feeding, fathering, and taking care of your baby at night. Chapter 10 concentrates on avoiding mother burnout. Chapter 11 refutes the argument to let babies "cry it out" by describing the "shutdown syndrome;" patient anecdotes are used for illustration. Sears' attitudes toward disciplining high need children along with "the pay-off" or benefits of attachment parenting are the focus of chapters 12 and 13. Chapter 14 is a case history of a family with a high need child.

Evaluation:
If the reader is open to the concept of attachment parenting and is the parent of a "colicky" baby, this resource is a "must read." Although some of the book's content is duplicated in Sears' *The Baby Book*, this book includes more detail. The following sections are especially enlightening: Chapter 11, describing "shutdown syndrome" or the result of babies crying it out; Chapter 12, focusing on disciplining the high need child; and Chapter 13, for those who worry that attachment parenting will lead to a dependent child. Sears, along with his other books, supplies the reader with numerous anecdotes from other family situations; these examples can only comfort a parent who is struggling with a child that others describe as difficult. Sprinkled throughout this book, particularly in chapters 5–9, are tips and tricks for soothing your baby. Sears states that "being fussy and demanding has survival benefits for these babies. If they didn't fuss, their needs might not be met." Parents of high need babies, then, will find this resource valuable, both for meeting the needs of the baby and their own.

Where To Find/Buy:
Bookstores and libraries.

BABY MASSAGE
A Practical Guide To Massage And Movement For Babies And Infants

Description:

This reference consists of four chapters detailing the benefits of baby massage. Chapter One talks about the importance of touch and explaining the healing potential of massage. Chapter Two includes general information about massage (supplies needed (oils), when not to do it, etc.) along with the specific benefits of baby massage; also included is a massage technique for newborn infants as well as a full body routine for infants two months and up. In Chapter Three parents will find how movement and flexibility exercises combined with massage can help children through the developmental stages of sitting, crawling and walking. The final section, Chapter Four, highlights how massage can help children with special needs, as well as how it can be used to assist with a few of the most common childhood illnesses, such as constipation, wind, colic, and congestion. There is an index and worldwide "Useful Addresses" for mother-to-mother support groups, childbirth education information, breastfeeding, and more.

Evaluation:

For readers whose interest lies in this subject, this 128 page book will surely leave you satisfied. With more than 100 beautifully detailed full color photographs and line drawings, readers unfamiliar with massage techniques will come away from this book confident and charged to try the author's "soothing caresses." This is a well-written, easy-to-read guide extolling the virtues of touch between infant and parent. The information is based upon the author's ten years of experience as a physical therapist attending hundreds of mothers and babies. The book is meant to be read cover to cover. The author is careful to stress gentleness, patience, and consistency. The how-to instructions are clear and concise; a novice will have no trouble picking up the author's suggestions on how to calm an infant or encourage their flexibility and strength as they begin more movements. Parents eager to try new ways to work with a fussy baby or capitalize on the bonding period will no doubt find a treasure trove of tips here.

Where To Find/Buy:

Bookstores and libraries.

Overall Rating
★★★
Unique approach with emphasis on the nurturing qualities of a gentle touch for babies

Design, Ease Of Use
★★★★
Table of contents vague, but index makes for easy navigation; beautifully illustrated

1–4 Stars; N/R = Not Rated

Media Type:
Print

Price:
$16.95

Principal Subject:
Care

Age Group:
Infants (0–1)

ISBN:
0312145454

Edition:
1995

Publisher:
St. Martin's Griffin (St. Martin's Press)

Author/Editor:
Peter Walker

About The Author:
(From Cover Notes)
Peter Walker is a physical therapist with over fifteen years of experience in working with children, parents, and parents-to-be. He offers baby massage workshops to midwives and other health-care professionals throughout the United Kingdom.

Overall Rating
★★★★

Innovative recipes for parents of infants and toddlers emphasizing taste and nutrition

Design, Ease Of Use
★★★★

Cross-referenced ingredients in index; mealplanner charts a plus; delightful illustrations

1–4 Stars; N/R = Not Rated

Media Type:
Print

Price:
$15.00

Principal Subject:
Care

Age Group:
Infants & Toddlers (0–3)

ISBN:
0671750194

Edition:
1992

Publisher:
Fireside (Simon & Schuster)

Author/Editor:
Annabel Karmel

About The Author:
(From Cover Notes)
Having studied at the Cordon Bleu School of Cookery, this is Annabel Karmel's first book. She is also an accomplished musician and actress and has made numerous television appearances. She lives with her husband, Simon, and family in London.

Care: Nutrition & Eating

HEALTHY BABY MEAL PLANNER (THE)
Mom-tested, Child-approved Recipes For Your Baby And Toddler

Best Resource For:
Nutritional information and baby food recipes

Recommended For:
Care

Description:

This 192 page guide includes many recipes containing fresh ingredients, low animal fat, and little or no sugar or salt. There are five chapters, an index, and a listing of acknowledgments. Chapter One provides parents with information on milk (breastfeeding, bottlefeeding, cow's milk), why fresh foods are best to use in recipes, facts on the six essential nutrients for a child, and food allergies. Chapters Two, Three, Four, and Five contain age-specific recipes broken into the following age groups: four to six months, six to nine months, nine to twelve months, and toddlers. Each recipe contains a check box with a smiling face and a gloomy face to record a child's opinion of that recipe. An introduction precedes each chapter offering advice on various subjects such as meal planning, dealing with picky eaters, which quantities work best for specific age groups, and more. The index contains cross-references under each ingredient so that parents can access additional recipes that contain the same given ingredient.

Evaluation:

This is a upbeat recipe book offering many really good, nutritious, and fairly easy to make meals. The humorous illustrations add to the book's lightheartedness. The author has tried to serve the dietary needs of the whole family starting when the baby is about nine months old. This resource contains some very useful information. Tips on freezing storage times, the age at which some foods may be introduced, when to start weaning, and how to learn patience at mealtimes are just some highlights. The recipes are simple and well written. For busy parents, the author's inclusion of the smiling-gloomy faces at the end of each recipe will help serve as a reminder for which meals were successful and which were not. The age-specific meal planners are particularly helpful. Each planner is laid out day by day for one week, and includes breakfast, lunch, dinner, snacks, and bedtime food if appropriate.

Where To Find/Buy:

Bookstores and libraries.

SMALL HELPINGS
A Complete Guide To Feeding Babies, Toddlers And Young Children

 ***Best* Resource For:**
Nutritional information and recipes

 Recommended For:
Care

Description:

This 160 page hardcover book aims to provide nutritional recipes for parents of young children to establish a pattern of healthy eating that can be carried on through their lives. The author's premise is that a recipe has to be easy for busy parents; all use fresh, natural ingredients. The Table of Contents contains four sections, the first of which includes information on basic nutrition, food allergies, and sugar's effect on children's teeth. Section 2 focuses on introducing solids to babies and presents food ideas for babies 4 months to 12 months of age. The third section offers ideas for feeding toddlers. It contains information about encouraging toddlers to eat good food, easing up on salt, eating out, and recipes including vegetables, pasta, fish, chicken, meat, and fruit. The final section discusses food for young children. Lunch box ideas, snacks, cookies, special treats, and "healthy fast food" are some of the topics discussed. Advice and "handy timesaving tips" are provided throughout for each stage of a child's development.

Evaluation:

Whimsical drawings and bordered pages help make this recipe book a fun, easy to use manual. All of the basic food groups are covered and there is also information offered on meat alternatives and vegetarian diets. The recipes are elementary, but imaginative and each includes a portion count. The only objection we found in the book was the author's advice regarding "weaning." She did not reflect current info about when to start babies on cow's milk or solids. Interesting tips, notes, and advice are added for many of the recipes; for example, the author suggests mixing vanilla bean to simmering fruit as a way of adding sweetness without extra sugar, and using lemon juice on apples to help keep them from turning brown. Parents will get a sense from this well-written guide that regardless of which recipe they choose, it will be nutritious and most likely their child will like it! From "Mermaid Morsels" to "Tofu and Peanut Butter Stir-Fry," parents will find something in this guide to suit even the most discriminating of tastes.

Where To Find/Buy:

Bookstores and libraries.

Overall Rating
★★★★
Nutritionally sound with quick and easy recipes using fresh, natural ingredients

Design, Ease Of Use
★★★
Simple, easy to reference; index good but not comprehensively cross-referenced

1–4 Stars; N/R = Not Rated

Media Type:
Print

Price:
$14.95

Principal Subject:
Care

Age Group:
All Ages (0–5)

ISBN:
1564260771

Edition:
1995

Publisher:
Cole Publishing Group (BBC Books/BBC Worldwide)

Author/Editor:
Annabel Karmel

About The Author:
(From Cover Notes)
Annabel Karmel, a best-selling author of previous cookbooks, has three young children.

Overall Rating
★★★
Good application of nutrition basics to healthful recipes for each age group (6–36 mos.)

Design, Ease Of Use
★★★★
Spiral-bound layout helpful; weekly meal planning charts; recipe index would be nice

1–4 Stars; N/R = Not Rated

Media Type:
Print

Price:
$9.95

Principal Subject:
Care

Age Group:
Infants & Toddlers (0–3)

ISBN:
089480300X

Edition:
1987

Publisher:
Welcome Enterprises (Workman Publishing)

Author/Editor:
Rena Coyle with Patricia Messing

About The Author:
(From Cover Notes)
Coyle is a mother and chef and Messing is a nutritionist.

BABY LET'S EAT

Best Resource For:
Nutritional information and recipes for toddlers

Recommended For:
Care

Description:

Presented in five chapters, this 128 page recipe book offers recipes for baby and toddler foods. Chapter One discusses nutritional basics including information on proteins, carbohydrates, fats, vitamins, minerals, and more; a food chart for children ages 1 to 3 years old is provided with suggested serving sizes and recommended daily servings. Also discussed are various food preparation methods, foods to avoid (sugars, salts, fats, caffeine, dangerous), storing, etc. The next four chapters are divided by ages: 6 to 12 months, 12 to 18 months, 18 to 24 months, and 24 to 36 months. Within each chapter, the authors, one a chef and the other a nutritionist, detail hurdles and solutions specific to that age child along with a weekly menu chart for meal planning. The corresponding recipes (20–25) from the weekly menu chart then complete each chapter and are designed for use with the whole family. Recipes include breakfast foods, lunch items, dinner entrees, and snacks; they emphasize the use of non-sugar substitutes. The amount of preparation and cooking time are given along with how long the food can be stored in the refrigerator or freezer.

Evaluation:

The strength of this recipe book that differentiates it from its counterparts is that it emphasizes family recipes along with the use of non-sugar substitutes, whole foods, and spices in lieu of salt. With its convenient spiral-bound design, colored recipe headings, and weekly meal planning charts for each age group, parents will find this guide easy to use. Whimsical illustrations accompany many recipes adding a light touch to a sometimes dull subject matter. The only difficulty some parents may find with this guide is that many recipes involve rather elaborate preparations, some uncommon ingredients, and lengthy preparation times of 30–45 minutes (not including cooking times). If parents consider the entrees to be family fare and not just menus to satisfy their toddlers' nutritional requirements, then this time may be well-spent. Otherwise, between busy schedules and finicky behaviors on the part of many toddlers, this time involved will become a source of frustration. However, if parents want to change their eating habits and prepare some healthful menus for their family, this is the book that can guide them.

Where To Find/Buy:

Bookstores and libraries.

FEED ME! I'M YOURS

Description:

Lansky has included in her book's third edition "new information, but it is still basically the same book." Recipes have been collected for "their nutrition, convenience, and fun." This 143+ page book is divided into 11 sections. The first couple of sections include information on preparing baby and finger foods. Following these sections are menus for toddler meals (breakfast, lunch, dinner, veggies, dessert, beverages) and snacks. Other chapters in this guide center on seasonal recipes, activities to do in the kitchen (crafts, various dough recipes, finger paints, paste, etc.), and birthday party ideas for children ages one to five. The final section is a "potpourri" of ideas and information from other parents. Some included tips are methods for removing stains, first aid tips, traveling tips, and information on poisons. There is an index, which precedes an ingredient substitution list, and weights and measurements conversion list. Several pages of other selected print resources available from the publisher round out the book.

Evaluation:

Divided into approximately eight main segments, this toddler baby food guide makes a wonderful addition to one's cookbook collection. This resource not only shows one how to blend and store fresh baby food, but also describes safe and nutritious finger foods, along with ways to add variety and balanced ingredients at mealtimes. There are recipes for teething biscuits, quick low sugar desserts, and recipes for specific seasons of the year. Some highlighted summer recipes include yogurt popsicles, water ices, and ideas for summer picnics; some of the recipes for winter include toasted pumpkin seeds and snow mousse. The birthday section offers insights on what activities are appropriate for specific ages, ideas for snack foods, cake ideas, and some fun preschool games. This is a delightful, helpful, and entertaining book that any parent concerned with their baby or child's nutrition and health will appreciate.

Where To Find/Buy:

Bookstores and libraries, or order direct by calling 1-800-338-2232.

Overall Rating
★★★
Fun and imaginative recipes for parents helping meet their child's nutritional needs

Design, Ease Of Use
★★★★
Straightforward with bold headings; spiral comb binding makes it easy to lay flat

1–4 Stars; N/R = Not Rated

Media Type:
Print

Price:
$9.00

Principal Subject:
Care

Age Group:
Infants & Toddlers (0–3)

ISBN:
0671884433

Edition:
3rd (1994)

Publisher:
Meadowbrook Press (Simon & Schuster)

Author/Editor:
Vicki Lansky

About The Author:
(From Cover Notes)
Vicki Lansky has authored over 25 books, and is well-known for her column in "Family Circle" magazine and "Sesame Street Parents' Guide Magazine." She has also appeared on national TV shows like "Donahue," "Oprah," and "Today.

Overall Rating
★★★
An excellent overview of natural foods, nutritional requirements, and food substitutes

Design, Ease Of Use
★★★★
Easily cross-referenced with large bold subheadings, numerous charts, bulleted tips

1–4 Stars; N/R = Not Rated

Media Type:
Print

Price:
$9.99

Principal Subject:
Care

Age Group:
Infants & Toddlers (0–3)

ISBN:
155870373X

Edition Reviewed:
2nd (1995)

Publisher:
Betterway Books (F&W Publications)

Author/Editor:
Susan Tate Firkaly

About The Author:
(From Cover Notes)
Susan Tate Firkaly is a lecturer and an assistant professor in the School of Medicine at the University of Virginia. She is also the associate director for Health Promotion in the Department of Student Health.

INTO THE MOUTHS OF BABES
A Natural Foods Nutrition And Feeding Guide For Infants And Toddlers

Description:
With over 175 "economical, easy-to-make, vitamin-packed, preservative-free" recipes, this 160 page guide offers information on nutrition and natural foods for infants and children up to age three. There are fourteen chapters. Chapters One, Two and Three address the reasoning behind making your own baby food, what you'll need in your kitchen, and tips on shopping for whole foods (vs. processed foods). The next two chapters discuss nutrition during pregnancy and for infants. Chapter Six contains information about breastfeeding, bottle-feeding, eating disorders, and introducing new foods. Information on food allergies can be found in Chapter Seven. The next four chapters include age-specific recipes for children ages six months to three years. Family recipes, recipes for children with allergies, and information on poisonous materials are contained in the final chapters. Many tables and charts are provided throughout. A bibliography, a list of further resources, a general index, and a recipe index are also given.

Evaluation:
Much more than just a cookbook, this resource is a well-written guide on the preparation of natural foods and why they should be the cornerstone of nutrition for your family. This book's second edition offers excellent alternatives for parents wishing to steer their children away from a diet of sugar, salt, chemical additives, and high animal protein foods. This new version also includes updated nutritional information reflecting the currently recommended "food pyramid" as opposed to the four food groups. In this resource, parents will find a useful chart of food groups for those who chose not to eat meat, a timetable for introducing new foods, and a list of foods that can cause problems, such as choking and allergies. The recipes are easy, convenient, and tasty. Although these recipes contain no meat, this resource offers plenty of information for parents to decide which foods are best for their families. After reading this book, parents might feel compelled to take advantage of these great recipes and change their diet forever.

Where To Find/Buy:
Bookstores and libraries, or order direct by calling 1-800-289-0963.

SUGAR-FREE TODDLERS
Over 100 Recipes Plus Sugar Ratings For Store-Bought Foods

 Recommended For:
Care

Description:

Three main sections, supported by eight chapters, comprise this 170 page recipe book. The first section offers basic information on toddlers and nutrition, the plight of child obesity, and a toddler's nutritional requirements. The case for sugar-free foods is also presented. Chapter 2 in this section contains information on common ingredients, nutritional quotients, a note about preparation times, and tips on freezing foods. Section Two (Chapters 3–8) includes over 100 of the authors' sugar-free recipes. These are grouped into categories that include: main dishes; biscuits, crackers, muffins and breads; drinks; snacks; sauces, syrups, and spreads; and cookies, cakes, and bars. Following Chapter 8 is a section entitled "Sugar Ratings For Store-bought Foods" which offers side-by-side product evaluations. This section includes which sweetener has been used, a "Toddler Rating," (toddler-tested evaluation), calorie count, and further comments on the store-bought product. An index completes the book.

Evaluation:

The author emphasizes that although she worked full-time when her daughter was young, she wasn't "fanatical about health food," but she was concerned about finding nutritious alternatives to highly refined food. This is a situation many parents will appreciate. With over 100 recipes, this guide strives to suggest nutritional, good-tasting food with no refined sugars or refined flours. Each recipe lists the toddler rating, prep time, nutritional quotient (based on an approximation of a toddler's daily nutritional requirements), and servings count. Simple black line illustrations enhance the overall "toddler" theme. The recipes are clear and well-organized. There are useful hints for preparing day care lunches as well as brown bag lunches. The author has done a fine job of providing substitutions such as carob, nonfat dry milk powder, and hints on using vegetable cooking spray as an alternative. For parents concerned about their child's sugar intake, this book will be a welcome addition to their kitchen library.

Where To Find/Buy:

Bookstores and libraries, or order direct by calling 1-800-234-8791.

Overall Rating
★★★
User-friendly recipes with consistent ingredients; includes nutritional quotients

Design, Ease Of Use
★★★★
Easy to flip through; helpful index

1–4 Stars; N/R = Not Rated

Media Type:
Print

Price:
$9.95

Principal Subject:
Care

Age Group:
Toddlers (1–3)

ISBN:
0913589578

Edition Reviewed:
1991

Publisher:
Williamson Publishing

Author/Editor:
Susan Watson

Overall Rating
★★★
For do-it-yourselfers interested in economics & health benefits of homemade baby food

Design, Ease Of Use
★★★
Small print; indexed separately by topic & recipe; numerous charts given (growth, etc.)

1–4 Stars; N/R = Not Rated

Media Type:
Print

Price:
$4.99

Principal Subject:
Care

Age Group:
Infants (0–1)

ISBN:
0553291831

Edition Reviewed:
3rd (1992)

Publisher:
Bantam Books (Bantam Doubleday Dell)

Author/Editor:
Sue Castle

About The Author:
(From Cover Notes)
Sue Castle, the author of several parenting books, currently writes and produces television programming on parenting, childcare, and nutrition issues. Castle has a B.A. in psychology form Smith College and an M.A. in Social Psychology from Columbia University.

COMPLETE NEW GUIDE TO PREPARING BABY FOODS (THE)

Description:

Beginning with "Nutrition" and ending with "Finger Foods," this 385 page book contains 14 chapters on how to prepare foods for your baby. Chapters 1, 2, and 3 speak to the importance of good nutrition, how to get the most for your money (including reading the labels), and information on feeding your baby (breastfeeding, introducing solids, balanced menu, digestive difficulties, etc.). Chapter 4 offers advice on the best equipment for easy preparation. Chapters 5 and 6 address safe storage for food and a "Baby Food System," which offers suggestions on ways to plan and save time, how to use leftovers, and how to modify recipes. Chapters 7 through 12 provide information on the four basic food groups (cereals, fruits, vegetables, proteins) along with desserts and beverages. The last two chapters offer recipes for "quick" baby foods and finger foods. There are 3 appendices, a bibliography, a section on how to prevent choking, and several child growth charts. A general index and a separate recipe index are also given.

Evaluation:

Here is a very complete and well-written guidebook with a great deal of supporting information and additional resources. By providing practical easily made recipes, she strives to guide parents and caregivers towards a more balanced diet. The general principles of good nutrition are presented along with food selections that provide the essential calories, proteins, carbohydrates, fats, vitamins, and minerals that young children need. The book then goes further and explains the concept and process of introducing solids and/or new foods to your baby and how to avoid digestive and allergic reactions. There are over 100 nutritious and economical recipes for baby foods that parents can make at home. Even if parents only use a few recipes from this book, it will be money well-spent. It will start their baby off on developing the good feeding habits they probably wished they had learned as a child.

Where To Find/Buy:

Bookstores and libraries, or order direct from Bantam Books, Dept. HN 12, 2451 S. Wolf Road., Des Plaines, IL 60018.

THE BABY COOKBOOK, REVISED EDITION
Tasty And Nutritious Meals For The Whole Family That Babies And Toddlers Will Also Love

★★★

Description:

This 368 page guide provides information on the importance of healthy nutrition. This revised edition incorporates updated vitamin and mineral charts, info on fluoride, childhood obesity, microwave cooking, and crockpot cooking. Including 250+ recipes to be used for the whole family, this resource is divided into two parts. Part 1 contains basic information on nutrition (proteins, fats, cholesterol, fiber, etc.) and its importance to infants; dairy products, nursing bottle syndrome, allergies, introducing solids, and childhood obesity are also addressed. "Balanced menus" for baby and toddler breakfasts, lunches, dinners, and snacks are also included. Part 2 provides recipes for the family and "special children's recipes" for: vegetables, legumes, tofu, cheese and eggs, fish, poultry, meats, grains and pasta, soups, breads, desserts, fruit and milk drinks, and stocks and sauces. The pros and cons of microwave cooking are given along with crockpot recipes. Growth and feeding charts, a general index, and a recipe index are also provided.

Evaluation:

This well-written nutrition/feeding/recipe guide will serve as a valuable resource to start a child off on a smart and healthy way of eating. When to offer, what to feed, and how to prepare are all facets covered in this book. Recipes have been prepared with thought to nutrition, cost, and convenience in mind. The author includes a personal diary of her own baby's feeding progression so that parents can also keep their own child's feeding patterns in perspective. There are recipes for light meals, family meals, safe microwave meals, and slow crockpot cooking recipes; over 100 recipes are new to this edition. Vitamin tables, protein charts, and a twelve month summary of when to introduce solids are just some of the enhancements of this book. The recipes are practical, nutritious, and simple to execute. Grouped by categories, the recipes are low in sodium and contain almost no sugars. Addressing the needs of the baby as well as the family, this cookbook will most likely see much use when added to the family library.

Where To Find/Buy:

Bookstores and libraries.

Overall Rating
★★★
Strong in providing information on the merits of nutrition coupled with 250+ recipes

Design, Ease Of Use
★★★
Clear, well-organized; non-threatening textbook format

1–4 Stars; N/R = Not Rated

Media Type:
Print

Price:
$13.00

Principal Subject:
Care

Age Group:
Infants & Toddlers (0–3)

ISBN:
0688103588

Edition Reviewed:
2nd (1992)

Publisher:
Quill (William Morrow & Company)

Author/Editor:
Karin Knight, R.N. and Jeannie Lumley

About The Author:
(From Cover Notes)
Kari Knight is a registered pediatric nurse who has worked in the public health system in the Los Angeles area. Jeannie Lumley is employed by a major recording company in their public relations department.

Overall Rating
★★
Overview of young children's growth and nutritional needs but best for childcare setting

Design, Ease Of Use
★★★
Organizational elements at their best; information though is in a textbook format

1–4 Stars; N/R = Not Rated

Media Type:
Print

Price:
$37.50

Principal Subject:
Care

Age Group:
All Ages (0–5)

ISBN:
0028020898

Edition Reviewed:
1995

Publisher:
Glencoe (McGraw-Hill)

Author/Editor:
Roberta L. Duyff,
Susan C. Giarratano, and
Mary F. Zuzich

NUTRITION, HEALTH AND SAFETY FOR PRESCHOOL CHILDREN

Description:

Divided into four parts, this 447 page guide focuses on young children's nutrition, health, and safety and is intended for caregivers and educators. How nutrition, safety, and health are interrelated is given in an overview along with the role heredity and environment play. Part 1 offers basic information about the nutritional needs of young children. Topics discussed here include food patterns, nutrition basics (nutrients, vitamins, proteins, etc.), and meal planning. Part 2 presents information about the growth and development of children. Separate chapters within this part focus on the nutritional needs of infants, toddler, preschoolers, and children with special nutritional needs (developmental delays, obesity, etc.). Part 3 presents health and safety issues of the childcare setting including policies, procedures, dealing with infectious diseases, and more. Ways to teach children and parents about health, nutrition, and safety are given in Part 4 along with four appendices offering information about recommended daily allowances, nutritive value of foods, growth charts, and federal food programs.

Evaluation:

This textbook illustrates the advantage of using good organizational tools. Each chapter lists the chapter's learning objectives along with a list of terms defined both within the chapter and in the book's glossary. Additional organizers provided throughout include sidebar tips, bulleted highlights, bold colored subheadings, tables of information, chapter summaries, review questions, and hypothetical situations to use for discussion purposes. Also given in each chapter are three sections (cultural diversity, promoting healthy habits, communicating) that offer practical suggestions for caregivers and teachers. Examples here include ways to incorporate kosher foods, holiday and birthday foods, field trips, fire drills, home safety, playground safety, etc. Also given are sidebar recipes on suggested "wholesome snacks." Other "recipe-type books" offer similar dietary information but in a more diluted form. Pricey and not necessarily an easily read book for busy parents, this book will be more useful to caregivers.

Where To Find/Buy:

Bookstores and libraries.

THE WELL-FED BABY
Easy Healthful Recipes For The First 12 Months

Description:

This guide was the result of Sweet and Bloom's adoption of a six month old Russian baby who was malnourished and suffering from rickets. Supported by seven major sections with an introduction and concluding index, this 190 page resource strives to instill healthy cooking techniques and nutritional recipes for parents of infants. Chapter One discusses the changing feeding and diet requirements of babies and toddlers. Recommendations and advice are given in an age-specific format for children ages 6 months to 12 months of age. Chapter Two offers recipes for breakfasts. How to prepare your own grains is a highlight of this chapter. Chapters Three, Four, and Five include recipes for breads, lunches, and dinners, respectively. Chapters Six and Seven follow with the topics of soups, snacks, and desserts. At the conclusion of the book, there are two additional sections which contain advice for eating out with young children and a listing of contributing chefs.

Evaluation:

Parents will certainly find this to be a good resource in providing information on healthy ways to prepare nutritious meals. Based upon the input from professional chefs and other food professionals, and tested within numerous families, a lot of good basic information is provided in this resource. Tips are given on food sanitation and safety; avoiding cross-contamination, such as the transfer of salmonella bacteria; food allergies; a feeding guide on food texture; and more. The recipes are simple and easy to execute, listing serving amounts for each along with age-specific recommendations. Each recipe is laid-out in a step-by-step format. One refreshing item about this book is it's global approach in terms of its recipe content. Parents will appreciate such diverse recipes as tabbouleh salad, rice congee, and basmati rice and chicken as inspired by some of the most accomplished chefs.

Where To Find/Buy:

Bookstores and libraries.

Overall Rating
★★
Encourages healthy creative cooking from scratch

Design, Ease Of Use
★★
Font of subheadings sometimes difficult to read; "block-cut" illustrations are attractive

1–4 Stars; N/R = Not Rated

Media Type:
Print

Price:
$12.00

Principal Subject:
Care

Age Group:
Infants (0–1)

ISBN:
0020453701

Edition Reviewed:
1994

Publisher:
Macmillan (Prentice Hall Macmillan)

Author/Editor:
O. Robin Sweet and Thomas Bloom

About The Author:
(From Cover Notes)
Sweet is an author, childbirth educator, and former pediatric nurse for 10 years. Bloom is an author, food educator, and former Professor of food science and food management at the University of Minnesota, The University of Wisconsin, and Florida State University.

Overall Rating
★
Tasty recipes that often involve elaborate preparation or unhealthy ingredients

Design, Ease Of Use
★★
Grouped by category (23) in the table of contents with no back-up index

1–4 Stars; N/R = Not Rated

Media Type:
Print

Price:
$12.95

Principal Subject:
Care

Age Group:
All Ages (0–5)

ISBN:
1570710309

Edition Reviewed:
1995

Publisher:
Sourcebooks

Author/Editor:
Sheila Ellison and
Dr. Judith Gray

About The Author:
(From Cover Notes)
Ellison, with a BA degree in psychology from USC, has volunteered on behalf of children, and founded community youth groups and mentoring programs. Gray is internationally known as an author, teacher, and speaker on future trends in education.

365 FOODS KIDS LOVE TO EAT

Description:

Offering their "practical, comprehensive, easy-to-follow" cookbook, the authors of this 365+ page book list 365 one page recipes "designed with kid's palates and appetites in mind." The book begins with sections offering tips on "table management for families" (manners), some suggestions for healthful eating ("trim fats from meats," etc.), and food substitutions and equivalences; a list of measuring conversions is provided at the back of the book. The table of contents lists all recipes which are grouped by category (23) including: baby foods, beverages, breads and muffins, breakfast, fruits, do-it-yourself, peanut butter, lunch boxes, salads, sandwiches, soups, snacks, cookies, designer foods, pasta, vegetables, meats, poultry, fish, desserts, parties, holidays, and foreign foods. Each category includes a facing page that lists the recipes included within that section. Some recipes include a one sentence "note" (offering the authors' personal anecdote or advice) or a suggested activity to do while preparing the food. There is no index.

Evaluation:

There is a plethora of available cookbooks to help parents prepare recipes that not only provide children with healthy eating habits, but can also be prepared quickly and easily. Not so with this one. Recipes in this guide contain many ingredients that children will certainly like—corn syrup, sugar, and chocolate to name a few—but not generally accepted as healthy. Additionally, many of the recipes involve quite elaborate steps. Since children's eating desires fluctuate dramatically from one day to the next, commonsense dictates that spending considerable time preparing a child's food is time ill-spent. The food prepared using these recipes is good, but it would be better presented to the entire family with possible success for the toddler or preschooler child. Some ingredients for the baby food recipes are ill-advised. Some recipes call for milk, suggesting breast or formula milk until the baby is 6 months old (and then what?), others include egg or honey with no warning about allergies. Look to other better researched guides to feeding your child.

Where To Find/Buy:

Bookstores and libraries.

FAMILY BED (THE)
An Age Old Concept In Child Rearing

 Recommended For:
Care

Description:

The author, the mother of two children and a former La Leche League counselor, wrote this book from her experience with her daughter who would not sleep alone, and after discovering that many parents solved this problem by ". . . tak(ing) the child to bed . . ." This book explores the benefits of allowing babies and older children to sleep with their parents, and the modern "taboo" against the practice. The first five chapters discuss current beliefs and attitudes towards shared sleeping, why and how parents began allowing their children to sleep with them, concerns and fears about it, and the psychological importance to the child. The next two chapters include a history of shared family sleep from medieval times onwards, and observations of sleep arrangements in various cultures throughout the world. Chapters 8–10 discuss the needs of the infant and older child, how siblings fit into the picture, and marital relations. The last three chapters discuss special circumstances (hospitalization, adopted children), nighttime parenting (discipline) as a continuum of daytime parenting, and the benefits of the family bed.

Evaluation:

Of the many ways in which modern society alienates its members, putting a baby to sleep in a separate room, some argue, may be one of the most subtle. As we learn from this book, the concept of shared sleep is hardly new—families have been sharing beds since the beginning of time. Many of the "scientific" reasons of why shared sleeping is so bad are discredited here, and experts and parents alike have been looking twice at the practice. Sharing sleep, the author argues, is practical (no more getting up in the middle of the night to breastfeed) and psychologically beneficial (babies and young children may feel more secure); it also ends the difficulty of putting a child to bed—when they are secure enough to sleep by themselves, they will. Especially interesting is the "brief history" of family sleeping, and the gradual rise of "sterile child rearing" that reached its zenith in the 1940s. Parents interested in or curious about the idea of the shared family bed will find this a persuasive and informative read.

Where To Find/Buy:

Bookstores and libraries.

Overall Rating
★★★
Persuasively presents the practical and psychological benefits of shared family sleep

Design, Ease Of Use
★★★★
Extremely well written and researched

1–4 Stars; N/R = Not Rated

Media Type:
Print

Price:
$9.95

Principal Subject:
Care

Age Group:
All Ages (0–5)

ISBN:
0895293579

Edition Reviewed:
1987

Publisher:
Avery Publishing Group

Author/Editor:
Tine Thevenin

About The Author:
(From Cover Notes)
The author began this book as a research report before it grew into a book manuscript. She was born in the Netherlands, and is the mother of two children. She has also been a counselor for La Leche League.

Overall Rating
★★★
Rationale and tips for finding a "sensitive solution to your baby's sleepless nights"

Design, Ease Of Use
★★★★
All subtopics listed under chapter headings in table of contents; useful photographs

1–4 Stars; N/R = Not Rated

Media Type:
Print

Price:
$11.95

Principal Subject:
Care

Age Group:
All Ages (0–5)

ISBN:
0452264073

Edition Reviewed:
1987

Publisher:
Penguin Books USA (Plume)

Author/Editor:
William Sears, M.D.

About The Author:
(From Cover Notes)
Sears, "one of America's most renowned pediatricians," has been in practice for 20 years and authored 10 books. Currently, he's a clinical assistant professor of pediatrics at USC School of Medicine.

NIGHTTIME PARENTING
How To Get Your Baby And Child To Sleep

Best Resource For:
Dealing with sleep issues

Recommended For:
Care

Description:

Sears has written this guide to answer the question, "Should I let my child cry it out at night, or console my crying child?" His goal, in this 203 page, 17 chapter book, is "to help parents and children achieve sleep harmony" . . . "lessening your child's night-waking and increasing your ability to cope." Sears draws on both his experience as a father of 8 and from returns of a questionnaire sent to patients. The foundation of the book, as with all of Sears' books, lays in the tenets of attachment parenting (where babies and caregivers best form a secure relationship by being very connected to each other's cues); chapter 1 explains this in detail. Other chapter topics deal with the difference between baby and adult sleep, where baby should sleep, dealing with night-waking, food that helps sleep, nighttime fathering, demands of the high need child, SIDS, sleep disorders, nap times, single nighttime parenting, and more. Sears asserts throughout his book the importance of babies and young children "sharing sleep" with their parents; in other words, sleeping in the parents' bed.

Evaluation:

Does Sears answer the question, "Should I let my child cry it out at night?" You bet. His points are well-made, using both research findings and anecdotes from parents. Everyone agrees that a baby's cries are a baby's language. However, as Sears asserts, "if the baby's cries fall on deaf ears, he is less motivated to cry" . . . "the baby loses trust that the caregiver will respond." One can always find arguments to defend any parenting style; parents and advisors to parents should read all the viewpoints and choose one that resonates with them. Sears' book represents a point of view that some parents will strongly embrace and others will just as strongly reject, research or no research. A weakness of this book, however, is that some areas need updating. For example, since 1987 (its copyright date), new research has come to light regarding SIDS, including the pros and cons of sleeping with your baby. Also, special situations, such as working mothers, need some extended suggestions and support, especially since this is the norm for many households.

Where To Find/Buy:

Bookstores and libraries.

SLEEP
How To Teach Your Child To Sleep Like A Baby

Description:

This six chapter, 214 page book aims to answer the question "How can I get my child to sleep through the night?" Based on "in-depth interviews with more than two dozen of today's leading experts in sleep research, pediatric medicine, and child psychology," the author has also conducted a "thorough" review of the research that has been done; the "experts" are listed in the Acknowledgments and literature reviewed is cited in the Resources section. Chapter One reviews children's sleep patterns and problems. Then Chapter Two describes ways to deal with "bedtime battles" while Chapter Three offers techniques for managing "middle-of-the-night awakenings." Chapter Four focuses on what to do to help children who have nighttime fears. "Where should your child sleep?" is the topic of Chapter Five outlining pros and cons of various sleep locations (family bed, bassinet, crib, big bed, etc.). "Special Situations" are addressed in Chapter Six and include circumstances that interfere with a child's sleep (siblings, twins, babysitter, travel, divorce, preemies, sleep disorders, etc.). No index is given.

Evaluation:

This book's intention is admirable given the amount of discussion today focusing on sleep issues and how many experts can't agree on how to handle sleep problems. Supplying parents with information on all the different methods that are available allows parents to compare methods and make their decision based on their family's needs. To this goal, organization elements in this book would have made this search more rewarding. Yet, there are no details in the table of contents and there is no index. Instead, parents will need to read the entire text, write down names and page numbers of methods, and jot down notes because there are no other ways to relocate the information. The author does highlight various sections within the chapters with titles such as "The Beat-Him-To-The-Punch Approach" or "The Reassuring Approach," but this offers little real help. A comparison chart that contrasts such things as amount of parental involvement or absence, the length of time needed to resolve sleep problems, etc. would be more helpful along with cross-references to page numbers. Parents should use this as a start but keep their paper and pen handy.

Where To Find/Buy:

Bookstores, libraries, or order direct by contacting Mail Order Department, Simon & Schuster, 200 Old Tappan Road, Old Tappan, NJ 07675.

Overall Rating
★★★
Useful for cross-examining the various methods available for teaching children to sleep

Design, Ease Of Use
★
No index, minimal table of contents makes searching for specific methods impossible

1–4 Stars; N/R = Not Rated

Media Type:
Print

Price:
$5.99

Principal Subject:
Care

Age Group:
All Ages (0–5)

ISBN:
0671880381

Edition Reviewed:
1996

Publisher:
Pocket Books (Simon & Schuster)

Author/Editor:
Tamara Eberlein

About The Author:
(From Cover Notes)
Eberlein has written over 200 articles on parenting, health, and psychology. Her work has appeared in magazines such as *Redbook, Good Housekeeping, Family Circle,* and more. She is a graduate of the Georgetown University School of Languages and Linguistics.

Overall Rating
★★
Good overview of sleep issues, pros and cons of various methods, and practical tips

Design, Ease Of Use
★★★★
Easily read with bulleted tips, inset blocks of advice and parental quotes; succinct

1–4 Stars; N/R = Not Rated

Media Type:
Print

Price:
$6.95

Principal Subject:
Care

Age Group:
All Ages (0–5)

ISBN:
0916773191

Edition Reviewed:
2nd (1991)

Publisher:
The Book Peddlers

Author/Editor:
Vicki Lansky

About The Author:
(From Cover Notes)
Lansky is a mother and author. She can also be read regularly in *Sesame Street's Parent Guide* section and in *Family Circle* where she writes the "HELP!" column.

GETTING YOUR CHILD TO SLEEP. . . AND BACK TO SLEEP
Tips For Parents Of Infants, Toddlers, And Preschoolers

Description:

The ten chapters of this 131 page guide highlight many of the facets of children's sleep. Chapter One discusses a baby's sleep patterns during the first six months while Chapter Two offers tips on developing bedtime routines for a baby. Chapters Three and Four focus on how to deal with baby's cries and colic. Chapter Five offers tips for getting a "night waker" back to sleep. Whether or not to allow a baby or child to share the parents' bed is the topic of Chapter Six. Helping parents cope with loss of sleep is Lansky's focus in Chapter Seven. "Naptime" how-tos and suggestions for older children are discussed in Chapter Eight, while Chapter Nine discusses "reasonable bedtime routines" for older children. The last chapter offers strategies for helping children handle their nighttime fears, bad dreams, and night terrors. A one page index concludes the book as well as a list of other resources. Each chapter contains bulleted tips, blocked insets of highlighted advice and parental quotes, and sometimes organizational contacts or products.

Evaluation:

Lansky has provided an overview here of all prevailing theories on how to deal with sleep issues from having baby "cry it out" to sleep arrangements in "the family bed." Although she presents the pros and cons of these sleep issues, most often Lansky's opinion is center stage following her line of reasoning that she had "made peace with the fact that sleep as [she] had known it was no longer to be part of [her] life" and "it was somehow okay." While this may not bide well with those who want sleep training methods to teach their baby to sleep, Lansky, does, however, offer strategies and support to overcome the tiredness plaguing many parents in the early months and years. She balances her opinions with quotes from parents who have tried the reverse of Lansky's suggestions and also had success. While not a definitive guide, Lansky's guide gives parents a plan for dealing with sleep issues. Parents will get practical tips ("play a radio, with an automatic shut-off timing feature . . .") and support ("learn to make jokes about your lack of sleep"). They can then look to other resources if necessary for additional support or how-tos.

Where To Find/Buy:

Bookstores, libraries, or order direct by calling (612) 475-3527 or 1-800-255-3379.

SOLVE YOUR CHILD'S SLEEP PROBLEMS

Description:

This 250 page book addresses the issues of sleeplessness and how it affects the parents as well as the child. Part 1, "Your Child's Sleep," describes the tired, frustrated and often angry responses of parents with a young child who will not settle into the normal routines of the family. Reassurance is given to the parents that the problem has nothing to do with poor parenting, nor is it a "stage" that must be waited out. Instead, each kind of sleep disorder is discussed to help the parent identify its cause and its treatment. Treatments for the common problems of "sleepless children" include new schedules, routines, and ways of handling the child that set appropriate expectations and limits. The goal is to use a consistent, firm, and fair technique, tailored to the child, the family, and the particular sleep disorder. There are cases where medical factors are involved, and this book identifies these so that parents can seek the appropriate assistance. Issues such as sleeptalking, sleepwalking, thrashing, and terrors are explained, as well as headbanging, noisy breathing, sleep apnea and narcolepsy.

Evaluation:

This book explains sleep, what is normal, and what is not in a child's behavior. Chapter 2, "What We Know About Sleep," explains REM and non-REM sleep and provides a good foundation for the rest of the book. The details given throughout the book, however, are somewhat dense. Much of the book is focused on how to develop good sleep patterns, which the author identifies as the most common cause of sleep issues in young children. Bedtime rituals, ways the child is comforted to sleep, and where the child sleeps are addressed in a straightforward way. The author suggests that a child should learn ways to "self-comfort," with no dependence on rocking, touching, bottles, or pacifiers; that this fundamental assumption is best for infants is disputed by many. Some parents may find some of Ferber's suggestions lack compassion, such as, if a child cries hard enough to vomit, parents should clean the bed and child, then continue the routine. Since not all problems can be solved by routine and firmness, attention is given to medical causes of poor sleep and how medical intervention and regulating the child's sleep patterns can help.

Where To Find/Buy:

Bookstores and libraries.

Overall Rating
★★
Informative, dry description of ways to regulate children's sleep habits

Design, Ease Of Use
★★★
Clear, easy to reference, helpful appendices and index

1–4 Stars; N/R = Not Rated

Media Type:
Print

Price:
$12.00

Principal Subject:
Care

Age Group:
All Ages (0–5)

ISBN:
0671620991

Edition Reviewed:
1985

Publisher:
Fireside (Simon & Schuster)

Author/Editor:
Richard Ferber, M.D.

About The Author:
(From Cover Notes)
Ferber, widely recognized as the nation's leading authority in the field of children's sleep problems, directs the Sleep Lab and the Center for Pediatric Sleep Disorders at Children's Hospital in Boston. He also teaches at Harvard Medical School and is a pediatrician.

Overall Rating

★

Considers child's developmental issues, but backed up only by personal research

Design, Ease Of Use

★★★★

Well-organized, concrete steps presented for each age; each chapter stands on its own

1–4 Stars; N/R = Not Rated

Media Type:
Print

Price:
$11.95

Principal Subject:
Care

Age Group:
All Ages (0–5)

ISBN:
0385192509

Edition Reviewed:
1985

Publisher:
Main Street Books (Doubleday/Bantam Doubleday Dell)

Author/Editor:
Joanne Cuthbertson and Susie Schevill

About The Author:
(From Cover Notes)
Cuthbertson and Schevill are both mothers and married to pediatricians.

HELPING YOUR CHILD SLEEP THROUGH THE NIGHT
A Guide For Parents Of Children From Infancy To Age Five

Description:

Written by two mothers, this 246 page resource is "devoted to showing you how to establish and maintain good sleeping habits for your children." An introduction outlines various elements of sleep including the "science of sleep" (bio rhythms, physiology), security objects, possible locations of sleep, bedtime rituals, and more. The remaining five chapters highlight the authors' sleep training methods, advice, and discussions of sleep disruptions (in light of habits, development, and specific situations) for various age groups: from birth to 4 months, 5 to 9 months, 10 to 18 months, 18 months to 3 years, and 3 years to 5 years. Each chapter is designed to stand on its own. It is suggested, however, that parents, read the introduction prior to turning to the chapter that corresponds to their child's age. A Q & A segment is included at the end of each chapter. A bibliography, suggested bedtime books for children, and an index conclude the resource.

Evaluation:

Of the various sleep training methods that exist, this resource considers reasons for sleep interruptions along with the child's developmental stage. The main problem we found, however, with this method is that it has not been tested by large controlled studies. It is based on the authors' reading and experience with their own children and friends' children. One concern in particular we had involves training a 3 day old newborn. It is suggested that after the newborn receives their "focal feeding" (at about 11 pm), upon waking later they should be comforted to sleep, and if need be, offered a bottle of water (or glucose water), and then placed in bed. This "stretching" the time between feedings is the heart of the authors' method. Many pediatricians, though, advise newborns be fed on demand. Nursing mothers are also advised not to use a bottle for several weeks due to nipple confusion on the part of the infant. And what if the baby, who, research states, is naturally inclined to be drawn to sweet tastes, decides the glucose water is a fine substitution for milk? Look to other more sound resources for help in getting your child to sleep.

Where To Find/Buy:
Bookstores and libraries.

Care: All-Inclusive

BABYSENSE
A Practical And Supportive Guide To Baby Care

 Best Resource For:
Overview of infant care

 Recommended For:
Care

Description:

In its 2nd edition, this well-known guide to baby care includes updated information about breast- vs. bottle-feeding, child care, the adjustment to motherhood, and more. In the introduction, the author states, "I spent a lot of time . . . working out solutions to problems that had been worked out before by countless other parents." The book's basis is that "parents are the ultimate experts" on baby care. Written for the first-time mother separated from extended family networks, this guide includes common-sense advice her mother would give her in a warm, personable tone. The first section of six discusses newborns, feeding (breast, bottle, solids), and such "comfort" matters as interpreting the baby's crying, colic, sleep, bathing, and clothing. The next two parts discuss coping with motherhood and childcare. The last section contains a hodgepodge of "practical matters," from traveling with your baby to childproofing your house, health care, and "playing and learning." Interspersed throughout are anecdotes and tips from real mothers, forming, as the author puts it, "the backbone of the material in this book."

Evaluation:

New mothers looking for a single book offering excellent information about baby care with warmth and support need look no further than here. It is wonderfully written, presenting practical how-tos clearly and effectively. It offers both breadth and depth, running the gamut of baby care issues from getting to know one's newborn to a recipe for home-made playdough. Recent SIDS findings are not included, so information on newborn sleeping positions is inaccurate; also, some breastfeeding guidance is outdated. Most readers will appreciate the author's belief that parents are the real experts on their baby's care, avoiding professional opinions that leave parents feeling "inadequate and imperiled." You'll find lots of helpful tips from real mothers, as well as a memorable account of the author's own 12-hour day with her firstborn. Useful drawings show everything from positions to nurse and burp babies to the safest ways to hold a baby during bath time. In an age when a first-time mother may not have someone to show her how to swaddle a baby or reassure her when she feels she's reached the end of her tether, this book makes a heroic attempt to give both practical advice and a sense of community to mothers.

Where To Find/Buy:

Bookstores and libraries.

Overall Rating
★★★★
An excellent, sensitive, and "human" guide to baby care; needs updating regarding SIDS

Design, Ease Of Use
★★★★
Wide pages, personable tone makes reading enjoyable; many chapters use Q & A format

1–4 Stars; N/R = Not Rated

Media Type:
Print

Price:
$16.95

Principal Subject:
Care

Age Group:
Infants (0–1)

ISBN:
0312050569

Edition Reviewed:
2nd (1991)

Publisher:
St. Martin's Press

Author/Editor:
Frances Wells Burck

About The Author:
(From Cover Notes)
Frances Wells Burck is the author of another book on parenting, *Mothers Talking: Sharing the Secret*. She lives outside New York City with her husband and three daughters.

★★★★

Overall Rating
★★★★
Excellent resource combining sight and sound for first-time or prospective parents

Design, Ease Of Use
★★★★
Visually pleasing art backdrops, inspiring quotes, and video clips; navigation a breeze

1–4 Stars; N/R = Not Rated

Media Type:
CD-ROM

Price:
$34.95

Principal Subject:
Care

Age Group:
Infants (0–1)

Edition Reviewed:
1996

Publisher:
PARENTING/Time Publishing Ventures

YOUR PREGNANCY, YOUR NEWBORN
The Complete Guide For Expectant And New Mothers

Best Resource For:
CD-ROM focusing on infants' care and development

Recommended For:
Care

Description:

For Mac (3.1+, 68040/33+), Windows/DOS (3.1+,5.0+; 486/66+). Created by the editors of *PARENTING* magazine, this CD-ROM is divided into five main sections. The first three focus on pregnancy with information on how to plan for pregnancy (work, exercise, health, etc.), a month-by-month description of pregnancy (baby development, changes in the mother, doctor relations), and labor & delivery (options, pain relief). Section Four highlights the newborn. Subtopic discussions include: the newborn's appearance, warning signs, senses, reflexes, communication, bonding, breastfeeding, bottlefeeding, and more. Section Five offers parents advice for "Life With Baby." Mom's needs, dad's needs, and baby's needs (feeding, sleeping, bathing, crying, etc.) are outlined. Also provided are baby health and safety tips from immunizations to first aid to car and home safety. A discussion of childcare options and issues is also given. An interactive pregnancy calendar is available, as well as an index and gift registry (Fisher-Price items).

Evaluation:

This is a must for prospective parents. Although it comes with a pretty high price tag, it will prove valuable for calming the fears of new parents-to-be as they gain confidence in their parenting. Combining visually stunning backdrops, realtime video clips, and audio advice from experts, this CD-ROM fills a need not addressed elsewhere. Numerous experts and parents from *PARENTING* are made available to parents offering their advice about maternity leave rights, birth and delivery, the older mom's experience, exercise, breastfeeding, choosing childcare, and more. Two areas which lack depth, however, deal with how to start breastfeeding and administering first aid. For both of these areas, video clips would be an asset. More expensive than most print resources, but it will satisfy the needs of many parents.

Where To Find/Buy:

Bookstores or computer software stores.

YOU AND YOUR NEWBORN BABY
A Guide To The First Months After Birth

 Recommended For:
Care

Description:

Written by a childbirth educator with twenty years experience, this book reflects a growing desire on the part of participants in her childbirth classes to focus on what one is to expect **after** the birth. Consequently, it offers ideas on things one can do to make the time after birth easier. The book consists of three major parts: "The Newborn Mother," "The Newborn Baby" and "The Newborn Family." The "Newborn Mother" part addresses questions about how the mother can take care of herself physically and emotionally before and after the birth. "The Newborn Baby" part focuses on health care of the baby, her/his development of sensory and motor skills, and basics regarding feeding, bathing and diapering. The final part, "The Newborn Baby," encourages the family to keep their relationships strong with the birth of a new family member. Special attention is given in this section to the "postpartum father" and to other children in the family.

Evaluation:

In the United States, where nearly 99% of women give birth in hospitals, the time that a mother and her baby remain in the hospital after the birth continues to shrink. In fact, by the year 2000, discharge from the hospital within 24 hours of the birth will probably become the norm. This trend challenges the family of the newborn as they alone face the postpartum experience, cut off from trained personnel who, in many other countries, are there to teach parenting skills, assess the mother's and baby's health, and provide moral support. This book, then, is meant to fill that gap. Its tone is that of a well educated, sensitive, reassuring professional who is vicariously there to help the family who feels so happy, but also overwhelmed and disorientated as they go home with a new child. The book also contains well drawn illustrations of breastfeeding, diaper changing, swaddling, etc. And so, if one is desperately searching for no-panic "operations manual" to substitute for the public health nurse who will not be there, this short, easy to read book fits the bill.

Where To Find/Buy:

Bookstores and libraries.

Overall Rating
★★★★
Concise, sensitive "operations manual" for arriving home with the new baby

Design, Ease Of Use
★★★
Well drawn illustrations, helpful charts and index

1–4 Stars; N/R = Not Rated

Media Type:
Print

Price:
$6.95

Principal Subject:
Care

Age Group:
Infants (0–1)

ISBN:
1558320547

Edition Reviewed:
1993

Publisher:
Harvard Common Press

Author/Editor:
Linda Todd, M.P.H.

About The Author:
(From Cover Notes)
Linda Todd, M.P.H. is coordinator of prenatal education at Fairview Riverside Medical Center in Minneapolis. She has been a faculty member for the International Childbirth Education Association's workshops and is the author of *Labor and Birth: A Guide for You.*

Overall Rating
★★★
Vast amount of concise info provided on topics from pregnancy to baby's first year

Design, Ease Of Use
★★★
Cumbersome subtopic list (often 100+) only listed alphabetically but worth the search

1–4 Stars; N/R = Not Rated

Media Type:
Internet

Principal Subject:
Care

Age Group:
Infants (0–1)

BABYCENTER
Complete Pregnancy & Baby Information

Description:
Launched in November 1997, this site offers seven main areas of parenting information. Their goal is to be "the most trusted and complete resource for new parents and parents-to-be." Information is organized under the headings of "Pregnancy," "Baby Care," "Family Life," "Mother Care," "Exercise/Nutrition," and "Working Parents." Various articles are listed alphabetically within each of these areas. Cross-references to Bulletin Board topics, "Great Debates," "Polls," and more are also given. Within "Baby Care," 100+ subtopics were offered from air bags and toy safety to development and immunizations; also provided is connection to the "Pampers Parenting Institute" online experts. "Family Life" and "Working Parents" host articles focusing on such topics as maternity leave, choosing childcare, insurance, marriage issues, and more. "Pregnancy" and "Mother Care" primarily centers on pregnancy while "Exercise/Nutrition" offers pregnancy and postpregnancy information. Online shopping is available as well.

Evaluation:
This ambitious new site certainly deserves a visit from prospective and new parents. The site's creators (editors, designers, engineers, and marketers) are obviously well-versed on the elements needed to make a site user-friendly. The site's main areas are very well-organized, offering complete cross-references. For example, parents seeking information on a baby's development will also be given links to related topics, other sources (websites and print references), and other parents. Some subtopics ("baby sleeping through the night") also reference bulletin boards on the same topic ("babies and sleep") and "great debates" ("baby sleeps alone vs. the family bed") offering the pros and cons on an issue, experts' advice, and more. The only area needing some help is in the access of these articles. Parents will need to read through a rather wieldy list of titles (often 100+) although a search can be conducted. The site is constantly asking for feedback in each area. Use it now with confidence but keep checking back for updates.

Where To Find/Buy:
On the Internet at the URL: http://www.babycenter.com.

Internet URL:
http://www.babycenter.com

BABYCARE FOR BEGINNERS

Description:

This 96 page book's spiral-bound, cardboard-stand format allows it to open upright on a changing surface, table, or bath leaving parents' hands free as they take care of their baby. Offering numerous step-by-step color photographs on each page with additional information on the flipside (once it's standing upright), this baby care guide is divided into 10 parts of how-tos with an additional 4 page illustrated first aid section (choking, CPR, etc.), a detailed table of contents, and an index. Instructional tips and photographs for taking care of baby include: handling, carrying, soothing, feeding, diaper changing, dressing, sleeping, cleaning/bathing, daily care routines, and signs of illness. Photographs within the ten parts include specific instructions for breastfeeding (positioning, pumping/expressing), bottlefeeding (sterilizing, mixing, feeding), getting baby into a sling or other type of carrier, cutting nails, brushing teeth, cleaning a girl, cleaning a boy, and more.

Evaluation:

New parents who have very little access to others' help and hands will appreciate this book's format and how-to instructions. Although some topics are treated lightly (signs of illness, amusing your baby, soothing your crying baby, etc.) and some suggestions are not advised for safety reasons (carrot sticks for an infant), most of the photographs are detailed enough to guarantee parents confidence and success. The format and information in this baby care guide will be most helpful for parents of newborns but less so for parents of older babies. These parents will need to look to other resources for additional information and suggestions surrounding the topics of feeding solids, playing with their baby, bathing in the tub, etc. Although the user of this resource may enjoy a format which frees up an extra set of hands while conducting certain baby care tasks, other resources can be easily found which also address the how-tos of newborn care along with tips for continued care throughout their first year.

Where To Find/Buy:

Bookstores and libraries.

Overall Rating

★★

Offering step-by-step photos to help parents learn to take care of their newborn baby

Design, Ease Of Use

★★★★

Large color photographs, bold headings; vertical standing format, spiral bound

1–4 Stars; N/R = Not Rated

Media Type:
Print

Price:
$16.95

Principal Subject:
Care

Age Group:
Infants (0–1)

ISBN:
0062731041

Edition Reviewed:
1996

Publisher:
Carroll & Brown Limited (Harper Perennial/ HarperCollins Publishers)

Author/Editor:
Dr. Frances Williams

Overall Rating
★★
Best used for parenting classes to introduce newborn care; incomplete for home use

Design, Ease Of Use
★★★
Well-organized and laid-out with numbered highlights on screen, segment headings

1–4 Stars; N/R = Not Rated

Media Type:
Videotape

Price:
$29.98

Principal Subject:
Care

Age Group:
Infants (0–1)

Edition Reviewed:
1995

Publisher:
Creative Outlook

PARENT'S OWNER'S MANUAL: NEWBORN
Volume 1: A Child Care Series

Description:
Creative Outlook's goal is to "ease your transition into parenting and enhance your comfort level in this new role." To that end, they have broken this 55 minute videotape into various segments: baby furniture (essentials), different ways of holding and picking up a baby, what to do when baby cries, using a pacifier, swaddling, feeding (breastfeeding, bottlefeeding), burping, diapering (pros and cons of cloth/disposables, how-tos), buying the layette (safety and comfort constraints), dressing, bathing (sponge bath, infant bath), sleeping (how-tos, sleep positions), nail trimming, "the medicine box" (essential supplies, medical aids), playtime, and packing the diaper bag for outings. Each segment includes live footage taken of parents as they illustrate the narrator's dialogue. In many cases, numbered highlights appear on the screen to isolate main points. Freeze frame techniques are also used to capture highlights in various segments.

Evaluation:
Parents who are visual learners and work best with live hands-on instructions may appreciate this tape. Others will do better to invest their money in other resources that offer more in-depth information about the same topics. Although this tape's intent is applaudable, once parents have seen it a few times, they'll wonder why they invested time and money in it at all. This tape's primary value would be in its use for new parents-to-be perhaps as a follow up for a parenting class on newborn care. For home use, however, its possibilities are limited. Viewers will also note subtle biases: the discrepancy between the details given for bottlefeeding compared to those for breastfeeding, advice to increase response time to baby's cries, and advice on training a baby to sleep on its own. Additionally, sleep positions described do not reflect new SIDS research. Parents will find that this videotape is not a complete "owner's manual" but is better used as a catalyst for seeking other sources offering more in-depth information and advice.

Where To Find/Buy:
Bookstores, libraries, videotape dealers, or order direct by calling 1-800-97-KIDS-1.

KIDZ ARE PEOPLE TOO PAGE (THE)

Description:

Pregnancy, childbirth, breastfeeding, and infant care are some of the major topics at this website created by a Christian mother of one. Her site's focus is that "children should be treated with respect, too." Each topic includes an introduction offering her helpful tips and advice. Links to other sites are also offered for further info. Pregnancy links include those offering general overviews, nutrition, low tech ways to conceive, etc. Also included are essays and brochures detailing an unborn child's right to life and sites offering alternatives to abortions. Birth stories are offered at "Childbirth"; users of the site may submit their own stories. Links at this topic include VBAC births (stories, info), water births, home births, Bradley method, doulas, midwives, and more. Areas linked under "Infant Care" include diaperings, wearing your baby, understanding your baby's cries, the family bed, and more. "Why breast is best" is offered at "Breastfeeding" along with links to articles supporting that choice; also included are tips on starting solids, nursing toddlers, etc. Excerpts from the Bible are offered to support the site's focus and beliefs.

Evaluation:

Two distinctive approaches to parenting have evolved. One approach, "attachment parenting," believes in heeding the baby's every cry, sharing sleep with one's baby, breastfeeding, etc. The second approach (termed by some "detachment parenting") believes that a baby needs to be taught to be independent, cry it out, learn to sleep by himself/herself, etc. This site takes both elements into account. In doing so, it uses quotes from the Bible, couples this guidance with the author's own experiences and attitudes, and supplies additional informational sources. Although one must link (often many times) to get the information one may be in search of, this site is positive, well-organized, and straightforward in its approach. The only valuable arena omitted is an opportunity for Christian parents to discuss parenting issues. Currently, the only avenue for parents to contribute is by offering their birth stories. Hopefully, future plans will encourage discussions to make this site even more useful.

Where To Find/Buy:

On the Internet at the URL: http://www.geocities.com/Heartland/8148.

Internet URL:

http://www.geocities.com/Heartland/8148

Overall Rating
★★
Offers Christian parenting perspectives

Design, Ease Of Use
★★
Straightforward, succinct; numerous links to get more info; needs to add discussion forum

1–4 Stars; N/R = Not Rated

Media Type:
Internet

Principal Subject:
Care

Age Group:
Infants (0–1)

Overall Rating
★
Info far too concise to be of much practical use; some info currently not recommended

Design, Ease Of Use
★★★★
Short interview-type vignettes; icons for accessibility; recaps at end of each segment

1–4 Stars; N/R = Not Rated

Media Type:
Videotape

Price:
$9.98

Principal Subject:
Care

Age Group:
Infants (0–1)

Edition Reviewed:
1985

Publisher:
J2 Communications/Ripps Communication

YOUR NEWBORN BABY WITH JOAN LUNDEN
Everything You Need To Know

Description:

Narrated by *Good Morning America*'s Joan Lunden and featuring her family pediatrician, Dr. Jeffrey Brown, this 60 minute videotape outlines topics concerning newborn infant care. Eleven segments are introduced by cartoon vignettes with a corresponding icon in the lower right hand corner also displayed on the videotape jacket. These icons are designed to be used with search/scan features of VCRs to locate information. Topics included in the discussions are: choosing your baby's doctor, decisions to think about before birth (breastfeeding, rooming-in, circumcision, etc.), preparing for baby (equipment, layette, packing for the hospital), "the magic moment" (hospital birth), newborn appearances and senses, feeding your baby (breastfeeding, bottlefeeding), diapering and caring for baby's bottom, bathing, how to deal with baby's cries, what to expect for baby's sleep, and when to call your baby's doctor. The guidelines in this 1985 videotape are based on recommendations from the American Academy of Pediatrics.

Evaluation:

Parents viewing this videotape will have the uncanny sense they are viewing episodes from *Good Morning America*. Produced in an interview format either with prospective mothers, the featured pediatrician, or parents of newborns, Lunden interjects her personal experiences along with professional advice. These short, concise segments may appeal to some, but most new parents will find the topics are treated too lightly to be of much value. Some sections are done well including the segments on the how-tos of breastfeeding (endorsed by La Leche League), when to call your doctor, and how to prepare for baby's arrival (includes what to pack for the hospital). However, due to the video's outdated copyright, some advice is currently considered to be unacceptable practice (putting a baby to sleep on their stomach), unnecessary (sterilizing bottles with a sterilizing device), or missing (how to deal with colic). The tape has an attractive sticker price, but parents will find their money better spent on more useful and up-to-date resources.

Where To Find/Buy:

Bookstores, libraries, and videotape dealers.

BABY JOURNAL (THE)
Your Weekly Guide To Baby's First Year

Description:

The companion book to *The Maternal Journal*, this resource "is designed to provide you with an enriched experience of your baby's first year of life." Accompanied by color illustrations, *The Baby Journal* provides developmental milestones, facts, tips, and selected information about one's baby from his/her first month through the fourteenth. Presented in a wall-calendar style, it also has a little space (about 1" x 1") for writing notes about the baby's developments from day to day. Special highlighted tips (roughly half a page) include information on giving massage to one's baby, skin care, bathtime, getting more sleep for the parent and the baby, exercise tips for mothers, introducing solid foods, babyproofing one's home, emergencies/first aid, playtime, weaning, choosing toys, avoiding gender stereotypes when choosing toys, and interacting with one's child.

Evaluation:

As this "journal" aims more at entertainment than information, an introduction warns the reader that it is "by no means intended to be a comprehensive encyclopedia of all existing data on raising children . . ." With that in mind, potential consumers must weigh this book's value against the more extensive information the same money would purchase in another resource. Advice offered here is really on the slim side. Additionally, there is hardly any space for mothers to actually write notes or journal entries, an activity that many parents may find useful and cathartic. The illustrations are amusing, and it makes a colorful wall-hanging. But parents should save their dollars and buy either a real journal with adequate space, a good book on baby care, or even a nature/art calendar that your baby will enjoy looking at too.

Where To Find/Buy:

Bookstores and libraries, or order direct by calling 1-800-338-2232.

Overall Rating
★
Entertaining but not really informative

Design, Ease Of Use
★★
Some useful tips and amusing color illustrations

1–4 Stars; N/R = Not Rated

Media Type:
Print

Price:
$10.00

Principal Subject:
Care

Age Group:
Infants (0–1)

ISBN:
0671867776

Edition Reviewed:
1992

Publisher:
Meadowbrook Press

Author/Editor:
Matthew Bennett

Overall Rating
★★★★

The concept of "touchpoints" helps explain the dynamics involved as a child develops

Design, Ease Of Use
★★★★

Easy to read, well-illustrated, lots of open space, and well-indexed

1–4 Stars; N/R = Not Rated

Media Type:
Print

Price:
$16.00

Principal Subject:
Growth & Learning

Age Group:
Infants & Toddlers (0–3)

ISBN:
020162690x

Edition Reviewed:
1992

Publisher:
Addison Wesley Publishing (Merloyd Lawrence)

Author/Editor:
T. Berry Brazelton, M.D.

About The Author:
(From Cover Notes)
T. Berry Brazelton, M.D. is Associate Professor of Pediatrics at Harvard Medical School and Chief of the Child Development Unit at the Boston Children's Hospital Medical Center. Dr. Brazelton is considered a leading authority on child development.

Growth & Learning: Child Development

TOUCHPOINTS
Your Child's Emotional And Behavioral Development

Best Resource For:
Guide to infant development

Recommended For:
Growth & Learning

Description:

Dr. Brazelton introduces his book as a "map of infancy and of early child development." The purpose of this map is to help parents navigate the predictable ups and downs, and spurts and stalls that happen along the way in raising a child. This book maps out not only the physical growth of a child, but psychological development as well, helping parents achieve an understanding of what happens as a child struggles to reorganize and incorporate each new achievement. As such, this book illustrates in three parts the "touchpoints" of development (from the newborn to the three-year-old child), challenges to development (discipline, fears, sleep problems, and more), and the child's allies in development (grandparents, friends, etc.). "Touchpoints" is a concept that Dr. Brazelton has developed to label the predictable times that occur just before a surge of rapid growth. At this time, a child's behavior falls apart and he becomes difficult to understand. "Touchpoints," in his words, become a window for viewing the "great energy that fuels a child for learning," that pushes him toward greater autonomy.

Evaluation:

Touchpoints, Dr. Brazelton's latest book on child development, includes much of the information found in his other books (such as *Mothers and Infants* and *The Earliest Relationship*). While those books targeted professionals who would be offering support or services to parents, this book is specifically for parents. As such it is less technical and easier to read. The same amount of comprehensive detail is provided, but it is arranged in a much more digestible manner. Breaking the book into three sections also makes it easier to reference when one is trying to solve problems and particular parental challenges, from headaches and stomach aches to television. The final section on "Allies in Development" is light, only 40 pages out of this 480 page book. This could be a whole additional book, since it addresses the value of interactions in a child's life—the past and how it is passed on (parents, grandparents), and the child's evolving relationships with peers and others. Many valuable insights and new research findings are interpreted in this book; it is a good book to have as new parents.

Where To Find/Buy:

Bookstores and libraries.

TOUCHPOINTS, VOLUME 2
The First Month Through The First Year

 Best Resource For:
Videotape focusing on infant development

 Recommended For:
Growth & Learning

Description:

This is the second videotape in a series of 3 hosted by T. Berry Brazelton, "America's preeminent baby doctor." Here he illustrates ways that families can understand their new baby from 1 month to 15 months of age. Five families are the focus of this 45 minute videotape, all of which were presented in the first videotape: a family with a "trying" child and older sibling, a single mom, a couple with a very busy dad and toddler, a couple who had a premature baby, and older first-time parents. Throughout the videotape, Brazelton expands upon the various "touchpoints" these families encounter. Touchpoints are "periods of time that precede a rapid growth in learning for both child and parent." As Brazelton explains, "Touchpoints are predictable and can help parents make decisions on how to handle their children." The camera and Brazelton detail certain age ranges—1–4 months, 5–6 months, 7–8 months, 9–12 months, 12–15 months—and the 15+ touchpoints included within these age groupings. Touchpoints include sleeping, feeding, motor skills, cognitive development, negativism, teasing, and more.

Evaluation:

Brazelton's charismatic manner once again holds the segments of the tape together as he introduces each new "touchpoint." Again, the honesty and humanness of the families involved contribute to the personal and warm tone of this film. The viewer is bound to find his/her baby in this film, whether that baby be fussy, calm, sleepy, or alert, The viewer can't help but benefit from watching the struggles and joys these families experience which are common to all parents, especially new parents. With his familiar tone and sunny attitude, Brazelton walks you through the babies' various milestones—object permanence, stranger anxiety, pincer grasp, sitting up, standing, walking, etc.—and does a fine job of explaining their importance in light of the babies' cognitive, emotional and physical growth. In fact, this video very neatly sums up the contents of his TV show and gives you the highlights in a tidy brief clip.

Where To Find/Buy:

Bookstores and libraries, or order direct by calling 800-756-8792.

Overall Rating
★★★★
Details major milestones babies encounter from one month of age to 15 months

Design, Ease Of Use
★★★★
Split screen w/ parents & baby; narration closely coincides with babies' actions

1–4 Stars; N/R = Not Rated

Media Type:
Videotape

Price:
$29.99

Principal Subject:
Growth & Learning

Age Group:
Infants (0–1)

ISBN:
1878983105

Edition Reviewed:
1991

Publisher:
Pipher Films

Overall Rating
★★★★
Combines research & concrete examples of toddlers' thoughts, feelings and responses

Design, Ease Of Use
★★★
Textbook-like at times, but offers bulleted highlights, clear headings, bold case studies

1–4 Stars; N/R = Not Rated

Media Type:
Print

Price:
$12.00

Principal Subject:
Growth & Learning

Age Group:
Toddlers (1–3)

ISBN:
0028740173

Edition Reviewed:
1995

Publisher:
The Free Press (Simon & Schuster)

Author/Editor:
Alicia F. Lieberman

About The Author:
(From Cover Notes)
Lieberman is professor of psychiatry at the University of California, San Francisco, and senior psychologist of its Infant-Parent Program. She is world-renowned for her work on mother-child attachment.

EMOTIONAL LIFE OF THE TODDLER (THE)

Best Resource For:
Guide to toddler development

Recommended For:
Growth & Learning

Description:
Lieberman, a senior psychologist who has studied mother-child attachments, presents her research and observations of how a toddler "thinks, feels, and responds to the challenges of growing up, and how parents can help them meet these challenges with greater self-confidence and joy." This 244 page book is divided into ten chapters with an index and a chapter-by-chapter reference section. Chapters 1–3 explore the toddler and his need to reconcile his new-found yearning for independence with his need for his parents' secure base. Chapters 4–6 explain the varieties in toddler temperaments (easy, slow to warm up, active, difficult) along with how parents' temperaments can interplay; separate chapters illustrate the developments of the active and shy toddler. The next two chapters focus on toddlers' anxieties and how specific age-related anxieties (toilet training, siblings, nighttime fears, separation, etc.) can be addressed. The impact of divorce on the toddler is the topic of Chapter 9 while Chapter 10 focuses on the effects of placing a toddler in childcare.

Evaluation:
Don't be taken aback by the textbook-like manner in which this book is presented. Lieberman does an excellent job of stating the scientific background and research for her generalizations while at the same time illustrating her points through specific toddler "case study" examples. She presents an interesting proposition in stating that the extreme fluctuations in toddler moods often mirror feelings parents had in their own childhood that may or may not have been successfully dealt with and that now result in anxious parental reactions. Lieberman does an excellent job of bringing the toddler's behavior back into the here-and-now, however, by offering concrete tips in bulleted highlights where appropriate and necessary. This is not a book on discipline although parents will naturally strive to better handle their toddler's actions with reactions that are based on an in-depth understanding of the toddler's drives and needs. Parents will certainly get that understanding within this book.

Where To Find/Buy:
Bookstores and libraries.

KNOW YOUR CHILD
An Authoritative Guide For Today's Parents

 Best Resource For:
Understanding children's temperament

 Recommended For:
Growth & Learning

Description:

Based on the underlying theme of temperament, this resource is divided into three major parts. Part I focuses on the differences in children and parents. Human development, the significance of temperament, parenting styles (secure, insecure, intimidated, over-interpretive, etc.), and the "goodness of fit" between parenting styles (attitudes and expectations) and children's temperament are some of the topics addressed in this first section. Part II discusses the developing child from infant to adolescent. Some of the topics covered include social, cognitive development, and emotional development along with gender identity, and the child's self-esteem. The final section, Part III, focuses on family issues. Content in this section addresses children with special needs, the debate over IQ scores, roles of parents and siblings, and the effect of working mothers. An extensive reference section and index conclude this 397 page resource.

Evaluation:

Based on the authors' 30 year longitudinal study, their 20 years of experience editing the annual volume of *Progress in Child Psychiatry and Child Development*, and their 40+ years of teaching and consulting practice, this book is exceptionally strong on research with advice for direct application. With its intent to cover the wide span of research that has been done on this subject, this guide does have a tendency sometimes to get weighted down with much theory and explanation. Parents may want more content on specific subjects upon reading this volume. There are several important themes running through this book. One, that babies are different from the start and one difference is their temperament. Also, infants are equipped with the necessary biological makeup that allows them to socially interact with the world around them. Finally, there are many good ways to be a good parent and what is important is the "goodness of fit." A very strong advocate of the parent, this resource offers useful information for those parents who "*know their children*, and are not bewildered by the contradictory advice they read and hear."

Where To Find/Buy:

Bookstores and libraries.

Overall Rating
★★★★
Strong advocate of "fit" between parents and child; good mix of research & application

Design, Ease Of Use
★★★
Although textbook like at first glance, reads well and is concise; easily referenced index

1–4 Stars; N/R = Not Rated

Media Type:
Print

Price:
$40.00

Principal Subject:
Growth & Learning

Age Group:
All Ages (0–5)

ISBN:
1568218346

Edition Reviewed:
2nd (1996)

Publisher:
Jason Aronson

Author/Editor:
Stella Chess and Alexander Thomas

About The Author:
(From Cover Notes)
Stella Chess and Alexander Thomas, both professors of psychiatry at New York University Medical Center, founded the modern study of temperament in 1956. They received an award from the Society for Research in Child Development for contributions to child development.

★★★★

Overall Rating
★★★★
In-depth study of five temperaments of children and how to adapt parenting styles

Design, Ease Of Use
★★
Reads much like a textbook but organizational structure helps break it up

1–4 Stars; N/R = Not Rated

Media Type:
Print

Price:
$12.00

Principal Subject:
Growth & Learning

Age Group:
All Ages (0–5)

ISBN:
0201441934

Edition Reviewed:
1995

Publisher:
Merloyd Lawrence (Addison-Wesley Publishing)

Author/Editor:
Stanley I. Greenspan, M.D. with Jacqueline Salmon

About The Author:
(From Cover Notes)
Greenspan is Clinical Professor of Psychiatry, Behavioral Sciences, and Pediatrics at the George Washington University Medical School. He has also written other books on early childhood as well as other scholarly and popular books.

THE CHALLENGING CHILD
Understanding, Raising, And Enjoying The Five "Difficult" Types Of Children

Description:
Based upon the author's research and that of others, this 318 page book focuses on the temperaments and needs of the difficult or challenging child. The author explains that infants and children have traits that differ in how they respond to the sensations around them. Because of this, some children are at risk for certain kinds of psychological or learning problems. However, Greenspan states these traits are not fixed and parents can significantly change these outcomes based upon the type of early and late experiences they have with their child. Five different personality patterns are described within this 10 chapter book including separate chapters on the highly sensitive child, the self-absorbed child, the defiant child, the inattentive child, and the active/aggressive child. Chapter 2 defines Greenspan's "stages of childhood" in which he offers a "road map" of the abilities children need to master from one stage to the next along with the challenges they may face. The rest of the book then describes various strategies parents may use to tailor their approaches to their child's characteristics and these changing developmental needs.

Evaluation:
This is a most fascinating study of just how different children's personalities can be and how to focus on children's strengths by readjusting parent-child interactions. Although designed specifically for the parents of children who are challenging, Greenspan also states that parents of non-challenging children will benefit from his philosophy too. The book reads much like a textbook articulating development theory, physiological roots of the behaviors, and emotional responses to stimuli. But all that aside, Greenspan does an excellent job of painting a picture of what parenting each of the various five temperaments entails. Greenspan's message throughout will offer reassurance and direction to parents who are most likely worn out, focusing on the negative characteristics of their child. He illustrates constructive ways parents can change their parenting styles while easing their child into more flexible adaptive modes. This resource not only offers parents an understanding about temperament as an interplay between heredity and environment, but also focuses on how traits can be molded, viewed in a positive light, and appreciated.

Where To Find/Buy:
Bookstores and libraries.

THE HURRIED CHILD
Growing Up Too Fast, Too Soon

Description:

This 217 page guide is divided into two main parts. Part I—"Our Hurried Children"—contains four chapters. These chapters describe the concept of childhood, attributes of the "hurried child," the influence of parents, education, and the media on children and adolescents' development, and the myth of the "Superkid." Part II—"Hurried Children: Stressed Children"—has five chapters. These chapters identify children's responses to responsibilities that contradict numerous developmental recommendations. The achievements and limitations of the major stages of child development are highlighted, as well as how "hurrying" a child has negative effects on their "normal" course of development intellectually, emotionally, and socially. Suggestions and advice are also given on how families might socialize children and how to help children in distress. Bold sub-headings, sample contract sheets (to track adult expectations), and bulleted facts and information are given. A notes section (by chapter) and index conclude the text.

Evaluation:

Although its copyright is dated, this classic continues to warrant attention. Elkind states that certain societal changes have caused parents to believe in the "Superkid," one who is more competent (than development shows) and can take on new responsibilities emotionally, socially, and intellectually. In effect, he says, we hurry their growth in our own best interests, then rationalize our decisions, and ignore the gross effects our decisions have on our children. He cites examples such as early childcare, latchkey kids, greater home responsibilities, early schooling, etc. At first glance, he appears to make sweeping generalizations ("The truth is that children . . . are less well off today that they were a couple of decades ago.") or project his strong opinions ("those who would teach young children about AIDS, nuclear war, and child abuse are really dealing with their own anxieties and fears . . ."). But upon closer examination, he backs up his statements with research studies, statistical evidence, and news headlines. This is an insightful, if not alarming, view that parents should include in their research about childcare and early schooling.

Where To Find/Buy:

Bookstores and libraries.

Overall Rating
★★★★
Often opinionated with generalizations, but backed by solid research & statistics

Design, Ease Of Use
★★
Larger type; but must be read cover to cover to find its "needle-in-a-haystack" points

1–4 Stars; N/R = Not Rated

Media Type:
Print

Price:
$14.00

Principal Subject:
Growth & Learning

Age Group:
All Ages (0–5)

ISBN:
0201073978

Edition Reviewed:
2nd (1988)

Publisher:
Addison-Wesley Publishing

Author/Editor:
David Elkind, Ph.D.

About The Author:
(From Cover Notes)
David Elkind, a worldwide advocate for the protection of childhood, is a professor of child study and senior resident scholar at the Lincoln Filene Center of Tufts University.

Overall Rating
★★★
An interesting and in-depth examination at a child's first two years of development

Design, Ease Of Use
★★★★
Very well-organized with chart and narrative summaries; boxed hints throughout

1–4 Stars; N/R = Not Rated

Media Type:
Print

Price:
$14.95

Principal Subject:
Growth & Learning

Age Group:
Infants & Toddlers (0–3)

ISBN:
0716724995

Edition Reviewed:
1994

Publisher:
W. H. Freeman

Author/Editor:
Claire B. Kopp, Ph.D. with Donna L. Bean

About The Author:
(From Cover Notes)
Dr. Claire B. Kopp is a noted developmental psychologist and a professor at the University of California at Los Angeles. This book is the result of her nearly three decades of work with children and parents, as well as her own experiences as a mother and grandmother.

BABY STEPS
The "Whys" Of Your Child's Behavior In the First Two Years

 Recommended For:
Growth & Learning

Description:
This 279 page resource focuses on understanding the behavior of infants and young children as related to their development. Four main sections, or "Previews," divide the book into monthly segments from birth to three months, four to seven months of age, and eight to twelve months of age; babies' development at fifteen to twenty-four months is divided into three month intervals. Each section contains a developmental overview for the entire preview period (roughly a 3–4 month period) followed by a "snapshot" summarizing the major milestones of this age. Additional subsections describe motor skills, visual perception, language, cognitive skills, social skills, emerging self-concepts, and emotions. Boxed "Hints" are provided throughout in the margins. A "Developmental Close-Up" at the end of each age group offers detailed discussions on age-relevant topics (grasping, toilet-training, etc.). Charts of developmental milestones for the first two years (divided into each skill type) completes the book along with additional reading and reference lists, and an index.

Evaluation:
This very comprehensive, well-organized resource may seem at first glance to be yet another textbook, but parents will find it to be extremely user-friendly. Many resources focus on children's behavior and how to deal with it; they often gloss over the impact a child's development has on his or her behavior. This resource takes a different stance, albeit at times in a roundabout way, that certain behaviors are normal if better understood. Parents need to make judicious use of the developmental milestone charts at the end of each Preview. These charts also list behaviors that may not be appropriate, thereby suggesting possibly delayed development. Parents are advised to contact their pediatrician; every child is unique and the guidelines given are merely guidelines. With this understanding, this book is definitely a resource well worth a parent's time.

Where To Find/Buy:
Bookstores and libraries.

INFANTS AND MOTHERS
Differences In Development

 Recommended For:
Growth & Learning

Description:
Dr. Brazelton has recorded in this book a narrative on the first year of life for three different baby types. Through this book's 300 pages, Brazelton traces the month-by-month reactions of three different types of babies—average, quiet, and active. The first chapter (of fourteen) explains the importance of noticing, understanding, and accepting each infant's individuality and unique differences. Through each succeeding chapter, Dr. Brazelton tries to illustrate the learning process that both parent and infant undertake as they take in new information, digest it, and organize it for later use. By understanding how each child is essentially "wired" at birth to respond to stimulation, parents are better equipped to adapt their parenting styles and the environment they provide their babies. Through each chapter, he illustrates how parents and infants learn from each other. He also reveals how over-stimulation can be "tuned-out" by the baby, and how under-stimulation can actually slow the baby's development. This revised edition reflects the changing status of the family, including single parents and working mothers and fathers.

Evaluation:
Brazelton's running commentary of his observations and evaluations as he interacts with infants makes this book unique. A mother who feels overwhelmed and unsure if she is adequate will appreciate the insights offered on a new baby's internal conflicts. As a new parent, you won't find advice, specific support, or techniques for the challenges of parenthood. Nor does this book seek to intellectualize the process of becoming a parent. It is, rather, an illustration of how three families (with different types of babies) adapted to and cared for their babies while the babies adapted to their new world; what the families did and how they felt are highlighted. This book, then, this quite interesting, but it is very detailed and most new parents will not have the time or attention span to get through it. It is better read in retrospect or to have read while waiting for the birth of a new infant. Professionals working with parents of infants will also find it to be a useful tool.

Where To Find/Buy:
Bookstores and libraries.

Overall Rating
★★★
A valuable book illustrating the individual needs of different "types" of infants

Design, Ease Of Use
★★★★
Well done, easily followed and easily referenced; loaded with photographs of babies

1–4 Stars; N/R = Not Rated

Media Type:
Print

Price:
$16.95

Principal Subject:
Growth & Learning

Age Group:
Infants (0–1)

ISBN:
0440506859

Edition Reviewed:
2nd (1983)

Publisher:
Bantam Doubleday Dell
(Merloyd Lawrence)

Author/Editor:
T. Berry Brazelton, M.D.

About The Author:
(From Cover Notes)
T. Berry Brazelton, M.D. is Associate Professor of Pediatrics at Harvard Medical School and Chief of the Child Development Unit at the Boston Children's Hospital Medical Center. Dr. Brazelton is considered a leading authority on child development.

★★★

Overall Rating
★★★

Great general discussion (sometimes typecast) of what to expect from a 4 year old

Design, Ease Of Use
★★★★

Easily read, some humor; good Q & A segment at end of book; black and white photos

1–4 Stars; N/R = Not Rated

Media Type:
Print

Price:
$10.95

Principal Subject:
Growth & Learning

Age Group:
Preschoolers (3–5)

ISBN:
0440506751

Edition Reviewed:
1976

Publisher:
Dell Trade (Dell Publishing/ Bantam Doubleday Dell)

Author/Editor:
Louise Bates Ames, Ph.D. and Frances L. Ilg, M.D.

About The Author:
(From Cover Notes)
Ames is a lecturer at the Yale Child Study Center and assistant professor emeritus at Yale University. Both Ilg and Ames are co-founders of the Gesell Institute of Child Development at Yale.

YOUR FOUR-YEAR-OLD
Wild And Wonderful

 Recommended For:
Growth & Learning

Description:

Written by co-founders of the Gesell Institute, this 9 chapter, 150 page resource highlights the development of four year olds. Chapter 1 describes general characteristics of four year olds—their attitudes, responses to situations, and motor, language, social, and emotional development. Chapter 2 focuses on interactions with other children, while "techniques" for dealing with the four year old's "wilder ways" are offered in Chapter 3. Chapter 4 highlights major "accomplishments and abilities" (language, motor, visual, language, adaptive play, etc.) of a typical 4 year old. Chapter 5 describes "The Four-Year-Old Birthday Party" with advice on the who, what, when, and hows of hosting a successful birthday party. Chapter 6 outlines typical daily routines (eating, sleeping, elimination, bath and dressing, tensional outlets), while Chapter 7 focuses on the four year old mind with a warning of "Don't Push Your Preschooler." Chapter 8 describes individual differences, and Chapter 9 offers "Stories from Real Life." Lists of toys and books for children are included in the 3 appendixes, as well as books for parents of four year olds.

Evaluation:

Overall, parents will find a generous amount of information here to introduce them to their "wild and wonderful" preschooler. In particular, Chapters 1–3 offer support and guidance by illustrating what parents can expect from their child, along with ways to work around their sometimes bothersome behaviors (profanity, supersilliness, boasting, etc.). Although no specific discipline strategies are presented, the techniques in Chapter 3 are very positive, often humorous, and address discipline in terms of "setting up the child's life situation so that good, effective, desirable behavior becomes possible." However, we found the discussion in Chapter 8 tended to typecast children. The authors state that individual differences in attitudes, reactions, and abilities occur due to a child's anatomical structure (endomorph, ectomorph, mesomorph). More current discussions focus on children's temperament, and the roles of parenting style, environment, and biology; this is mentioned, albeit very briefly (1/2 a page), and as an aside. Great for an overall description of the four year old, other resources will greatly complement this guide.

Where To Find/Buy:

Bookstores, libraries, or order direct by contacting Dell Readers Service, Box DR, 1540 Broadway, New York, NY 10036.

YOUR THREE-YEAR-OLD
Friend Or Enemy

 Recommended For:
Growth & Learning

Description:

Written by co-founders of the Gesell Institute, this 9 chapter, 167 page resource highlights the development of three year olds. Chapter 1 describes general characteristics of three year olds—their attitudes, responses to situations, their developing sense of self, and more. Chapter 2 focuses on interactions with other children, while "techniques" for dealing with the three year old's "very hard to handle" ways are offered in Chapter 3. Chapter 4 highlights major "accomplishments and abilities" (language, motor, visual, language, adaptive play, etc.) of a typical 3 year old. Chapter 5 describes "The Three-Year-Old Birthday Party" with advice on the who, what, when, and hows of hosting a successful birthday party. Chapter 6 outlines typical daily routines (eating, sleeping, elimination, bath and dressing, tensional outlets), while Chapter 7 focuses on the three year old mind and "How He Sees the World." Chapter 8 describes individual differences, and Chapter 9 offers "Stories from Real Life." Lists of suggested toys and books for children are included in the 3 appendixes, as well as books for parents of three year olds.

Evaluation:

This book, on the whole, is straightforward and easily read, candidly describing the mindset and behaviors of a preschooler. However, be advised that it does take a rather bleak view of the behaviors exhibited during the preschooler's disequilibrium stage at 3 1/2 years old. Warnings are issued about what to expect ("you may need all the help you can get, and then some!"), parents (especially mothers) are advised to line up daycare or babysitters as a way to "reduce the time you will need to spend together," and attending nursery school is strongly recommended. Unlike other books in the series, the discussion in Chapter 8—"Individuality"—will prove enlightening for many parents trying to "read" their child. Children's reactions and behavior are presented in light of the authors' work and Dr. Stella Chess' studies of children's temperament and personality characteristics. This book will prove useful as a starting guide to preschoolers' development. It presents a good overview of what to expect during the preschool years and describes ways for parents to positively contribute to their child's development.

Where To Find/Buy:

Bookstores, libraries, or order direct by contacting Dell Readers Service, Box DR, 1540 Broadway, New York, NY 10036.

Overall Rating
★★★
Presents a straightforward, candid description of the 3 year old, rather bleak at times

Design, Ease Of Use
★★★★
Succinct, easily read; well-organized; Q & A segment reiterates authors' points

1–4 Stars; N/R = Not Rated

Media Type:
Print

Price:
$10.95

Principal Subject:
Growth & Learning

Age Group:
Preschoolers (3–5)

ISBN:
0440506492

Edition Reviewed:
1985

Publisher:
Dell Trade (Dell Publishing/ Bantam Doubleday Dell)

Author/Editor:
Louise Bates Ames, Ph.D. and Frances L. Ilg, M.D.

About The Author:
(From Cover Notes)
Ames is a lecturer at the Yale Child Study Center and assistant professor emeritus at Yale University. Both Ilg and Ames are co-founders of the Gesell Institute of Child Development at Yale.

Overall Rating
★★★
Thorough discussion of the "terrific and terrible" twos; minimal info of temperament

Design, Ease Of Use
★★★★
Easily read; chapters broken up by subtopics or ages; many black and white photos

1–4 Stars; N/R = Not Rated

Media Type:
Print

Price:
$10.95

Principal Subject:
Growth & Learning

Age Group:
Infants & Toddlers (0–3)

ISBN:
0440506387

Edition Reviewed:
1976

Publisher:
Dell Trade (Dell Publishing/ Bantam Doubleday Dell)

Author/Editor:
Louise Bates Ames, Ph.D. and Frances L. Ilg, M.D.

About The Author:
(From Cover Notes)
Ames is a lecturer at the Yale Child Study Center and assistant professor emeritus at Yale University. Both Ilg and Ames are co-founders of the Gesell Institute of Child Development at Yale.

YOUR TWO-YEAR-OLD
12 To 24 Months

 Recommended For:
Growth & Learning

Description:

Written by co-founders of the Gesell Institute, this 148 page resource highlights the development of a two year old; much of the book is directed toward the "disequilibrium" age of 2 1/2 years, or "the terrible twos." Divided into 9 chapters, the first two chapters describe the transition into toddlerhood along with general characteristics of toddlers in terms of motor, language, social, and emotional changes. Chapter 3 focuses on toddlers' social interactions with others, while "techniques" for dealing with toddlers' behavior on "difficult days" are offered in Chapter 4. Chapter 5 describes major "accomplishments and abilities" (language, motor, visual, language, adaptive play, etc.) of the 2 year old and the 2 1/2 year old. Chapter 6 outlines typical daily routines (eating, bath and dressing, bedtime, and elimination), while Chapter 7 focuses on the "mental life" of toddlers, or how they view the world. Chapter 8 describes differences in children's development. Chapter 9 offers "Stories from Real Life." Lists of toys, equipment, and books for children are included in the 4 appendixes, as well as books for parents of two year olds.

Evaluation:

As the second in a series of ten books, this one outlines the toddler's development and behavior better than the first of the series. Here, parents will find not only a sensitive portrayal of the tender, yet tumultuous two year old, but also some positive concrete tips for dealing with toddler behavior, especially in Chapter 4. Suggestions, such as how to take advantage of the toddler's ritualistic tendency, accepting security measures (teddy bears, blankets, etc.), giving face-saving commands, avoiding certain things (terms like "later"), using distractions, etc., are clearly described. Chapter 6 offers help for handling daily routines with the Q & A segment in Chapter 9 underscoring this chapter's advice. Although Chapters 2, 3, 4, and 6 highlight what to expect from toddlers, no discussion is afforded the role of discipline. Parents will need other resources to supplement this topic. Also, the discussion in Chapter 8 is minimal; the role of temperament in explaining the range of toddler behaviors is ignored. Good for a general discussion, this resource offers parents an overall scan of their toddler's development and behaviors.

Where To Find/Buy:

Bookstores, libraries, or order direct by contacting Dell Readers Service, Box DR, 1540 Broadway, New York, NY 10036.

A JOURNEY THROUGH THE FIRST YEAR OF LIFE

★★★

Description:

Narrated by Dr. Burton L. White, an educational psychologist, and Judith Nolte, editor of *American Baby* magazine, this 45 minute videotape affords parents a sequential glimpse into their child's development during the first year of life. Divided into 6 segments from "Hello World" (the first month) to "Walking Tall" (the 11th and 12th months), this video illustrates baby's milestones concerning motor skills (gross and fine), sensory development (hearing, sight, sound, touch), language development, problem-solving skills (cause-effect, etc.), and social and emotional development. Each segment includes a brief introduction by the two narrators followed by footage of babies illustrating each concept. Brief parent interviews are interjected throughout. A preview heading signals the onset of the next stage along with a written synopsis of what's achieved, for example, "Sitting On Top of the World"—sitting up the 7th and 8th months. A recap is given after each discussion before the next stage is introduced.

Evaluation:

White, known for his extensive research (38+ years) in the arena of child development, along with Nolte, whose magazine is well-known by most new parents, offer this good, but canned, description of a baby's first year. Parents will find direct examples to help understand their baby's development along with indirect advice on ways to enhance their baby's discovery of their world. Although not focusing on how to take care of a baby, this video would be a helpful tool in a parenting education class on understanding the developmental needs of newborns and babies. The examples are very well-done, the information is succinct, and the parent narratives, although lacking spontaneity, are appropriate venues for the narrators' discussions. The only negative element of this tape is its canned, prepackaged nature of presentation. However, it offers valuable informative, it's not too expensive compared to other videos available, and it would be a good shower present for first-time parents.

Where To Find/Buy:

Bookstores, libraries, video stories, or order direct by calling 1-800-VHS-TAPE.

Overall Rating
★★★
Offers developmental tidbits on baby's first year milestones

Design, Ease Of Use
★★★
Succinct w/ segment headings; great exs. of baby's development; canned presentation

I–4 Stars; N/R = Not Rated

Media Type:
Videotape

Price:
$19.98

Principal Subject:
Growth & Learning

Age Group:
Infants (0–1)

ISBN:
1560940883

Edition Reviewed:
1985

Publisher:
Congress Entertainment, Ltd.

Overall Rating
★★★
A great take-along book to help teach young children "social studies"/social skills

Design, Ease Of Use
★★★
Complete table of contents & "quick-find" index; chapter divisions difficult to discern

1–4 Stars; N/R = Not Rated

Media Type:
Print

Price:
$10.95

Principal Subject:
Growth & Learning

Age Group:
All Ages (0–5)

ISBN:
0316034665

Edition Reviewed:
1996

Publisher:
Little, Brown and Company

Author/Editor:
Linda Allison and Martha Weston

About The Author:
(From Cover Notes)
Linda Allison and Martha Weston have been authoring and illustrating children's books since 1975. They test their ideas on many parents, children, and teachers. Both women reside with their families in San Francisco, California.

HOWDY DO ME AND YOU
Getting-Along Activities For You And Your Young Child

Description:

There are 48 pages of activities, games, and tips to help develop a preschooler's social skills. This book focuses on easing your child into basic "getting-along" behavior—cooperation, confidence, self-reliance, empathy, and discussing feelings. The table of contents is divided into 5 sections with an index. Sections include the following topics: "Me," "Family," "Community," "Sharing, Caring, Getting Along," and "Celebrating It All." A set of "Learning Notes" introduce information for each section. For instance, in the Learning Notes in the "Family" section address a child's sense of belonging in a family. The subsequent subchapters offer activities such as making family photo albums, drawing and talking about family, making family refrigerator magnets, and making a family card game. There are comic-like color illustrations of children and family on every page. The authors have drawn on experiences with family and friends to compile these activities focusing on preschool children.

Evaluation:

This upbeat book will be a humorous and worthwhile addition for parents seeking to enhance their child's social learning through creative games and activities. Many of these interactions will help them build their child's self image, teaching them confidence, acceptance and perseverance. Every page is filled with whimsical illustrations and things to do. The "Community" section invites them to make a map of their neighborhood, teach preschoolers about Earth Day, and take their child to their workplace. The layout of the book might be perplexing as it shifts from chapter to chapter. They are not numbered and the reader must be very careful to catch the "Learning Notes" BEFORE each chapter to recognize the division. By concentrating on sharing, caring, and respecting others, this book will help preschoolers learn to accept the differences in people. It discusses how to enjoy the diversity of different cultures in a brief and lighthearted way. It is an appropriate book to add to one's shopping cart.

Where To Find/Buy:

Bookstores and libraries.

NEW FIRST THREE YEARS OF LIFE (THE)
The Completely Revised And Updated Edition Of The Parenting Classic

Description:

Based on White's thirty-eight years of observation and research, this 384 page book consists of two sections. The first section details "The Seven Phases of the First Three Years of Life." This includes an initial section offering guidelines for a child's first 8 months and a concluding overview of educational developments that occur within the first three years. The seven phases are broken down into age groups: birth to 6 weeks, 6 to 14 weeks, 3 1/2 to 5 1/2 months, 5 1/2 to 8 months, 8 to 14 months, 14 to 24 months, and 24 months to 36 months. Each phase begins with an introduction, then describes a child's general behavior, apparent interests, educational/learning developments, recommended and not recommended child-rearing practices, recommended materials, and behaviors triggering the onset of the next phase. Section Two spotlights child rearing topics such as spoiling, sibling rivalry, discipline, substitute child care, older first-time mothers, toilet training, and more. An index is included as well as a list of recommended readings.

Evaluation:

White's book is one of the few books based on natural observations of children in their homes. His methodology is well-outlined and somewhat scientifically founded. However, as White states in his concluding remarks, a project designed to carry out his ideals was incorrectly set up due to government misinterpretation. Final test results then, comparing children in this project with others in terms of their achievement in language, intelligence, and social behavior, were incorrect. This leaves parents questioning whether or not his suggestions actually work—can parents avoid the "terrible twos" by following his philosophy as he promises? All that aside, White offers a valid in-depth glimpse at the inner workings of the young child. If parents can distinguish between his personal opinion and child development facts, they will relish reading about the changes their child goes through. His writing style is down-to-earth, although sometimes textbook-like. Offering a balance between strict authoritarian styles of parenting and laissez-faire, this book has stood the test of time in its popularity with parents.

Where To Find/Buy:

Bookstores and libraries.

Overall Rating
★★★
Presents a balance between strict and permissive parenting based on 38 years of research

Design, Ease Of Use
★★★
Excellent index, ample table of contents; differentiation between subheadings awkward

1–4 Stars; N/R = Not Rated

Media Type:
Print

Price:
$14.00

Principal Subject:
Growth & Learning

Age Group:
Infants & Toddlers (0–3)

ISBN:
0684804190

Edition Reviewed:
4th (1995)

Publisher:
Fireside (Simon & Schuster)

Author/Editor:
Burton L. White

About The Author:
(From Cover Notes)
Burton L. White is the director of the Center for Parent Education in Newton, Massachusetts, and the designer of the Missouri New Parents as Teachers Project. He is the father of four (now grown) children and he lives in Waban, Massachusetts.

Overall Rating
★★★
An interesting and in-depth look at child development

Design, Ease Of Use
★★
Rather heavy text but it is easily cross-referenced; graphics would help the monotony

1–4 Stars; N/R = Not Rated

Media Type:
Print

Price:
$17.00

Principal Subject:
Growth & Learning

Age Group:
Infants & Toddlers (0–3)

ISBN:
0394714369

Edition Reviewed:
2nd (1983)

Publisher:
Alfred A. Knopf

Author/Editor:
Penelope Leach

About The Author:
(From Cover Notes)
Penelope Leach was educated at Cambridge University and the London School of Economics, where she received her Ph.D. in Psychology and lectured on psychology and child development. For four years she ran a study on the effects of babies on their parents.

BABYHOOD
Stage By Stage, From Birth To Age Two: How Your Baby Develops Physically, Emotionally, Mentally

Description:

Babyhood is a book of over 400 pages and thirty-one information-loaded chapters. Written from the point-of-view of the developing child, it aims to create an ideal model of care, contact and communication between child and parents. The information is arranged to cover five age periods (first 6 weeks, to 3 months, to six months, to 12 months, to toddler). Similar topics are reviewed in each section, noting what has changed and how the child has developed. Each age period is introduced with a discussion of the child's normal patterns, or in the case of newborns, the lack of pattern, and how to help ease a child's distress as she settles into them. Within each period particular patterns are explained. For example, the physical patterns of feeding, sleeping, elimination, and crying may be discussed followed by the development of motor control, sensory input and meaning-making, hearing and making sounds, (the beginning of language development), and so on. Each of the age-periods is summarized and a table included in each chapter to help you review normal behaviors, stages, and comments for the child's development to this point.

Evaluation:

Outdated in some respects, this book does not go into the details of how to hold or feed or clean a baby. Instead it addresses the larger view of where a baby is at each stage of her development, i.e. physically, emotionally, and mentally. Its goal is to teach a new parent how to assess their child, offering baselines for a "good" physical state, as well as emotional and mental states. While the first 70 pages or so review what parents need to know on diet, sleep needs, normal crying, and elimination, the more interesting material begins with Chapter 5 on the "difficulties of getting settled." Using her descriptions of "miserable babies, jumpy babies, sleepy babies and wakeful babies," Leach illustrates how a parent can benefit from understanding and assessing their baby's development. As patterns begin to make sense, the reader is tempted to flip forward to the next section to see what comes next about a given topic, like language, sleeping, etc. We believe you'll find that Leach has managed to create a fascinating book on child development and an intimate look at the parent-child interaction that goes into that development.

Where To Find/Buy:

Bookstores and libraries.

FIRST FEELINGS
Milestones In The Emotional Development Of Your Baby And Child

Description:

This 247 page, six chapter book focuses on the emotional development of children from birth to 48 months of age. The authors, a psychiatrist and child development researcher, offer advice on how parents can take an active role in understanding the emotional stages in their child's life. Subheadings within each chapter include: "Observing Your Baby," "Creating a Supportive Environment," and "Reviewing Your Support." Six emotional milestones and various "Dimensions of Human Emotion" are given in the introduction. Chapter 1 (0–3 months) discusses baby's personality and parental personality styles. The second chapter (2–7 months) deals with forming relationships and attachment periods. Chapter 3 (3–10 months) contains info on communication, while Chapter 4 (9–18 months) delves into the emergence of a child's sense of self. Chapter 5 (18–36 months) and Chapter 6 (30–48 months) include topics such as emotional thinking and expression, how a child's personality functions, emotional memory, repression, and more.

Evaluation:

This resource aims to orient parents "to the broader issues that must be addressed before a solution to the particular drama or problem is found." Using years of research and clinical experience, the authors present an abundance of information from studies that support the theories contained in this guide. Although the book reads like a textbook or doctoral thesis at times, it helps bridge the gap found in resources that simply address a child's physical and cognitive growth. By considering this guide's "milestones" that mark the emotional development of a child, parents will be able to more clearly identify some of the more common difficulties encountered along a specific stage in their child's development and find ways to help them deal with events more effectively. Parents will also be better able to appreciate their child's special abilities by taking a look at and understanding their child's first feelings in life. This is a well-written, well-researched book worthy of every parent's attention.

Where To Find/Buy:

Bookstores and libraries, or order direct from Penguin Books by Mail, Dept. BA Box 999, Bergenfield, NJ 07621-0999.

Overall Rating
★★★
Based on research, this book fills a need not often addressed by other resources

Design, Ease Of Use
★★
Heavy, reads like a textbook at times; small type on newsprint makes reading difficult

1–4 Stars; N/R = Not Rated

Media Type:
Print

Price:
$12.95

Principal Subject:
Growth & Learning

Age Group:
Infants (0–1)

ISBN:
0140119884

Edition Reviewed:
1985

Publisher:
Penguin Books

Author/Editor:
Stanley I. Greenspan, M.D., and Nancy Thorndike Greenspan

About The Author:
(From Cover Notes)
Stanley Greenspan, M.D., is a practicing psychiatrist and chief of the Clinical Infant and Child Development Research Center of the Division of Maternal and Child Health and the National Institute of Mental Health. Nancy Thorndike Greenspan is a health economist.

Overall Rating
★★
Good overall discussion of toddlers' development and this "often difficult year of life"

Design, Ease Of Use
★★★★
Easily read; chapters broken up by subtopics or ages; many black and white photos

1–4 Stars; N/R = Not Rated

Media Type:
Print

Price:
$10.95

Principal Subject:
Growth & Learning

Age Group:
Infants & Toddlers (0–3)

ISBN:
0440506727

Edition Reviewed:
1982

Publisher:
Dell Trade (Dell Publishing/ Bantam Doubleday Dell)

Author/Editor:
Louise Bates Ames, Ph.D., Frances L. Ilg, M.D., & Carol Chase Haber, M.A.

About The Author:
(From Cover Notes)
Ames is a lecturer at the Yale Child Study Center and assistant professor emeritus at Yale University. Both Ilg and Ames are co-founders of the Gesell Institute of Child Development at Yale. Haber, a school psychologist, is a trained and qualified Gesell Examiner.

YOUR ONE-YEAR-OLD
The Fun-Loving, Fussy 12- To 24-Month-Old

Description:

Written by co-founders of the Gesell Institute, this 178 page resource highlights the development of a toddler; much of the book is directed toward the median age of 18 months. Divided into 11 chapters, the first two chapters describe the transitions from babyhood into toddlerhood. Chapter 3 offers general characteristics of toddlers including motor, language, social, and emotional changes; the "disequilibrium" apparent between 15 and 21 months is also discussed. Chapter 4 describes major "accomplishments and abilities" (language, fine motor, large motor, etc.) and is divided into 3 month age segments from 12–24 months. Chapter 5 focuses on toddlers' social interactions with others, while Chapter 6 outlines typical daily routines (sleeping, feeding, elimination, bath and dressing). "Techniques" to deal with emerging behavior for this "often difficult year of life" are offered in Chapter 7. Chapter 8 focuses on the "mental life" of toddlers. Chapter 9 describes differences in children's development. Chapters 10 and 11 offer "real stories" and a quiz for parents. Lists of toys and books for children and adults are included in the 3 appendixes.

Evaluation:

Although some information in this book reflects the book's copyright date, parents will glean a good overall picture of the young toddler's emerging abilities, personality, and behavior. Written in a straightforward manner, this guide reflects the historical practices of Dr. Arnold Gesell who was instrumental in child observational studies from the 1930s onwards. While most areas are still pertinent in terms of a toddler's development, some areas should be taken lightly, such as the advice to introduce toddlers to reading at 15 to 18 months; most experts nowadays suggest a much earlier age of 3 to 6 months. Additionally, we found the discussion in Chapter 9 rather bizarre as it described variances in children's development. Theories presented suggest that these individual differences occur due to a child's anatomical structure (endomorph, ectomorph, mesomorph), basic level of health, mother-child match, or other reasons; current discussions focus on children's temperament, and the roles of parenting style, environment, and biology. Good as a general guide, we suggest parents use this with other resources to learn about their young toddler.

Where To Find/Buy:

Bookstores, libraries, or order direct by contacting Dell Readers Service, Box DR, 1540 Broadway, New York, NY 10036.

EARLIEST RELATIONSHIP (THE)
Parent, Infants, And The Drama Of Early Attachment

Description:

This 250 page book is written for professionals from a variety of disciplines with the goal of alerting these professionals to the need for care of the parent and child as a unit. The authors say that professionals who care for infants can benefit from knowledge of parental emotions and conflicts that affect the parent-child bond. "A baby cannot exist alone, but is essentially part of a relationship." The book's 31 chapters go into detail on the aspects of this relationship. The book is broken into five parts tracing the evolution of attachment from "Pregnancy: The Birth of Attachment," "The Newborn as Participant," and "Observing Early Interaction" to "Imaginary Interactions" and ". . . A Complementary Approach to Infant Attachment." Subtopics covered include: the "prehistory of attachment," assessing the newborn, early interactions and observations, giving meaning to infant behavior, projection, assessing "imaginary interactions," assessing interaction, and more. The book ends with nine case studies and interventions used to assist in healing the parent-child bond. A 10 page reference list and an index are included.

Evaluation:

This book is a fascinating look at the work that has been done on developmental observation; it also reflects the progress made in the holistic treatment of the parent and child. Well-organized and well-written, this book informs the reader thoroughly in each stage, so that even someone who has not had an education in psychology can understand the terminology, findings, and conclusions. That said, it is still not a "light" book. This book is targeted at various professionals—pediatricians, nurses, psychoanalysts, social workers, etc. The authors highlight an infant's normal development and point out that anxieties and ambivalences are the fuels that drive growth, and should not be singled out; normal development and pathology intermingle all the time and should be a part of any assessment. At the same time, the crises of parenthood generate a need for parents to learn and self-correct, so they can adapt. Professionals aware of this relationship can offer support and insight that will positively assist the parent-child bond. The reader will find that this book sheds light on these insights in a very informative way.

Where To Find/Buy:

Bookstores and libraries.

Overall Rating
★★
Strong plea for professionals working with parents to care for parents & child as a unit

Design, Ease Of Use
★★★
Clear, well-organized; textbook structure and jargon may turn some off

1–4 Stars; N/R = Not Rated

Media Type:
Print

Price:
$12.00

Principal Subject:
Growth & Learning

Age Group:
All Ages (0–5)

ISBN:
0201567644

Edition Reviewed:
1990

Publisher:
Addison-Wesley Publishing (Merloyd Lawrence)

Author/Editor:
T. Berry Brazelton, M.D. and Bertrand G. Cramer, M.D.

About The Author:
(From Cover Notes)
T. Berry Brazelton, M.D., is an internationally known pediatrician, an advocate for children, and the author of many best-selling books. Bertrand G. Cramer, M.D. is Professor of Psychiatry at the University of Geneva, Switzerland and a practicing psychoanalyst.

Overall Rating
★★
Good for general overview of a toddler's growth and development

Design, Ease Of Use
★★★
Meager index but detailed table of contents suffices; user-friendly language and tone

1–4 Stars; N/R = Not Rated

Media Type:
Print

Price:
$14.95

Principal Subject:
Growth & Learning

Age Group:
Toddlers (1–3)

ISBN:
0937858536

Edition Reviewed:
1985

Publisher:
Newmarket Press

Author/Editor:
Marilyn Segal, Ph.D. and Don Adcock, Ph.D.

About The Author:
(From Cover Notes)
Both authors are development psychologists. Segal is the director of the Family Center at Nova University in Florida and also a professor of human development. Adcock, a professor of early childhood development, is the associate director at the Family Center.

YOUR CHILD AT PLAY: ONE TO TWO YEARS
Exploring, Daily Living, Learning, And Making Friends

Description:

One in a series of four, this 219 page resource details the development of toddlers from the age of one to two. Divided into three parts and 12 chapters, this book was written by two developmental psychologists "as a practical guide for parents who are faced with the everyday challenges of living with a toddler." The book is organized according to topics rather than ages to allow for differences in toddlers' rates of growth. Each part delivers advice to parents as they try to handle the "competing objectives" their toddler faces, such as independence vs. independence, learning vs. playing, and so on. Part 1—"Exploration"—focuses on the various ways toddlers explore their environment along with issues that arise as parents want to encourage exploration but keep it in bounds. Part 2—"Everyday Living"—focuses on the toddler's strife for independence through daily routines such as sleeping, eating, etc. Part 3—"Play and Learning"—explores what the toddler learns through different kinds of play such as physical games, toys, reading books, and interactions with adults, children, and pets.

Evaluation:

Parents looking for a basic overview of their toddler's growth and development will find it here. This resource, although dated, offers an assortment of short tips from "hundreds of families." It contains advice ranging from how to reasonably accommodate a toddler's desire to play with water to how to maintain one's sanity while going out in public. Not an end-all for subjects such as discipline, beginning toilet training (featured in the next book of the series), or sibling relationships, nonetheless, this book does a good job of reassuring parents that the behaviors their toddler is displaying are most likely "normal." User-friendly in tone, each chapter begins with a typical dialog scene between parents and a toddler highlighting the characteristics discussed in that chapter. Numerous black and white photographs are also included. Providing a general perspective on what to expect or reassurance for behaviors already encountered, this book is good as a starter for other resources that provide more details.

Where To Find/Buy:

Bookstores and libraries.

MY TODDLER
The Beginning Of Independence

Description:

This 217 page guide is from the "Stepping-Stones" series for Christian parents by Dr. Paul Warren of the Minirth Meier New Life Clinics. There are seven chapters primarily focusing on a toddler's development from age one to three. Physical Development is the focus of Chapter 1 including the topics of what to expect, how to deal with eating habits, potty training, safety, and more; brief highlights of the changes engulfing the "terrible twos" are also given. Chapter 2 deals with the toddler's need for independence and dependence; a toddler's negativism, ways to promote their independence, and the caregiver's role are discussed. Social development, language development, and reducing stress in a parent's life are addressed in Chapters 3, 4, and 5. Chapter 6 offers discipline strategies—how to control a one-year-old, historical roots of discipline, the Biblical roots of discipline, positive discipline, and more. Chapter 7 are the author's closing comments. There is no index. An anecdote format is used throughout.

Evaluation:

While many other resources detail a toddler's growth and development in more a textbook-like fashion, many readers will appreciate this book's narrative short story format. Dr. Warren's humor and friendly writing tone immediately sets the reader at ease. The book's larger print makes it more easily read than other resources. The table of contents neatly lists major subtopics within the book and the bold subheadings help delineate issues. However, an index would have proved a supportive backup as would bulleted tips, highlights, or chapter summaries. This guide is based on the new King James Version of the Bible and reflects those teachings in a subtle fashion aiming for a balanced approach to childrearing. Warren's underlying message is that parents can build trust and independence within young children by understanding toddlers' physical, mental, social, and emotional needs and development. Parents will find many good tips and strategies here but they'll need other resources for back-up.

Where To Find/Buy:

Bookstores and libraries, or order direct by calling 1-800-NEW-LIFE.

Overall Rating
★★
Good basic info on understanding and encouraging toddlers with a Christian theme

Design, Ease Of Use
★★
Easy to read; table of contents highlights major subtopics but an index would be helpful

1–4 Stars; N/R = Not Rated

Media Type:
Print

Price:
$10.99

Principal Subject:
Growth & Learning

Age Group:
Toddlers (1–3)

ISBN:
0785283471

Edition Reviewed:
1994

Publisher:
Thomas Nelson Publishers

Author/Editor:
Dr. Paul Warren

About The Author:
(From Cover Notes)
Paul Warren, M.D. is a behavioral pediatrician, adolescent medicine specialist, medical director of the Minirth Meier New Life Clinic in Richardson, Texas, and maintains an active outpatient practice. He is a popular speaker on child and adolescent issues.

Overall Rating
★★
Interesting glimpse at a child's social development but based on a questionable study

Design, Ease Of Use
★
Textbook-like; vague table of contents; good summaries at end of chapters; index given

1–4 Stars; N/R = Not Rated

Media Type:
Print

Price:
$11.00

Principal Subject:
Growth & Learning

Age Group:
Infants & Toddlers (0–3)

ISBN:
0684801345

Edition Reviewed:
1995

Publisher:
Fireside (Simon & Schuster)

Author/Editor:
Burton L. White

About The Author:
(From Cover Notes)
White is the director of the Center for Parent Education in Newton, Massachusetts, and the designer of the Missouri New Parents as Teachers Project. He is the father of four (now grown) children and lives in Waban, Massachusetts.

RAISING A HAPPY, UNSPOILED CHILD

Description:
Based upon White's 38 years of observation, this 253 page book focuses on a child's social development and "how to raise an absolutely wonderful 22 month old child." White found that two-year-olds who were socially capable retained those qualities at the age of 6 compared with those children who were "overindulged and spoiled." His study then focused on parent-child interactions in the early months to see how to avoid dealing with the "terrible twos." The introduction explains his methodology. The book is divided into seven chapters. Chapters 1–5 are divided by age range (birth–5 1/2 months, 5 1/2 months–7 1/2 months, 7 1/2 months to 14 months, 14–22–30 months, and 22–30–36 months) and offer development information and suggestions. Subtopics within each chapter include discussions of normal social development, the development of a social style, how to guide your child through this stage, and more. Chapter 6 presents "Special Topics" such as "hazards" (late parenting, prematurity, etc.), effects of caregivers and grandparents, and more. Chapter 7 offers White's concluding remarks.

Evaluation:
White's research is one of the few studies based on natural observations of children in their homes. His research methodology is well-outlined, extensive, and somewhat scientifically founded; White admits that neither he nor anyone else has developed a reliable measure for the many facets of a baby's social development. This leaves the reader questioning the study's objectivity especially when reading what seems to be White's personal opinion at times. Will White's suggestions actually work—can parents avoid the "terrible twos" by following his advice as they "discipline" their baby at the critical stage from 5 1/2 months to 7 1/2 months? It's up to parents to read his work and adopt or reject his philosophy according to their own parenting beliefs. His writing style tends to be heavy textually, not making for light reading. But all that aside, White offers an in-depth glimpse at the inner workings and interactions of the young child. If parents can distinguish between White's personal opinion and child development facts, they will enjoy reading about the changes their child goes through.

Where To Find/Buy:
Bookstores and libraries.

THE SEVEN SPIRITUAL LAWS FOR PARENTS
(Audiotape)
Guiding Your Children To Success And Fulfillment

Description:

Read by the author, this 90 minute audiotape is an abridged version of his book by the same title. His philosophy, based on a 5,000 year old system of mind/body medicine (Ayurvedic principles), embodies the belief that parents want their children to be successful and that the most direct way to success is through spirit. Success depends on what you are and not on what you do, states Chopra. He emphasizes that parents mistakenly confuse success with materialistic accomplishments. After exploring the topic of spirituality in general terms, Chopra then directs his discussion to "the journey of spirit" based on living in harmony with natural law. He states seven general "laws," as detailed in his book *The Seven Spiritual Laws of Success*, and then restates them in less abstract terms for children (ex: "everything is possible," "if you want to get something, give it," "you are here for a reason," etc.). Each law is explained and then matched up to a day of the week on which parents and children practice these spiritual skills.

Evaluation:

Parents sold on Chopra's set of beliefs will find this tape rather hypnotic and affirming thanks largely to Chopra's gentle voice, soothing tone, and spiritual message. However, we recommend this tape for those who are familiar with the book, but need a refresher course from time to time, or for those parents who learn better auditorially. Somewhat random flowing and repetitive at times, this tape follows the book quite well. A lot of information about how to raise children spiritually is tendered here and having the book as either a base or back-up will further parents' understanding. Chopra does a fine job of illustrating his points although much of the information and suggestions are geared more towards the parents of school-age children (6 and up). Crossing most conventional western religions, Chopra creates a balanced approach toward instilling spirituality within children. Earmarking given days of the week to practice this spirituality will give many parents some concrete tools from which to work.

Where To Find/Buy:

Bookstores and libraries, or order direct by calling 1-800-726-0600.

Internet URL:

http://www.randomhouse.com

Overall Rating
★★
Offers a spiritual base for some parents or excursion for others of western religions

Design, Ease Of Use
★
Message given in rather rambling fashion; best used as refresher or back-up to the book

1–4 Stars; N/R = Not Rated

Media Type:
Audiotape

Price:
$14.00

Principal Subject:
Growth & Learning

Age Group:
All Ages (0–5)

ISBN:
0679460411

Edition Reviewed:
1997

Publisher:
Random House

Author/Editor:
Deepak Chopra, M.D.

About The Author:
(From Cover Notes)
Chopra, who has practiced endocrinology since 1971, is the former chief of staff of New England Memorial Hospital in Stoneham, Massachusetts. He is also the president of the American Association for Ayurvedic Medicine. He is the author of 19 books.

Overall Rating
★★
Offers a spiritual base for some parents or excursion for others of western religions

Design, Ease Of Use
★
Heavy text style that must be read cover to cover; each "law" includes a synopsis

1–4 Stars; N/R = Not Rated

Media Type:
Print

Price:
$16.95

Principal Subject:
Growth & Learning

Age Group:
All Ages (0–5)

ISBN:
060960077X

Edition Reviewed:
1997

Publisher:
Harmony Books (Crown Publishers/Random House)

Author/Editor:
Deepak Chopra, M.D.

About The Author:
(From Cover Notes)
Chopra, who has practiced endocrinology since 1971, is the former chief of staff of New England Memorial Hospital in Stoneham, Massachusetts. He is also the president of the American Association for Ayurvedic Medicine. He is the author of 19 books.

THE SEVEN SPIRITUAL LAWS FOR PARENTS
(Print)
Guiding Your Children To Success And Fulfillment

Description:

Chopra's philosophy, based on a 5,000 year old system of mind/body medicine (Ayurvedic principles), embodies the belief that parents want their children to be successful and that the most direct way to success is through spirit. Success depends on what you are and not on what you do, states Chopra. He emphasizes that parents mistakenly confuse success with materialistic accomplishments. After exploring the topic of spirituality in Part One of his 156 page book, Chopra then discusses "the journey of spirit" which is based on living in harmony with natural law. He states the seven "laws" as detailed in his book *The Seven Spiritual Laws of Success*, and then restates them in less abstract terms for children (ex: "everything is possible," "if you want to get something, give it," "you are here for a reason," etc.); brief overviews are given for developmental stages and ages (birth to 15 years old). In Part Two, each law is outlined and then assigned a day of the week on which parents and children practice these spiritual skills.

Evaluation:

This book was written in response to pleas from parents who had read Chopra's book *The Seven Spiritual Laws of Success* and desired to translate these lessons to their children. Parents sold on Chopra's beliefs will no doubt find this book helpful. Crossing most conventional western religions, Chopra creates visions of an ideal world with his approach toward spirituality. A lot of information about how to raise children spiritually is tendered here but few concrete suggestions; parents trying to bring spirituality down to earth for their child will need to hunt a bit. Parents need to read this resource cover to cover several times to best comprehend Chopra's generalities. Written in a heavy text style, it's somewhat random and repetitive at times. Many of the suggestions are geared more for parents of school-age children (6 and up) with some input for parents of younger children. On the plus side, earmarking given days of the week to practice spirituality will give many Chopra followers some concrete tools from which to work.

Where To Find/Buy:

Bookstores and libraries.

Internet URL:

http://www.randomhouse.com

CHILD DEVELOPMENT: THE FIRST TWO YEARS
A Comprehensive Guide To Enhancing Your Child's Physical And Mental Development

Description:

Divided into five age segments, this 47 minute videotape describes developmental changes for babies and toddlers. The first segment (birth to 3 months) offers general information about physical development, feeding (breastfeeding and bottlefeeding), the importance of touching and bonding, and ways to stimulate your baby. Segment Two (3 to 6 months) discusses the how-tos of introducing solids along with advice on using playpens and interacting with your baby. The next segment illustrates the developmental changes that occur between the ages of 6 and 12 months as many babies gain head and lower body control, added mobility, and motor skills such as crawling, pulling to stand, and walking. Tips on childproofing, introducing finger foods, and language acquisition are provided. The final two age segments are combined (12 to 18 months; 18–24 months) and feature developmental information about toddlers. Suggested milestones for physical development, language skills, and emotional development are given.

Evaluation:

As parents watch this video, they will no doubt be captivated by the engaging footage of babies going about the process of growing up. However, the accompanying information is bleak and does not do justice to such an important topic. For example, considerable footage is used to show a baby exploring his food bowl, yet little time is given to how language develops (other than constant reminders to talk to your baby). Extensive time is afforded to how to read a commercial baby food jar, while insignificant time is allowed for discussing children's cognitive development; no mention is made of cause-effect relationships, object permanence, and other facets important for baby's mental growth and social development. The video is divided into neat little age packages, but the narration jumps around. One minute the narrator discusses a baby's early growth, but the next minute, she discusses a toddlers' physical development. A continuum of how a baby changes into a toddler is useful but in this videotape it gets confusing. Other videotapes offer more in-depth information on this important subject. Check out those resources over this one.

Where To Find/Buy:

Bookstores, libraries, videotape dealers, or order direct by calling (212) 674-5550.

Overall Rating
★
Minimal information on many facets of child development

Design, Ease Of Use
★★
Engaging videotape footage; narration confusing (jumps around age group to age group)

1–4 Stars; N/R = Not Rated

Media Type:
Videotape

Price:
$24.98

Principal Subject:
Growth & Learning

Age Group:
Infants & Toddlers (0–3)

ISBN:
0803015232

Edition Reviewed:
1993

Publisher:
V.I.E.W.

Overall Rating
★
Informative guide but primarily useful for parents of school age children or adolescents

Design, Ease Of Use
★★
Table of contents format wieldy with all questions listed; index not comprehensive

1–4 Stars; N/R = Not Rated

Media Type:
Print

Price:
$12.95

Principal Subject:
Growth & Learning

Age Group:
All Ages (0–5)

ISBN:
1577490053

Edition Reviewed:
1995

Publisher:
Fairview Press

Author/Editor:
Gerald Deskin, Ph.D., M.F.C.C., and Greg Steckler, M.A., M.F.C.C.

About The Author:
(From Cover Notes)
Gerald Deskin, Ph.D.,M.F.C.C., is a licensed psychologist and licensed marriage, family, and child therapist. Greg Steckler, M.A., M.F.C.C., is a marriage, family, and child therapist and is founding director of the Halcyon Center for Child Studies, Inc.

PARENT'S ANSWER BOOK (THE)
Over 101 Most-Asked Questions About Your Child's Well-Being

Description:
Divided into five sections, this 216-page answer book centers on offering advice and suggestions on 100+ child and adolescent development issues. The first section answers questions related to family development. Some of these issues include: how to tell if your child is ready to drive, dealing with sibling rivalry, what to do when your child wants things that you can't afford, how to tell if your child is over-scheduled, and more. The second section answers questions about school and learning problems. The next two sections offer advice on social and emotional development, and the final section deals with physical development. A sampling of issues in these last three sections address subjects such as depression, weight problems, dealing with stress, sleep disorders, etc. Questions are listed in the table of contents, delineated in bold within each section, and follow-up, explanatory subtopics are also given in bold. An index is also included.

Evaluation:
Ask a question, any question, and this book is sure to have an answer—at least on most of the more frequently addressed issues for school-aged child and adolescents. This book does an excellent job of answering significant questions, even answers to questions such as what to do if your son has impregnated a girl, what to do if you find out your child has been sexually involved or abused, how to get your child to attend religious services, how far away should you live from your ex-spouse, how to find out if your child is in a gang, and more. The authors answer all questions in a complete, no-nonsense manner, with a "Recommendations" section included that highlight the authors' main points on each question. The book's candor is refreshing and parents of school age children and adolescents will find themselves referring to it time and time again. Parents of preschoolers or younger, however, will have to hunt carefully for any applicable information within this book and will end up turning to other better resources.

Where To Find/Buy:
Bookstores and libraries, or order direct by calling 1-800-544-8207.

THE MAGIC YEARS
Understanding And Handling The Problems Of Early Childhood

Description:

Written by a past professor of child psychoanalysis, this 305 page resource discusses childhood fears, anxieties, and neurosis in its aim to promote mental health within children. Divided into five parts, with nine chapters, this guide relies heavily on the writings of Anna Freud (ego psychology, early childhood development), Rene Spitz (psychology of infancy), Heinz Hartmann and Ernst Kris (psychoanalytic ego psychology), and Jean Piaget (child's construct of reality). The author states that the information provided comes from case studies in which the child's history has allowed emotional disturbances to develop, but that it is difficult to definitively describe how to avoid these disturbances. Part One focuses on anxiety, the ego, mental health, and more. Parts Two, Three, and Four respectively discuss characteristics and conflicts facing the child during the first eighteen months, from 18 months to 3 years, and from 3 years to 6 years of age. A conclusion is provided in Part Six along with a 3 page index.

Evaluation:

Not a book for the faint of heart who haven't the time to concentrate and discern the author's intent, this book is packed with psychoanalytical jargon and heavy rhetoric. For those parents who prefer theory mixed with suggested practice, we recommend they select other resources offering a more balanced approach in discussing children's cognitive, emotional, and social development. The bottom line premise of this book is good. It concludes that "parents need not be paragons; they may be inexperienced, they may be permitted to err . . . to employ sometimes a wrong method or an unendorsed technique," but that as long as the bonds between parent and child are strong, they have a good chance of rearing a mentally healthy child. Unfortunately, this message often gets lost in the shuffle between the author's espousing of her psychoanalytic background and the case studies she presents. Suited more for the educator who can deliver this message more concretely to parents, save this one for when you have ample time on your hands, the ability to concentrate, or nothing better to read.

Where To Find/Buy:

Bookstores and libraries.

Overall Rating
★
Strictly based on psychoanalytic studies, this resource emphasizes parent-child bond

Design, Ease Of Use
★
Heavy rhetorical text with substantial psychoanalytic discussions; minimal index

1–4 Stars; N/R = Not Rated

Media Type:
Print

Price:
$12.00

Principal Subject:
Growth & Learning

Age Group:
All Ages (0–5)

ISBN:
0684825503

Edition Reviewed:
1996

Publisher:
Fireside (Simon & Schuster)

Author/Editor:
Selma H. Fraiberg

About The Author:
(From Cover Notes)
Fraiberg was professor of child psychoanalysis and director of the Infant-Parent Program of San Francisco General Hospital, University of California School of Medicine. Her articles were published widely in professional and popular magazines.

Overall Rating
★

Site lacks any real substance at the moment even though their goals are admirable

Design, Ease Of Use
★

None of the given information can be printed at the site making it fairly useless

1–4 Stars; N/R = Not Rated

Media Type:
Internet

Principal Subject:
Growth & Learning

Age Group:
Infants & Toddlers (0–3)

ZERO TO THREE
Young Explorers

Description:
Zero To Three, a nonprofit national organization founded in 1977 and "dedicated solely to advancing the healthy development of babies and young children," offers two avenues of parenting information at their homepage. Parents will find a "tip of the week," developmental milestones (birth–8 months, 8 months–18 months, 18 months–2 years), advice on choosing quality child care, and more. Options available to professionals include info on the National Training Institute's program (December 5th–7th, 1997), a newsroom with press releases and articles from ZTT's bimonthly bulletin, and more. Options available for both parents and professionals include ZTT's online bookstore and the results of a telephone poll of 1,022 parents of children under the age of three. Results are shown in both narrative and graph form highlighting the differences in what parents know about various areas of their child's development (physical vs. emotional, social, intellectual), how parents feel about their role and abilities, and more.

Evaluation:
This site's premise centers on seven key characteristics that "need to be developed in young children to ensure their success in school": confidence, curiosity, self-control, ability to relate to others, capacity to have an impact and be persistent, capacity to communicate, and cooperation. To that end, this site would seem worth exploring. The week we visited, the "tip of the week" involved "curiosity" and the tip centered on a visit to your local library's storytime. The tips are neat, tidy, concise, and manageable by most parents. Where this site falls short however is in an overall direction. So you've gone to the library. What else can you do besides that to foster curiosity? Suggested ways to simultaneously integrate the other 6 characteristics would be beneficial. Defining and detailing these seven key qualities for parents, offering a plan for developing them, and providing a history of tips already presented would be more useful. This site's goal is admirable and they're still growing. Check back later.

Where To Find/Buy:
On the Internet at the URL: http://www.zerotothree.org/. Publications can be ordered by calling 1-800-899-4301.

Internet URL:
http://www.zerotothree.org/

STOP STRUGGLING WITH YOUR CHILD

 Best Resource For:
Videotape focusing on children's behavior and discipline strategies

 Recommended For:
Growth & Learning

Description:

Reiterating the points of their book by the same title, these "parenting experts" detail their four-step process for minimizing family conflicts and maximizing a child's self-esteem. The ultimate goals of this method are to help parents move from major power struggles to minor ones and, by doing so, increase a child's self-concept. The four steps are: "Don't Use Your Mouth, Use Your Routine"; "Treat 'Em As A Team"; "Make A Correction With A Connection"; and "See The Small Successes Along The Way." They suggest that if parents change their own behavior, children will change theirs. They also suggest that following these steps gives children opportunities to become cooperative, to practice problem-solving, and to take responsibility for themselves. Parents are encouraged to separate themselves from the problem, to not get hooked into fights, and to think with reason, not anger. At the end of this 30 minute tape, the authors offer "Quick Tips" for solving conflicts such as not picking up belongings, fights in the car, not doing chores, clothing choices, and more.

Evaluation:

This would be a marvelous tape to use in a parent education class. It clearly outlines the major points involved in most current positive discipline resources in a succinct, concise manner. By combining footage from the authors' workshop and from real-life family scenarios, the authors do a good job at identifying major conflicts parents face. The connection they make between parent-child power plays and self-esteem is well made and is one not often addressed in other resources. By realizing that power struggles often earmark a child's need for attention, but also noting that reducing conflicts helps to bolster a child's self-esteem, many parents will have a reason to want to change their own behavior. Parents can increase their own self-esteem by taking themselves out of the fight and stepping back to watch their child become more responsible. Although this video is a bit pricey for at-home viewing, busy parents will appreciate its conciseness and application.

Where To Find/Buy:

Bookstores, libraries, video stores, or order directly by calling (310) 577-8581.

Overall Rating
★★★★
Excellent for beginning a discussion on discipline in a parenting education class or forum

Design, Ease Of Use
★★★★
To the point with major necessary tips highlighted; includes a wrap-up & quick tips

1–4 Stars; N/R = Not Rated

Media Type:
Videotape

Price:
$29.98

Principal Subject:
Growth & Learning

Age Group:
All Ages (0–5)

Edition Reviewed:
none given

Publisher:
TMW Media Group

★★★★

Overall Rating
★★★★
Offers parents verbal cues for staying in control of potential conflicts with their child

Design, Ease Of Use
★★★
Rambles at times, but fairly succinct in identifying main points; concrete examples given

1–4 Stars; N/R = Not Rated

Media Type:
Audiotape

Price:
$11.95

Principal Subject:
Growth & Learning

Age Group:
All Ages (0–5)

ISBN:
0944634311

Edition Reviewed:
1996

Publisher:
The Love and Logic Press

Author/Editor:
Jim Fay and Foster W. Cline, M.D.

About The Author:
(From Cover Notes)
Foster W. Cline, MD is a child and adult psychiatrist. He specializes in working with difficult children. Jim Fay has 31 years of experience as an educator and principal. He is an educational consultant and won many awards in the education field.

AVOIDING POWER STRUGGLES WITH KIDS

Best Resource For:
Audiotape focusing on children's behavior and ways to avoid power struggles

Recommended For:
Growth & Learning

Description:

The authors of *Parenting with Love and Logic* highlight their parenting technique—that "love" allows children to grow through their mistakes while "logic" allows children to live with the consequences of their choices. This 65 minute audiotape focuses on the "Science of Control." The authors believe that if parents take all the control away from kids, kids will fight to get control in negative ways (power struggles); conversely, the more control parents give away, the more control they will have. The authors give four steps to dealing with potential power struggles. First, parents need to diffuse a problem by saying something like "no problem." Then, they need to use "thinking words" (what the parent will do) as opposed to "fighting words" (what the child has to do). Next, children should be given choices that the parent can live with, and finally, the authors state that "parents should hope and pray" the child makes the wrong decision so they will receive some real world learning experience when "it's affordable." Tips for dealing with specific situations are given (bedtime, eating, chores, watching TV, schoolwork, and more).

Evaluation:

Parents who don't have the time to read the authors' book will glean the important points through this audiotape. It generally tends to be succinct, although the authors do ramble at times leaving the listener wondering where they are going. Most parents will appreciate how this technique doesn't focus on them solving problems but instead focuses on their child. The authors state that this will still keep the parent in control but avoid the "brain drains" and conflicts. Parents are taken out of the hotbed of anger, lectures, and threats which tend to make children resentful of them. Instead, the parent becomes available to offer empathy for the child's mistakes (but no "I-told-you-sos"). The authors make a good point about encouraging children to make choices (without danger involved) and live with the consequences at an early age—when "it's affordable" and not devastating to their lives. Of particular use for many parents will be the numerous verbal examples given for what to say in given situations. Parents will find this tape a good reflection of the authors' key points and worth their time and money.

Where To Find/Buy:

Bookstores and libraries, or order direct by calling 1-800-338-4065.

PARENTING WITH LOVE AND LOGIC (Print)
Teaching Children Responsibility

 Recommended For:
Growth & Learning

Description:

Divided into two parts, this 225 page book centers on using love and logic while parenting. The authors define love as not permissive or tolerant of disrespect, but that which allows children to make mistakes and live with the logical consequences; logic is centered in the consequences themselves. Parenting then becomes an issue of offering your child choices along with empathy if your child makes mistakes in the process. The first part of the book discusses general parenting issues: self-concept, setting limits, offering choices, consequences, etc. Each chapter in part one recites a proverb, specific to the topic. The second part focuses on 41 love and logic "Pearls" (tips) for dealing with problems parents encounter during the first twelve years of their children's lives. Included here is advice about dealing with peer pressure, temper tantrums, fears and monsters, negative body language, and more. The second part is intended to be used in conjunction with part one. An index is included along with information about "Love and Logic" seminars.

Evaluation:

This book's approach focuses on providing children the "opportunity for a joyful, productive, and responsible adult life." The book's relaxed writing style sets a comfortable, down-to-earth mood and it is easily read. The author has thoughtfully anticipated and incorporated important parental issues in the index which are not clearly noted in the detailed table of contents. For instance, drug use, runaways, diseases, and suicide are all generally included in Pearl 8—"Crisis Situations"— but are also listed separately in the index. The two part format allows the "Love and Logic Parenting Pearls" to validate the first section. The book offers many interesting issues with sound advice not often included in other books with the same subject material. Some of these issues include pet care, back seat car battles, table manners, bossiness, teeth brushing, and telephone interruptions. Other resources offer positive approaches to dealing with children's behavior; this book's unique approach makes it a helpful resource to be used in conjunction with them.

Where To Find/Buy:

Bookstores and libraries.

Overall Rating
★★★★
Relaxed approach includes tips for specific problems based on logical consequences

Design, Ease Of Use
★★★
Lots of story copy to get beyond; good cross-referencing in index

1–4 Stars; N/R = Not Rated

Media Type:
Print

Price:
$18.00

Principal Subject:
Growth & Learning

Age Group:
All Ages (0–5)

ISBN:
0891093117

Edition Reviewed:
1990

Publisher:
Pinon Press

Author/Editor:
Foster Cline, M.D. and Jim Fay

About The Author:
(From Cover Notes)
Foster W. Cline, MD is a child and adult psychiatrist. He specializes in working with difficult children. Jim Fay has 31 years of experience as an educator and principal. He is an educational consultant and won many awards in the education field.

★★★★

Overall Rating
★★★★
Emphasizes communication, respect, and dignity between parents and children

Design, Ease Of Use
★★★
Numbered highlights, bulleted tips, summaries useful; must be read cover-to-cover

1–4 Stars; N/R = Not Rated

Media Type:
Print

Price:
$11.00

Principal Subject:
Growth & Learning

Age Group:
All Ages (0–5)

ISBN:
0345402510

Edition Reviewed:
3rd (1996)

Publisher:
Ballantine Books (Random House)

Author/Editor:
Jane Nelsen, Ed.D.

About The Author:
(From Cover Notes)
Nelsen is a licensed marriage, family, and child therapist, and was an elementary school counselor and a college instructor in child development for ten years. She is the mother of seven children and has thirteen grandchildren.

POSITIVE DISCIPLINE (Print)
Revised Edition

 Best Resource For:
Understanding behavior and appropriate ways to discipline

 Recommended For:
Growth & Learning

Description:
Drawn from the beliefs of Alfred Adler and Rudolf Dreikurs, "positive discipline" is defined as firmness with dignity, kindness, and respect. The goals are twofold: to teach children self-discipline, responsibility, cooperation, and problem-solving skills; and to always be positive with no humiliation for the child or the adult. Key concepts to this discipline practice include: treat mistakes as opportunities to learn, seek solutions to problems together as a family (rather than blame), believe that children do better when they feel better, the "significant seven" of successful people ("I am capable," etc.), children listen to parents when they feel listened to, and more. Nelsen's newly revised edition contains more examples of how to use encouragement to motivate children along with her emphasis on understanding and applying the importance of "social interest" (concern for others, the community, and the environment). The chapter on natural and logical consequences has also been revised.

Evaluation:
This 258 page, ten chapter resource offers a combined approach of understanding family dynamics (parenting styles, birth order/siblings, etc.) and child temperament, so that a better understanding of the child's goal/behavior is reached and communication patterns improved. Parents will not only learn ways to interpret their child's mistakes differently but also ways to enhance their family interactions. By offering parents constructive ways to approach a child's mistake, through developing problem-solving strategies as a family and by making decisions together, Nelsen offers strong alternatives to techniques that no longer work for parents, such as punitive discipline. If parents are looking for solutions to specific problems, they might well read one of her other books, *Positive Discipline A–Z*. The questions at the end of each chapter help to refocus parents (or parent groups) into the essential ingredients of Nelsen's method. The book must be read cover-to-cover to understand the philosophy and gain its benefits, but these benefits will outweigh the time needed to digest the material and practice its suggestions.

Where To Find/Buy:
Bookstores, libraries, or order direct by calling 1-800-456-7770.

RAISING A THINKING CHILD

Help Your Young Child To Resolve Everyday Conflicts And Get Along With Others—The "I Can Problem Solve" Program

 Recommended For:
Growth & Learning

Description:

This 210 page book is intended to help your child become a thinking, considerate individual. There are two parts to this guidebook. Part One centers on helping your child think through problems. Some subtopics within this section include "Playing with Words," Understanding Feelings," "Considering Consequences," and "ICPSing." ICPS, a program developed by the author, is an acronym for "I Can Problem Solve." The ICPS approach teaches children how to think, not what to think or do. Part One follows a family as they progress through each stage of the ICPS program; it is a composite of actual families Shure has encountered professionally. Part Two focuses on putting together the techniques in Part One and fine-tuning those skills. This section includes ICPS games, activities, and dialogues. Three appendices are included (a self-evaluation checklist, a list of things for parent and child to think about, and ICPS dialogue reminders). Selected references are noted and there is a comprehensive index.

Evaluation:

The ICPS program, developed by Dr. Shure 25 years ago, has proven successful with thousands of children (up to age 12) with varied IQ levels from both urban and suburban schools; ICPS has received several national awards; this guidebook is based on ICPS research and experiences with parents of children up to age seven. ICPS is a positive childrearing approach that places the onus of problem solving within the child. Included is a useful index on "Common Problems" (hitting, grabbing, bedtime, etc.) where parents can quickly locate information on a specific problem. This resource is well-researched and fairly easily read; bolder subchapter headings would help. The program is not designed to tell children what they should do or how they should behave. Rather it shows how parents can affect their child's social adjustment and encourage them to think; ICPS research claims that better social adjustment allows for better academic skills. This book definitely offers a fresh approach in a methodical, yet practical way.

Where To Find/Buy:

Bookstores and libraries, or write directly to: Mail Order Department, Simon & Schuster Inc., 200 Old Tappan Road, Old Tappan, NJ 07675.

Overall Rating
★★★★
Practical guide to behavior that places responsibility of discipline within the child

Design, Ease Of Use
★★★
Thorough research base;"common problems" cross-referenced; bolder headings needed

1–4 Stars; N/R = Not Rated

Media Type:
Print

Price:
$12.00

Principal Subject:
Growth & Learning

Age Group:
All Ages (0–5)

ISBN:
0671534637

Edition Reviewed:
1994

Publisher:
Pocket Books (Simon & Schuster)

Author/Editor:
Myrna B. Shure, Ph.D. with Theresa Foy DiGeronimo, M.Ed.

About The Author:
(From Cover Notes)
Shure is a developmental psychologist, professor of psychology at Allegheny University of Health Sciences (Philadelphia), and a media consultant on mental health issues and behavior problems. DiGeronimo has coauthored more than a dozen books on parenting.

Overall Rating
★★★
An upbeat and concise guide on how to deal with and overcome challenging behaviors

Design, Ease Of Use
★★★★
Clear format for each chapter using icons, catchy titles, compact; light-hearted tone

1–4 Stars; N/R = Not Rated

Media Type:
Print

Price:
$14.00

Principal Subject:
Growth & Learning

Age Group:
All Ages (0–5)

ISBN:
0517884631

Edition Reviewed:
1996

Publisher:
Three Rivers Press (Crown Publishers/Random House)

Author/Editor:
Barbara Chernofsky, M.S. and Diane Gage

About The Author:
(From Cover Notes)
Barbara Chernofsky, M.S., is a child-care specialist for the NBC affiliate KNSD-TV, in San Diego. Diane Gage has written eight books and is the Director of Corporate Relations for Sharp HealthCare in San Diego.

CHANGE YOUR CHILD'S BEHAVIOR BY CHANGING YOURS
13 New Tricks to Get Kids To Cooperate

 Recommended For:
Growth & Learning

Description:
This 198 page guide is divided up into three parts. The book is based on two premises of "proactive parenting" which are listed in Part One: changing adult behavior will change a child's behavior, and children's inappropriate behavior is mostly age-appropriate. Part Two offers tips on how to handle thirteen of challenging behaviors for children from birth to age 6 (bedtime, siblings, eating, going places, etc.). Part Three discusses the relationship between parents, childcare providers, and teachers. Each chapter follows the same format: a scenario of a child-parent conflict, a description of the developmental trait that provides impetus for the behavior, a section explaining typical parental reactions, a section which relates the child's behavior to a similar adult behavior, and a section suggesting alternative reactions to a child's behavior. Each chapter includes a "Bibliotherapy" section which lists reading resources to be used between parent and child to teach about that particular behavior.

Evaluation:
The authors suggest that if parents look at their own adult behavior, they will be able to understand more clearly the behaviors of their children; "adults throw tantrums, pout, take revenge, and refuse to cooperate. It's just that our actions are cloaked in adult rhetoric. . . ." This resource's unique approach is positive, upbeat, and refreshing; it offers parents encouragement and motivational techniques to change their adult behavior. Although all behaviors aren't addressed, this guidebook offers great concise advice and suggestions for "on-the-go" parents. Of special interest are the sections within each chapter titled "Stop! Rewind Your Own Tape." These snippets relating adult behaviors to the child's will not only help parents relate to what is going on with their child, but may also in effect offer parents alternatives for communicating with their child. This guide's use of icons and consistent formatting makes it very user-friendly and a quick read. For busy parents on the fly, this book will prove to be a big help.

Where To Find/Buy:
Bookstores and libraries.

DISCIPLINE BOOK (THE)
Everything You Need To Know To Have A Better-Behaved Child—From Birth To Age Ten

 Recommended For:
Growth & Learning

Description:

This 316 page book includes 19 chapters on discipline strategies for young children. The book centers on ten principles. These include a healthy relationship between parent and child ("attachment parenting"), knowing your child, (understanding age appropriate behavior), being respectful of authority, setting limits, obedience expectations, modeling discipline, nurturing self-confidence, shaping your child's behavior, raising compassionate children, and communicating effectively. To expound on these principles, the book is divided into three parts. Part 1 focuses on promoting desirable behavior; 11 chapters deal with child development, temper tantrums, anger, sleep, and more. Part 2, with 5 chapters, highlights pros and cons of methods for correcting undesirable behavior (spanking, timeout, etc.) along with specific situations (hitting, whining, bad language, etc.). Part 3 discusses lifelong discipline, including morals and manners, sexuality, and disciplining special children. A sample discipline plan is also offered.

Evaluation:

This is most certainly one of the better books on discipline. William Sears, M.D. and Martha Sears, R.N. have combined their professional and personal experiences (parents of 8 children) to develop a philosophy of discipline whose purpose is to equip children with the tools they will need to succeed in life. The philosophy is backed up with practical advice. It is well-researched, well-written, and easily comprehended. The book is both advocate and champion of parents looking for answers to questions about behavior, beginning with the "connection" of breastfeeding, then carrying through to a lifelong discipline plan. And because discipline has many facets, it provides general guidelines for parents to analyze behavior problems within their families as well as providing a definitive and positive approach to raising well-adjusted, well-behaved children; solutions to some specific behavior problems will need to be found elsewhere. This book has much to offer parents so they can feel confident as they raise their child.

Where To Find/Buy:

Bookstores and libraries.

Overall Rating
★★★
This sound practical and philosophical guide will complement any home library

Design, Ease Of Use
★★★★
Detailed table of contents; anecdotes throughout; highlighted blocks of info

1–4 Stars; N/R = Not Rated

Media Type:
Print

Price:
$13.95

Principal Subject:
Growth & Learning

Age Group:
All Ages (0–5)

ISBN:
0316779032

Edition Reviewed:
1995

Publisher:
Little Brown and Company

Author/Editor:
William Sears, M.D., and Martha Sears, R.N.

About The Author:
(From Cover Notes)
William Sears, M.D., is a Clinical Assistant Professor of Pediatrics at the University of Southern California School of Medicine. Martha Sears, R.N., is a registered nurse and certified childbirth educator.

Overall Rating
★★★
Relaxed approach includes tips for specific problems based on logical consequences

Design, Ease Of Use
★★★★
Abridged version "reads" more smoothly than the book; table of contents given for tapes

1–4 Stars; N/R = Not Rated

Media Type:
Audiotape

Price:
$24.95

Principal Subject:
Growth & Learning

Age Group:
All Ages (0–5)

ISBN:
0944634389

Edition Reviewed:
1997

Publisher:
The Love and Logic Press

Author/Editor:
Foster Cline, M.D. and Jim Fay

About The Author:
(From Cover Notes)
Foster W. Cline, MD is a child and adult psychiatrist. He specializes in working with difficult children. Jim Fay has 30+ years of experience as an educator and principal. Both are the authors of over 90 books, tapes, and articles on parenting and positive discipline.

PARENTING WITH LOVE AND LOGIC (Audiotape)
Teaching Children Responsibility

 Recommended For:
Growth & Learning

Description:
Adapted from the book by the same name, this audio version is divided into four tapes with a total running time of about 3 1/2 hours. The authors' philosophy centers on using love and logic while parenting. The authors define love as not permissive or tolerant of disrespect, but that which allows children to make mistakes and live with the logical consequences; logic is centered in the consequences themselves. Parenting then becomes an issue of offering a child choices along with empathy if the child makes mistakes in the process. The first part of the audio discusses general parenting issues: self-concept, setting limits, offering choices, consequences, etc. The second part focuses on 30 (the book contained 41) love and logic "Pearls" (tips) for dealing with problems parents encounter during the first 12 years of their child's life. Included here is advice about dealing with anger, bedtime, chores, temper tantrums, fears and monsters, television watching, and more. The second part is intended to be used in conjunction with Part One.

Evaluation:
The love and logic approach focuses on providing parents the opportunity to "put the fun back into parenting" while raising responsible children. The narration on the tape, like the writing style of the book, sets a comfortable, down-to-earth mood and the information is easily digested. Whereas the book contains too many stories that tend to muffle the information, this abridged version is succinct and flows quite well. The two parts of the audiotape not only present the philosophical elements of "love and logic" but also validate these concepts with practical tips and real-life examples; numerous sample dialogues are given for how to talk with one's child. The audiotape also highlights many issues not often included in other resources on the same subject. Some of these issues include back-seat car battles, table manners, bossiness, allowances/money, and telephone interruptions. Other resources also offer positive approaches to dealing with children's behavior; this tape would be a helpful resource to be used in conjunction with them.

Where To Find/Buy:
Bookstores and libraries, or order direct by calling 1-800-338-4065.

POSITIVE DISCIPLINE A–Z
1001 Solutions To Everyday Parenting Problems

 Recommended For:
Growth & Learning

Description:

This 354-page reference book is divided into three parts. Part 1 offers "basic positive discipline parenting tools." Some of the 27 topics discussed within this part include: family meetings, choices, consequences, follow-through, humor, special time together, and more. Part 2 offers "positive discipline solutions." Some of the issues addressed include adoption, bedtime hassles, disrespect, divorce, materialism, defiance, whining, and more. Part 3 offers "short tips" (one paragraph each) for avoiding common problems encountered by parents of young children and teenagers. Each issue is discussed and a plan detailed using the bold subheadings: "Understanding Your Child, Yourself, and the Situation"; "Suggestions"; "Planning Ahead to Prevent Future Problems"; "Life Skills Children Can Learn"; "Parenting Pointers"; and "Booster Thoughts." A "How to Use This Book" section offers six guidelines to help your child gain courage, confidence, and life skills. A comprehensive index is also included.

Evaluation:

Although certainly not addressing ALL of a preschoolers' discipline problems, this book directs parents to advice and suggestions on some of the most common. This well-written, easily understandable resource offers 1000+ solutions to issues such as birth order, cruelty to animals, masturbation, tattling, and more. Its value lies in that it offers not only advice, but also encourages parents by presenting "pointers" and reinforcing "Booster Thoughts" for each discipline solution. The authors' purpose is twofold: to enable parents to increase their self-confidence while solving problems with their children; consequently their children will be presented with positive models so they can become successful at problem-solving on their own. The authors stress that parents need to focus on enjoying their child by using understanding, compassion, and wisdom, instead of seeking perfection as a goal. Offering logical and practical advice, parents should look to this resource as one of the better guides for teaching discipline to their child.

Where To Find/Buy:

Bookstores and libraries, or order direct by calling (916) 632-4400 or 1-800-456-7770. FAX orders can be placed by dialing 1-800-377-2811.

Overall Rating
★★★
Short, simple "what to do" solutions that not only support the parent but also the child

Design, Ease Of Use
★★★★
Alphabetical listing of "problems"; consistent, bold headings separate sections

1–4 Stars; N/R = Not Rated

Media Type:
Print

Price:
$14.95

Principal Subject:
Growth & Learning

Age Group:
All Ages (0–5)

ISBN:
1559583126

Edition Reviewed:
1993

Publisher:
Prima Publishing

Author/Editor:
Jane Nelsen, Ed.D., Lynn Lott, M.A., M.F.C.C., and H. Stephen Glenn

About The Author:
(From Cover Notes)
Jane Nelsen, Ed.D. is a lecturer and has authored previous books. Lynn Lott, M.A., M.F.C.C. is a speaker and therapist. H. Stephen Glenn pioneered the Developing Capable People course which teaches skills for living and building strong relationships.

Overall Rating
★★★
Offers parents verbal cues for staying in control of potential conflicts with their child

Design, Ease Of Use
★★★
Rambles at times, but fairly succinct in identifying main points; concrete examples given

1–4 Stars; N/R = Not Rated

Media Type:
Audiotape

Price:
$11.95

Principal Subject:
Growth & Learning

Age Group:
All Ages (0–5)

ISBN:
0944634354

Edition Reviewed:
1996

Publisher:
The Love and Logic Press

Author/Editor:
Jim Fay with Foster W. Cline, M.D.

About The Author:
(From Cover Notes)
Jim Fay, with over 30 years experience in education, is one of America's most sought-after consultants and presenters. He is the author of over 90 books, tapes, and articles on parenting and positive discipline.

LOVE ME ENOUGH TO SET SOME LIMITS
Building Your Child's Self-Esteem With Thoughtful Limit Setting

Description:

Using an interview format, the writers of *Parenting with Love and Logic* highlight their parenting technique. They believe that "love" allows children to grow through their mistakes while "logic" allows children to live with the consequences of their choices. This 65 minute audiotape explains how to set limits and offer children choices. Tips for dealing with specific situations are also given (homework, bedtime, clothes, music, friends, chores, using the car, curfews, sibling fights). The authors believe that setting firm limits builds children's self-concept and self-esteem and that children "desperately need limits." They differentiate between "fighting words" (telling them what not to do) and "thinking words" (giving them choices while implying the consequences will always be there). Fay states that if parents use thinking words, dignity, and respect, then their children will treat their parents the same way. A "direct correlation" between good school performance and setting limits on early behaviors is also suggested.

Evaluation:

Parents who don't have the time to read the authors' book will glean the important points through this audiotape. It generally tends to be succinct, although the authors do ramble at times leaving the listener wondering where they are going. Several concrete examples of how to deal with certain situations are given, a quality lacking in one of their other tapes. Although mostly directed at parents of teenagers, parents of younger children will be able to pick out main ideas; in fact, Fay states that limits are established when parents begin responding to children's cries. Of particular use for many parents will be the numerous verbal examples given for what to say in given situations. Emphasis was on parents doing mental preparation by rehearsing what they will do and say to their child before a repeated behavior occurs. They state that this will put the parent in control and avoid "brain drains" and arguments. Parents will find this tape a good reflection of the authors' key points and worth their time and money.

Where To Find/Buy:

Bookstores and libraries, or order direct by calling 1-800-338-4065.

POSITIVE DISCIPLINE (Audiotape)
Teaching Children Self-Discipline, Responsibility, Cooperation, And Problem-Solving Skills

Description:

In this 90 minute audiotape taken from one of her workshops, Nelsen discusses concepts from her book *Positive Discipline*. The tape begins by discussing three parenting styles (authoritarian, permissive, democratic) and then illustrates Nelsen's method. Drawn from the beliefs of Adler and Dreikurs, "positive discipline" is defined as firmness with dignity, kindness, and respect. Its goals are twofold: to teach children self-discipline, responsibility, cooperation, and problem-solving skills; and to always be positive with no humiliation for the child or the adult. Key practices and concepts include: treating mistakes as opportunities to learn, seeking solutions to problems together as a family (rather than blame), believing that children do better when they feel better, the "significant seven" of successful people ("I am capable," etc.), children listen to parents when they feel listened to, and more. Consisting of audience Q & A's along with a lecture-type format, Nelsen interjects stories from her personal experience as a mother of seven children along with other narrative examples to illustrate her points.

Evaluation:

Parents will be drawn into Nelsen's tape from the beginning as she presents examples of how various situations are handled based upon three different parenting styles; many parents will perhaps be surprised that "positive discipline" does not imply permissiveness, or what Nelsen refers to as "anarchy." Nelsen does a fine job of pointing out how positive discipline offers parents constructive ways to approach a child's mistake, techniques to develop problem-solving strategies as a family, and tips on how to make decisions together. In effect, Nelsen's strategies work toward enhancing family communication skills and may offer strong alternatives to discipline techniques that no longer work for parents. This tape mirrors the generalities of positive discipline coupled with some specifics (dealing with morning, mealtime, bedtime hassles, etc.). If parents are looking for solutions to specific problems, we suggest they read her book, *Positive Discipline A–Z*. This resource is best used for auditory learners and/or large groups of parents.

Where To Find/Buy:

Bookstores and libraries, or order direct by calling 1-800-456-7770.

Overall Rating
★★★
Straight-forward approach that treats mistakes as chances to learn, not punitive

Design, Ease Of Use
★★★
Rambling at times, examples are excellent; best used in conjunction with the text

1–4 Stars; N/R = Not Rated

Media Type:
Audiotape

Price:
$10.00

Principal Subject:
Growth & Learning

Age Group:
All Ages (0–5)

Publisher:
Empowering People Books, Tapes & Videos

Author/Editor:
Jane Nelsen, Ed.D.

About The Author:
(From Cover Notes)
Nelsen, a licensed family/marriage therapist and former elementary school counselor, has ten years experience as a college instructor in Child Development and was the Director of Project ACCEPT (Adlerian Counseling Concepts for Encouraging Parents and Teachers).

Overall Rating
★★★
Effectively shows the value of setting boundaries & alternatives to punitive discipline

Design, Ease Of Use
★★★
Concise table of contents with follow up Index

1–4 Stars; N/R = Not Rated

Media Type:
Print

Price:
$14.00

Principal Subject:
Growth & Learning

Age Group:
Preschoolers (3–5)

ISBN:
1559584971

Edition Reviewed:
1995

Publisher:
Prima Publishing

Author/Editor:
Jane Nelsen, Ed.D., Cheryl Erwin, and Roslyn Duffy

About The Author:
(From Cover Notes)
Nelson is a lecturer and author. Erwin is the parenting education trainer for a non-profit family resource center (Reno, Nevada). Duffy is the director and founder of the Better Living Institute (Seattle, Washington) and director of a Montessori school since 1979.

POSITIVE DISCIPLINE FOR PRESCHOOLERS
For Their Early Years—Raising Children Who Are Responsible, Respectful And Resourceful

Best Resource For:
Understanding preschoolers' behavior and appropriate ways to discipline

Description:
Each of the 20 chapters in this 315 page book focuses on setting appropriate boundaries for young children from birth on. Advice and insight are offered for raising a responsible, respectful, and resourceful child. This guide provides possible solutions to mastering preschooler challenges, such as sleeping, eating, and potty training issues, with the goal being to encourage positive behavior and teach independence. Chapters 3 and 4 highlight a child's first and second year of life. Emotional development, nursing, self-trust, and sleeping with parents are several of the topics covered in these chapters. Chapters 5 and 6 afford perspective on a preschooler's temperament and includes positive discipline skills; Chapter 15 addresses the differences between discipline and punishment. Other sections offer information for children who need special help (ADD, ADHD, etc.). Chapter 20 focuses on establishing a support system—learning from the wisdom of others, taking care of yourselves, and focusing on the joys of parenthood.

Evaluation:
This book is all about learning from mistakes and turning them into positive successes. It is just one of eight books in the "Developing Capable People Series." The authors want to convey to the reader that this book is about children, how each of them is different, and how this book will help one to know what the world is like for the child. Highlights of this book are Chapter 6's discussion on the nine temperaments of children (varying degrees of active and passive characteristics) and Chapter 10—"The Messages of Misbehavior." The former dispels the myth of "the perfect child" while the latter offers help on understanding the roots of and solutions to "misbehavior." The book is filled with anecdotal information which can only help the parent to raise children who are "responsible, respectful and resourceful."

Where To Find/Buy:
Bookstores and libraries, or order direct by calling 1-800-456-7770 or (916) 632-4400.

POSITIVE DISCIPLINE (Videotape)

Description:

Presented in a two-part, two hour video, Nelsen discusses concepts from her book *Positive Discipline* as presented from one of her workshops for parents and teachers. Consisting of bulleted points and a lecture-type format, Nelsen interjects stories from her personal experience as a mother of seven children along with classroom stories to illustrate her points. Drawn from the beliefs of Adler and Dreikurs, "positive discipline" is defined as firmness with dignity, kindness, and respect. The goals of positive discipline are twofold: to teach children self-discipline, responsibility, cooperation, and problem-solving skills; and to always be positive with no humiliation for the child or the adult. Key concepts to this discipline practice include: treat mistakes as opportunities to learn, seek solutions to problems (rather than blame) together as a family, believe that children do better when they feel better, the "significant seven" of successful people ("I am capable," etc.), children listen to parents when they feel listened to, and more.

Evaluation:

Nelsen does a fine job here illustrating the key concepts of "positive discipline." Parents will not only learn ways to interpret their child's mistakes differently but also ways to enhance communication skills as a family. Offering parents constructive ways to approach a child's mistake, developing problem-solving strategies as a family, and by making decisions together, Nelsen offers strong alternatives to techniques that no longer work for parents. However, if parents are looking for solutions to specific problems, they might well read her book, *Positive Discipline A–Z*. A "study guide" accompanies these tapes and will be useful in zeroing in on the crucial elements of Nelsen's message. This workbook's format gives parents the opportunity to reflect on how they have used the various principles, along with ways of visualizing different future responses, thereby allowing parents to process the material and not rely on it as a step-by-step program. This resource is best used for auditory learners and/or large groups of parents.

Where To Find/Buy:

Bookstores, libraries, videotape dealers, or order direct by calling 1-800-456-7770.

Overall Rating
★★★
Relays key concepts and practice of positive discipline; best used for large parent groups

Design, Ease Of Use
★★★
Rambling at times due to personal stories; key concepts written on cue cards for review

---

1–4 Stars; N/R = Not Rated

Media Type:
Videotape

Price:
$49.95

Principal Subject:
Growth & Learning

Age Group:
All Ages (0–5)

Edition Reviewed:
1988

Publisher:
Empowering People

Author/Editor:
Jane Nelsen, Ed.D.

About The Author:
(From Cover Notes)
Nelsen, a licensed family/marriage therapist and former elementary school counselor, has ten years experience as a college instructor in Child Development and was the Director of Project ACCEPT (Adlerian Counseling Concepts for Encouraging Parents and Teachers).

Overall Rating
★★★
Excellent companion to positive discipline focusing on emotions underlying behavior

Design, Ease Of Use
★★★
Easily read, but should be read cover to cover; self-tests given; numerous anecdotes

1–4 Stars; N/R = Not Rated

Media Type:
Print

Price:
$22.00

Principal Subject:
Growth & Learning

Age Group:
Toddlers & Preschoolers (1–5)

ISBN:
0684801302

Edition Reviewed:
1997

Publisher:
Simon & Schuster

Author/Editor:
John Gottman, Ph.D., with Joan DeClaire

About The Author:
(From Cover Notes)
Gottman is a professor of psychology at the University of Washington. Since 1979 he has held a National Institute of Mental Health Research Scientist Award. DeClaire is a senior editor for Microsoft's *Pregnancy and Childcare*, an on-line consumer health-info service.

THE HEART OF PARENTING (Print)
How To Raise An Emotionally Intelligent Child

Description:
Gottman coins the term "Emotion Coaching" to describe his five-step process of teaching children how to understand and manage their emotions. This 239 page guide is divided into seven chapters with an appendix of recommended children's books on emotions, a notes section, and an index. Chapter One outlines the benefits of using Emotion Coaching along with details of Gottman's study (two 10 year studies of 120+ families). Chapter Two describes four different parenting styles (dismissing, disapproval, laissez-faire, emotion coaching) and their responses to children's emotions; an 81 item self-test is provided to determine your parenting style. The five key steps of Emotion Coaching are outlined in Chapter Three. Chapter Four presents some strategies to deal with possible communication blocks between parent and child. Chapter Five discusses marriage, divorce, and children's emotions. "The Father's Crucial Role" is outlined in Chapter Six and how to continue Emotional Coaching as your child grows is the topic of Chapter Seven.

Evaluation:
Defining emotional intelligence as being able to "concentrate better, have better peer relationships, higher academic achievement, and good health," Gottman's study doesn't focus on how to teach children to behave. It doesn't teach parents how to discipline. Instead, Emotion Coaching may help lead some parents to more constructive ways of dealing with emotional outbursts from their child and open better lines of communication. With numerous personal and professional anecdotes, he explains the five steps: become aware of the child's emotion, recognize the emotion as a chance for intimacy and teaching, listen empathetically and validate the child's feelings, help the child label the emotion, and set limits while problem-solving. Bordering sometimes on the edge of psycho-babble, nonetheless, Gottman's message is well-founded. Providing evidence of how emotional intelligence can affect children's school performance, their physiological responses to stress, and the ability to withstand difficult social situations in middle childhood, this process may supply added strategies for dealing with children's behavior and emotions.

Where To Find/Buy:
Bookstores and libraries.

WITHOUT SPANKING OR SPOILING
A Practical Approach To Toddler And Preschool Guidance

Description:

Based on parent effectiveness training, behavior modification, transactional analysis, and the Adlerian-Dreikurs approach, the methods in this guidebook are designed for use with toddlers and preschoolers. This 126 page guide is separated into seven chapters. Chapter 1 focuses on three "support skills" for guiding children: parental values, developing reasonable parental expectations, and encouraging self-esteem. Chapter 2 offers a problem-solving approach for dealing with challenging behaviors. Chapters 3, 4, 5, and 6 detail strategies for avoiding conflicts, encouraging appropriate behavior, instilling new behaviors, and modifying inappropriate behavior. Chapter 7 integrates these strategies by showing how two parenting situations were resolved using the author's techniques. Appendix One offers "150 ideas for common problems" with ten examples of how to use the techniques in the book to solve problems. Appendix Two includes summary sheets for the book's featured "Ten Tools." An index is also given.

Evaluation:

By offering 32 alternatives to spanking, and over 150 ways to resolve many of the conflicts parents experience today, this is truly a working resource. The numerous worksheets, exercises, and charts included in this resource will be of great help to many parents, caregivers, and teachers. By helping to isolate and break down problem behaviors, parents will be more apt to take a proactive stance rather than reacting negatively to issues. Parents are encouraged to determine what their goals are for their children, then choose the best course of discipline, and develop their own "effective, loving style of parenting." Although not necessarily an easily-read book, it is a resource well worth parents' time if they are finding themselves in a quandary about which type of discipline is best. Based upon the personalities of the parent and child, this book may offer parents some welcome relief and additional ideas for how to deal with conflicts that arise.

Where To Find/Buy:

Bookstores and libraries, or order direct by calling 1-800-992-6657.

Overall Rating
★★★
Lots of information for dealing with early childhood problems in a workbook format

Design, Ease Of Use
★★★
Table of Contents is comprehensive but best read cover to cover; numerous worksheets

1–4 Stars; N/R = Not Rated

Media Type:
Print

Price:
$14.95

Principal Subject:
Growth & Learning

Age Group:
Toddlers & Preschoolers (1–5)

ISBN:
0943990742

Edition Reviewed:
2nd (1993)

Publisher:
Parenting Press

Author/Editor:
Elizabeth Crary

About The Author:
(From Cover Notes)
Elizabeth Crary is a parent educator who has over 20 years of experience in teaching parenting classes. She currently teaches at North Seattle Community College in Seattle, Washington.

Overall Rating
★★★
Unique approach clearly presented and well-illustrated; expect long-term use

Design, Ease Of Use
★★
Adequate table of contents & index; heavy text style, caps in chapter subheadings help

1–4 Stars; N/R = Not Rated

Media Type:
Print

Price:
$12.00

Principal Subject:
Growth & Learning

Age Group:
All Ages (0–5)

ISBN:
0380719541

Edition Reviewed:
1994

Publisher:
Avon Books (Hearst Corporation)

Author/Editor:
Barbara Coloroso

About The Author:
(From Cover Notes)
Barbara Coloroso, a former schoolteacher, is an internationally known speaker in the areas of parenting, teaching, positive school climate, and nonviolent resolution.

KIDS ARE WORTH IT!
Giving Your Child The Gift Of Inner Discipline

Description:
This book is based upon the author's parenting theory of teaching children to believe, think, and respect themselves, thus, becoming responsible, resourceful, resilient, and loving individuals who have the gift of inner discipline. She shows how to do this in 14 chapters. Chapter 2 speaks to three kinds of families: "Brickwall," "Jellyfish," and "Backbone" and the characteristics of each; how they respond to various situations is explained throughout the rest of the book. Chapter topics include: keeping your cool, dealing with serious problems (getting your child out of jail, etc.), money, toilet training, sexuality, and more. The author demonstrates that her "answer [to these situations] is more an approach to parenting than a collection of techniques." The author further states that having an attitude in which parents believe kids are worth it, treating them in a way parents would want to be treated, and behaving in a way that leaves dignities intact will provide an environment to help children develop self-discipline.

Evaluation:
The underlying theme in this book is "The Golden Rule." Drawing from her experience as a nun, and now as a parent of teenagers, the author outlines an approach that allows the child to be responsible for themselves instead of being reliant on external rewards, incentives, and punishments. It is a refreshing point-of-view, and clearly outlined and illustrated. The book's 253 pages offers insights on why discipline is not learned through threats and bribes, offering instead the impetus to teach children HOW to think. The book also provides good news about the strong-willed child, and how to buffer your child from the dangers of sexual promiscuity, drug abuse, and other self-destructive behavior. Although heavy with text at times, this book and its inspirational quotes, will help parents find alternative ways to deal with "problems." Although superficially more relevant for parents of teenagers, parents of young children will glean a well-thought out foundation for "disciplining" their toddler or preschooler.

Where To Find/Buy:
Bookstores and libraries.

THE HEART OF PARENTING (Audiotape)
Raising An Emotionally Intelligent Child

Description:

Gottman coins the term "Emotion Coaching" to describe his five-step process of teaching children how to understand and manage their emotions. This abridged version of his book is presented in two audiotapes with a running time of 3 hours. The benefits of Emotion Coaching are discussed along with details of his study (two 10 year studies of 120+ families). Four different parenting styles are described (emotion coaching, dismissing, disapproval, laissez-faire) and their responses to children's emotions; a self-test booklet accompanies the tapes with an 81 item self-test to determine your parenting style. The five key steps of Emotion Coaching are outlined (awareness of the child's emotion, recognize it as a chance for intimacy and teaching, listen with empathy and validate the child's feelings, label the emotion, and set limits while problem-solving) as well as strategies to deal with possible communication blocks between parent and child. The effects of marriage and divorce on children's emotions are also presented. The father's crucial role is explained as well as advice on how to continue Emotional Coaching as your child grows.

Evaluation:

Defining emotional intelligence as being able to "concentrate better, have better peer relationships, higher academic achievement, and good health," Gottman's study doesn't focus on how to teach children to behave. It doesn't teach parents how to discipline. Instead, Emotion Coaching may help lead some parents to more constructive ways of dealing with emotional outbursts from their child. With numerous personal and professional anecdotes, Gottman's advice sometimes borders on the edge of psycho-babble, but nonetheless, his message is well-founded. Providing evidence of how emotional intelligence can affect children's school performance, their physiological responses to stress, and the ability to withstand difficult social situations in middle childhood, this process may supply added strategies for dealing with children's behavior and emotions. Would we recommend the book over the audiotape? Gottman's voice is disappointing in its rather monotonous quality. The audiotape is convenient for those who "read" while driving or while doing other tasks, but a cross-referencing guide to the book would have been an added bonus.

Where To Find/Buy:

Bookstores and libraries, or order direct by calling 1-800-452-5589.

Overall Rating
★★★
Excellent companion to positive discipline focusing on emotions underlying behavior

Design, Ease Of Use
★★
Read by Gottman rather monotonously (3 hours); self-tests given in companion booklet

1–4 Stars; N/R = Not Rated

Media Type:
Audiotape

Price:
$17.95

Principal Subject:
Growth & Learning

Age Group:
Toddlers & Preschoolers (1–5)

ISBN:
1559274352

Edition Reviewed:
1997

Publisher:
Audio Renaissance Tapes (CPU)

Author/Editor:
John Gottman, Ph.D., with Joan DeClaire

About The Author:
(From Cover Notes)
Gottman is a professor of psychology at the University of Washington. Since 1979 he has held a National Institute of Mental Health Research Scientist Award. DeClaire is a senior editor for Microsoft's *Pregnancy and Childcare*, an on-line consumer health-info service.

Overall Rating
★★★
Practical down-to-earth tips to guide communications between parent and child

Design, Ease Of Use
★
Lots of information presented in a cluttered, rather distracting format

1–4 Stars; N/R = Not Rated

Media Type:
Print

Price:
$12.00

Principal Subject:
Growth & Learning

Age Group:
All Ages (0–5)

ISBN:
0380570009

Edition Reviewed:
1980

Publisher:
Avon Books (Hearst Corporation)

Author/Editor:
Adele Faber and Elaine Mazlish

About The Author:
(From Cover Notes)
Adele Faber and Elaine Mazlish are both graduates of New York University, and have taught at the New School for Social Research in New York and the Family Life Institute of Long Island University.

HOW TO TALK SO KIDS WILL LISTEN & LISTEN SO KIDS WILL TALK

Description:

This guidebook presents communication methods that "affirm the dignity and humanity of both parents and children." This 242 page, 7 chapter book is based on the authors' 6 years of experience with parents in their workshops. Numerous exercises, sample dialogues, and cartoon "dos" and "don'ts" are given for each chapter. The authors suggest that parents first flip through the book, but then progress through the chapters slowly in order doing the exercises as they go; they advise parents not to skip over any of the activities. The first chapter is about helping children deal with their feelings. Chapter 2 focuses on cooperation. Chapters 3 and 4 include alternatives to punishment and encouraging autonomy, respectively. Chapter 5 highlights ways to praise children. Chapter 6 discusses how to free children from "playing roles," i.e., self-fulfilling statements. Chapter 7 shows parents how to put to use the suggestions from the book. A summary, some additional resources, and an index conclude the book.

Evaluation:

This resource offers valid parenting points and great problem-solving strategies, but it tends to be a laborious read. Sample conversations interspersed throughout, response "fill-ins" for the reader, and amateurish cartoons make deciphering information a difficult and fatiguing operation. Despite inclusion of an index, readers may need to re-review the material in order to ferret out tips for specific topics. For some issues, the authors have written "scenes" to help the reader understand the proposed principles. Instead, these dialogues are confusing. The authors try to recoup in each chapter by including "A Quick Reminder" that sums up major points, but these lead to overkill and the weary search for information plods on amongst the poor style format. If parents are intent on reviewing this book, they need to thoroughly peruse the "How to Read and Use" section at the beginning.

Where To Find/Buy:

Bookstores and libraries.

TODDLERS AND PARENTS
A Declaration Of Independence

Description:

Brazelton, a pediatrician and parenting advocate, offers advice to parents and caregivers working with toddlers. Within the 249 pages of his book, he intermixes narrative paragraphs, set in a story-type format, with explanations of a toddler's actions and interactions. The book is divided into 11 chapters. The first chapter deals with the one year old's "Declaration of Independence" while the next 3 chapters focus on 15 month old toddlers in family day care, in sibling relationships, and living with a single parent (single mother, single father, working single mother). Subsequent chapters deal with the toddler at 18 months old, at two years old, and at thirty months old. Three of these chapters outline family scenarios and characteristics of the "Withdrawn Child," the "Demanding Child," and the "Unusually Active Child." A chapter is devoted to the 30 month old toddler's experience at day care, followed by chapters describing a toddler's sense of self and inner control; the importance of setting limits, the value of fantasy and imaginative play, language acquisition, role playing, and more are also described.

Evaluation:

While other resources have a tendency to be read much like a textbook, this one reads more like a novel. As a result, the toddler's behavior comes alive via the story vignettes used throughout to introduce Brazelton's responses to discipline situations, developmental issues, and more. However, this method of delivery results in a book that can't be read lightly; parents will need to read it from cover to cover to get the information and advice they need to help them through this tumultuous time and they will be unable to just jump in anywhere to get concise, succinct answers to their questions. Although an index is available, cross-references won't be of any assistance, if parents haven't read the chapter from the start to understand the dynamics of the sample family and the issues Brazelton addresses. On the other hand, if parents have the time to absorb Brazelton's engaging story telling style, they will glean some good advice and answers to their concerns. Otherwise, they need to look to other better organized resources that offer information in parent-sized bites.

Where To Find/Buy:

Bookstores and libraries.

Overall Rating
★★★
Interesting interplay between fictional stories, professional advice, and description

Design, Ease Of Use
★
Rambling, must be read cover to cover to get exact information; table of contents vague

1–4 Stars; N/R = Not Rated

Media Type:
Print

Price:
$17.95

Principal Subject:
Growth & Learning

Age Group:
Toddlers (1–3)

ISBN:
0440506433

Edition Reviewed:
2nd (1989)

Publisher:
Dell Trade (Dell Publishing/ Bantam Doubleday Dell)

Author/Editor:
T. Berry Brazelton, M.D.

About The Author:
(From Cover Notes)
Brazelton is clinical professor of pediatrics at Harvard Medical School and Chief of the Child Development Unit at the Boston Children's Hospital Medical Center. He is a leading authority on child development and a parent/ family advocate.

Overall Rating
★★
Concise dos and don'ts of 30 common behavior problems presented in a "first-aid" style

Design, Ease Of Use
★★★★
Table of contents lists all behaviors; easily read (bold headings, consistent format)

1–4 Stars; N/R = Not Rated

Media Type:
Print

Price:
$6.00

Principal Subject:
Growth & Learning

Age Group:
All Ages (0–5)

ISBN:
0671544640

Edition Reviewed:
1984

Publisher:
Meadowbrook Press (Simon & Schuster)

Author/Editor:
Jerry Wyckoff, Ph.D. and Barbara C. Unell

About The Author:
(From Cover Notes)
Jerry Wyckoff is a family therapist and adjunct professor in the Human Development and Family Life Department of the University of Kansas. Barbara Unell has written numerous articles, three books, and is an editor for "Twins" magazine.

DISCIPLINE WITHOUT SHOUTING OR SPANKING
Practical Solutions To The Most Common Preschool Behavior Problems

Description:
Containing 30 of the most common behavior problems, this 135 page guidebook offers nonviolent suggestions for disciplining preschoolers. A glossary of discipline terms begins the book followed by an outline of developmental milestones for children one to five. The authors suggest that parents read this first to understand their child's developmental stage so they can determine whether a certain kind of behavior is appropriate or not. The remainder of the book contains "chapters" of typically 3 pages each focusing on a given behavioral problem (aggression, messiness, dawdling, sibling rivalry, etc.). Each chapter offers a description of the problem, ways to prevent the behavior from occurring in the first place, ways to solve the problem (dos and don'ts), and a closing narrative that details a real-life situation in which parents successfully handled the problem. The two appendices include a checklist for childproofing your home and a feeding guide for young children. There is also a follow-up index.

Evaluation:
This handy book is for parents seeking brief, immediate, and direct practical answers to parenting questions concerning behavior and discipline. Based on over twenty years of behavioral research and the principal of "separating the child from the behavior," this book stresses nonviolent solutions while instilling self-esteem. It is well-laid out, in a quick, easy-to-read format. In their introduction, the authors thoughtfully guide you through the text describing how best to use this resource. Seven "ABCs" of disciplined parenting are offered to help focus parents: determine the specific behavior to be changed, describe to the child exactly how you would like them to change their behavior, praise, avoid power struggles, supervise children's play, and don't dwell on bad behavior. Although parents won't find in-depth answers here for solving more extreme behavioral problems (lying, stealing, etc.), parents will find it a helpful and handy reference used in conjunction with other behavioral guides.

Where To Find/Buy:
Bookstores and libraries, or order direct by calling 1-800-338-2232 or (612) 930-1100.

PARENT'S PRESCHOOLER DICTIONARY (THE)
Commonsense Solutions To Early Childhood Behavioral Problems

Description:

With topics listed alphabetically in the table of contents, this 274 page "Dictionary" includes 97 articles to help parents resolve behavior problems and answer questions about their young child. An index is included to locate "problems" cross-referenced under a different name. Each article, or topic, begins with a short introductory explanation, followed by a longer "What to Expect" section. This explains the commonality of the problem as well as why the problem occurs. Bulleted "How to Help" sections offer "Dos" and "Don't" advice on how to solve the problem. The author suggests that if you follow one of her suggestions, your child's "troublesome action will happen less often. If you follow all of the suggestions, the behavior will be gone within two weeks." A sampling of topics include: adoption, autism, mother and father absence, fear, selfishness, sexual molestation, thumbsucking, and twins. Topic discussions typically average 2–3 pages in length.

Evaluation:

Parents, caregivers, and teachers will find this resource helpful, due to its concise, innovative and easy to follow suggestions which will assist them in dealing with preschooler and toddler conduct. Verville has skillfully compiled answers and suggestions on a variety of issues to help parents build the confidence they need in dealing with those trying moments. The alphabetical table of contents affords rapid access, backed by a comprehensive cross-referenced index. All topics are noted on their pages by a corresponding letter in the alphabet to allow for the "dictionary" format. The "Dos" and "Don'ts" of the "How to Help" section contain suggestions that a parent can immediately apply. A unique feature of the book are the "Remember" paragraphs at the conclusion of each topic; they offer a short final word in a positive constructive tone rather like an adage. There is, however, a concern about this book: the author **guarantees** that problems will disappear if the reader follows her suggestions. Isn't that a bit presumptive?

Where To Find/Buy:

Bookstores and libraries.

Overall Rating
★★
Good reference when you need a quick decision

Design, Ease Of Use
★★★★
Topics listed alphabetically with a comprehensive cross-referenced index

1–4 Stars; N/R = Not Rated

Media Type:
Print

Price:
$24.50

Principal Subject:
Growth & Learning

Age Group:
Preschoolers (3–5)

ISBN:
0896032930

Edition Reviewed:
1995

Publisher:
Humana Press

Author/Editor:
Elinor Verville, Ph.D.

About The Author:
(From Cover Notes)
Elinor Verville earned her Ph.D. in clinical psychology from the University of Wisconsin. Her practice is dedicated to the behavioral problems in children. Dr. Verville currently resides in Tulsa, Oklahoma. She and her husband have three children.

Overall Rating
★★
Treats parents' role as that of a "wild animal trainer"; emphasis is on the "system"

Design, Ease Of Use
★★★
Good combination of seminar lecture, parent testimonials, role played scenes; expensive

1–4 Stars; N/R = Not Rated

Media Type:
Videotape

Price:
$44.98

Principal Subject:
Growth & Learning

Age Group:
Toddlers & Preschoolers (1–5)

ISBN:
0963386131

Edition Reviewed:
1990

Publisher:
Child Management

Author/Editor:
Thomas W. Phelan, Ph.D.

About The Author:
(From Cover Notes)
Phelan is a nationally renowned expert and lecturer on child discipline and ADD. He is a registered Ph.D. Clinical Psychologist and appears frequently on both radio and TV, and has been engaged in full-time private practice since 1972.

1-2-3 MAGIC (Videotape)
Effective Discipline For Children 2–12

Description:

This 120 minute videotape offers highlights from the book by the same title as developed by the author, a clinical psychologist, in 1984. The author's intent is to arm parents with a discipline method for children ages 2 to 12 which involves no shouting, arguing, or spanking. Believing that the two biggest mistakes parents make involve too much talking (rationalizing) and too much emotion (yelling, nagging, etc.), Phelan emphasizes that parents need to assume the role of a "Wild Animal Trainer" rather than thinking of their child as a "Little Adult." Some of the issues presented include controlling obnoxious actions, testing/manipulations children use, encouraging good behavior, tantrums, and more. The "1-2-3 Magic" system relies on, as the author states in his book, the belief that children "are born unreasonable and selfish, and it is our job to help them become the opposite." In his videotape, he further details the method's use for behaviors that parents want stopped (hitting, etc.) or started (chores, etc.), the six types of testing and manipulation children use, variations of "1-2-3," and more.

Evaluation:

"1-2-3" is a step process of disciplining children in a positive, caring environment. For example, when parents encounter unreasonable behavior, they say, "That's 1" (first warning). If no change occurs in the child's behavior, parents then hold up another finger and say, "That's 2." If there still is no change, then "3, take 5" sends the child off to his room for the "time out" of 5 minutes after which nothing further is said about the behavior. Combining footage from Phelan's seminar along with parent testimonials and acted out scenes, the videotape does a fine job showing the major points and the application of his method. The main problems we found with the tape are its cost, its length, and its tendency to drift at times. Much emphasis is placed on the "system" with little emphasis placed on communicating little more than "do as I say." Although this is yet another "cure-all" for inappropriate behavior, it may prove useful to those with an authoritarian style of parenting looking for alternatives to spanking. We recommend, however, that parents check out more than this resource for a more balanced view.

Where To Find/Buy

Bookstores, libraries, videotape dealers, or order direct by calling 1-800-442-4453.

365 WACKY, WONDERFUL WAYS TO GET YOUR CHILDREN TO DO WHAT YOU WANT
Tools For Everyday Parenting Series

Description:

This is a 102-page "idea book," offering 365+ suggestions for encouraging positive behavior in young children. The table of contents supports 9 sections. Each section is further divided into 3–5 subtopics. The first section is a review of "Magic Tools" and the ideas in the book are based on five points. These points include acknowledging good behavior, avoiding problems, setting limits, accepting feelings, and reducing power struggles. Other sections of the book involve developmental issues (saying "no," throwing food, etc.), safety conflicts (sharp knives, etc.), trouble with other kids (hitting, not sharing, etc.), everyday problems (whining, won't go to bed, etc.) and parenting in public (won't leave the park, tantrum in stores, etc.). Each subtopic includes a statement and definition of the problem, ideas of how to solve the problem, and a list of other resources. A "Just For Parents" section discusses ideas for alleviating frustration. The final section offers a list of additional resources for parents, followed by an index.

Evaluation:

Here is a light-hearted, comical look at how parents can solve inappropriate behavior in their young child and still keep their sense of humor. This book gives parents idea after idea on how to keep their sanity and still maintain a relationship with their children. Easy-to-read and in an unconventional format (5.5" x 8.5" soft cover), this "wacky" book delivers short, numerous, "pick-and-choose" suggestions for a wide variety of common, everyday problems. This resource also includes several development charts, reflective notes, and a brief index. The suggestions and ideas are always set to the positive side, while the reinforcing cartoons add a humorous approach that simply reiterates the text. It would have been more useful to use the cartoon format to illustrate other ways to deal with the problem other than simply repeating the text's message. Although not a comprehensive "text," this book would make for good conversation or a springboard for other tried-and-true methods within a parent forum.

Where To Find/Buy:

Bookstores and libraries, or order direct by calling 1-800-992-6657.

Overall Rating
★★
Light-hearted & entertaining book offering practical suggestions for everyday problems

Design, Ease Of Use
★★★
A quick read; both the contents and index are helpful; cartoons fun but rather repetitive

---

1–4 Stars; N/R = Not Rated

Media Type:
Print

Price:
$9.95

Principal Subject:
Growth & Learning

Age Group:
All Ages (0–5)

ISBN:
0943990793

Edition:
1995

Publisher:
Parenting Press

Author/Editor:
Elizabeth Crary

About The Author:
(From Cover Notes)
Elizabeth Crary has been a parent educator for 20 years and the author of 27 other books for parents and children.

Overall Rating
★★
Short, concise solutions probably won't satisfy most parents' needs for in-depth advice

Design, Ease Of Use
★★
Strong chapter subheadings & bulleted highlights useful; index would be helpful

1–4 Stars; N/R = Not Rated

Media Type:
Print

Price:
$6.00

Principal Subject:
Growth & Learning

Age Group:
All Ages (0–5)

ISBN:
0671527010

Edition:
1995

Publisher:
Meadowbrook Press (Simon & Schuster)

Author/Editor:
Dawn Lighter, M.A.

About The Author:
(From Cover Notes)
Dawn Lighter, M.A., is a family therapist. She has an M.A. in Family Counseling from the University of San Diego.

GENTLE DISCIPLINE
50 Effective Techniques For Teaching Your Children Good Behavior

Description:
This 107 page book is based on three steps toward growth: awareness, learning new skills, and getting support. It focuses on a nonviolent, gentle approach to discipline. The book has five parts. Part One offers parents ten ways of avoiding conflicts with their child (ignoring, walking away, choices, humor, etc.). Parts Two and Three center, respectively, on improving communication (clear commands, family meetings, etc.) and shaping your child's environment (simplify, enrich, limit, and organize). General guidelines for children, with positive and negative consequences, are given in Part Four, and Part Five closes with ten ways parents can meet their own needs. There is a listing of further suggested readings and resources as well as a two page bibliography. Each of the 50 techniques typically is covered in one page and the age groups for which this technique works best are given at the end of the explanation. Most of the techniques are suitable for the 2–19 year age range. No index is provided.

Evaluation:
Offering 50 simple, effective techniques for disciplining your child, this book focuses on teaching children good behavior, rather than simply punishing bad behavior. Many valuable solutions are given for parents on correcting misbehavior using a nonviolent authoritative approach. These solutions, however, are quite concise; parents wishing more in-depth examples will need to look elsewhere. Not only addressing the child's behavior, this guide is unique by taking into account parental bad habits as well; topics such as avoiding alcohol, not undermining your partner's authority, and recognizing when to seek psychological help are addressed in Part Five. The author also recommends various ways parents can stay in shape, physically and psychologically, so they can function better as a parent. The book is logical and sequential. It speaks to all families, regardless of lifestyles or environment, and would be useful in everyone's family library combined with other resources on behavior and discipline.

Where To Find/Buy:
Bookstores and libraries, or order direct by calling 1-800-338-2232.

NO MORE TANTRUMS
A Parent's Guide To Taming Your Toddler And Keeping Your Cool

Description:

Offering a "helpful compilation of parent-tested, child-tested solutions to . . . troublesome areas in child rearing," this 168-page, 18 chapter book strives to help parents deal with toddlers' behaviors. Chapter 1 offers parents tips on how they can keep calm during a child's outburst. Chapters 2 through 5 discuss sibling issues. These include how to manage a sibling's behaviors towards a new baby (sulking, pouting, etc.), along with how parents can include the older child in the care of the new baby. Most other chapters address situations where tantrums may erupt. These situations include sharing with other children, talking back, nagging and whining, tattling, name-calling, as well as lying and stealing, to name a few. Some of the suggestions are in the form of dialogue, while "starred" paragraphs offer the authors' insight, alternatives, and advice. Also included are tips on getting a child to bed at the appropriate time and establishing accepted behaviors in public places. The book supports a full index.

Evaluation:

Although the book's concise advice sometimes lacks depth, this upbeat guidebook does a good job of addressing toddler misbehavior. The book offers multiple solutions towards resolving sibling disputes, disciplining effectively, establishing rules, and encouraging positive habits in a sensitive, compassionate manner. The authors have wisely used humor in dealing with this subject matter, leaving the reader in a comfortable, no-stress environment. This approach shows parents the effectiveness of stepping back and thinking about their child's behavior first, before reacting to the heat-of-the-moment tantrum. Handling one's own temper first helps to eliminate the frequency of temper tantrums, suggest the authors. The book is easy to use with a larger print format. The index is a good back-up for a rather obscure table of contents with titles such as "The Taming of Some Shrews" and "War and . . . War." This resource will be best used to complement other books dealing with both the "whys" and "hows" of toddler behavior.

Where To Find/Buy:

Bookstores and libraries.

Overall Rating
★★
Lighthearted tips for dealing with toddler behavior but solutions could use more depth

Design, Ease Of Use
★★
Spread out larger print is great; vague chapter titles aided by comprehensive index

1–4 Stars; N/R = Not Rated

Media Type:
Print

Price:
$12.95

Principal Subject:
Growth & Learning

Age Group:
Toddlers & Preschoolers (1–5)

ISBN:
0809230704

Edition:
1997

Publisher:
Contemporary Books (NTC/Contemporary Publishing)

Author/Editor:
Diane Mason, Gayle Jensen, and Carolyn Ryzewicz

About The Author:
(From Cover Notes)
Diane Mason, Gayle Jensen, and Carolyn Ryzewicz are parents with a history of credits in journalistic, entrepreneurial, and educational endeavors.

Overall Rating
★★
Surface explanations for understanding a child's behavior; emphasis is on "the system"

Design, Ease Of Use
★
No index; somewhat obscure table of contents

1–4 Stars; N/R = Not Rated

Media Type:
Print

Price:
$12.95

Principal Subject:
Growth & Learning

Age Group:
Toddlers & Preschoolers (1–5)

ISBN:
0963386190

Edition:
2nd (1995)

Publisher:
Child Management

Author/Editor:
Thomas W. Phelan, Ph.D.

About The Author:
(From Cover Notes)
Dr. Thomas W. Phelan is a lecturer on child discipline and Attention Deficit Disorder. He is a registered Ph.D. Clinical Psychologist who founded the Illinois Association for Hyperactivity and Attention Deficit Disorder. He also appears on both radio and TV.

1-2-3 MAGIC (Print)
Effective Discipline For Children 2–12

Description:
This 180 page, 9 chapter guidebook highlights "one of the most popular child rearing programs in the country" developed by the author, a clinical psychologist, in 1984. The book's intent is to arm parents with a discipline method for children ages 2 to 12 that involves no shouting, arguing, or spanking. Some of the issues presented include controlling obnoxious actions, testing/manipulations children use, encouraging good behavior, tantrums, and more. The "1-2-3 Magic" system relies on, as the author states, the belief that children "are born unreasonable and selfish, and it is our job to help them become the opposite." He further details the method's use for behaviors that parents want stopped (hitting, etc.) or started (chores, etc.), the six types of testing and manipulation children use, and more. This newer edition also includes four new chapters for teachers of preschool to junior high, a chapter on dealing with behaviors in public, active listening, building self-esteem, and more. There is no index.

Evaluation:
The intent of the 1-2-3 system is a step process of disciplining children in a positive, caring environment. For example, when parents encounter unreasonable behavior, they say, "That's 1"; this is the first warning. If no change occurs in the child's behavior, parents then hold up another finger and say, "That's 2." If there still is no change, then "3" sends the child off to his room for the "time out." The book further explains how to get him to his room and other facets of the process. After the timeout, nothing further is said about the behavior. The guide is easy to understand, sometimes using a dialogue style format for clarity. So much emphasis is placed on the "system" that the book falls short on giving depth to the real issues of discipline. Very short, basic explanations are given for a variety of topics. An index would have helped for a rather obscure table of contents. This is just another attempted "cure-all" for inappropriate behavior in children. Check out more than this resource for a more balanced view.

Where To Find/Buy:
Bookstores and libraries, or order direct by calling 1-800-442-4453.

HOW TO READ YOUR CHILD LIKE A BOOK

Description:

There are five "developmental stages" to this resource guide. Stage 1 addresses "Trust" and includes information on children ages birth to eighteen months. It focuses on topics such as crying, fear, irritability, and more. Each topic is further divided into five subtopics: "Your Child's Behavior," "What Your Child May Be Thinking or Feeling," "What It Means," "What To Do," and "What Not To Do." Stage 2 addresses "Identity" issues for children eighteen months to three years old. Some of the topics covered are feelings, aggressive behavior, separation anxiety, and more. Stage 3 focuses on the "Competence" of three to four year olds and stage 4 explores "Power"—how four and five year olds test and push limits. Stage 5 discusses issues of "Self-Control" for children five to six years of age. Following these sections is a section on "Parting Remarks" which talks about responsible parenting. The book concludes with an "Assessment Checklist for Preschoolers" and a resource list. There is no index.

Evaluation:

This 213-page book does a good job of trying to help the reader comprehend each of the five developmental stages, presenting information in a logical, understandable sequence. However, some of the advice is rather concise and parents may find themselves asking for more information on a specific issue. The table of contents is vague with subtopic titles such as, "Expanding Interests," "Making Things Happen," etc.; a supporting index would have greatly helped this guide. Variances in children's personalities and developmental levels have not been keenly addressed in this guide. The reader will need to look beyond the author's concise suggestions keeping in mind that there is more than one way to address these developmental issues depending upon the personality of their child. Parents will most likely find this resource guide a better companion to a more comprehensive reference, instead of being used as a stand alone cure-all.

Where To Find/Buy:

Bookstores and libraries, or order direct by calling 1-800-338-2232.

Overall Rating
★★
Good content, although too concise for most subjects

Design, Ease Of Use
★
Vague titles in table of contents; book follows sequentially and smoothly along; no index

1–4 Stars; N/R = Not Rated

Media Type:
Print

Price:
$8.00

Principal Subject:
Growth & Learning

Age Group:
All Ages (0–5)

ISBN:
0671521241

Edition Reviewed:
1997

Publisher:
Meadowbrook Press (Simon & Schuster)

Author/Editor:
Lynn Weiss, Ph.D.

About The Author:
(From Cover Notes)
Lynn Weiss, Ph.D., is a child and adult psychotherapist, as well as a marriage, family, and mental health counselor. She also hosts a radio talk show in Dallas/Fort Worth and is a frequent commentator for CNN.

Overall Rating
★★
Useful tips & support for parents trying to balance authoritarian and attachment styles

Design, Ease Of Use
★
Table of contents vague, subheadings absent in some chapters; Q & A format for each topic

1–4 Stars; N/R = Not Rated

Media Type:
Print

Price:
$8.95

Principal Subject:
Growth & Learning

Age Group:
Toddlers (1–3)

ISBN:
0836228111

Edition Reviewed:
1993

Publisher:
Andrews and McMeel
(Universal Press Syndicate)

Author/Editor:
John Rosemond

About The Author:
(From Cover Notes)
John Rosemond is a family psychologist and director of the Center for Affirmative Parenting (CAP) in Gastonia, North Carolina. CAP is a national organization whose purpose is to provide families with advice and guidance in the raising of their children.

MAKING THE "TERRIBLE" TWOS TERRIFIC!

Description:
This 184 page book is based on Rosemond's "benevolent dictatorship" disciplinary style. As he states, successful parenting includes "Management, as opposed to punishment; Proactivity, as opposed to reactivity; Assertiveness, as opposed to anger; Consistency, as opposed to unpredictability; and Communication, as opposed to confusion." He aims to provide parents with a resource that is "low on theory and high on service" as their child moves through the "terrible twos." This guide supports seven chapters. Chapters 1, 2, and 3 discuss ways to understand a two-year-old, how to encourage their healthy development, and methods of managing discipline. Chapter 4 talks about toilet training, and the final chapters, 5, 6, and 7, contain information on bedtime routines, aggressive behaviors, and day care vs. parent care. Most chapters focus on the author's point of view primarily based on books by Dr. Burton White. Chapters contain parent anecdotes about the given topic and finish in a question and answer format.

Evaluation:
Rosemond interjects humor, his professional experience in psychology, and his consistent principles to help parents understand and cope with their two-year-old's development. His point is that a household must be parent-centered, not child-centered. Successful parenting in his terms means three things need to happen: that children need to "pay more attention to the adult than the adult does to the child," children need to do as told, and parents must have the last word ("because I told you so"). He also offers tips on how to discipline (spanking is acceptable and defined). This guide must be read cover to cover since the titles in the table of contents and chapter subheadings are rather vague. Rosemond also has a tendency to ramble while dismissing others' points of views and espousing his own. The Q & A format at the end of each chapter is helpful for focused input on any given subject. Parents looking to strike a balance between an authoritarian parenting style and an attachment style may find their answers in this guidebook.

Where To Find/Buy:
Bookstores and libraries.

SETTING LIMITS
How To Raise Responsible, Independent Children By Providing Reasonable Boundaries

Description:

Mac Kenzie's discipline approach is aimed at helping parents "teach their children how to make acceptable choices and to truly understand the consequences of unacceptable behavior." Aimed primarily at schoolage children, these methods are also illustrated from age 2 through the teenage years. This 334 page guide contains twelve chapters. The first three chapters of the book are focused on "the family dance" and what doesn't work when establishing and learning rules. Chapters 4–8 illustrate ways that encourage cooperation, accountability, successful problem solving skills, and consequences. Chapter 9 shows parents how these methods can be applied to teenagers, with Chapters 10 and 11 offering suggestions on how these methods can be used to conquer conflicts involving chores and homework. Chapter 12 offers advice on how to implement this approach and how to deal with problems inherent in making this change. Advice on how to start a parent help group, a list of additional resources, and an index complete the book.

Evaluation:

Although this book is intended as a discipline guide for parents, teachers, and caregivers, it can also be helpful for anyone interested in improving the way they communicate with children. Emphasis in this method is placed on teaching rules and expectations for acceptable behavior without sending mixed or conflicting messages. Using many staged examples and diagrams to illustrate a point, the author has managed to meld the techniques together in a complementary progressive approach; useful for many will be the way he contrasts various parental responses to a given situation (permissive, democratic, punitive). All chapters conclude with a summary and a list of "Parent Study Group Questions" that provide parents and caregivers with useful skill-training exercises. However, parents will need to read the book cover-to-cover and stay focused to fully benefit from this technique. If they can clearly see the author's points and direction through the multitude of parent-child stories, it is worth their time.

Where To Find/Buy:

Bookstores and libraries, or order direct by calling (916) 632-4400.

Overall Rating
★★
Concepts and methods illustrated through numerous situational anecdotes

Design, Ease Of Use
★
Must be read cover to cover; chapter summaries useful but bulleted tips would also help

1–4 Stars; N/R = Not Rated

Media Type:
Print

Price:
$15.00

Principal Subject:
Growth & Learning

Age Group:
Toddlers & Preschoolers (1–5)

ISBN:
1559582200

Edition Reviewed:
1993

Publisher:
Prima Publishing

Author/Editor:
Robert J. Mac Kenzie, Ed.D.

About The Author:
(From Cover Notes)
Robert J. Mac Kenzie, Ed.D., an educational psychologist and family therapist has more than 13 years experience working with family behavioral problems. He provides family counseling and leads parent/teacher training workshops nationwide.

Overall Rating
★
Offers a historical basis, sprinkled with some scripture, for using corporal punishment

Design, Ease Of Use
★
Chapter titles in table of contents are rather obscure; does not contain an index

1–4 Stars; N/R = Not Rated

Media Type:
Print

Price:
$12.99

Principal Subject:
Growth & Learning

Age Group:
All Ages (0–5)

ISBN:
0884861775

Edition Reviewed:
1997

Publisher:
Inspirational Press (BBS Publishing)

Author/Editor:
James Dobson, Ph.D.

About The Author:
(From Cover Notes)
James C. Dobson, Ph.D., is founder and president of Focus on the Family. He has served as a consultant to the White House on family matters, has a national radio program, and was Associate Clinical Professor of Pediatrics at the USC School of Medicine for 14 years.

DR. JAMES DOBSON ON PARENTING
The Strong-Willed Child And Parenting Isn't For Cowards

Description:

This book contains two complete books written by Dobson. Reference notes follow each book. The first book, *The Strong Willed Child* (copyright 1978), has nine chapters. These include discussions about "Shaping the Will," "Protecting the Spirit," common parenting errors, sibling rivalry, hyperactivity, an evaluation of effecting parenting, and more. The second book, *Parenting Isn't For Cowards* (copyright 1987), has 12 chapters. This book discusses the challenge of parenthood, offers feedback from 35,000 parents about their children and themselves, gives suggestions for parents of young children, ways to handle "power games," and more. It also provides suggestions and advice to parents of adolescents, a question and answer chapter, and finishes with Dobson's inspired "Final Thought." There is an appendix following the second book consisting of a questionnaire/survey. There are numerous tables and explanatory charts interspersed throughout the book.

Evaluation:

This book rests primarily on Dobson's stated purpose to "verbalize the Judeo-Christian tradition regarding discipline of children and to apply those concepts to today's families." We would then hope that numerous scripture verses would be quoted to support his position, perhaps coupled with results from more recent child development studies regarding behavior and discipline. Instead, Dobson takes on a decidedly defensive posture lambasting many respected child development theorists. Dobson's first book begins with a story of how he taught his willful dog to obey commands by striking him. Dobson continues this analogy stating that "corporal punishment [a small switch or belt] . . . is a teaching tool by which harmful behavior is inhibited. . . ." He further states that he makes no attempt to validate or prove his suggestions and perspectives. If one wants a historical perspective on behavior and discipline, this resource can be helpful. Otherwise, other books offer a more well-rounded Christian base from which to parent.

Where To Find/Buy:

Bookstores and libraries.

PREVENTIVE PARENTING WITH LOVE, ENCOURAGEMENT, AND LIMITS
The Preschool Years

Description:
The authors define preventive parenting as an approach that requires parents to pay attention to their children's needs, interests, and behavior, and take into account what their children are learning from the way parents respond to situations. Within this 126 page book, parents will find eight chapters dealing with behavior and discipline. The authors recommend parents read the book cover to cover sequentially. The chapters have been designed to be read in about 10 minutes. A story vignette introduces each chapter with a concluding summary and home practice activities which are divided into two sections—a basic skill and an advanced skill. Chapter topics focus on: observing parent-child interactions ("key events"), teaching cooperation, focusing on positive behavior, using incentives, setting limits, using consequences and time out, "coaching children's friendships," and establishing family cohesiveness. No index is provided. A one page list of resources is given.

Evaluation:
Saving harried parents time is an admirable goal, since their time is at a premium. But, there's inherently a danger in not giving parenting topics the time they rightly deserve and, in effect, simplifying things too much, as it has been done in this resource. Certainly parents can handle more than a 10 minute slice of advice for understanding the roots of their child's behavior and how best to approach discipline. Yet, the authors dedicate little time here and too much time explaining the hows, whys, and why-nots of using incentives to change behavior. The authors place great importance on "key events," but rarely deal with them in-depth opting instead for the most obvious explanation or a convenient acronym to guide parents—"the PIE recipe for incentives." Parents reading this guide will get the impression that most behaviors can be modified by using a sticker, a star chart, or a cute keyword. They will most likely be left with more problems than they started with, like how to get rid of those stickers and star charts.

Where To Find/Buy:
Bookstores, libraries, or order direct by calling (541) 343-4433 or contacting Castalia Publishing, P. O. Box 1587, Eugene, OR 97440.

Overall Rating
★
Most advice is obvious and too simplistic; heavy reliance on acronyms for some messages

Design, Ease Of Use
★
Consistent chapter format nice, but has a vague table of contents with no index to help

1–4 Stars; N/R = Not Rated

Media Type:
Print

Price:
$10.95

Principal Subject:
Growth & Learning

Age Group:
Toddlers & Preschoolers (1–5)

ISBN:
0916154130

Edition Reviewed:
1996

Publisher:
Castalia Publishing

Author/Editor:
Thomas J. Dishion, Ph.D. and Scot G. Patterson

About The Author:
(From Cover Notes)
Dishion is a child psychologist, family therapist, and research scientist at the Oregon Social Learning Center. He is also an associate professor of counseling at the University of Oregon. Patterson has a BS in psychology and has been a coauthor of other books.

Overall Rating
★
Strong on the author's philosophy without offering alternatives for discipline

Design, Ease Of Use
★
Contains no index; difficult to find specific information through all of the fluff

1–4 Stars; N/R = Not Rated

Media Type:
Print

Price:
$12.99

Principal Subject:
Growth & Learning

Age Group:
All Ages (0–5)

ISBN:
0842305068

Edition Reviewed:
2nd (1992)

Publisher:
Tyndale House Publishers

Author/Editor:
James Dobson

About The Author:
(From Cover Notes)
James Dobson, a licensed psychologist, is president of Focus on the Family. He has earned several honorary doctorates and holds a Ph.D. in child development. He resides in Colorado with his wife. They have two grown children.

THE NEW DARE TO DISCIPLINE

Description:
These eleven chapters convey the author's approach towards disciplining children, which is based on his "understanding of the Judeo-Christian concept of parenting that has guided millions of mothers and fathers for centuries." Chapter One gives the author's premise by stating that, in order to be successful, parents must have courage, consistency, conviction, diligence, and enthusiasm. Chapters Two and Three discuss philosophies and methods as well as examining five concepts the author refers to as "commonsense" child rearing. Chapter Four is set in a question/answer format, and Chapters Five and Six discuss reinforcement principles. Chapters Seven, Eight, and Nine focus on the discipline needed in learning situations and the barriers involved. Chapter Ten discusses morality and Chapter Eleven offers suggestions on how mothers can cope with the rigors of parenting. Also included are a "Notes" section and an appendix listing narcotic drugs, their costs, indications of use, and slang vocabulary.

Evaluation:
This revised 277 page edition centers on the author's strong feelings about discipline and how parents should employ his techniques based upon the Scripture. He rarely backs up his premises, however, with quotes from the Bible. Focusing heavily on the author's ego and less so on parents' and children's needs, many parents will come away annoyed. Many of the concepts in this resource border on the ridiculous. For example, although the author suggests that corporal punishment should be an "infrequent occurrence," he belabors the hows, whens, whys, and whats (paddle or switch) of spanking throughout his book in an obviously defensive posture. He even has an opinion on how long a child should be allowed to cry after discipline (with the caveat that maybe the child needs another spanking). No back-up rationale for discipline is tendered other than Dobson's opinion. Other experts in the field treat misbehavior in a more well-founded manner.

Where To Find/Buy:
Bookstores and libraries.

TODDLERS
Love And Logic Parenting For Early Childhood

Description:

The authors, "internationally recognized parenting experts," offer their technique referred to as "love and logic parenting." "Love" allows children to grow through their mistakes while "logic" allows children to live with the consequences of their choices. This 114 minute audiotape (in two parts) is conducted in an interview-type format with numerous anecdotal stories. The authors believe that parents lay the foundation for their child's ability to internalize appropriate behavior and that this can be developed from the time a child is 6 months old; the critical period is when they are 8–12 months old. Descriptions of what parents do wrong and how they can better deal with issues (tantrums, testing limits, public displays, etc.) are given. Key practices involve: creating a parent-centered environment (where parents "say what they mean and mean what they say"); dealing with situations without anger, frustration, or threats; not rescuing children from consequences; treating situations with consistency; and more.

Evaluation:

The authors suggest that raising a toddler is not unlike training an animal. In fact, they state that one of the two things parents should do is to take a good dog discipline course. Although, this philosophy may help put some frustrated parents back in control who feel powerless, other parents may feel even more frustration. Numerous stories are given about what parents do wrong with warnings that the teenage years will then be troubled and riddled with drugs, disrespect, and other problems. Few positive examples are offered, and few practical strategies are given for dealing with situations; for example, for problems while shopping, it's suggested that someone else come along separately so they can drive the child back home if need be. The format flows like a Siskel & Ebert episode with the authors playing off one another. This rambling tape fails to give parents constructive input and it's chockfull of warnings. Parents will be better served reading their book instead of wasting time and money on this medium.

Where To Find/Buy:

Bookstores and libraries, or order direct by calling 1-800-338-4065.

Overall Rating
★
Rather negative with emphasis on warning parents who don't follow this philosophy

Design, Ease Of Use
★
Authors/interviewees tend to ramble with numerous anecdotal stories

1–4 Stars; N/R = Not Rated

Media Type:
Audiotape

Price:
$17.95

Principal Subject:
Growth & Learning

Age Group:
All Ages (0–5)

ISBN:
0944634443

Edition Reviewed:
1997

Publisher:
The Love and Logic Press

Author/Editor:
Jim Fay and Foster W. Cline, M.D.

About The Author:
(From Cover Notes)
Foster W. Cline, MD is a child and adult psychiatrist. He specializes in working with difficult children. Jim Fay has 31 years of experience as an educator and principal. He is an educational consultant and won many awards in the education field.

★★★★

Overall Rating
★★★★
Excellent examples and professional advice for parents working through sibling rivalry

Design, Ease Of Use
★★★★
Flows well, recap summary at end of tape; good mix of parent stories and professional advice

1–4 Stars; N/R = Not Rated

Media Type:
Videotape

Price:
$24.98

Principal Subject:
Growth & Learning

Age Group:
All Ages (0–5)

Edition Reviewed:
1994

Publisher:
Skydance Productions

THOSE BABY BLUES
A Parent's Guide To Helping Your Child Adjust To The New Baby

 Best Resource For:
Videotape offering advice about sibling relationships

 Recommended For:
Growth & Learning

Description:

Reported by Marcia Ladendorff (board member of the Childbirth Education Association), this 30 minute videotape offers both family stories and professional advice (Dr. Brenda Wade, psychologist and contributor for "Good Morning America;" Dr. Glen Aylward, professor of child and family psychology). Designed to "help you consider the situations you'll face before you're in the thick of things," this tape focuses on an older sibling's reactions to a new sibling. Discussions include changes in behavior, throwing tantrums, aggression, hidden hostility, regression, "nothing's wrong," withdrawal, and depression. Family stories are relayed with film footage showing sibling interactions. Each professional's perspective and advice is offered on how to handle given situations. Emphasis is on parents knowing their child's personality and ways to help them cope, acknowledging their feelings, noting and rewarding positive behavior, and more. A complimentary videotape for siblings—"Oh, Baby"—accompanies this one and is specifically intended "to trigger discussion in a more removed, less threatening context."

Evaluation:

Parents who are either wrestling with how to help an older sibling adjust to the birth of a baby, or parents who are already "in the thick of things," will be pleased with the information and support in this tape. Seeing family members' interactions directly coupled with the professionals' advice works extremely well here. Responses of an older child are addressed along with an understanding of their response in adult terms. For example, Wade draws a comparison between an older sibling's feelings when parents bring a new baby home to having one's spouse bring home a new wife, saying "Isn't she cute? She's so little . . . You'll grow to really like having her around." Free-flowing at times, the video neatly recaps all major points at the end offering a list and brief overview of warning signs, what to do for your child depending on their personality, and other major tips. Also provided is a list of organizations for further information; one organization offers information about classes for older siblings. We highly recommend parents invest their time and money in this resource. They'll walk away refreshed.

Where To Find/Buy:
Bookstores, libraries, and videotape dealers.

LOVING EACH ONE BEST
A Caring And Practical Approach To Raising Siblings

 Best Resource For:
Guide to understanding the dynamics of sibling relationships

 Recommended For:
Growth & Learning

Description:

With ten chapters, three appendices, and an index, this 210 page resource contains advice for parents as they cope with sibling conflicts, handle the ensuing stress, and adjust their lifestyle to the addition of a new sibling. Chapters 1 and 2 contain information about what to expect before and after parents give birth to baby number two. The stress involved with being a full-time mother, the roles fathers play, and ways to relieve stress are explored in Chapter 3. Some of the topics discussed in Chapters 4–7 include sibling conflicts, fairness and jealousies, recognizing the differences between children, and what parents can do when they feel angry about parenting. Chapter 8 offers interviews with children as they tell their side of the story. The final Chapters, 9 and 10, suggest ways to approach daily life in an upbeat manner by savoring the "lovely moments" and good times that family life can provide. The appendixes offer a reading list along with parent and child questionnaires used in writing this book.

Evaluation:

With humor and insight, this book uses a compassionate, caring approach to raising siblings. This easily read reference is based on the author's parenting workshops throughout the U.S. and includes advice from real parents who have survived the "aggravating and mystifying aspects of raising more than one child." Whereas most books dealing with sibling relationships are primarily child-centered, this book also focuses on the adults involved thus offering parents a refreshing new perspective. With a thoughtful and reassuring tone, the author details how many parents cope with the stresses involved with having a new sibling. Many parents will feel relieved that their silent thoughts, fears, and feelings are echoed here. Useful examples of positive and negative parent-child dialogues are presented along with bulleted tips, numerous suggestions, and chapter wrap-ups. With no heavy text or tables to wade through, this book should be required reading for worried parents bringing home baby number two.

Where To Find/Buy:

Bookstores and libraries.

Overall Rating
★★★★
Provides excellent advice and information and is very supportive of parents' needs

Design, Ease Of Use
★★★
Small print, but good spacing; bolder highlights would make it more user-friendly

1–4 Stars; N/R = Not Rated

Media Type:
Print

Price:
$12.95

Principal Subject:
Growth & Learning

Age Group:
All Ages (0–5)

ISBN:
0553378341

Edition Reviewed:
1996

Publisher:
Bantam Books (Bantam Doubleday Dell)

Author/Editor:
Nancy Samalin with Catherine Whitney

About The Author:
(From Cover Notes)
Nancy Samalin, a parenting expert, has written several other books. She is a consulting editor and columnist for *Parents* magazine, and is director of Parent Guidance Workshops which are known throughout the United States and abroad.

Overall Rating
★★★★
Script examples, cartoons, and anecdotes are major conveyance of authors' advice

Design, Ease Of Use
★★★
Easy read; text has a tendency to ramble at times

1–4 Stars; N/R = Not Rated

Media Type:
Print

Price:
$12.00

Principal Subject:
Growth & Learning

Age Group:
All Ages (0–5)

ISBN:
0380799006

Edition Reviewed:
2nd (1998)

Publisher:
Avon Books (Hearst Corporation)

Author/Editor:
Adele Faber and Elaine Mazlish

About The Author:
(From Cover Notes)
Adele Faber and Elaine Mazlish are noted for their work in adult-child communication. Both are sought after for their lectures and group workshop programs. They live in Long Island, New York. Each of them has three grown children.

SIBLINGS WITHOUT RIVALRY
How To Help Your Children Live Together So You Can Live Too

 Recommended For:
Growth & Learning

Description:

Consisting of eight chapters, this 250 page resource focuses on strategies parents can use when intervening in sibling rivalries. Chapter 1 illustrates the past and present relationship of a brother and sister presented in a story format. Chapter 2 focuses on expressing feelings and explores inner negative feelings. Chapters 3 and 4 deal with equality and comparisons between siblings. Chapter 5 addresses sibling roles and how to avoid locking children into descriptive stereotypes ("messy," "clean," etc.). Chapter 6 explains how to successfully intervene in conflicts and Chapter 7 contains advice on "making peace" with sibling relationships in one's past. Chapter 8, new to this edition, highlights parents' stories that illustrate how they coped and encouraged appropriate behaviors between brothers and sisters; also given are expectations for children who are home alone due to their parents' employment. Charts, reminders, comic strip Dos and Don'ts, and Q & As are presented in many chapters. An index is also given.

Evaluation:

This book was first published ten years ago and it became a best seller almost immediately. Now, after ten years of communicating with parents through letters, TV and radio talk shows, the same authors have released a tenth anniversary edition of their book with the addition of several new chapters. A large part of this resource continues to be based upon the authors' combined experiences with their own families and with those who participated in their workshops. If fact, the reader has the sensation of being in a workshop through this book, learning from the expertise of the authors and fellow participants. As such, stories make up much of this book's content. And, like a workshop, the story telling is dynamic and somewhat disorganized. So, if one is looking for clear answers to specific questions bolstered by a great, organized layout, this is not the resource. But if the reader wishes to have the sense that he/she is a fellow seeker with other parents who are tackling one of the toughest problems parents have to handle and that this is done in the midst of story telling and anecdotes, this is an appropriate resource.

Where To Find/Buy:

Bookstores and libraries.

WELCOMING YOUR SECOND BABY

Description:

Six questions, separated and explained in six chapters, make up this 99 page reference on welcoming a second baby into your home. Chapters 1, 2 and 3 contain information to help parents best prepare their child for the birth of a new baby, ways to help them adjust to mom's absence while in the hospital, and options to consider when deciding whether or not children should be present at the birth of the new baby. Chapters 4, 5, and 6 discuss how parents can keep their older child from feeling left out, how to help them accept the new baby, and ways to help their child handle special circumstances, such as adoption or Cesarean birth. Throughout each chapter are additional resources, (descriptions of books, videos, etc. for children, divided by age groups and topic; self-help groups; etc.), tips ("Prepare postcards or notes to mail your child from the hospital"), and highlighted blocks of quotes from parents offering their personal stories, experiences, and words of encouragement. An index completes the book.

Evaluation:

This resource strives to put parents at ease struggling with such concerns as whether or not they will love their second child as much as their first, feeling "disloyal" to their firstborn, and wondering if their second child will be a competitor for their attention and love. Giving advice and suggestions to help prepare parents and their child for the new arrival, the author has collected ideas and presented them in a concise, matter-of-fact format for quick-fix solutions. Interspersed throughout each paragraph are tons of additional age-appropriate resources, with information on where to buy them (when available). This guide is unique and very easy to read in its no-nonsense, bulleted note format, a quality that a busy parent in the throes of their pregnancy will appreciate. The table of contents is adequate and the index does a fine job as back-up. Parents may spend some time searching for specific topics, but the hunt will be well worth it.

Where To Find/Buy:

Bookstores and libraries, or order direct from Practical Parenting at 1-800-255-3379.

Overall Rating
★★★
Noteworthy collection of helpful tips and advice

Design, Ease Of Use
★★★★
Highlighted blocks of parent anecdotes; bulleted tips; clear topic and subtopic headings

1–4 Stars; N/R = Not Rated

Media Type:
Print

Price:
$6.95

Principal Subject:
Growth & Learning

Age Group:
All Ages (0–5)

ISBN:
916773124

Edition Reviewed:
3rd (1995)

Publisher:
The Book Peddlers

Author/Editor:
Vicki Lansky

About The Author:
(From Cover Notes)
Vicki Lansky has authored over 25 books, and is well-known for her column in "Family Circle" magazine and "Sesame Street Parents' Guide Magazine." She has also appeared on national TV shows like "Donahue," "Oprah," and "Today."

Overall Rating
★★
Helpful for understanding sibling dynamics, less useful for how to deal with rivalry

Design, Ease Of Use
★★★★
Clear, well-organized, well-referenced and indexed

1–4 Stars; N/R = Not Rated

Media Type:
Print

Price:
$10.00

Principal Subject:
Growth & Learning

Age Group:
All Ages (0–5)

ISBN:
0449906450

Edition Reviewed:
1995

Publisher:
Fawcett Columbine Book (Ballantine Books/Random House)

Author/Editor:
Judy Dunn

About The Author:
(From Cover Notes)
Judy Dunn is an international authority on childhood development, Distinguished Professor of Human Development at Pennsylvania State University, and also the recent recipient of a Guggenheim Fellowship. She has done extensive research in the field of sibling relations.

FROM ONE CHILD TO TWO
What To Expect, How To Cope, And How To Enjoy Your Growing Family

Description:
This 217 page guide contains three main sections with twelve chapters. The first two years of caring for two children, second pregnancies, how to prepare for the arrival of a second child, coming home from the hospital, the evolving sibling relationship, and more are all discussed in Part One's 7 chapters. Part Two contains 2 chapters. Sibling conflicts and competition, as well as violence and anger that arise in families are addressed. Part Three offers 3 chapters. These contain information about the differences between children, information about twins and siblings, and what to expect in terms of children's behavior in the coming years. Each chapter concludes with a summary of bulleted tips. An Appendix listing organizations, a one page bibliography, and a comprehensive index complete the book. The suggestions contained within the book are based upon the author's personal experience (twins and toddler under the age of 18 months) and 15 years of observing family and sibling relationships.

Evaluation:
If the reader's fears center on whether their older child can adjust to a new sibling, then this resource is worth checking into. This book's strength lies in the extensive observational research done by the author culminating in this book and others. It offers practical suggestions and advice on introducing a second child into the family. Parental burnout, the father's changing role, coping with the changing demands of a marriage, and ways of juggling schedules are just some of the issues addressed. Parents often wonder if they'll be able to love the second child just as much as the first without taking anything from the first. This book answers such concerns as these in a direct, reassuring, and practical manner. The summary at the end of each chapter with bulleted tips is quite helpful. The index is very extensive making up for the lack of bolder subheadings within the book. Coupled with other resources that offer more in-depth strategies for handling sibling rivalry, this book will prove an indispensable guide.

Where To Find/Buy:
Bookstores and libraries.

SURVIVING SIBLING RIVALRY
Helping Brothers And Sisters Get Along

Description:

One in a series entitled *Lee Canter's Effective Parenting Books*, this 48 page guide is all about warding off sibling conflicts. The book is divided into ten sections, beginning with questions and answers that parents most often ask. Some of these concern issues such as: jealousy, being fair, and establishing family rules. Sections following include information on why siblings argue and fight, how to create a positive environment, ways to prevent conflicts, and what do to when children continue to fight. The remaining sections suggest ways to resolve continuing problems and how to speak to your child so they will listen. There are interactive worksheets, such as a "Family Rules" chart, a "Cooperation Station" chart, a "Colossal Cooperation Award," and a "Sibling Contract" that are to be used in conjunction with the authors' suggestions within the sections. The book closes with the "Top 10 'Sibling Rivalry' Reminders" consisting of guidelines to help put sibling conflicts into perspective. This book does not contain an index.

Evaluation:

For parents at their wits' end with sibling squabbles and who are seeking a quick-fix, this positive book might offer welcome relief. It describes ways that families can cope with everyday stresses and it offers advice on how to keep conflicts to a minimum. The book seeks to help parents understand why conflicts evolve and what they might do to avoid ensuing confrontations. It also provides reassurance that sibling rivalry can be constructive and, as the authors state, siblings should be given the chance to work things out first before parental intervention. Several highlighted asides offer insight and advice on ways to create a positive environment. This guide offers good conflict management tools for parents through a role-play format with a stated "solution" following each proposed problem; verbal cues are provided for parents in most cases. Although the information here is given in concise "bits," parents will find it's worth a measure of their time.

Where To Find/Buy:

Bookstores and libraries, or order direct by calling 1-800-262-4347 or (310) 395-3221.

Overall Rating
★★
At times too concise; but provides good information especially for busy parents

Design, Ease Of Use
★★★★
Easy read despite not having an index; sibling contracts, charts, & awards provided

1–4 Stars; N/R = Not Rated

Media Type:
Print

Price:
$5.95

Principal Subject:
Growth & Learning

Age Group:
All Ages (0–5)

ISBN:
0939007770

Edition Reviewed:
1993

Publisher:
Lee Canter & Associates

Author/Editor:
Lee Canter and Marlene Canter

About The Author:
(From Cover Notes)
Lee and Marlene Canter are from the educational consulting firm Lee Canter & Associates. They are nationally renowned for their work in parenting and education.

Overall Rating
★★
Child-oriented approach that should allay siblings' fears and answer their questions

Design, Ease Of Use
★★★
Simplistic, easily shared; comic illustrations; reading level & larger print for older children

1–4 Stars; N/R = Not Rated

Media Type:
Print

Price:
$13.95

Principal Subject:
Growth & Learning

Age Group:
All Ages (0–5)

ISBN:
0818405783

Edition Reviewed:
1996

Publisher:
Lyle Stuart (Carol Publishing Group)

Author/Editor:
Cynthia MacGregor

About The Author:
(From Cover Notes)
Cynthia MacGregor is the editor of *Fresh Start*, and the author of many other parenting books. She lives in Lantana, Florida.

WHY DO WE NEED ANOTHER BABY?
Helping Your Child Welcome A New Arrival—With Love And Illustrations

Description:
This large format book, 9 1/2" x 9 1/2", is a children's book intended to be read aloud by adults to an older sibling. It has forty-three pages accompanied by full color comical illustrations. The print is large (approximately 1/4"). There is no table of contents. There is no index. There are several paragraphs of information written at a child's level on each page. This book acts as a vehicle for parents to answer the questions their children might have about a new baby coming into the family. Some sample questions presented include: "Do things seem a little different around your house lately?" and "If my parents love me so much, why do they need another child?" These are followed by simple explanatory information ("Maybe you've noticed that your mommy looks a little rounder . . . ") and then the book delves into the progression of pregnancy, birth, and siblings in general terms. This book centers on letting the older child know that parents can love more than one child and not be partial to the new baby.

Evaluation:
This is a whimsical resource meant to answer children's questions about a new baby in a charming, yet simple way. With humorous illustrations and the oversized print, this resource will most likely put to rest a child's fears and quell their anxieties about the new-baby-to-be. The book reassures the child that even though a new baby is joining the family, mommy and daddy still love him or her. It explains ways that siblings might interact with the new baby, such as reading to him or her, telling stories, or just feeling how great it is that babies always "look up" to an older brother or sister. Meant to be read by a parent to the other siblings, the book strives to include the older sibling in the care and feeding of the new baby. The illustrations are well done and entertaining. Children and adults alike should have fun with this book. Use it as an extension of other resources that offer parents strategies and advice for introducing a new baby into their established family life.

Where To Find/Buy:
Bookstores and libraries.

BABY AND I CAN PLAY & FUN WITH TODDLERS

Description:

This book is designed to help children play appropriately with their siblings. Using full page illustrations with one to two sentence captions, the book describes simple activities for children between the ages of 0–5. This guide suggests, for instance, that looking at a book together and making up stories about the pictures, is one activity siblings can do together. Part of the book is dedicated to solving problems commonly experienced by older siblings when a new baby is introduced into the family—jealousy, grabbing toys, hitting, etc. Parents are encouraged to read the book together with their child so that they may discuss and expand upon the activities and contribute ideas. The "Note To Parents" section in the back of the book offers questions to ask your child linked to page numbers within the book. Each question is followed by suggested activities for siblings and parents. The final page in the book lists problem solving books by other authors that may be ordered from the publisher.

Evaluation:

This book, while well-intentioned, is confusing at best and fails to explicitly identify a target audience—is it for the new baby, for parents, or for siblings? While the book may assume that very young children can read or that someone will read this book to them, comprehending its messages is another matter. The author woefully attempts in the back of the book to expand the illustrations' captions, buying into a clumsy "switch-back" referencing format. Many of the questions and comments listed in the "Note To Parents" section do not offer concrete solutions to the sibling problems discussed. Rather they are vague, repetitive, or condescending. This resource contains no table of contents or index. Readers must review, and re-review all 48 illustrated pages if they wish to seek specific activities. There is little unique information contained in this book. Other good books are available that target sibling relationships or activities to do with your baby. We recommend parents choose these resources instead.

Where To Find/Buy:

Bookstores and libraries, or order direct by calling 1-800-992-6657.

Overall Rating
★
Only useful for parents needing help with the basics of sibling interactions

Design, Ease Of Use
★
Difficult to reference; direction and intended audience confusing

1–4 Stars; N/R = Not Rated

Media Type:
Print

Price:
$7.95

Principal Subject:
Growth & Learning

Age Group:
Infants & Toddlers (0–3)

ISBN:
0943990564

Edition Reviewed:
1990

Publisher:
Parenting Press

Author/Editor:
Karen Henderickson

About The Author:
(From Cover Notes)
Karen Henderickson has worked as a special education teacher for preschools, and as a social worker in the public school system. She and her husband have two children.

Overall Rating

★

Simplistic answers (and reliance on a professional technique) to multi-faceted problems

Design, Ease Of Use

★

Amateurish quality; parent interview format doesn't work due to lack of solid advice

1–4 Stars; N/R = Not Rated

Media Type:

Videotape

Price:

$19.98

Principal Subject:

Growth & Learning

Age Group:

All Ages (0–5)

Publisher:

JVM Productions

SIBLING RIVALRY
The Healthy Parenting Series

Description:

Presented by "noted therapists and authors" Jean Rosenbaum and Veryl Rosenbaum, this 28 minute videotape is part of The Healthy Parenting series and focuses on sibling relations. Consisting of family interviews, parent stories, and interjections by the therapists, this video outlines various responses an older sibling may have to a new sibling. Reactions discussed include general reactions ("attention getting devices"—obnoxious noises, loud talking, hyperactivity, etc.), aggressive behaviors (hitting, excessive fawning, etc.), and regression (acting infant-like). Suggestions for how to handle negative sibling rivalry include: allowing the older child to express his negative feelings without fear of disapproval, inviting story-telling and drawings of the family as techniques for ridding aggression, encouraging opportunities for the older child to play with his peers, giving the older child special time with one or both parents, allowing the older child to participate with taking care of the infant, and more.

Evaluation:

A simplistic message using amateurish production techniques are the only way to best describe this tape. Parents want to know how to avoid sibling rivalry to begin with or they want some real answers to some real situations. The majority of the time spent on this tape, however, focused on one specific strategy (drawings by the child) credited by the therapist as the best way for ridding aggression. However, how many parents are trained to analyze children's drawings and the underlying emotions embedded within them? Other answers were far too obvious and simplistic. The narrator's first summary point was that an older child should feel loved and not be made to feel left out . . . pretty obvious. The narrator's second summary point was that an older child should be encouraged to express their feelings . . . again fairly obvious. Not quite as obvious is the narrator's third and final summary point that "the situation invariably resolves itself." Parents can more effectively resolve family squabbles by checking into better resources.

Where To Find/Buy:

Bookstores, libraries, videotape dealers, or order direct by calling 1-800-471-4109.

MOMMY I HAVE TO GO POTTY!
A Parent's Guide To Toilet Training

★★★★

 Best Resource For:
Guide to toilet training/learning

 Recommended For:
Growth & Learning

Description:

Based on four main points—respect, positive attitude, environment, and moderation, this 132 page book shows parents how to toilet train their child. There are nine chapters. Chapter 1 highlights "readiness" signs for toilet training; a checklist is given. Chapters 2 and 3 include toilet training in "Grandma's Day" and where to begin today. Chapters 4 through 6 discuss what do to if a parent's plan for training doesn't work, what kinds of reward systems do work, and how to deal with power struggles. Night Training and bedwetting are discussed in Chapter 7, and Chapter 8 focuses on problems such as constipation, bowel retention and encopresis. The final chapter summarizes all of the information by also discussing parenting styles and "final tips." Checklists, "Stories from the Bathroom" (parent narratives), and tables are interspersed throughout the book. Appendix A illustrates a graph showing "average children's toilet training progress." A suggested reading section and an index round out the book.

Evaluation:

With checklists, bulleted ideas and tips, and personal experience stories from parents, this resource is one of the better ones available to help parents toilet train their child. Faull states her advice is for today's broad-based group of parents. These are parents, she explains, who realize that there are differences in approaches from one generation to the next and that each child learns to use the toilet in their own unique way. Guidelines are given so parents can recognize developmental signs in their child. These will ensure that toilet training will be successful with "as little emotional upheaval as possible, in a time frame attuned to the child." Many parent narratives are given to introduce and support the author's message. This lends a personal, down-to-earth, easy-going style to the book. Although not all aspects of toilet training are addressed (twins/multiples, children with special needs), readers will glean a goodly amount of information to send them on their way towards success without diapers.

Where To Find/Buy:

Bookstores and libraries, or order direct by calling 1-800-992-6657.

Overall Rating
★★★★
Presents both toilet training philosophy & practice using a "parent-as-coach" attitude

Design, Ease Of Use
★★★★
Helpful index, excellent checklists, parent anecdotes, bulleted tips

1–4 Stars; N/R = Not Rated

Media Type:
Print

Price:
$13.95

Principal Subject:
Growth & Learning

Age Group:
All Ages (0–5)

ISBN:
0965047709

Edition Reviewed:
1996

Publisher:
Raefield-Roberts & Parenting Press

Author/Editor:
Jan Faull, M.Ed.

About The Author:
(From Cover Notes)
Jan Faull, M.Ed., is a parent educator with 20 years of experience teaching toilet training practices to parents. Author of a Q & A parenting column for the Online magazine "Family Planet," she is also a regular parenting expert on a local television station in Seattle, WA.

★★★

Overall Rating
★★★
A good amount of useful information sprinkled with humor in a concise book

Design, Ease Of Use
★★★★
Complete index; bulleted tips; lists of contacts for supplies and children's stories for aid

1–4 Stars; N/R = Not Rated

Media Type:
Print

Price:
$6.99

Principal Subject:
Growth & Learning

Age Group:
All Ages (0–5)

ISBN:
0553371401

Edition Reviewed:
2nd (1993)

Publisher:
Bantam Books (Bantam Doubleday Dell)

Author/Editor:
Vicki Lansky

About The Author:
(From Cover Notes)
Vicki Lansky has authored over 25 books, and is well-known for her column in "Family Circle" magazine and "Sesame Street Parents' Guide Magazine." She has also appeared on national TV shows like "Donahue," "Oprah," and "Today."

TOILET TRAINING
A Practical Guide To Daytime And Nighttime Training

 Recommended For:
Growth & Learning

Description:
Consisting of 107 pages and eight chapters, this guide presents information on toilet training your preschooler. Chapter 1 advises parents on how to tell if their child is ready. Chapter 2 details the choices available for toilet training (potty chairs, adult toilet adapter seats, footstools, and the family toilet). Chapters 3 and 4 discuss how to begin training along with opinions from noted child development experts (Brazelton, Leach, Ames, Azrin/Foxx). Chapter 5 includes advice on working with an uncooperative child. Chapters 6, 7, and 8 focus on toilet training under special circumstances, handling accidents, and dealing with bed-wetting. Interspersed throughout the book are bulleted tips, explanatory illustrations, and additional resources for parents along with lists of books, videos, games, and "surrogate" dolls that wet and use the toilet for children. Contact information for mail-order companies that carry potty seats and diapers is included. A single-page index completes the book.

Evaluation:
This is a basic, no nonsense guide offering clear advice for parents looking to toilet train their children. The author has done a fine job of defining toilet training, preparing parents for what to expect, and delivering a variety of solutions from which parents can choose, based upon their child's age and personality. This book thoughtfully includes the addresses and telephone numbers of valuable toilet training resources making it not only useful but unique. Of special interest to parents will be the six-page section that highlights further reading material for children; the publisher and telephone number are included for each book. This guide does well interweaving tips from parents, humorous illustrations, and bulleted advice. Parents of boys will appreciate the "For Boys Only" section which shows how much fun it can be turning the "blue" toilet bowl water green. With her usual humorous flair and concise advice, Lansky fans won't be disappointed. This guide is succinct and addresses all toileting issues.

Where To Find/Buy:
Bookstores and libraries, or order direct by calling 1-800-255-3379.

PARENTS BOOK OF TOILET TEACHING

Description:
The author of this 128 page guidebook on toilet teaching toddlers states that "the philosophy presented here is one of common sense and a balance between parents' rights and children's needs." The book has 10 chapters. Chapter 1 speaks to parents about when to start training their child—"Don't Start Too Early." The author then suggests reading Chapters 2 through 6 (in order). These chapters include a discussion of readiness, preparing your toddler for toilet learning, a step-by-step plan, dealing with "the learning period" and accidents, and staying dry during the night. Chapters 7 through 9 center on common difficulties, how the feelings and attitudes of parents can affect toilet teaching, and how to keep everything in perspective. The final chapter is a review of the book in the form of frequently asked questions from parents. There is a conclusive index, including references to other resources which are used throughout the guide.

Evaluation:
Well-organized and sensible, this resource nudges parents towards successfully teaching their young child how to use the toilet in an unhurried, natural progression. Parents are taught how to instill reassuring daily routines, how to ease into the transition from diapers to underpants, and how to talk to their child to reinforce success. Once parents have determined that their child is ready, chapter 4 offers a step-by-step plan that guides the transfer towards no diapers. Despite its copyright date, this guide book is very good at not advancing the process before the toddler is ready. It continues this reminder throughout with warnings not to proceed before following a previous step. For parents that are having difficulties with toilet teaching, such as bedwetting or late toilet learning, the book offers an address and home telephone number of a physician in this field. Even though the book's copyright date is 1983, we called this number and it works! This is a sensitive book worthy of your time.

Where To Find/Buy:
Bookstores and libraries.

Overall Rating
★★★
Succinct positive advice on toilet learning/teaching with good clarity of ideas

Design, Ease Of Use
★★
Small print; bold headings would help highlight info

1–4 Stars; N/R = Not Rated

Media Type:
Print

Price:
$5.99

Principal Subject:
Growth & Learning

Age Group:
All Ages (0–5)

ISBN:
0345343328

Edition Reviewed:
1983

Publisher:
Ballantine Books (Random House)

Author/Editor:
Joanna Cole

About The Author:
(From Cover Notes)
Joanna Cole is a former elementary school teacher and graduate of City College of New York with a BA in psychology. She is a writer specializing in books and articles for and about children.

Overall Rating
★★

Sorts out research info on "effective methods" in a simple easy-to-understand manner

Design, Ease Of Use
★★

A lot of information in a compact book, small print; table of contents & index are helpful

1–4 Stars; N/R = Not Rated

Media Type:
Print

Price:
$5.99

Principal Subject:
Growth & Learning

Age Group:
All Ages (0–5)

ISBN:
0451192125

Edition Reviewed:
2nd (1997)

Publisher:
Signet (Penguin Group/ Penguin Putnam)

Author/Editor:
Charles E. Schaefer, Ph.D. and Theresa Foy DiGeronimo

About The Author:
(From Cover Notes)
Dr. Charles Schaefer is a renowned child-care expert and the author and co-author of several books. Theresa DiGeronimo is an experienced medical writer and has a master's degree in education.

TOILET TRAINING WITHOUT TEARS

Description:

Separated into four sections, this 235 page resource offers parents several different toilet teaching methods in a "positive, nurturing" way. Part I carries information on basic toilet training. Besides teaching several approaches to toilet training, it also includes tips on establishing early hygiene habits. Approaches discussed include "The Readiness Approach," "The Early Approach," and "The Rapid Approach." Part II highlights special situations such as delayed toileting, toilet training the resistant child of three-and-a-half to five, helping children with delayed bowel and bladder control, and bedwetting. Part III offers tips for training caregivers and ways to toilet train children while traveling. Part IV addresses techniques in training the mentally and physically challenged child. There are two appendices. Appendix A lists toilet training products and Appendix B provides additional reading and video resources. The "Notes" section lists chapter by chapter references; with a concluding index.

Evaluation:

This resource encourages parents to take on the role of a teacher and encourage their child, avoiding the extremes of being either too strict or too lax. The author advises parents to maintain a warm and loving attitude, offering more positive than negative feedback. This is a well written, well-meaning book which gives the author's ten general guidelines while addressing "the most effective methods of toilet training." This allows parents to choose the one that fits their needs and their child's developmental readiness. This resource gives all methods fair treatment by offering both the advantages and disadvantages of the methods discussed. There are numerous charts, illustrations, and tables to help parents decide which method may work best for them. It is a practical guide without prejudice, offering parents suggestions and essential tips on how to effectively toilet train their child. For parents entering into this phase of their child's development, this resource may contain the information they're looking for.

Where To Find/Buy:

Bookstores and libraries, or order direct by calling 1-800-253-6476.

GOOD-BYE DIAPERS

Description:

This 192 page resource contains 13 chapters. Each chapter contains bold subheadings for specific topics covered. The first section focuses on attitude, the process of elimination is described next, followed by advice on choosing a potty. Chapter 4 discusses several approaches to toilet training, with chapters 5, 6, and 7 focusing on the "first steps," saying "good-bye" to diapers, and the one-day intensive approach (the Azrin-Foxx method). Information for toilet training the older child is offered in Chapter 8 with "General Tips" discussed in Chapter 9. Chapters 10 through 13 include ways to prevent bedwetting, encopresis (fecal soiling), toilet training the special needs child, and stories of parental experiences in toilet training their children. The stories are fictional but are inspired by real situations. They are presented to give parents examples of the various approaches outlined in the book. The author focuses on parental attitude throughout stating it makes toilet training either an "ordeal . . . or . . . a joyful challenge."

Evaluation:

This guide's main focus is on attitude first before introducing parents to toilet training techniques. The author does a good job of outlining various techniques, all approached with a positive attitude. Parents can then decide which are most appropriate for their child's needs and design a toilet training program specific to their child. The "Special Situations" section is sensitive to blind, deaf, and autistic children, as well as children with ostomies, spina bifida, cerebral palsy, mental retardation, attention deficit hyperactivity disorder, and more; also addressed are tips for toilet training twins and multiples. Good general information is provided in this resource to offer parents choices best suited for their situations. The type in this book is small, no illustrations are given for the various methods or the potty training equipment that are available, and no index is provided. Sympathetic towards families searching for answers to toilet training concerns, this guide may help parents get started, but they'll need other sources too.

Where To Find/Buy:

Bookstores and libraries, or order direct by calling 1-800-788-6262, ext. 1.

Overall Rating
★★
Approach emphasizes parental attitude; multiple techniques need elaboration

Design, Ease Of Use
★
No index, small print, and no graphics make the hunt for specific information difficult

1–4 Stars; N/R = Not Rated

Media Type:
Print

Price:
$4.99

Principal Subject:
Growth & Learning

Age Group:
All Ages (0–5)

ISBN:
0425141853

Edition Reviewed:
1994

Publisher:
Berkley Books (Berkley Publishing Group)

Author/Editor:
Batya Swift Yasgur

Overall Rating
★
Stress-free approach, but many parents may find it stressful as THEY become trained

Design, Ease Of Use
★★
Adequate but vague titles in table of contents; bold subheadings throughout chapters

1–4 Stars; N/R = Not Rated

Media Type:
Print

Price:
$5.95

Principal Subject:
Growth & Learning

Age Group:
All Ages (0–5)

ISBN:
0895296926

Edition Reviewed:
1996

Publisher:
Avery Publishing Group

Author/Editor:
Katie Van Pelt

About The Author:
(From Cover Notes)
Mother of three children, Katie Van Pelt draws from the potty training method handed down to her through three generations of her family, based on a commonsense approach and a loving environment.

POTTY TRAINING YOUR BABY
A Practical Guide For Easier Toilet Training

Description:
The author of this 119 page book believes that "potty training is more of a philosophy than a specific, step-by-step technique." General guidelines are given to toilet train children with "minimal stress." There are five chapters. Chapter 1 is dedicated to the "Early-Start Alternative." This approach is based on identifying the physical sensations of toileting to a child, practicing muscle control, and learning purposeful control. The author states that this technique can begin before the age of one and is generally completed by two years of age. Chapter 2 discusses the "elements" needed for toilet training—a relaxed attitude, a healthy baby, a baby that can sit up, and the right potty. Chapters 3 and 4 specifically deal with training a one year old and a two year old child. Chapter 5 focuses on bowel movements, and Chapter 6 offers the author's final thoughts (avoiding negatives and teasing, using the "big potty," and dealing with accidents). An index is included.

Evaluation:
Here is yet another opinion on toilet training based on a method that was handed down through three generations of the author's family. The author's intent was to gather and evaluate current information to show parents the success of her own method. The "Early-Start Alternative" bills toilet training as a time of bonding, learning, and enjoyment. It stresses patience, respect, and insight into your child's needs during this time in his development. There are, however, many contradictions in the author's statements. After stating that "potty training is more of a philosophy . . . ," she then proceeds to give parents the step-by-step instructions for toilet training. She also emphasizes "taking an easygoing attitude toward training" and yet, one stage of her technique includes marching your child off to the toilet every 20 minutes over a several hour period. Overall, this book outlines ways to toilet train the parent more than it offers ways to train the child. Parents looking for the opposite will need to look to other resources.

Where To Find/Buy:
Bookstores and libraries.

TOILET TRAINING IN LESS THAN A DAY

Description:

This guide is about the Azrin-Foxx method of toilet training children where spanking and anger are excluded. This book contains seven chapters. Chapter 1 outlines concerns parents have about toilet training; many letters from mothers are included. Chapter 2 details the method's background and success rate (children 20 months or older, who were "responsive to instructions, and whose parents desired the training, were trained . . ."). Chapters 3 through 5 discuss the general teaching plan, how to train your child, and what to expect and do after training. Chapter 6 is a mother's account describing her thoughts and actions while training her son using the new method. The final chapter includes a reminder list of 99 questions and answers, a list of training materials and supplies, and reminder sheets for prompting/inspection (during training) and after training inspections. One appendix focuses on toilet training children with mental retardation. A short reference section for further reading and an index complete the book.

Evaluation:

The authors claim "the average child required less than four hours to be trained . . . without assistance." Outdated, but still a bestseller, this book emphasizes a behavioral approach with a system of stimuli (the potty chair), rewards (candy, snacks), and punishment (verbal disapproval, but "spanking or other physical punishment is probably never necessary . . ."). The authors' method, first developed and successful for the profoundly retarded, was extended to address toilet training for all children. Their research states that children using this method learn fast because of the many factors the authors believe make learning pleasant, simple, and exciting. The training is intense and, in many ways, more a training for the parent than for the child. Areas not addressed that many newer resources include are nighttime training, bowel elimination, travel, medical problems that interfere with training, etc. Also not included are tips on weaning your child from the treats that reward toileting. Even though 2 million copies of this resource have been sold, there are currently better resources than this one available.

Where To Find/Buy:

Bookstores and libraries.

Overall Rating
★
Focus is on quickness of learning with rewards and punishment; some areas not addressed

Design, Ease Of Use
★★
Must read chapter by chapter to understand the entire method; small text; good pics

1–4 Stars; N/R = Not Rated

Media Type:
Print

Price:
$5.99

Principal Subject:
Growth & Learning

Age Group:
All Ages (0–5)

ISBN:
0671693808

Edition Reviewed:
1974

Publisher:
Pocket Books

Author/Editor:
Nathan H. Azrin, Ph.D., and Richard M. Foxx, Ph.D.

About The Author:
(From Cover Notes)
Azrin heads the Behavior Research Laboratory at Anna State Hospital, Anna, Illinois and is Professor of Rehabilitation at Southern Illinois University. Foxx is a research psychologist for the state of Illinois Department of Mental Health.

Overall Rating
★
Simple and basic but dumbing down the reader is irritating

Design, Ease Of Use
★
Outdated pics & text; most tips for parents are hidden in the child's guide for part 2

1–4 Stars; N/R = Not Rated

Media Type:
Print

Price:
$11.95

Principal Subject:
Growth & Learning

Age Group:
All Ages (0–5)

ISBN:
0316542377

Edition Reviewed:
1978

Publisher:
Little, Brown and Company

Author/Editor:
Alison Mack

About The Author:
(From Cover Notes)
Alison Mack is a parent and has written previous child development books.

TOILET LEARNING
The Picture Book Technique For Children And Parents

Description:

Organized in two parts, this 109 page book centers on toilet "learning," rather than toilet training, for young children reaching that development stage. The author suggests that "toilet learning presents a remarkable opportunity to evaluate your entire approach to child rearing as your personality and your child's become revealed to you." Part 1 includes nine topics. Some topics include a history of previous toilet training practices, the benefits of using the toilet, how to prepare yourself and your child for toilet learning, and more. There is also a sub-chapter entitled, "The Freud Complex," explaining the author's opinion of the psychiatrist Sigmund Freud and his theories on child care. This guidebook's second half—"Child's Guide to Toilet Learning"—uses a picture book technique to assist parents in helping their child get ready to use the toilet. It is an illustrated section explaining bodily functions to the child and how to use the toilet. A guide on how to use Part Two precludes this section. No index is given.

Evaluation:

The only benefit of this book is the advice to not rush your child into toilet "learning." The author does a fine job of "beating up" Sigmund Freud and other toilet training practices trying to validate her technique (she even references a 1914 infant care book). The book, copyrighted in 1978, is dated in many respects. Part 2, the child's guide, should include illustrations and text that capture a child's attention, especially since this is the crux of the author's message to young children. Instead this is where most of the parent information is housed. Marginally artistic, these illustrations show children, horses, and various wildlife relieving themselves outdoors, as well as portraying firemen, policemen, babysitters, and grandpa on the toilet. Using terms like "wee-wee" and "doo-doo" nearly insults the intelligence of parents in its attempt to "train" them how to "train" their young children about bodily functions. There are better, more informative resources available on this subject.

Where To Find/Buy:
Bookstores and libraries.

Growth & Learning: Age-Appropriate Activities

BABY GAMES
The Joyful Guide To Child's Play From Birth To Three Years

 Best Resource For:
Activities to do with toddlers

 Recommended For:
Growth & Learning

Description:

This revised and updated 183 page book is organized into twelve chapters and culls a wide variety of activities. The author suggests that the book be used as a play resource to find the child's and parent's own favorite games and rhythms of play. The first six chapters relate to activities in infancy and are broken down into three month time frames; subsequent chapters represent six month time frames because of the developmental pattern changes that occur at about eighteen months. The author, however, advises not limiting oneself to the book's timetables and categories, but rather to use the entire book depending upon the needs of the child and parent. Chapter 1, then, begins with activities for ages birth to 3 months, progressing through Chapter 9 with activities for children 30 to 36 months of age. Movement, water play, music, kitchen and art activities, indoor and outdoor games—all are presented. Chapter 10 lists recordings, television, video/computer programs, books, and public entertainment resources. Information about toys and birthday/holiday activities are also given.

Evaluation:

This book's strength lies in its organizational elements. The index, divided into ten sections, lists all activities for quick and easy use. The music section includes traditional folk songs and rhymes and the specific locality or country of origin has been indicated (when possible). Some unusual art activities include colored pasta, string painting, or Jell-O painting. Other sections include word play, changing/dressing games, and quiet activities. The "Calendar of Holidays" (within Chapter 12's "Birthdays, Unbirthdays, Holiday, and Other Excuses for a Party") gives a thoughtful and informative review of traditional holidays celebrated in various countries. Groundhog's Day, New Year's, Shrovetide, Afrikomen, Mardi Gras, and Sham-al-Nessin are but a sampling. Books, poems, songs, games, activities, and more are included for most holidays. This guidebook is well written with a wealth of information for parents, teachers, and caregivers. It is a helpful, entertaining resource to be kept close at hand.

Where To Find/Buy:

Bookstores and libraries, or order direct from the publisher (125 South Twenty-second Street, Philadelphia, Pennsylvania 19103).

Overall Rating
★★★★
Great comprehensive resource for all parents and caregivers—a "must have"

Design, Ease Of Use
★★★★
Age-appropriate contents; detailed chronological index useful for referencing

1–4 Stars; N/R = Not Rated

Media Type:
Print

Price:
$12.95

Principal Subject:
Growth & Learning

Age Group:
Infants & Toddlers (0–3)

ISBN:
0894716174

Edition Reviewed:
1988

Publisher:
Running Press Book Publishers

Author/Editor:
Elaine Martin

Overall Rating
★★★★
Outstanding array of activity categories, open-ended and based on discovery approach

Design, Ease Of Use
★★★★
Detailed table of contents makes up for lack of index; attractive with explicit drawings

1–4 Stars; N/R = Not Rated

Media Type:
Print

Price:
$12.00

Principal Subject:
Growth & Learning

Age Group:
Toddlers & Preschoolers (1–5)

ISBN:
0671528572

Edition Reviewed:
1997

Publisher:
Pocket Books (Simon & Schuster)

Author/Editor:
Amy Nolan

About The Author:
(From Cover Notes)
Nolan has a B.F.A. in art and an M.S. in elementary education. She has been affiliated with The Children's Museum in Boston for the past seven years, first as the manager of Playspace and later as a freelance writer.

GREAT EXPLORATIONS
100 Creative Play Ideas For Parents And Preschoolers From Playspace At The Children's Museum Boston

 Best Resource For:
Activities to do with young children

 Recommended For:
Growth & Learning

Description:

Developed by the manager of Playspace (part of the Children's Museum in Boston), this 245 page resource offers the center's favorite art, science, music, cooking, and dramatic play experiences. The age-appropriate activities focus on the "whole" child, emphasize a discovery-based approach to learning, are open-ended, and involve simple, inexpensive materials. The author's intent is for activities and materials to be "as accessible as possible to as many people as possible." Activities are grouped according to categories—arts and crafts, science, outside, seasonal, quiet, music and movement, pretend play, and cooking. Each activity usually is explained in 2 pages with a list of materials, recommended ages, length of time needed, directions, "what your child is learning," and ways to extend the activity. Additional sections offer information about Playspace's philosophy, the role of play in a child's development, the rationale behind the activities that were chosen, how to get started, what basic supplies should be kept on hand, how to set up the activities, where to buy supplies, how to display a child's work, and more.

Evaluation:

Parents won't find any other book of activities that beats this one. It's chockfull of a wide range of activities, not just placing emphasis on art, language, or other areas that are generally the focus of other resources. For example, many other resources neglect some categories and skills such as science, pretend play, self-expression, mathematics, cooking, and problem-solving. This guide includes all these arenas and more. All activities are developmentally sound with the process highlighted and not the product. The author offers parents the opportunity to extend the activities inviting a continuation of the learning experience. Although designed specifically for children between the ages of 18 months and 5 years, the author also provides a section that explains how activities can be adapted for younger and older children. Some of the activities may take a little more parent time in getting set up than others, but this book offers parents and their child excellent ideas for engaging in play together.

Where To Find/Buy:

Bookstores, libraries, or order direct by contacting: Mail Order Department, Simon & Schuster, Inc., 200 Old Tappan Rd, Old Tappan, NJ 07675.

PRESCHOOL ART
It's The Process, Not The Product

★★★★

Best Resource For:
Art activities to do with preschoolers

Recommended For:
Growth & Learning

Description:

This art resource's emphasis on "process not product" invites children to explore art materials without an adult "sample" or finished product to direct their activity. The guidebook offers over 250 pages of art activities. The table of contents lists these activities in chart form, divided into sections: title, page, medium, age, preparation (time), help, caution, and author's favorite. Each activity then includes icons to make the projects "more usable and accessible" for caregivers, teachers, and parents. The activities are further divided up in the table of contents into "The Basics" and seasons. The "Basics" section includes projects for any time of the year and focus primarily on introducing basic art ideas (41), such as crayon rubbing, yeast dough, chalk drawing, and more. The remaining projects within the season divisions build on these basic art ideas. Every activity contains a "Hint" which offers advice for how to extend the activity. The index is divided into three sections by project, materials, and art medium.

Evaluation:

Parents will be not only impressed but inspired in finding this 260 page resource. The projects are not only age specific, but also well-organized and well laid-out; how much time to allow for planning and preparing the activity, red-flagging activities that need extra attention, and extending activities are necessities often neglected in other resources. Each page includes a materials' list, explanation of the process, possible variations, and a detailed line drawing. The "Hint" notes offer additional tips and advice. Most of the materials can be found around your home. The projects cover all mediums, from shoe polish to corn cobs to bread sculptures! The index is most comprehensive, determined by either project, materials, or art medium. The book relies on true creativity by the child, allowing no sample finished projects to copy. The activities are easy to do, offering a high success rate; projects can easily evolve into great gift ideas for Grandmas and Grandpas or anyone. Highly recommended.

Where To Find/Buy:

Bookstores and libraries.

Overall Rating
★★★★
Containing hours of fun and creativity, this book will inspire artists both young and old

Design, Ease Of Use
★★★★
Icons, hints, and a "wow" index accompany excellent line drawings of each activity

1–4 Stars; N/R = Not Rated

Media Type:
Print

Price:
$19.95

Principal Subject:
Growth & Learning

Age Group:
Preschoolers (3–5)

ISBN:
0876591683

Edition Reviewed:
1994

Publisher:
Gryphon House

Author/Editor:
MaryAnn Kohl

About The Author:
(From Cover Notes)
MaryAnn Kohl is an educator and publisher whose interest in creative art comes from her experience teaching young children using both a whole language and learning center approach. She lives with her husband and two daughters in Bellingham, Washington.

Overall Rating
★★★★
300 commonplace and unusual games, many of them accompanied by songs or rhymes

Design, Ease Of Use
★★★
Activities listed alphabetically or by category; list of skills practiced would be useful

1–4 Stars; N/R = Not Rated

Media Type:
Print

Price:
$12.95

Principal Subject:
Growth & Learning

Age Group:
Toddlers & Preschoolers (1–5)

ISBN:
0876591829

Edition Reviewed:
1997

Publisher:
Gryphon House

Author/Editor:
Jackie Silberg

About The Author:
(From Cover Notes)
Silberg presents concerts, workshops and keynote addresses at early childhood conferences all over the U.S. She holds a MS degree in early childhood education from Emporia State University in Kansas where she is a Distinguished Alumna.

300 THREE MINUTE GAMES
Quick And Easy Activities For 2–5 Year Olds

 Recommended For:
Growth & Learning

Description:

Designed to be used as a companion to one of Silberg's many other books (*500 Five Minute Games*), this 191 page book offers 300 "stimulating games that challenge the imagination" and are age-appropriate for toddlers and preschoolers. Silberg is an "acclaimed speaker, teacher, and trainer on early childhood development and music." Activities within her book are grouped within 14 categories including animal games, bath games, book games, exercise games, imagination games, music games, outside games, quiet games, storytelling games, stuck inside games, stuffed animal games, thinking games, transition games, and waiting games. Poems, rhymes, or songs accompany most activities. Step-by-step directions are given along with occasional black line drawings. A skill or concept that is practiced by doing the activity is also provided. These skills range from "develops imagination" to "practices language skills" to "teaches about propulsion." An index lists activities alphabetically by name.

Evaluation:

This is definitely one of Silberg's better books. She does an excellent job here of compiling the more commonplace activities ("Playing in the Tub"—bring all sorts of unbreakable things into the tub) with the more unusual, often humorous activities ("Here's Some Soup"—pretend to make soup in the tub and add all sorts of vegetables while you stir it . . . but, with the admonition "Do not drink the bath water"). Not just for fun, these games are also developmentally sound. Heavy emphasis is placed on language skills and young children will delight in the rhythms of the poems, songs, and rhymes included with many of the activities. Silberg's other books list activities by recommended age of the child. This one does not, leaving the assessment of the activity's success up to the parent and child where it rightfully belongs since no two children's developments are alike. Many activities seem more geared toward the 2 and 3 year old range, but parents can, of course, adapt and expand these activities for the older preschooler. This would make a great gift for parents of toddlers or preschoolers at their child's birthday.

365 OUTDOOR ACTIVITIES YOU CAN DO WITH YOUR CHILD

Recommended For:
Growth & Learning

Description:

This 430 page book offers parents "activities that foster a love of learning and a sense of family, neighborhood, and community." The 365 activities fall into 25 categories. They are grouped alphabetically in the table of contents and the body of the book and by category in the index. Categories include: backyard fun, beach activities, environmental activities, gardening, imagination games, natural science, old-fashioned games, seasonal activities, recycled/reused household materials, sports, toys and gadgets, and more. Each activity is fully contained on one page and includes a list of materials in the margin along with safety reminders and optional materials when applicable. Also included is a small illustration for each activity along with a narrative description of how to do the activity. The authors' safety tips are included in the introduction along with suggested tips for outdoor play ("tailor the competition to your child," "foster team spirit," etc.). Advice is also given on how to use this book to reduce indoor TV watching.

Evaluation:

Not involving a lot of preparation, the ideas in this compact (4" x 6") little book will be of great help for parents intent on either reliving games and adventures from their youth and/or or intent on eliminating (or limiting) their family's TV watching and/or coming up with fun, spontaneous ways of interacting with their children outdoors. Although many of the activities are designed more for elementary school-aged children, creative parents of toddlers and preschoolers will be able to adapt many of these activities for their child. The suggested activities are open-ended, prepared easily and spontaneously, and complete with understandable directions. Many activity resources focus on arts and crafts. This resource, then, is a great idea book about what one can do with one's child outside the house and fills the gap left by other resources.

Where To Find/Buy:

Bookstores and libraries.

Overall Rating
★★★★
Fun, easily prepared games and adventures generally using very little materials

Design, Ease Of Use
★★★
Arranged alphabetically and by category; age group categories would be helpful too

1–4 Stars; N/R = Not Rated

Media Type:
Print

Price:
$6.95

Principal Subject:
Growth & Learning

Age Group:
All Ages (0–5)

ISBN:
1558502602

Edition Reviewed:
1993

Publisher:
Adams Media

Author/Editor:
Steve Bennett and Ruth Bennett

About The Author:
(From Cover Notes)
Steve Bennett has written more than 35 books in the fields of parenting, family computing, and business management. Ruth Bennett is a landscape architect who has designed parks, playgrounds, and public places in many U.S. cities. They have 2 children and live TV-free.

★★★★

Overall Rating
★★★★
Fun, easily prepared ideas (many for older children) using common household items

Design, Ease Of Use
★★★
Arranged alphabetically and by category; age group categories would be helpful too

1–4 Stars; N/R = Not Rated

Media Type:
Print

Price:
$7.95

Principal Subject:
Growth & Learning

Age Group:
Preschoolers (3–5)

ISBN:
1558505857

Edition Reviewed:
2nd (1996)

Publisher:
Adams Media

Author/Editor:
Steve Bennett and Ruth Bennett

About The Author:
(From Cover Notes)
Steve Bennett has written more than 55 books in the fields of parenting, family computing, and business management. Ruth Bennett is a landscape architect who has designed parks, playgrounds, and public places in many U.S. cities. They have 2 children and live TV-free.

365 TV-FREE ACTIVITIES
You Can Do With Your Child

 Best Resource For:
Activities to do with preschoolers

 Recommended For:
Growth & Learning

Description:

This 425 page book offers parents "games and activities that require little or no preparation, yet provide hours of entertainment and play that might otherwise be spent in front of the tube." The 365 activities fall into 16 categories. They are grouped alphabetically in the table of contents and the body of the book and by category in the index. Categories include: arts and crafts, food stuff, math and numbers, recycled/reused household materials, science, words and language, toymaking, and more. Each activity is fully contained on one page and includes in the margin a list of materials along with safety reminders and optional materials when applicable. A small illustration is also included for each activity along with a narrative description of how to do the activity. The introduction contains a list of suggested materials to keep on hand in the "TV-Free Activity Supply Center" consisting of common household items such as boxes, toilet paper tubes, magazines, junk mail and catalogs, bottle and container lids, and more.

Evaluation:

Not involving a lot of preparation, the ideas in this compact (4" x 6") little book will be of great help for busy parents intent on either limiting their family's TV watching, weaning their children completely from the tube or just plain looking for creative ways to spend time with their children. While most activities tend to address the developmental levels of elementary school children, parents of toddlers and preschoolers—with some creativity—can most likely adapt many of these activities for their child. Most suggested activities are open-ended and easy to prepare with understandable directions. Because many activity books usually focus on arts and crafts, this one will offer ideas to fill in the gaps left by those other resources.

Where To Find/Buy:

Bookstores and libraries, or order direct by calling (781) 767-8100 or 1-800-872-5627.

Internet URL:

http://www.adamsmedia.com

ACTIVE LEARNING FOR INFANTS

 Best Resource For:
Activities to do with infants

 Recommended For:
Growth & Learning

Description:

This 193 page activity guidebook is one of five in Addison-Wesley's "Active Learning Series." This comprehensive, concise, informative book is made up of four activity sections and a planning guide for those working with infants, newborn to 12 months of age. Section 1—"Planning for Infants"—includes ideas for developing a schedule, making interest centers, and an environment that is positive; a sequential developmental list of what "Baby Can" do are also offered. Section 2, "Activities for Listening and Talking," contains activities (books, pictures, conversation, etc.) that promote talking and listening. "Activities for Physical Development" offers ideas to develop babies' large and small muscles. Section 4—"Creative Activities"—uses art, blocks, dramatic play, and music to develop babies' senses, imagination, and art enjoyment. The final section, "Activities for Learning from the World Around Them" focuses on nature, numbers, the five senses, size, shape, and color. Separate indexes are included for each section. Each activity contains an icon corresponding to the age range (0–5 months, 5–9 months, 9–12 months) appropriate for the activity.

Evaluation:

One of Addison-Wesley's "Active Learning Series," this reference specifically focuses on the newborn to one year old infant. It provides numerous developmental activities covering the areas of creativity, community, listening and talking, physical development, and learning about the environment. The book does not have an overall index but it does have a detailed table of contents and section indexes. Each activity includes: skills the baby will need, where the activity can be done (indoors, outdoors), how long it could take, and how many babies can do the activity; the icons give a quick visual cue for caregivers trying to find an age-appropriate activity. Although designed primarily for educators of young infants, this guidebook will also be a useful reference for parents seeking ideas and suggestions on things to do with their baby. The checklists and materials lists are invaluable sources for organizing one's self and guiding an infant's education. Parents will benefit from buying the series; these will be a much used resource.

Where To Find/Buy:

Bookstores and libraries.

Overall Rating
★★★★
Comprehensive guide primarily beneficial for caregivers and educators of infants

Design, Ease Of Use
★★★
Icons show ages for activities; good table of contents & section indexes, no main index

1–4 Stars; N/R = Not Rated

Media Type:
Print

Price:
$23.25

Principal Subject:
Growth & Learning

Age Group:
Infants (0–1)

ISBN:
0201213346

Edition Reviewed:
1987

Publisher:
Addison-Wesley Longman (Addison-Wesley Publishing)

Author/Editor:
Debby Cryer, Thelma Harms, and Beth Bourland

About The Author:
(From Cover Notes)
Ms. Cryer, Harms, and Bourland are with the Frank Porter Graham Child Development Center, University of North Carolina, Chapel Hill, North Carolina

Overall Rating
★★★★
Excellent combination of theory, practice, and concrete examples to encourage reading

Design, Ease Of Use
★★★
Laborious reading in first half, the Treasury and various indexes are well-organized

1–4 Stars; N/R = Not Rated

Media Type:
Print

Price:
$13.95

Principal Subject:
Growth & Learning

Age Group:
All Ages (0–5)

ISBN:
0140469710

Edition Reviewed:
4th (1995)

Publisher:
Penguin Group (Penguin Books USA)

Author/Editor:
Jim Trelease

About The Author:
(From Cover Notes)
Trelease, a graduate of the University of Massachusetts, was an award-winning artist and writer for *The Springfield Daily News* for 20 years. He works full-time addressing parents, teachers, and professional groups on the subjects of children, literature, and TV.

READ-ALOUD HANDBOOK (THE)

 Best Resource For:
Books to share with young children

 Recommended For:
Growth & Learning

Description:
Trelease's 387 page, ten chapter handbook is two books in one. The first half presents evidence that supports reading aloud to children while the second half contains his "Treasury of Read-Alouds." Chapters 1 and 2 focus on why and when parents should read to their child. Chapter 3 presents the progressive stages for reading aloud based upon the child's development; also listed are the types of books that are recommended for a child's given age (wordless books, picture books, etc.). The "Dos and Don'ts of Read-Aloud" is the subject of Chapter 4 while Chapter 5 highlights various programs that have implemented read-alouds and had positive results. Chapter 6 deals with setting up home, school, and public libraries. The drawbacks of TV are covered in Chapter 7 while the benefits of Sustained Silent Reading (SSR) are explained in Chapter 8. Chapter 9 explains how to use Chapter 10—the Treasury (200+ pages). Books are separated by type (wordless, predictable, picture, etc.). Each book includes a one paragraph synopsis, suggested age range, other books by that author, other books that are related to the subject, and more.

Evaluation:
Now in its fourth edition, this book has remained a timeless classic. Recently revised with updated statistics, new research and anecdotes, and current children's literature additions, this book continues to appeal to parents and teachers. Although quite a bit of the book's first half is dedicated to children of school-age, we recommend parents of babies and young children wade through it. Some of the reading is tedious and laborious, bordering on the feel of a textbook. However, Trelease does a great job interjecting numerous family and classroom examples to break up the serious tone of his message—"a nation that doesn't read much doesn't know much." His treatise is that children should be read to from the time they are a few months old if for nothing else than to hear the sounds of language. The Treasury is well-organized allowing parents to either seek out other books by the same author or books along the same theme. Well-researched and with tons of great ideas for young readers, this one would be a great shower present for a new mother or father.

Where To Find/Buy:
Bookstores and libraries.

PEEKABOO AND OTHER GAMES TO PLAY WITH YOUR BABY
Tools For Everyday Parenting Series

Description:

This 120 page book is a collection of over 100 activities and baby games that parents and caregivers can use for interacting with their infant or toddler. Separated into 15 age-specific sections (by month from newborn to 12 months old, then by 12–15 months and 15–18 months), it also includes a section on choosing or making age-appropriate toys and a section on reading with babies and toddlers. A half page of information introduces each section with highlights of that stage of development. Also included are simple songs, rhymes, and numerous illustrations. A materials list is provided for each activity and usually includes everyday household items (magazines, cardboard, glue, etc.). Book resource lists for parents, babies, and toddlers are provided at the end of the book. The "Subject Index" concludes the book and separates the games and activities described in the book into seven sections (language games, learning games, movement games, sensory games, sound games, things to make, and visual games).

Evaluation:

This is a whimsical book with ideas for activities and games that children and adults will find fun to do together. The author has carefully tried to put together simple games that involve the five senses of sight, sound, touch, taste, and smell. Differences in children's personalities and safety concerns have also been considered. The book sports a generalized table of contents divided by baby's age month-by-month and the "Subject Index" does a great job of backup. Parents will find many unique activities in this concise guide from making collages by taping contact paper with the sticky side out on the refrigerator to "painting" with shaving cream, and more. Each activity capitalizes on the developmental milestones at a particular age. Descriptions include a list of materials along with additional information to ensure success. The book is in a non-standard 8.5 x 5.5 size, with an easy-to-read typeface and bold subheadings. This entertaining collection should provide many good times between parents and children.

Where To Find/Buy:

Bookstores and libraries, or order direct by calling 1-800-992-6657.

Overall Rating
★★★
Simple everyday games based on child's developmental level using household items

Design, Ease Of Use
★★★★
Table of contents arranged by baby's age, index arranged by subject

1–4 Stars; N/R = Not Rated

Media Type:
Print

Price:
$9.95

Principal Subject:
Growth & Learning

Age Group:
Infants & Toddlers (0–3)

ISBN:
0943990815

Edition Reviewed:
1995

Publisher:
Parenting Press

Author/Editor:
Shari Steelsmith

About The Author:
(From Cover Notes)
Shari Steelsmith and her husband are the parents of two sons. This is Ms. Steelsmith's first activities book for children. She is also the author of *How to Open and Operate a Home-Based Day-Care Business.*

★★★

Overall Rating
★★★
Complete listings of annotated children's resources based on defined criteria

Design, Ease Of Use
★★★★
Arranged alphabetically by title with 5 indexes listing resources by subject, age, etc.

1–4 Stars; N/R = Not Rated

Media Type:
Print

Price:
$30.00

Principal Subject:
Growth & Learning

Age Group:
All Ages (0–5)

ISBN:
0835230198

Edition Reviewed:
1992

Publisher:
R.R. Bowker (Reed Reference Publishing)

Author/Editor:
James L. Thomas

PLAY, LEARN, & GROW

An Annotated Guide To The Best Books And Materials For Very Young Children

 Recommended For:
Growth & Learning

Description:

Stating that it is a "highly selective, evaluative collection development resource guide," this 439 page guide highlights books and other media (not games or toys) for use with children under the age of 5. Over 5,000 print and non-print titles were evaluated by librarians and early childhood educators in compiling this list. The importance of the parent/adult's role in engaging a child to read begins the book. The next sections discuss the importance of choosing quality materials, a "developmental portrait" for infants through five year olds (characteristics, what they enjoy, sample book titles), criteria used for selecting the book's content, and more. The remainder of the book contains the annotated list of books and media arranged alphabetically by title, with bibliographic information, an assigned general category (wordless, concept, etc.), age range, and more. Three appendices are included (professional resources, publisher contacts, organizations) along with five indexes to access entries (by name, subject, age/category, age/purchase priority, and format).

Evaluation:

Reading aloud is certainly an activity that young children and infants enjoy with their parents. At first glance though, it seems that this bulky text, with all its resources arranged alphabetically, will provide endless agony. Do parents have to wade through all the annotations to find appropriate books for their child? Fortunately not. This inherent problem can be circumvented if parents make good use of the indexes as they search for materials pertinent to their needs, such as a search for "all books for a preschooler that have to do with dinosaurs." Parents will find the information contained within this resource complete, easily accessible in a variety of ways, and well-summarized. It should prove helpful to parents struggling with what to buy in the bookstore or what to search for in the local library. However, its primary target audience is early childhood educators and those involved with library media. It's pricey for parents and other resources are available that offer similar (even more current) listings for less money. We recommend parents use these editions over this text.

Where To Find/Buy:

Bookstores and libraries.

ACTIVE LEARNING FOR FIVES

★★★

Description:

This 450 page activity guidebook is one of six in Addison-Wesley's "Active Learning Series." This comprehensive, concise, informative book is made up of four activity sections and a planning guide for those working with children between 60 and 72 months of age. Section 1—"Planning for Fives"—includes ideas for developing a schedule, ways to avoid potential problems, and an environment that is positive; how to plan activities around topics is also included. Section 2, "Activities for Listening and Talking," offers activities (books, pictures, pre-reading, pre-writing, etc.) that foster talking and listening. "Activities for Physical Development" offers ideas to develop children's large and small muscles. Section 4—"Creative Activities"—uses art, carpentry, blocks, dramatic play, and music to develop children's senses, imagination, and enjoyment. The final section, "Activities for Learning from the World Around Them" focuses on science and nature, size, shape, and numbers. Separate indexes are included for each section.

Evaluation:

This series, developed at the Frank Porter Graham Child Development Center in Chapel Hill, North Carolina, was tested in 17 daycare centers by those working with five-year-olds. With over 500 activities, this guidebook is an excellent resource for both parents and caregivers. Besides excellent resource information, the activities are supported by sample units, activity tips, checklists, activity plans, and materials indexes. This easy-to-use text offers activities that can be done with one child or a small group of children; the "Fives Can . . . " lists help caregivers choose age-appropriate activities. All sections are divided by a "divider" which hosts an index allowing parents to effortlessly find specific activities. Primarily for educators and caregivers, this resource also offers sample schedules, advice on self-directed and teacher-directed activities, and weekly morning and afternoon activity plans makes this guidebook an invaluable resource. Parents will find this resource useful for a quick guide to their child's development and a source for endless fun and learning with their preschooler.

Where To Find/Buy:

Bookstores and libraries.

Overall Rating
★★★
Mainly for educators, but parents will discover great tips & age-appropriate activities

Design, Ease Of Use
★★★
Planning guides & schedules are a commitment, but worth it; separate section indexes

1–4 Stars; N/R = Not Rated

Media Type:
Print

Price:
$23.25

Principal Subject:
Growth & Learning

Age Group:
Preschoolers (3–5)

ISBN:
0201494019

Edition Reviewed:
1996

Publisher:
Innovative Learning Publications (Addison-Wesley Publishing)

Author/Editor:
Debby Cryer, Thelma Harms, and Adele Richardson Ray

About The Author:
(From Cover Notes)
Ms. Cryer, Harms, and Ray are with the Frank Porter Graham Child Development Center, University of North Carolina, Chapel Hill, North Carolina

★★★

Overall Rating
★★★
Offers a wealth of activities and organizational tools along with supporting rationale

Design, Ease Of Use
★★★
Comprehensive table of contents makes up for a lack of index; section indexes provided

1–4 Stars; N/R = Not Rated

Media Type:
Print

Price:
$23.25

Principal Subject:
Growth & Learning

Age Group:
Preschoolers (3–5)

ISBN:
0201494000

Edition Reviewed:
1996

Publisher:
Innovative Learning Publications (Addison-Wesley Publishing)

Author/Editor:
Debby Cryer, Thelma Harms, Adele Richardson Ray

About The Author:
(From Cover Notes)
Debby Cryer, Thelma Harms, and Adele Richardson Ray collaborated with the Frank Porter Graham Child Development Center (University of North Carolina) in Chapel Hill, North Carolina in the development of this guidebook.

ACTIVE LEARNING FOR FOURS

Description:

Boasting 402 pages, this guidebook contains five sections of activities for four-year-olds. "Planning for Fours" suggests ideas for setting up a schedule and positive environment that promotes quality care and avoidance of problems; how to plan activities around topics is also given. The second section includes activities to help those working with four-year-olds make the best use of listening and talking skills along with pre-writing and pre-reading activities. Section three includes exercises and activities for large and small muscles such as: kicking, catching, riding a tricycle, some simple games (basketball, beanbag toss, etc.), tying knots, cutting, making bead patterns, and more. Section four deals with art and carpentry, blocks, dramatic play, and music. The final section focuses on activities involving science and nature, size, shape, and numbers. An index precedes each Section followed by a rationale of why the activities are important, a materials and notes list, and an activity checklist.

Evaluation:

This reference is one of the Addison-Wesley "Active Learning Series" specifically focused on the four-year-old preschooler. It provides a wonderful source of developmental activities covering the areas of creativity, community, listening and talking, physical development, and learning about the environment. The book does not have an overall index but it does have a detailed table of contents and separate section indexes. Each activity has an approximate time completion, with a suggested optimal number of children participating. Also noted is whether the activity is more appropriately experienced indoors or outdoors. Although designed primarily for educators of young children, this guidebook can also serve as a quality reference for parents seeking ideas and suggestions on things to do with their four-year-old. The checklists and materials lists are invaluable sources for organizing one's self and guiding a four-year-old's education. Buy the series; these will be a much used resource.

Where To Find/Buy:

Bookstores and libraries.

ACTIVE LEARNING FOR ONES

Description:

This 218 page activity guidebook is one of four in Addison-Wesley's "Active Learning Series." This comprehensive, concise, informative book is made up of four activity sections and a planning guide for those working with children between 12 and 24 months of age. Section 1—"Planning for Ones"—includes ideas for developing a schedule, making interest centers, and an environment that is positive; how to write an activity plan for each child is also included. Section 2, "Activities for Listening and Talking," assists you with activities (books, pictures, conversation, etc.) that promote talking and listening. "Activities for Physical Development" offers ideas to develop children's large and small muscles. Section 4—"Creative Activities"—uses art, blocks, dramatic play, and music to develop children's senses, imagination, and art enjoyment. The final section, "Activities for Learning from the World Around Them" focuses on nature, the senses, size, shape, color, and numbers. Separate indexes are included for each section.

Evaluation:

This reference is one of the Addison-Wesley "Active Learning Series" specifically focused on the one-year-old toddler. It provides a wonderful source of developmental activities covering the areas of creativity, community, listening and talking, physical development, and learning about the environment. The book does not have an overall index but it does have a detailed table of contents and section indexes. Each activity has an approximate time completion, with a suggested optimal number of children participating. Also noted is whether the activity is more appropriately experienced indoors or outdoors. Although designed primarily for educators of young children, this guidebook can also serve as a quality reference for parents seeking ideas and suggestions on things to do with their one-year-old. The checklists and materials lists are invaluable sources for organizing one's self and guiding a one-year-old's education.

Where To Find/Buy:

Bookstores and libraries.

Overall Rating
★★★
Comprehensive guide primarily beneficial for caregivers & educators of one-year-olds

Design, Ease Of Use
★★★
No main index, but detailed table of contents and section indexes ease navigation

1–4 Stars; N/R = Not Rated

Media Type:
Print

Price:
$18.60

Principal Subject:
Growth & Learning

Age Group:
Toddlers (1–3)

ISBN:
0201213354

Edition Reviewed:
1987

Publisher:
Addison-Wesley Longman (Addison-Wesley Publishing)

Author/Editor:
Debby Cryer, Thelma Harms, and Beth Bourland

About The Author:
(From Cover Notes)
Ms. Cryer, Harms, and Bourland are with the Frank Porter Graham Child Development Center, University of North Carolina, Chapel Hill, North Carolina

★★★

Overall Rating
★★★
Primarily for educators, this guide serves as an excellent and comprehensive resource

Design, Ease Of Use
★★★
Planning guides & schedules are a commitment, but worth it; separate section indexes

1–4 Stars; N/R = Not Rated

Media Type:
Print

Price:
$23.95

Principal Subject:
Growth & Learning

Age Group:
Preschoolers (3–5)

ISBN:
0201213370

Edition Reviewed:
1988

Publisher:
Addison-Wesley Longman
(Addison-Wesley Publishing)

Author/Editor:
Debby Cryer, Thelma Harms, and Beth Bourland

About The Author:
(From Cover Notes)
Ms. Cryer, Harms, and Bourland are with the Frank Porter Graham Child Development Center, University of North Carolina, Chapel Hill, North Carolina

ACTIVE LEARNING FOR THREES

Description:

This 354 page activity guidebook is one of six in Addison-Wesley's "Active Learning Series." This comprehensive, concise, informative book is made up of four activity sections and a planning guide for those working with children between 36 and 48 months of age. Section 1—"Planning for Threes"—includes ideas for developing a schedule to avoid potential problems and an environment that is positive; ways of helping three-year-olds develop self-discipline are included. Section 2, "Activities for Listening and Talking," assists you with activities (books, pictures, puppets, etc.) that promote talking and listening. "Activities for Physical Development" offers ideas to develop children's large and small muscles. Section 4—"Creative Activities"—uses art, blocks, dramatic play, and music to develop children's senses, imagination, and art enjoyment. The final section, "Activities for Learning from the World Around Them" focuses on nature, the senses, size, shape, color, and numbers. Separate indexes are included for each section.

Evaluation:

This series, developed at the Frank Porter Graham Child Development Center in Chapel Hill, North Carolina, was tested in 17 daycare centers by those working with three-year-olds. With over 400 activities, this guidebook is an excellent resource for both parents and caregivers. Besides excellent resource information, the activities are supported by sample units, activity tips, checklists, activity plans, and materials indexes. This easy-to-use text offers activities you can do with one child or a small group of children; the "Three Can . . ." lists help caregivers choose age-appropriate activities. All sections are divided by a card stock colored "divider" which hosts an index allowing you to effortlessly find specific activities. Sample schedules, advice on self-directed and teacher-directed activities, and weekly morning and afternoon activity plans makes this guidebook an invaluable resource.

Where To Find/Buy:

Bookstores and libraries.

ACTIVE LEARNING FOR TWOS

Description:

Boasting 330 pages, this guidebook contains five sections of activities for two-year-olds. "Planning for Twos" suggests ideas for setting up an environment conducive for "good care and avoid(ing) problems;" this section also shows how to plan activities so that things will run smoothly. The second section includes activities to help those working with two-year-olds make the best use of listening and talking skills. Large and small muscle activities comprise section three. There are exercises and activities for using your legs, arms, and back through walking, running, climbing, and balancing, as well as developing the muscles in your hands and fingers. Section four deals with art, blocks, dramatic play, and music. The final section focuses on activities involving nature, the senses, size, shape, color and numbers. Materials lists (and suggested "notes") and "Activity Checklists" accompany each section. Each Section has its own index preceding the section along with a rationale on why the activities are important.

Evaluation:

This reference is one of the Addison-Wesley "Active Learning Series" specifically focused on the two-year-old toddler. It provides a wonderful source of developmental activities covering the areas of creativity, community, listening and talking, physical development, and learning about the environment. The book does not have an overall index but it does have a detailed table of contents and section indexes. Each activity has an approximate time completion, with a suggested optimal number of children participating. Also noted is whether the activity is more appropriately experienced indoors or outdoors. Although designed primarily for educators of young children, this guidebook can also serve as a quality reference for parents seeking ideas and suggestions on things to do with their two-year-old. The checklists and materials lists are invaluable sources for organizing one's self and guiding a two-year-old's education. Buy the series; these will be a much used resource.

Where To Find/Buy:

Bookstores and libraries.

Overall Rating
★★★
Offers a wealth of activities and organizational tools, along with supporting rationale

Design, Ease Of Use
★★★
Comprehensive table of contents makes up for a lack of index; section indexes provided

1–4 Stars; N/R = Not Rated

Media Type:
Print

Price:
$23.25

Principal Subject:
Growth & Learning

Age Group:
Toddlers (1–3)

ISBN:
0201213362

Edition Reviewed:
1988

Publisher:
Addison-Wesley Longman
(Addison-Wesley Publishing)

Author/Editor:
Debby Cryer, Thelma Harms, Beth Bourland

About The Author:
(From Cover Notes)
Debby Cryer, Thelma Harms, and Beth Bourland collaborated with the Frank Porter Graham Child Development Center (University of North Carolina) in Chapel Hill, North Carolina in the development of this guidebook.

Overall Rating
★★★
Most activities are unusual and capitalize positively on what toddlers like to do

Design, Ease Of Use
★★★
Comprehensive index and bold headings make it easily read; graphics would help

1–4 Stars; N/R = Not Rated

Media Type:
Print

Price:
$14.95

Principal Subject:
Growth & Learning

Age Group:
All Ages (0–5)

ISBN:
091028704X

Edition Reviewed:
1984

Publisher:
Telshare Publishing Company

Author/Editor:
Karen Miller

About The Author:
(From Cover Notes)
Karen Miller has spent over 20 years in the child care field. She has been a teacher for Head Start, a director of child care centers, and has held numerous other child care positions, one involving curriculum development for two major child care organizations.

THINGS TO DO WITH TODDLERS AND TWOS

Description:

This 167 page guide contains 10 chapters, organized according to different types of toddler behaviors (sticking fingers in holes, climbing, etc). It is a compilation of ideas and activities and designed to set up a foundation for interactive fun between caregiver and child. Chapters 1 through 4 explore games and activities involving cause and effect, playing with water, noise makers (toys that shake, rattle, bang, twang, etc.), and art activities. Chapter 5 highlights activities that use the senses (textures, taste, etc). Pretending and dramatic play are covered in Chapter 6, while Chapter 7 focuses on language development (singing, fingerplays, things to do with pictures, etc.). Chapters 8 and 9 offer activities that show how things work together (stacking and puzzles) and various types of movement (climbing, throwing, pushing, crawling, etc.). Chapter 10 discusses "special problems" of toddlers in groups. These include clinging, sharing, frustration, and attention to name a few. An appendix, bibliography, and index conclude the resource.

Evaluation:

The author's intent is to describe activities that will provide a stimulating environment for toddlers. She resists applying age-specific guidelines to those activities, however, leaving that up to the parent; she is also adamant that the book is not a discussion of child development. However, she suggests that various activities she has described can enhance a toddler's newly acquired capabilities or offer a positive redirection of unacceptable behaviors. Many activities are unusual (marbles/bubble in a tube, pulleys, record player art, etc.) and sure to capture the interest and fascination of any toddler. Many capitalize on themes of science, math, reading, and other subject areas without appearing too intrusive or instructional. All activities involve open-ended exploration and are derived from the author's observation of what toddlers like to do. This is an unusual basis not often found in other activity resources which focus more on the teachable objective rather than the discovery element. Sure to offer fun experiences whether used in a home or in an educational context, this resource has much to offer.

Where To Find/Buy:

Bookstores, libraries, or order direct by calling 1-800-343-9707.

BABIES NEED BOOKS
Sharing The Joy Of Books With Children From Birth To Six

Description:

This book focuses on the why, what, when, and hows of introducing children to reading and books. It contains 261 pages, seven chapters with age-specific book lists, a conclusion, supplemental book lists, and an index. Chapter 1 offers supportive testimony of why children should be involved with books, with Chapter 2 plunging into the mechanics of reading with babies. The following chapters, 3 through 7, offer information in a progressive format for children up to age five. Different aspects of children's books are highlighted, such as the value of various illustration methods, the types of books to choose from (board books, alphabet, collections, etc.), the benefits of "theme" and "story" books for children, and more. Some of the book lists for each age category offer a short synopsis of the books, as well as the author and publisher. The concluding "Supplementary Book lists" section has been prepared by children's literature specialists and is intended to be used as a complementary supplement to the main book. There is an extensive index.

Evaluation:

This is a handy and valuable resource that focuses solely on the early childhood years. The author's intent is admirable—to list books that will involve children deeply, spark their imagination and curiosity, and establish a lifelong habit and appreciation of reading. There are old and new books, best-sellers, classics, and hard-to-find books, and all are worthy and respected. The shortcomings of this resource can only be found in its abruptness in stopping at six years of age, but its compact package makes it handy to carry around. We also wish the author had supplied ISBNs for recommended books to make searches a bit easier for parents, librarians, and bookstores. It is very well-presented, well-written with supportive information, and easily navigable. Although the author is most adamant about reading and this dominates the book (sometimes intrusively), the lists and evaluation of the books are great resources. Parents will find their time floundering at the bookstore cut drastically.

Where To Find/Buy:

Bookstores and libraries.

Overall Rating
★★★
Useful book lists (based on author's favorites) and valuable support for reading aloud

Design, Ease Of Use
★★
Book lists need highlights; no ISBNs provided for suggested books

1–4 Stars; N/R = Not Rated

Media Type:
Print

Price:
$15.95

Principal Subject:
Growth & Learning

Age Group:
All Ages (0–5)

ISBN:
0435081446

Edition Reviewed:
2nd (1998)

Publisher:
Heinemann (Reed Elsevier)

Author/Editor:
Dorothy Butler

About The Author:
(From Cover Notes)
A native of New Zealand, Dorothy Butler is a teacher, bookseller, and author, as well as a worldwide recognized children's literature advocate.

Overall Rating
★★★
Many, many ideas for playing with your baby

Design, Ease Of Use
★
"Flip-through" style with no index; recommended ages not included on activities

Media Type:
Print

Price:
$12.95

Principal Subject:
Growth & Learning

Age Group:
Infants & Toddlers (0–3)

ISBN:
1570711100

Edition:
1996

Publisher:
Sourcebooks

Author/Editor:
Sheila Ellison and Susan Ferdinandi

About The Author:
(From Cover Notes)
Sheila Ellison is the author of the '365' series of parenting books, including "365 Days of Creative Play." Susan Ferdinandi is the Assistant Director and teacher at the Little School in Benicia, CA. Both are experienced mothers, and are also sisters.

365 DAYS OF BABY LOVE
Playing, Growing And Exploring With Babies From Birth To Age 2

Description:
The authors, two experienced mothers who also happen to be sisters, state in their introduction, "We believe that the magic of childhood lives in the everyday moments." This book aims at offering a wide variety of games, toys, crafts, interactions, and exercises to help you fill those everyday moments with meaningful activities. Filled throughout with children's drawings, this book is organized in an easy-to-use style with one activity per page, often with enclosed "Wit & Wisdom" captions with tips from other parents across the country. The book contains 26 individual sections, with many ideas included in each section for such areas as "Caregiving," "Language and Sound," "Everyday Toys," "Nature," "Art," "Dad's Time," and "Food and Nutrition." Each of the 26 sections starts with activities appropriate for infants and progresses up through activities for two year olds; no age specifications are listed for each activity to account for individuals' variations. When necessary to the activity, a list of materials precedes the activity's description.

Evaluation:
Readers will find in this book a plethora of interesting games, activities, and interactions to engage in with their baby. This book emphasizes a baby's need to make choices and exercise his/her will, with activities that promote a baby's interactive abilities and development. The toys, crafts, and music sections are particularly valuable, including such cheap, easy-to-make items as a "permanent photo," created by keeping a series of school photos in one frame, or "finger tapping" devices created by sewing buttons on a child's old pair of gloves. Some of the other activities, however, feel too directed for both babies and mothers. The magic of motherhood lies in the spontaneity and freedom of being able to structure time with one's child in unique ways. But, if a mother is looking for ideas which can be tailored to her interactions with her child and/or she does not have an extended family to rely on, this resource can be a lifesaver now and then.

Where To Find/Buy:
Bookstores and libraries.

BABY SIGNS
How To Talk With Your Baby Before Your Baby Can Talk

Description:

This 163 page 10 chapter reference focuses on how to take advantage of your baby's non-verbal communication, their signs and gestures, and teach them to "talk" before they can. Chapters 1 and 2 give a brief overview of the meaning of "baby signs," and how babies use it to communicate before they are old enough to speak. Chapters 3, 4, and 5 contain information on how to begin teaching baby signs ("hat," "bird," "flower," "fish," "more") and how to progress toward more advanced baby signs; emphasis is on selecting a non-verbal cue that is mutually understood between parent and child. Stories about babies who sign are highlighted in Chapter 6, while Chapter 7 discusses the transition from signing to speech. The final three chapters include answers to parents' questions, an illustrated section of suggested baby signs, and interactive poems using baby signs. There is list of suggested books at the close of the book for parents interested in learning more about infant sign language research. This resource contains no index.

Evaluation:

Enhanced by black and white photographs and whimsical illustrations, this guide offers parents ways to enrich their interactions with their child through early signing. Based on ten years of research with families, the authors believe that a baby's ability to create and respond to gestures ("bye-bye," "no," "yes," etc.) can lead to better communication. By teaching children "baby signs," parents can hasten the process of learning to talk, jump start their child's intellectual development, enhance their self-esteem, and form a stronger bond between parent and child. This book provides a comprehensive argument for and interesting case studies of early communication which, when employed and practiced regularly, can certainly help parents meet their babies' needs early on. Hopefully later editions will include an index making this guide quite a bit easier to explore. Emphasizing that there are no "correct" signs except those established between parent and child, this book, however, is worth struggling through.

Where To Find/Buy:

Bookstores and libraries.

Overall Rating
★★★
Comprehensive argument, backed up by case studies, for teaching early communication

Design, Ease Of Use
★
Lack of index makes it difficult to find specifics; large subheadings somewhat useful

1–4 Stars/ N/R = Not Rated

Media Type:
Print

Price:
$12.95

Principal Subject:
Growth & Learning

Age Group:
Infants & Toddlers (0–3)

ISBN:
0809234300

Edition:
1996

Publisher:
Contemporary Books (NTC/ Contemporary Publishing)

Author/Editor:
Linda Acredolo, Ph.D. and Susan Goodwyn, Ph.D.

About The Author:
(From Cover Notes)
Acredolo is a Professor of Psychology at the University of California at Davis. Goodwyn is an Associate Professor of Psychology at California State University, Stanislaus. Both have been teaching Baby Signs to parent, teachers, and pediatricians for the past 10 years.

Overall Rating:
★★
Over 100 toddler games described, many of which are commonplace—"playing ball"

Design, Ease Of Use
★★★★
Well-organized with easy-to-use cross-referencing; listing the game's objective is useful

1–4 Stars; N/R = Not Rated

Media Type:
Print

Price:
$14.95

Principal Subject:
Growth & Learning

Age Group:
Toddlers (1–3)

ISBN:
0876591632

Edition:
1993

Publisher:
Gryphon House

Author/Editor:
Jackie Silberg

About The Author:
(From Cover Notes)
Silberg, an acclaimed speaker, teacher, trainer of early childhood development and music, is also a regular columnist for "Instructor" magazine. She is an adjunct lecturer in preschool education at Emporia (Kansas) State University, and has hosted a children's TV program.

GAMES TO PLAY WITH TODDLERS

Description:
This 285 page book includes ten sections of activities for children ages 1 to 2 years. Sections include: growing & learning games, teddy bear games, the kitchen, the outdoors, laughing & having fun, art & singing, car games, special bonding, bath & dressing, and finger & toe games. Silberg uses her experience as a teacher and trainer in early childhood development to detail games for toddlers ages 12–15 months, 15 to 18 months, 18 to 21 months, and 21 to 24 months. Originating from a variety of cultures and ethnic backgrounds, the games selected for each age group focus on coordination, language, observation, listening skills, imitation, nature appreciation, creativity, and other areas. The games progress in a step-by-step format with their intended objective—"What your toddler will learn"—noted at the bottom of each page. Also included are "Guidelines for Growth" a list of specific actions that illustrate toddler growth in motor, auditory & visual skills, language & cognitive skills, and self-concept skills.

Evaluation:
Readers will be pleased at the opportunity to "pick and choose" games based upon skill set/objective and interest. Additionally, grouping activities by age makes it relatively easy for parents/caregivers to determine where their child falls in terms of their developmental growth. For example, a 14 month old child might succeed at a game that is "appropriate" for an 18 month old. Or if a caregiver wishes to help a child in a certain area, like language skills, progressive games are given to serve that purpose. But remember these are, as always, "average" developmental guidelines. The games encompass both indoor and outdoor activities. Care is made to utilize common objects which are used in everyday situations. Alternative methods of play are offered for most games encouraging further creativity and exploration. Many of the games, however, are fairly commonly known: playing catch, throwing beanbags, Thumbkin, etc. Other books offer unique alternatives; this resource can be used to back up some of these.

Where To Find/Buy:
Bookstores and libraries.

INVOLVING PARENTS THROUGH CHILDREN'S LITERATURE
Preschool–Kindergarten

Description:

The author, with a background in teaching and as a reading specialist, offers 40 books to "demonstrate all the magic, creativity, and imagination that can be shared and enjoyed in books." An additional list of 99 children's books is given in the appendix. The book's intent is to present quality literature along with activities to promote enjoyable parent-child involvement to then encourage positive literacy development. The book's introduction outlines the criteria used for the selected titles and encompasses input from children's librarians, teachers, reading specialists, students, award-winning books, and more. This guide is presented in an 8 1/2" x 11" format for reproduction use by teachers. Each book title includes a story summary, a list of open-ended discussion questions, activities that are related to the book, and other children's books that can be used to extend the reading; a project is included for some books. Each title is typically covered in 1–2 pages. Three sample letters for teachers to send to parents are provided in the appendix.

Evaluation:

This book answers the question of "what do I do after a read a book aloud to my child?" Not simply a guide to choosing quality children's literature, this book extends the parent-child connection by applying the concepts within the book to other situations. The discussion questions involve more than rote memory and usually ask the child to engage in creative thinking by applying the book's theme to their own life—"what would you do if you swallowed a fly?" (from *I Know An Old Lady*). The extensions incorporate science concepts, math foundations, creative writing, arts and crafts, and more. Although some of the projects and activities (mainly the creative writing ones) are intended for older school-age children, they can certainly be adapted to preschoolers. Only 40 selections from children's literature are listed in this guide, but the activities may prompt a parent to think of ways to extend alternative reading materials too. This is definitely a must for educators and a possibility for parents wanting to creatively extend children's literature.

Where To Find/Buy:

Bookstores and libraries.

Overall Rating
★★
Offers parents creative applications to 40 selected book titles, but mostly for educators

Design, Ease Of Use
★★★★
Detailed table of contents, consistent format; sample letters to use with parents

1–4 Stars; N/R = Not Rated

Media Type:
Print

Price:
$15.00

Principal Subject:
Growth & Learning

Age Group:
Preschoolers (3–5)

ISBN:
1563080222

Edition Reviewed:
1993

Publisher:
Teachers Ideas Press
(Libraries Unlimited)

Author/Editor:
Anthony D. Fredericks

About The Author:
(From Cover Notes)
Fredericks, with a master's and doctor of education degrees in reading, has also been a classroom teacher and reading specialist in public and private schools for more than 15 years. He is also an associate professor of education at York College, York, Pennsylvania.

Overall Rating
★★
Useful activities to stimulate toddlers without digging into their parents' pocketbooks

Design, Ease Of Use
★★★★
Small size makes it easy to use; loaded with illustrations and written concisely

1–4 Stars; N/R = Not Rated

Media Type:
Print

Price:
$9.95

Principal Subject:
Growth & Learning

Age Group:
Toddlers (1–3)

ISBN:
1884734006

Edition Reviewed:
1995

Publisher:
Parenting Press

Author/Editor:
Sandi Dexter

About The Author:
(From Cover Notes)
Sandi Dexter is a parent and teacher who has been involved with preschoolers for 12 years. She is a collector of odds and ends from around her home and community, putting them to good use for toddler play and learning.

JOYFUL PLAY WITH TODDLERS
Recipes For Fun With Odds And Ends

Description:

This resource contains 126 pages of things to make and do with toddlers utilizing everyday "odds and ends." It begins with ideas for improving parenting skills by explaining how young children learn and explore. There is a brief (one page) checklist on how to babyproof your home, as well as a list of those items not suitable for making toys. The second chapter talks about setting limits, behavior, acknowledging feelings, power struggles, and regaining calm. The book progresses onto toys and games with suggestions of safe household items to use and how toddlers and parents might turn them into playthings. These include games using boxes, milk cartons, old clothes, kitchen utensils, and more. The "Activities" segment includes water and outdoor play, make-believe adventures, music and art, and cooking. An index is included. The book's main intent is to offer suggestions for on-the-spot games and activities for toddlers.

Evaluation:

Parents, teachers, and caregivers will find this quick idea guide a useful resource. It offers simple activities, such as bird watching, listening to sounds, and ladder stepping, as well as more advanced activities, such as cooking and threading pasta necklaces. There is also advice on how to find free or inexpensive art materials. The book is unique in its dedication of describing a set of fun and creative games utilizing household items. Each activity is easily accessible via the Table of Contents and Index. Safety tips concerning water activities and how to babyproof your home are invaluable saves. This guidebook is full of practical, fun ideas and would make a worthwhile addition to your family library.

Where To Find/Buy:

Bookstores and libraries, or order direct by calling 1-800-992-6657.

THE JOYFUL CHILD
A Sourcebook Of Activities And Ideas For Releasing Children's Natural Joy

Description:

This book centers on releasing the inner joy within ourselves and our children. Incorporating quotes throughout from philosophers, authors, and the Bible, this 257 page guide is divided into three parts. Part One discusses various philosophies and ideas for releasing "Natural Joy." Subtopics include defining joy and exploring the foundations of joy; self-esteem, values, and universal principles; teaching relationships (parents, child, teachers) along guidelines for the transmission of consciousness and attitudes; and looking at four different types of children—DISC (Dominate, Influencing, Supportive, and Conscientious). Part Two suggests activities in art, music, games, and more. Part Three shows parents how to bring it all together by focusing on creating a lesson plan, discussing the value of prayer, and the joy of serving. An Appendix portrays Dr. Robert Muller's "World Core Curriculum." A 10 page reference and resources section is included as well as an 8 page index.

Evaluation:

Jenkins' book details her argument for helping children and parents release their inner joy to become more caring and compassionate individuals. "Joy, as an expression of love, is a healing energy much needed by humanity and the planet at this time," and this is the author's stated purpose. Gleaning information from various philosophies on the topics of joy and inner peace, this guidebook expounds upon the virtues of "The Golden Rule" and how parents can modify their behavior as well as their children's towards this end. Despite the book's heavy spiritual flavor and sometimes preachiness, many families will find valuable information to interweave into their daily lives. The author's global approach helps extend the joyful child's awareness beyond national boundaries to understand their interconnection with everyone and everything. The author has taken great care to give a variety of resources for each chapter.

Where To Find/Buy:

Bookstores and libraries, or order direct by calling the publisher at (707) 542-5400, or Joyful Child, Inc. at (602) 494-3383.

Overall Rating
★★
Refreshing global approach; a bit heavy on rhetoric

Design, Ease Of Use
★★★★
Detailed table of contents, thorough reference and index sections, bold subheadings

1–4 Stars; N/R = Not Rated

Media Type:
Print

Price:
$16.95

Principal Subject:
Growth & Learning

Age Group:
All Ages (0–5)

ISBN:
0944031668

Edition Reviewed:
1996

Publisher:
Aslan Publishing

Author/Editor:
Peggy Jenkins, Ph.D.

About The Author:
(From Cover Notes)
Peggy Jenkins is the founder and director of a nonprofit educational service organization called "Joyful Child Inc." Dr. Jenkins is also a seminar leader in parent/teacher education, and a consultant in the area of behavior/learning styles.

Overall Rating
★★

Light on developmental info, but offers novel activities for parents and five-year-olds

Design, Ease Of Use
★★★

Convenient calendar format to hang up on the wall with monthly ideas

1–4 Stars; N/R = Not Rated

Media Type:
Print

Price:
$3.99

Principal Subject:
Growth & Learning

Age Group:
Preschoolers (3–5)

ISBN:
1570290482

Edition Reviewed:
1995

Publisher:
Totline Publications (Frank Schaffer Publications/Warren Publishing House)

Author/Editor:
Theodosia Spewock

About The Author:
(From Cover Notes)
Spewock has been an educator since 1978 as a reading specialist, parent educator, and a member and past president of Pennsylvania's Reading Association. She hosts a local radio story hour and is the author of other parenting books.

A YEAR OF FUN: JUST FOR FIVES
Fun Seasonal Activities, Songs, Poems, And Fingerplays—Plus Practical Advice For Parents

Description:
Created by a veteran educator, this 32 page guide includes developmental information and age-appropriate activities for those working with five-year-olds. One in a series of six and presented in a calendar-type format, it includes generic calendar segments designed to be hung up, used in any sequence, and repeated as often as parents would like. The first two pages highlight the author's introduction along with "typical behavior of fives" and a kindergarten readiness checklist. Each section thereafter includes a two-page spread for each month of the year. Blocked descriptions of activities (12–20) are included along with recipes, fingerplays, songs, rhymes, and other activities. The ideas often center on a monthly theme such as the season, holidays, etc. Each month also includes a development reminder which is highlighted in a colored block. Development topics focus on cognitive, language (listening, speaking, writing), motor, emotional growth, and more. A list of toys and books for five-year-olds is also given. Black and white illustrations are included throughout.

Evaluation:
This guide's strength lies in its presentation and inclusion of unusual activities. There are not hundreds of activities, but parents will find the ideas novel, easily prepared, and excellent fun for parent-child involvement. The directions are simple (one paragraph long), and even though the objective and materials are not listed, as many other guides do, parents will have little trouble getting ready. The author's obvious strength, however, lies in creating activities that foster a child's growth, but not in the area of describing a child's growth. Information is far too succinct to invite confidence or knowledge. Parents will need other resources to give them a developmental overview of a five-year-old child's growth. The author does, however, offer some good basic advice to parents as they get their child ready for kindergarten; she discusses "school lingo" ("line up," "give me your ears," etc.), visiting the school beforehand, and more. The price is right, its format makes it readily accessible, and no doubt parents and children will find many activities to enjoy together.

Where To Find/Buy:
Bookstores and libraries.

A YEAR OF FUN: JUST FOR FOURS
Fun Seasonal Activities, Songs, Poems, And Fingerplays—Plus Practical Advice For Parents

Description:
Created by a veteran educator, this 32 page guide includes developmental information and age-appropriate activities for those working with four-year-olds. One in a series of six and presented in a calendar-type format, it includes generic calendar segments designed to be hung up, used in any sequence, and repeated as often as parents would like. The first two pages highlight the author's introduction along with "typical behavior of fours." Each section thereafter includes a two-page spread for each month of the year. Blocked descriptions of activities (12–20) are included along with recipes, fingerplays, songs, rhymes, and other activities. The ideas often center on a monthly theme such as the season, holidays, etc. Each month also includes a development reminder which is highlighted in a colored block. Development topics focus on cognitive, language (listening, speaking, writing), motor, emotional growth, and more. A list of toys and books for four-year-olds is also given. Black and white illustrations are included throughout.

Evaluation:
This guide offers a novel approach in a field of many resources that strive to offer parents a combination of developmental information and activities to enhance a child's growth. This guide's strength lies in its presentation and inclusion of unusual activities. The directions are simple (one paragraph long), and even though the objective and materials are not listed (as many other guides do), parents will have little trouble getting ready. There are not hundreds of activities, but parents will find the ideas novel, easily prepared, and excellent fun for parent-child involvement. Although the activities are certainly age-appropriate, the author's obvious strength lies in creating activities that foster a child's growth, but not in the area of describing a child's growth. Information is far too succinct to invite confidence or knowledge. Parents will need other resources to give them a developmental overview of a four-year-old child's growth. But, the price is right, its format makes it readily accessible, and no doubt parents and children will find many activities to enjoy together.

Where To Find/Buy:
Bookstores and libraries.

Overall Rating
★★
Novel activities to engage parents and four-year-olds, but light on development info

Design, Ease Of Use
★★★
Convenient calendar format to hang up on the wall with monthly ideas

1–4 Stars; N/R = Not Rated

Media Type:
Print

Price:
$3.99

Principal Subject:
Growth & Learning

Age Group:
Preschoolers (3–5)

ISBN:
1570290474

Edition Reviewed:
1995

Publisher:
Totline Publications (Frank Schaffer Publications/Warren Publishing House)

Author/Editor:
Theodosia Spewock

About The Author:
(From Cover Notes)
Spewock has been an educator since 1978 as a reading specialist, parent educator, and a member and past president of Pennsylvania's Reading Association. She hosts a local radio story hour and is the author of other parenting books.

Overall Rating
★★
Connects daycare providers through email contact and hosts numerous activities

Design, Ease Of Use
★★★
Email access may elicit 100+ responses daily; activity lists printable but extensive

1–4 Stars; N/R = Not Rated

Media Type:
Internet

Principal Subject:
Growth & Learning

Age Group:
All Ages (0–5)

DAYCARE PROVIDERS HOME PAGE

Description:
Developed by a home daycare provider for the "sharing of information and ideas concerning the providing of professional services by daycare/ childcare providers," this site offers two options at their homepage along with numerous links to child-related sites. The first option is connection to "The Daycare Provider's Mailing List." This email access offers daycare providers, parents, and others an opportunity to enter into discussions and share ideas. Instructions are given on how to subscribe and how to leave the list; a warning is offered that subscription often brings over 100 messages each day. The second option—"Cindy's Cardfile—Circle, Craft and Activity Ideas"—presents 12 sections of activities ranging from "drama, fairy tales, families, and flowers" to "shapes, space, stories, transportation, and weather." Activities within these sections can be printed and include activity title, materials needed, and the procedure. Roughly 3 activities are given per page.

Evaluation:
Although this site states it is for daycare providers, it offers the visitor a wide range of activities that a parent can do with his/her child. A wide variety of choices can be found under several headings. Unlike many print resources, however, these activities do not include stated objectives nor developmental skills that are meant to be enhanced. The activities vary from art-type projects and role-playing, to songs (based upon well-known tunes) and finger rhymes. The lists of activities can be printed, but are organized one right after the other, making it difficult to print one selected activity. Regardless, this site hosts a "cardfile" of possibilities. Of special interest, for example, are the suggested activities for the various seasons. Because the site is not designed to enhance particular developmental skills, however, it can only be recommended as serving parents' need for their "fun fillers" with their children during the day.

Where To Find/Buy:
On the Internet at the URL: http://www.icomm.ca/daycare/index.html.

Internet URL:
http://www.icomm.ca/daycare/index.html

EARLYCHILDHOOD.COM

Description:

Sponsored by a school supply store specializing in arts and crafts materials, this site offers information for both parents and early childhood education professionals. Options at the site include "arts-n-crafts," articles and resources, forums to share your ideas, post concerns and questions to others, and an avenue for individuals or organizations to publish articles and comments. A list of education-type links is also provided. Articles offer advice and information from "early childhood experts" such as Bev Bos, Evelyn Petersen, and others. Articles written specifically for parents focus on listening skills, reading to your children, and teaching thinking skills at home. Also given is narrative advice from Bev Bos along the topics of children's book literacy, music, "parenting basics," and separation anxiety. Other articles concentrate on issues that typically concern professionals—creating thematic curriculums, multi-age classrooms, assessment and evaluation, technology in the classroom, and more.

Evaluation:

This site has the feel of being fairly new on the scene. Its breadth is dependent on contributions from educators and parents making its contents and growth ambiguous. Not much is available currently for parents, but the few articles read well and are motivating. If you thrive on arts and crafts and enjoy sharing new ideas with your child, you should take a look at their offerings. Although the site is sponsored by a supply store, their presence is not overbearing. The art and craft ideas involve simple materials and supplies. Most projects are open-ended, and the process is emphasized, not the product, thereby contributing to your child's sense of accomplishment. Communication opportunities in the forums seem to be mainly between educators and not between parents. Hopefully, this site will encompass more direct conversations between parents in the future. Other sites can offer you more well-rounded advice when it comes to parenting. We suggest you use this site for a quick uplift or a quick craft idea.

Where To Find/Buy:

On the Internet at the URL: http://www.earlychildhood.com.

Internet URL:

http://www.earlychildhood.com

Overall Rating
★★
Some good information based upon contributors, but mostly fun for the craftsy parent

Design, Ease Of Use
★★★
Clear path through site; information succinct albeit without graphics

---

1–4 Stars; N/R = Not Rated

Media Type:
Internet

Principal Subject:
Growth & Learning

Age Group:
Toddlers & Preschoolers (1–5)

Publisher:
Discount School Supply

Overall Rating
★★

250+ baby games described, many of which are commonplace (peekaboo, shake, etc.)

Design, Ease Of Use
★★★

Clear format; simple instructions & illustrations; games listed alphabetically in index

1–4 Stars; N/R = Not Rated

Media Type:
Print

Price:
$14.95

Principal Subject:
Growth & Learning

Age Group:
Infants (0–1)

ISBN:
0876591624

Edition Reviewed:
6th (1993)

Publisher:
Gryphon House

Author/Editor:
Jackie Silberg

About The Author:
(From Cover Notes)
Silberg has authored numerous books on child development and is a regular columnist for the teacher magazine Instructor. She is also an adjunct lecturer in preschool education at Emporia (KS) State University, and has hosted her own children's television program.

GAMES TO PLAY WITH BABIES

Description:

Silberg uses her experience as a teacher and trainer in early childhood development to detail games for infants ages 0 to 3 months, 3 to 6 months, 6 to 9 months, and 9 to 12 months. This 286 page book includes eight sections of activities for babies, parents, and caregivers. Sections include: growing & learning games, special bonding games, kitchen games, laughing & having fun, art & singing, bath & dressing, finger & toe games, and going to sleep games. Originating from a variety of cultures and ethnic backgrounds, the games selected for each age group focus on hand-eye coordination, language, observation, listening skills, bonding, exploration, body awareness, and other areas. The games progress in a step-by-step format with their intended objective—"What your baby will learn"—noted at the bottom of each page. Also included are "Guidelines for Growth" a list of specific actions that illustrate babies' growth in motor, auditory & visual skills, language & cognitive skills, and self-concept skills.

Evaluation:

Being able to "pick and choose" activities based upon daily routines (sleep, having fun, bonding, etc.) and interest (fingers, toes, singing, etc.) will delight many parents. By listing the appropriate age for each activity along with the activity's intent, parents will find this resource a help in their child's development. Each game contains very easy instructions with minimal preparation time and planning. Most of the activities are fairly commonplace as those described in some of her other books—"Where Did It Go?" (covering a toy with a cloth), "Shake, Shake, Shake" (filling containers with objects), etc. Although some rhymes, songs, and poems are offered, other resources place more emphasis on language experiences. The black and white illustrations are adequate but incomplete. The page layouts make for quick navigation but are uninspiring. The alphabetical index is comprehensive. For parents searching for an impromptu game, this source will help. Other resources, however, offer a wider selection of unusual activities, along with the more commonplace, to keep a little one (and parents) focused and interested.

Where To Find/Buy:

Bookstores and libraries.

MORE GAMES TO PLAY WITH TODDLERS

Description:

This 271 page guide contains 200+ games and activities for toddlers and is divided into twelve sections. Each game is explained on one page and includes a recommended age. Step-by-step instructions are given with occasional illustrations. Each game notes what a child will learn from the activity. A "Guidelines for Growth" chart lists developmental skills in terms of motor, auditory, and visual skills; language and cognitive skills; and self-concept skills. The first four sections include block games, bouncing games, games involving color and shape, and language games. Quiet and outside games, rhyming games, games involving running and jumping, and seasonal games follow. The final sections include singing games, toy games, and social games which use cooperation, coordination and imitation skills. The Table of Contents lists all the games, which age the activity is appropriate for, and what skill is reinforced ("coordination," "listening," etc.). An annotated list of books for toddlers and an index are given.

Evaluation:

Caregivers, as well as parents, will certainly find this a useful book. Each game contains very easy instructions with minimal preparation time and planning. These games involve few materials, although most of the activities are just as commonplace as those described in her first book—walking around the house pointing out a given color, stacking blocks, etc. The novelty with this edition, however, is the emphasis on language with more rhymes, songs, and poems offered. By listing the appropriate age for each activity along with the activity's intent, parents will find this resource a help in their child's development. The black and white illustrations are adequate but incomplete. The page layouts make for quick navigation but are uninspiring. The index is comprehensive and cross-referenced. For parents searching for an impromptu game, this source will help. Other resources, however, will offer a wider selection of unusual activities, along with the more commonplace, to keep a busy toddler focused and interested.

Where To Find/Buy:

Bookstores and libraries.

Overall Rating
★★
A fun overview of some of the more common games for children ages 12 to 24 months

Design, Ease Of Use
★★★
Simply organized with clear instructions; some illustrations

1–4 Stars; N/R = Not Rated

Media Type:
Print

Price:
$14.95

Principal Subject:
Growth & Learning

Age Group:
Toddlers (1–3)

ISBN:
0876591780

Edition Reviewed:
1996

Publisher:
Gryphon House

Author/Editor:
Jackie Silberg

About The Author:
(From Cover Notes)
Jackie Silberg has a degree in education from the University of Missouri, Kansas City, and a master's degree in early childhood education from Emporia State University in Kansas. She is also a teacher, a keynote speaker, and an accomplished musician.

Overall Rating
★★
Offers multi-level activities for infants & toddlers, but not useful as a sole resource

Design, Ease Of Use
★★
Good bold headings; no illustrations; activity index by "invitation" would be helpful

1–4 Stars; N/R = Not Rated

Media Type:
Print

Price:
$16.95

Principal Subject:
Growth & Learning

Age Group:
Infants & Toddlers (0–3)

ISBN:
0893340383

Edition Reviewed:
1994

Publisher:
Humanics Limited

Author/Editor:
Kathryn Castle, Ed.D.

INFANT & TODDLER HANDBOOK (THE)
Invitations For Optimum Early Development

Description:

This 105 page book is organized in seven chapters, each with its own introduction. Chapter 1 includes information on infant/toddler social, motor, language, and cognitive development skills. Chapter 2 continues with information on designing an interesting and responsive environment encouraging exploration. Chapters 3 through 7 present age-specific learning "invitations"—to look & listen, touch, communicate, move, and discover & solve problems. The author defines "invitations" as a means of providing infants and toddlers with "appropriate learning opportunities, activities, and materials which help them grow in all areas of development." Each "invitation" includes the child's "emerging ability," the "caregiver role," and lists of activities related to that "invitation" divided by age groups (3 and 6 month breakdowns). Two appendices are also included. Appendix A includes a list of books, records, and other resources. Appendix B is a table for matching caregiving activities to a child's individual temperament.

Evaluation:

The layout of this book is methodical, and although there is no index, the table of contents serves as a clear path to tap the book's information. The author's suggestion—to convert the activities to cards, organize them in a file box, and use them according to a child's age and development—is a good one. The result of this would be a convenient curriculum guide for either caregivers or parents. Particularly well done are the "Role of the Caregiver" sections in Chapters 3, 5, and 7. Some research data is given to justify and validate the suggested activities. For example, information is provided on how language-related activities (talking, singing, reading) encourage the development of the left side of the brain; visual-spatial materials (mobiles, music, stacking toys) encourage the development of the right side of the brain. The author then offers activities to satisfy both kinds of experiences. Used with other more comprehensive activity guidebooks, caregivers in particular will find this book useful for creating a caring and interactive environment.

Where To Find/Buy:

Bookstores and libraries.

CHOOSING YOUR CHILDREN'S BOOKS
2 To 5 Years Old

Description:

Twelve "chapters" comprise this 78 page guide to children's literature developed by the author, an English teacher and school media specialist. Her introduction briefly highlights young children's literacy development along with suggestions for encouraging young readers. She also gives an overview of the types of books this age group enjoys. The children's books White recommends are arranged alphabetically within the following 12 categories: alphabet books, counting books, concepts, nature, rhymes, wordless, simple stories, stories, folk tales, bedtime books, families, and starting school. Bibliographic information is included for each along with a one paragraph annotation; illustrations from these annotated books are included at times. The guide is the author's personal selection and criteria used for selecting the materials was "by doing a lot of reading!" The book includes choices from the classics, award winners, multicultural, and modern stories. It is the first in a series of three.

Evaluation:

The author's husband states in his foreword that this book was created as a more simple version of the heavy reference books that are available about children's literature. Then he continues by saying that they envisioned a slim guide with large print that "could be easily brought to the bookshop or library to make a selection." Their vision is a reality here. This guide is slim, does have large print, and certainly can be easily packed for an outing. However, it won't take long for parents and children to read through all of the resources listed within this guide book. Each category roughly contains about 12–20 choices, certainly not an overabundance considering the hungry reading appetites of this age group. We do like the author's intent of having something a bit more portable. But we also know that parents and their children will be better served investing in one of the more extensive resources that are available. These won't cost much more but offer more choices and variety than contained within this volume.

Where To Find/Buy:

Bookstores and libraries.

Overall Rating
★
Limited choices for encouraging young readers, based on loose selection criteria

Design, Ease Of Use
★★★★
Large print, easily portable; organized first by category, alphabetically in the index

1–4 Stars; N/R = Not Rated

Media Type:
Print

Price:
$5.95

Principal Subject:
Growth & Learning

Age Group:
Toddlers & Preschoolers (1–5)

ISBN:
1882726103

Edition Reviewed:
1994

Publisher:
Bayley & Musgrave

Author/Editor:
Valerie White, B.A., Cert.Ed.

About The Author:
(From Cover Notes)
White is an experienced teacher of English and school media specialist. She holds a degree in English, with a Postgraduate Certificate in Education.

Overall Rating
★
Book's intent is admirable but activities are rather droll and uninteresting

Design, Ease Of Use
★★
Easy to read but wide margins and a lot of white space provide little text

1–4 Stars; N/R = Not Rated

Media Type:
Print

Price:
$17.95

Principal Subject:
Growth & Learning

Age Group:
All Ages (0–5)

ISBN:
0893340464

Edition Reviewed:
1994

Publisher:
Humanics Limited

Author/Editor:
Angie Rose, Ph.D; Lynn Weiss, Ph.D.

About The Author:
(From Cover Notes)
Angie Rose has a Ph.D. in early childhood development and education. She is also the specialist in Education for Responsible for Parenthood (EFRP) for the Dallas Independent School District. Weiss is a psychotherapist and hosts a daily radio call-in program.

SELF-ESTEEM ACTIVITIES
Giving Children From Birth To Six The Freedom To Grow

Description:

This 169 page book focuses on age-specific self-esteem activities for children age birth to six years. These games and activities are arranged to parallel the authors' suggested five steps of a child's emotional development. These five stages include trust, self-awareness, competence, power, and self control. The table of contents separates the activities for each of these five stages and orders them by age: birth to 18 months, 18 months to three years, three to four years, four to five years, and five to six years. There is no index. One activity or game is described on each page. Each activity includes the following information: its purpose, the materials needed, how to do the activity, what was learned, and ways to extend the activity (other projects or activities). The authors, Angie Rose, Ph.D., and Lynn Weiss, Ph.D. are professionals whose collective educational backgrounds include child development, effective parenting strategies, anthropology, and mental health.

Evaluation:

This guidebook provides parents a very simple approach for interacting with their children in an educational way. The introduction neatly explains the five developmental steps children experience as they become emotionally healthy, self-controlled individuals. The age-specific breakouts, separated by the five emotional development stages, allow parents to quickly find an appropriate game. It would have also been helpful to have an index to look for an activity based on the learned outcome from each game. The "What Next?" section at the end of each activity points towards a future goal, or next step, and serves as another way to measure your child's development and growth. All activities focus on building a child's self-esteem. They are easy to follow and well-planned, albeit often mundane and commonplace—blowing kisses, playing with playdough, etc. This resource, although well-intentioned for parents looking to develop a strong sense of self-esteem in their child, will only serve as a start.

Where To Find/Buy:

Bookstores and libraries.

365 DAYS OF CREATIVE PLAY
For Children 2 Yrs. & Up

Description:

With a brief introduction describing the benefits of a child's experiences with play, this 377+ page book describes 365 activities that can be done with children aged 2 years and older. Activities are grouped into 13 categories "all of which tap into the child's creative potential." The activities do not need to be done in order but a balance between all categories is included when the activities are done sequentially. Included categories are: Art, Construction, Craft, Dance, Education, Environment, Family, Foods and Cooking, Games, Horticulture, Make-Believe, Music, and Nature. There is no table of contents, but an index lists the activities and activity number by these categories. Suggested safety tips is provided along with a list of materials, supplies, and equipment. Each activity is fully explained on one page with a list of materials, directions, and a child's illustration of the activity also given. The authors also note that all the activities and their materials comply with safe environmental standards.

Evaluation:

Although the activities are designed "for children 2 years and up," that's convenient for selling the book but not a fair description of its contents. Most of the activities are designed for the older child or parent. Involving considerable adult preparation at times, these activities will creatively challenge the parent but do little for their child's self-confidence or self-esteem. The other problem with this book is in its organization. Additional information needs to be included for each activity such as: the activity's category, the suggested age range, and the objective/skill that is being enhanced. Listing the activities by category in the index, without a table of contents or general alphabetical listing, makes subsequent searches for an activity difficult. The "365 Days" format, of course, fits in neatly with doing one activity a day with your child. But the book is bulky (a spiral-bound format would be more useful) and some activities are fairly common (make popsicles with your child). Check out other resources that build on children's developmental abilities, not adults'.

Where To Find/Buy:

Bookstores and libraries.

Overall Rating
★
Great for enhancing the parent's creative potential, less so for the child's

Design, Ease Of Use
★
No table of contents, index lists activities by category only; needs a spiral format

1–4 Stars; N/R = Not Rated

Media Type:
Print

Price:
$12.95

Principal Subject:
Growth & Learning

Age Group:
Toddlers & Preschoolers (1–5)

ISBN:
1570710295

Edition Reviewed:
3rd (1995)

Publisher:
Sourcebooks

Author/Editor:
Sheila Ellison and Dr. Judith Gray

About The Author:
(From Cover Notes)
Ellison, with a BA degree in psychology from USC, has volunteered on behalf of children, and founded community youth groups and mentoring programs. Gray is internationally known as an author, teacher, and speaker on future trends in education.

Overall Rating
★★★★
Provides comparisons between preschool philosophies along with practical advice

Design, Ease Of Use
★★★★
Easily read w/ bulleted tips, highlighted blocks of information, checklists, and more

1–4 Stars; N/R = Not Rated

Media Type:
Print

Price:
$14.95

Principal Subject:
Growth & Learning

Age Group:
Preschoolers (3–5)

ISBN:
0816036772

Edition Reviewed:
1997

Publisher:
Facts On File

Author/Editor:
Marian Edelman Borden

About The Author:
(From Cover Notes)
Borden is a professional writer and journalist. She is also a frequent contributor to magazines featuring early childhood education and her articles have appeared in *American Baby*, *Healthy Kids*, *Parenting*, *Sesame Street*, and the *New York Times*.

SMART START
The Parents' Complete Guide To Preschool Education

 Best Resource For:
Selecting an appropriate preschool

 Recommended For:
Growth & Learning

Description:

This 222 page step-by-step guide to choosing a preschool is divided into 8 chapters. Chapter 1 lists philosophical and educational differences between various preschool programs. Pros and cons of each program are given (Piagetian, Montessori, parent co-op, and more) along with suggested guidelines to use when making a choice. Also addressed are concerns of parents of children with handicapping conditions, twins and multiples, and others. Chapter 2 focuses on evaluating and observing preschools; checklists and questions are provided. Chapter 3 provides advice for those families with children in daycare who wish to include preschool experiences in their child's day. Chapter 4–6 deal with the transition of getting your child ready for school, what a typical day at preschool might be like, and how to forge a positive relationship with your child's teacher. Chapter 7 offers information on the physical, intellectual, and emotional changes of children from the ages of 2–5. A checklist and discussion of kindergarten readiness are provided in Chapter 8. Appendices contain preschool evaluation sheets, immunization schedule, and resources.

Evaluation:

Any parent searching for a tool to help determine a preschool appropriate to their child's educational needs need look no further. This guidebook not only helps parents establish and refine their criteria, but also gives parents background information about the various choices available and how to make the transition go smoothly. The book is extremely well-organized with bold chapter subheadings, "bulleted" (a pencil icon) advice, and highlighted blocks of recommendations, tips, and strategies. Additionally, each chapter concludes with a question and answer segment that spotlights additional concerns parents may have. Other resources that address this subject offer little in terms of in-depth program comparisons. They usually help parents through the decision-making process but go no further. Tips for easing separation anxieties by helping parents and children make a successful transition and ways of assuring children continued success once they enter kindergarten are areas often not included. This book covers these issues and offers succinct, practical advice to help parents identify quality programs that match their needs.

Where To Find/Buy:
Bookstores and libraries.

PRESCHOOL AND YOUR CHILD
What You Should Know

Description:

Supported by four chapters, this 84 page resource provides parents with information about all of the aspects of a preschool program. Chapter One discusses the "Basic Ingredients" of a good early childhood program including types of schools, how to make comparisons, goals of schools, and terminology. Chapter Two explains to parents what things to consider when looking for a preschool: how to determine the right school for their child; health and safety issues; philosophy; financial considerations; and more. Admissions, publicly financed programs, and what to do if your child is not accepted by a desired school are some of the issues addressed in Chapter Three. Chapter Four focuses on a child's readiness for preschool with developmental information for parents to compare starting their child at age 2, 3, and 4; compatibility concerns between parents and the school are also discussed. An appendix lists additional organizations and resource centers, followed by a "Notes" section and a concluding index.

Evaluation:

Parents will find this book an adequate resource for finding a program to help their child grow up feeling confident and successful, developing at their own pace and in their own way. General guidelines, suggestions, and advice are offered on a myriad of topics from choosing a school to separating from your child. One premise of the book is that whether your child is ready or not for preschool, parents should always remember that childhood should never be hurried or rushed. Keeping this in mind, this book offers just enough information so parents can make an educated decision about a preschool based upon their child's individual development and personality; no specific details, however, are given about popular programs such as Montessori, Waldorf, or others. Parents will need to look further. Parents are given advice on how to match their goals and expectations with a particular program's philosophy and practice. This book offers a good first start with some interesting insights for parents ready to take this next big step.

Where To Find/Buy:

Bookstores and libraries.

Overall Rating
★★
A good basic primer on choosing a preschool and making it a positive experience for all

Design, Ease Of Use
★★
Well-stocked Table of Contents but with distracting bullets; question lists provided

1–4 Stars; N/R = Not Rated

Media Type:
Print

Price:
$7.95

Principal Subject:
Growth & Learning

Age Group:
Preschoolers (3–5)

ISBN:
0802774725

Edition Reviewed:
2nd (1995)

Publisher:
Walker & Company (Walker Publishing)

Author/Editor:
Diana Townsend-Butterworth

About The Author:
(From Cover Notes)
Diana Townsend-Butterworth has lectured to parents' organizations, and has appeared on national television and radio shows., and is a frequent contributor to *Family Circle, Women's World,* and other publications.

Overall Rating
★
Focuses on mainstreaming 4 year olds into schools; vicarious info about preschools given

Design, Ease Of Use
★★
Detailed table of contents, adequate index; heavily laden with research rhetoric

1–4 Stars; N/R = Not Rated

Media Type:
Print

Price:
$19.95

Principal Subject:
Growth & Learning

Age Group:
Preschoolers (3–5)

ISBN:
1853962708

Edition Reviewed:
1995

Publisher:
Paul Chapman Publishing

Author/Editor:
Marion Dowling

About The Author:
(From Cover Notes)
Dowling, an independent specialist in early years, has taught in primary schools, been a nursery headteacher, and worked as an advisory headteacher and senior primary adviser. She has contributed to early childhood education inservice courses in Britain and overseas.

STARTING SCHOOL AT FOUR: A SHARED ENDEAVOUR

Description:
Seven chapters comprise this 165 page book whose stated intentions are to highlight issues about a child's first year in school along with the needs of four-year-olds. It is written specifically for those working with preschool-aged children. Chapter 1 describes the roles of various educators from parents to preschool providers to teachers. How to select a school, adjust to the school environment, and more are presented in Chapter 2. Children's personal development and how they learn are the topics of Chapters 3 and 4. Chapters 5 and 6 discuss the characteristics of young children starting school and how to set up the various aspects of the curriculum (literacy, mathematics, science, etc.) to meet their needs. Chapter 7 concentrates on the role and implications of assessments (on entry to school, during the first few months after entry, etc.). Each chapter concludes with a "Suggested action" section consisting of the author's advice to those involved with young children's education (headteachers, parents, etc.).

Evaluation:
Unless parents are planning to live in Britain in their near future, don't bother to sightsee this guide. Although the title implies that the guide will perhaps help in choosing a preschool, in reality this guide focuses on the growing trend in Britain to mainstream children into their school system at the age of 4. It's heavy on the research rhetoric, heavy on how educators can accommodate four-year-olds, but light on concrete advice for parents offering generalized information and textbook answers instead. However, if parents read carefully (and they will need to read VERY carefully) between the lines in this guide, they will certainly decipher some criteria to use when looking for and evaluating various preschool programs, especially when comparing a four-year-old's needs with certain focused preschool programs. This author's stated intentions are honorable, but this guide will offer nothing of great consequence to those parents looking for definitive guidelines as they search for a preschool for their child.

Where To Find/Buy:
Bookstores and libraries.

EVERYTHING YOU ALWAYS WANTED TO KNOW ABOUT PRESCHOOL BUT DIDN'T KNOW WHOM TO ASK

Description:

This 31 page pamphlet is organized around parental questions arising from a preschool search. Twenty questions are listed in the table of contents and then addressed within the body of the booklet. No page numbers are given. Answers address such questions as: "Why should my child go to preschool?," "What makes a quality preschool program?," "What if my child doesn't want to leave me?," and "What does 'developmentally appropriate' mean, and how does it apply to my preschool?" Other areas discussed include what a typical day is like, recommended class sizes, how to prepare a child for their first school experience, the role of cultural diversity in the preschool, discipline procedures, parental involvement, kindergarten readiness, and more. Each question is typically answered in a one- or two-page spread and includes illustrations from preschoolers. Red highlighted text denote question subheadings and bold black text break up some of the text.

Evaluation:

This guide does a fine job presenting just about every question parents may ask as they begin their preschool search. The problem with this book lies in their answers. The authors give light treatment to answers that skirt primary issues and provide no checklists for evaluating schools leaving parents shortchanged. The book reads more like a promotional effort about preschools by preschools. Other resources give in-depth comparisons between various preschool programs (religious, Montessori, Piagetian, and more), offer evaluation checklists and questions to ask preschool directors, advice on making the transition successful for parents and child, and information on what kindergarten readiness means. This book offers the barest basics with commonsense pat answers. For example, in answering how to prepare a child for preschool, the authors advice parents to talk with their child about their feelings (with suggested book resources listed in the table of contents but not found in the pamphlet). Parents should use other resources to help them with this important decision.

Where To Find/Buy:

Bookstores and libraries.

Overall Rating
★
Barest info and commonsense answers to good questions concerning preschool selection

Design, Ease Of Use
★
Red highlights and bold text; no page numbers, no index, some info listed but not found

1–4 Stars; N/R = Not Rated

Media Type:
Print

Price:
$2.99

Principal Subject:
Growth & Learning

Age Group:
Preschoolers (3–5)

ISBN:
0590936018

Edition Reviewed:
1996

Publisher:
Scholastic

Author/Editor:
Ellen Booth Church with Deb Matthews

About The Author:
(From Cover Notes)
Church is an early childhood consultant for public and private schools specializing in curriculum development and programming. Matthews is an early childhood consultant for Head Start, other child-care organizations, and public schools.

Overall Rating
★★★★
A creative, sensitive, and insightful guide to helping children cope with grief and loss

Design, Ease Of Use
★★★★
Eloquent and readable

1–4 Stars; N/R = Not Rated

Media Type:
Print

Price:
$12.95

Principal Subject:
Growth & Learning

Age Group:
All Ages (0–5)

ISBN:
1558320512

Edition Reviewed:
1994

Publisher:
Harvard Common Press

Author/Editor:
Claudia Jewett Jarratt

About The Author:
(From Cover Notes)
The author is a child and family therapist and the author of another book about children, *Adopting the Older Child.*

HELPING CHILDREN COPE WITH SEPARATION AND LOSS

Best Resource For:
Understanding how children deal with grief and loss

Recommended For:
Growth & Learning

Description:

This 232-page book is intended to be read by parents and other primary caregivers, as well as "helping" adults such as therapists, school counselors, and teachers who wish to help a child work through the stages of recovery from loss. Various types of experiences are explored here, from the death of a parent, to special issues of adoption and foster care, to grief caused by parental divorce or separation. The book begins with a discussion about how to tell a child about a loss, and then moves in progressive chapters to the specific losses a child may face. Successive chapters trace the progressive stages of the grieving process, and typical and atypical reactions by children. Specific ways to help children work through these stages are also discussed, including creative games and discussions to help them understand their own feelings, and deal with problems of self-esteem, self-blame, and anxiety. The final chapter focuses on the grief process over time: the need to "revisit and readdress grief experiences" and the changing feelings of children as they themselves learn and grow.

Evaluation:

This is a sensitive and perceptive book about children's unique ways of coping with grief, written by a respected child and family therapist. Although its focus is not solely on children of divorce, this book is very useful reading for parents or therapists working with such children, as they too must undergo a grieving process—the "death of the family" and the loss of normal expectations of what a family should be. The best parts of this book include those which discuss how children perceive the world at various ages, which can determine how adults should speak to them about loss (such as the "magical thinking" stage until age 7, during which a child tends to believe that his or her thoughts and feelings directly affect the people around them). The book provides a number of lively, creative exercises designed to help a child identify and give voice to his/her feelings. This book, in contrast to many other books about children, looks at them from the inside-out, with empathy, intelligence, and feeling, and would be of help to any parent/caregiver who seeks to help a child through separation, divorce, or other trauma.

Where To Find/Buy:

Bookstores and libraries.

IT'S NOBODY'S FAULT
New Hope And Help For Difficult Children

Best Resource For:
Understanding and treatment of brain disorders

Recommended For:
Growth & Learning

Description:

The author, a child and adolescent psychiatrist, discusses symptoms, causes, and treatment for various brain disorders in this 303 page guide which is divided into three parts. Part One focuses on life with a child's brain disorder—what a brain disorder is and how it affects the child's life and those they come in contact with; the role of the health professional in treating these disorders is also presented. Part Two explains the causes of brain disorders ("DNA Roulette") and the role of medication. Part Three highlights 13 "no-fault brain disorders": ADHD, obsessive compulsive disorder, separation anxiety disorder, social phobia/shyness, generalized anxiety disorder, enuresis/bedwetting, tourette syndrome, bipolar disorder/manic depressive illness, major depressive disorder, eating disorders, schizophrenia, conduct disorder, and pervasive developmental disorder, autism, and Asperger's disorder. Symptoms, diagnosis, brain chemistry, treatment, and parenting are presented for each disorder. Story vignettes from the author's experience are used to illustrate various behaviors, treatments, and outcomes after treatment.

Evaluation:

The author's term "no-fault brain disorder" (that brain disorders exist because of how a child's brain works and not because of what his parents do) will offer welcome relief to the parents, families, and teachers struggling to work with a child that has a disorder. By additionally pointing out the discrepancy between calling some treatments "medication" (seen as beneficial) and others "drugs" (seen as debilitating), the author helps take away stigmas attached to disorders that he believes will benefit from medical treatment. Throughout the book, there is much emphasis placed on understanding the biological roots of a disorder and how the genetic chemistry of the brain precludes certain behaviors. Parents who have wrestled too long with their child's behavior and children who have wrestled ineffectively with their self-esteem should take a look at this author's advice. By presenting the "latest treatments" and a strong argument for medication (psychopharmacology), this resource may well afford some parents a new course of action that will better serve their child's needs and improve attitudes about themselves.

Where To Find/Buy:

Bookstores and libraries.

Overall Rating
★★★★
Emphasizes brain chemistry as root of 13 brain disorders rather than parenting styles

Design, Ease Of Use
★★★★
Story vignettes; incl. useful appendices (glossary, support groups, medication tables)

1–4 Stars; N/R = Not Rated

Media Type:
Print

Price:
$15.00

Principal Subject:
Growth & Learning

Age Group:
All Ages (0–5)

ISBN:
0812929217

Edition Reviewed:
1996

Publisher:
Times Books (Random House)

Author/Editor:
Harold S. Koplewicz, M.D.

About The Author:
(From Cover Notes)
Koplewicz is vice chairman of the Department of Psychiatry, director of the Division of Child and Adolescent Psychiatry at New York University Medical Center, and professor of clinical psychiatry at the New York University School of Medicine.

Overall Rating
★★★★

Comprehensive and supportive guide to assessing and treating learning disabilities

Design, Ease Of Use
★★★★

Good index backs up table of contents; visual aids, bullets, boxed-in stories provided

1–4 Stars; N/R = Not Rated

Media Type:
Print

Price:
$25.00

Principal Subject:
Growth & Learning

Age Group:
Preschoolers (3–5)

ISBN:
0684827387

Edition Reviewed:
1997

Publisher:
The Free Press (Simon & Schuster)

Author/Editor:
Corinne Smith, Ph.D. and Lisa Strick

About The Author:
(From Cover Notes)
Smith, associate dean of education at Syracuse University, is an expert in nonstandard assessment approaches on the topic of learning disabilities. Strick is a freelance writer who has produced many features on family and education for national magazines.

LEARNING DISABILITIES: A TO Z
A Parent's Complete Guide To Learning Disabilities From Preschool To Adulthood

Best Resource For:
Dealing with learning disabilities

Recommended For:
Growth & Learning

Description:

There are three parts to this 407 page book which outlines the causes, symptoms, and treatment of learning disabilities and is written by an "expert in nonstandard assessment approaches." Learning disabilities are neurological handicaps that affect the brain's ability to understand, remember, or communicate information. Part 1 focuses on defining learning disabilities including their causes and the various types that might arise. The authors emphasize that the cause is less important than knowing how it affects the child and how to find the right kinds of help. Types of learning disabilities that are highlighted include ADHD, visual perception disabilities, language processing disabilities, and fine motor disabilities. Part 2 presents various signs that are used to indicate learning disabilities. Also given is advice on how to get a competent assessment and how to become an "expert" on your child. Part 3 focuses on how to get an "appropriate" education for your child. Four appendixes offer benchmarks for normal development, common assessment measures, skills development (K–middle school), and a resource list.

Evaluation:

Parents who are seeking guidance in having their child's learning problems diagnosed and treated will appreciate the amount of solid information provided in this guide. In particular, parents and teachers will applaud the advice presented in Part 3. For example, the chapter on "Strategies for Promoting Personal Success," gives parents concrete tips for creating a positive environment for their child. Many other books ignore such elements as how to help a child with learning disabilities transition to living on their own, consider college, or find employment. This one fills that need. Concrete suggestions are offered throughout along with the reminder that although "learning disability" focuses on a child's weakness, the child's strengths should also be attended to. Although seemingly textbook-like at first, this guide's writing style and tone are user-friendly offering excellent visual aids such as children's drawings, schoolwork, and boxed-in story vignettes to illustrate the authors' points. This succinct, supportive guide deserves a place in any home where learning disabilities are being addressed.

Where To Find/Buy:

Bookstores and libraries.

PARENTING THE STRONG-WILLED CHILD
The Clinically Proven Five-Week Program For Parents Of Two- To Six-Year-Olds

Best Resource For:
Understanding strong-willed children

Recommended For:
Growth & Learning

Description:

This book is divided into four sections. Each of the first three parts describes a different dimension of the guide's five-week program strategy. Part I explains the factors that cause or contribute to strong-willed behavior. Considered factors include such topics as temperament, parenting styles, parental conflict, divorce, alcohol abuse, and television. Techniques of the five-week program are the focus of Part II broken down week by week, and day by day in some segments. Part III centers on ways to develop a more positive environment in the family and home. The purpose of this part is to show ways to enhance and maintain the positive behavior changes that occurred via the five-week program. The final section, Part IV, combines what parents have learned in the first three parts. It offers parents suggestions, advice, and strategies for managing specific behavior problems commonly occurring in young, strong-willed children (temper tantrums, aggression, bedtime and mealtime problems, etc.).

Evaluation:

This 256 page book focuses on the specific challenge of parenting a strong-willed child. Offering a five-week easily followed guide, this program is based on a clinical treatment program that is backed by over 30 years of collective research. Unusual to this study is that the authors have also done follow-up work 15 years later with families who have used their technique finding continued success. This approach uses a positive, step-by-step, clearly outlined strategy that discusses ways for parents to seek manageable solutions to their children's difficult behavior. This book will dictate your full attention and should not be used simply as a reference aid, although the comprehensive index makes for easy navigation in finding information on any specific topic. The tables, charts, and worksheets work hard to illustrate concepts, and are very useful for the success of the program. Parents who are anxious and frustrated about the behavior of their strong-willed child need to take a look at this useful resource.

Where To Find/Buy:

Bookstores and libraries.

Overall Rating
★★★★
Good information offered in a step-by-step format for a specific parenting dilemma

Design, Ease Of Use
★★★★
Highlighted advice with numerous charts and tables

1–4 Stars; N/R = Not Rated

Media Type:
Print

Price:
$14.95

Principal Subject:
Growth & Learning

Age Group:
Toddlers & Preschoolers (1–5)

ISBN:
0809232650

Edition Reviewed:
1996

Publisher:
Contemporary Books (NTC/Contemporary Publishing)

Author/Editor:
Rex Forehand, Ph.D. and Nicholas Long, Ph.D.

About The Author:
(From Cover Notes)
Forehand is a research professor of clinical child psychology and director of the Institute for Behavioral Research at the University of Georgia. Long is an associate professor of pediatrics and director of pediatric psychology at the University of Arkansas.

Overall Rating
★★★★
Combines research and experience in diagnosing and treating childhood depression

Design, Ease Of Use
★★
Heavy use of clinical terminology at times, useful story vignettes help break it up

1–4 Stars; N/R = Not Rated

Media Type:
Print

Price:
$11.95

Principal Subject:
Growth & Learning

Age Group:
All Ages (0–5)

ISBN:
0385476426

Edition Reviewed:
1995

Publisher:
Main Street Books
(Doubleday/Bantam
Doubleday Dell)

Author/Editor:
Barbara D. Ingersoll, Ph.D. and
Sam Goldstein, Ph.D.

About The Author:
(From Cover Notes)
Ingersoll, with a Ph.D. in clinical psychology, has treated hyperactive children and counseled their families for 20+ years. Goldstein is a clinical instructor in the Department of Psychiatry and has been in private practice since 1982.

LONELY, SAD AND ANGRY
A Parent's Guide To Depression In Children And Adolescents

 Best Resource For:
Understanding and treatment for childhood depression

 Recommended For:
Growth & Learning

Description:

This book, written by clinical psychologists, aims to offer "accurate and up-to-date information about depression and depressive disorders in children and adolescents." Divided into ten chapters, this 225 page book's intent is to provide a combined approach of scientific research and the authors' combined 40+ years experience working with troubled children and their families. Chapters 1–3 describe symptoms of childhood depression along with related emotional and behavioral problems, such as anxiety disorders, conduct disorder, oppositional defiant disorder, ADHD, and learning disabilities; various diagnostic scales to rate signs of depression are given. The causes of depression are discussed in Chapter 4 while Chapters 5–6 highlight psychological and medical treatments. Chapter 7 offers information on dealing with suicidal behavior and psychiatric hospitalization. Chapters 8–9 presents strategies for parents and teachers on how to help the depressed child. Chapter 10 includes the authors' perspective on societal factors that foster emotional illness and how to address these concerns in the future.

Evaluation:

While some books rely heavily on defining the biological causes of depression, this book offers a more well-rounded proposition, namely that it is a combination of nurture, nature, and environment. To justify this, the authors cite the inherent problems with some research seeking to simply blame the parents' parenting styles or the child's genetic background. In particular, we encourage parents to read Chapters 5 and 8. The pros and cons of the various types of psychotherapy are discussed in Chapter 5 while Chapter 8 focuses on how parents can handle their own emotions, keep their marriage intact, determine positive rewards and negative consequences, and more; appendixes offer parents a list of supportive organizations, ideas for fun rewards, and a depression symptom checklist. To help break up the text, the authors supply the reader with numerous parent-child stories that neatly capture their primary message. Although this book is not necessarily an easily read one due primarily to its use of psychiatric terminology, it does offer valuable insights warranting parental attention.

Where To Find/Buy:

Bookstores and libraries.

WHEN YOU WORRY ABOUT THE CHILD YOU LOVE

Emotional And Learning Problems In Children

 Best Resource For:
Understanding and treatment of children's emotional and learning problems

 Recommended For:
Growth & Learning

Description:

The author, defining himself as a "therapeutic optimist," focuses on how to deal with childhood problems. This 280 page, 11 chapter book offers a balanced approach of nature (genetic influences) and nurture (parents, environment) rather than laying blame on parental styles; it may be read in any order. Chapters 1–2 give specific examples of treatable emotional and/or learning problems that are genetically or biologically based; indicators are also provided. Chapter 3 gives "techniques of brain management" (25 tips for managing emotion and learning). Chapters 4–8 deal with conditions associated with the states of anger, sadness, fear, and confusion; the author believes that most childhood problems are related to one of these states. Some less common childhood problems are examined in Chapter 9 (social remoteness, trichotillomania, Tourette syndrome, fetal alcohol syndrome/effect). A discussion about medication follows in Chapter 10, and Chapter 11 offers resources and contacts for additional help.

Evaluation:

This book is an easy read and parents won't feel putdown because of psychiatric jargon or in-depth biological explanations. Just enough information is offered to make parents become informed without feeling overwhelmed. Chapter 1 is particularly well-done: the author has provided over 30 examples of childhood problems. Each of these includes a sentence describing the child's symptoms, followed by a one paragraph "snapshot" of the child's behavior, a possible diagnosis, at-home remedies, and professional treatment. Chapters 4–8 offer helpful input to parents and teachers in dealing with a child's anger, sadness, fear, or confusion. The only obstacle keeping this guide from being user-friendly is its lack of organizational aids. Bold highlights would be a big help; the author's tips are numbered but not spaced well making his points lost in the text. This book illustrates the fact that many causes of childhood problems are beyond parents' and children's control but parents can use this guide as a road map to help them cope with and treat their child's problems.

Where To Find/Buy:

Bookstores and libraries.

Overall Rating
★★★★
User-friendly guide of problems stemming from anger, sadness, fear, and confusion

Design, Ease Of Use
★★
Author's message and tips get lost in the text; bold subheadings or bullets would help

1–4 Stars; N/R = Not Rated

Media Type:
Print

Price:
$11.00

Principal Subject:
Growth & Learning

Age Group:
All Ages (0–5)

ISBN:
0684832682

Edition Reviewed:
1997

Publisher:
Fireside (Simon & Schuster)

Author/Editor:
Edward Hallowell, M.D.

About The Author:
(From Cover Notes)
Hallowell is a child and adult psychiatrist in private practice in Cambridge, Massachusetts, and on the faculty of Harvard Medical School. He lectures widely on topics related to children's emotional health as well as learning disabilities.

Overall Rating
★★★
Provides the basics on many problems that children and teenagers face

Design, Ease Of Use
★★★★
Simple, effective design; easy to maneuver around

1–4 Stars; N/R = Not Rated

Media Type:
Internet

Principal Subject:
Growth & Learning

Age Group:
All Ages (0–5)

Publisher:
American Academy of Child & Adolescent Psychiatry

About The Author:
(From Cover Notes)
The leading national professional medical association dedicated to treating and improving the quality of life for children, adolescents, and families affected by mental, behavioral, or developmental disorders.

FACTS FOR FAMILIES
To Educate Parents And Families About Psychiatric Disorders Affecting Children And Adolescents

Description:
This website contains information for parents and families on the effects that dozens of situations, influences, and disorders may have on children and adolescents. It provides a list of diverse topics, including: anxiety and depression; television; divorce; grief; sexual abuse; pregnancy; lead poisoning; and learning disabilities. Each topic is discussed briefly and a recommendation for seeking further professional help is always included. The website contains scores of pages of up-to-date information, available in English, Spanish, or French. It also provides a list of some 40 other organizations that deal with the issues affecting today's children, providing their URL addresses. This site includes much background on the American Academy of Child & Adolescent Psychiatry itself (the organization's involvement in research, training, and legislative issues). The site contains abstracts from the past two years of the Journal of the American Academy of Adolescent Psychiatry.

Evaluation:
An excellent website to glean a quick understanding of the complexities facing today's youth. This site is a great starting point on about any problem that may be affecting your child or teenager. The organization claims that between 7 and 12 million American youth suffer from mental, behavioral, or developmental disorders at any given time. If you have concerns about a particular issue, you're sure to find it among the list provided. Simply click on the topic that concerns you and you'll be provided with a one-page fact sheet outlining the basics, which usually includes a short list of trouble signs to watch for. This site provides a good general overview. However, you'll probably want to seek more detailed and specific information next. Unfortunately, the site doesn't link you directly from the topic you're exploring to sources of additional information—you'll have to do that additional research yourself.

Where To Find/Buy:
On the Internet, at the URL: http://www.aacap.org/web/aacap/factsfam/

Internet URL:
http://www.aacap.org/web/aacap/factsfam/

RAISING YOUR SPIRITED CHILD
A Guide For Parents Whose Child Is More Intense, Sensitive, Perceptive, Persistent, Energetic

Description:

The author distinguishes spirited children from others as "normal children who are more intense, persistent, sensitive, perceptive, and uncomfortable with change than other children." Labeled a "how-they" (as compared to a "how-to") book, this 302 page guide is based on a combination of the author's classes and "hundreds" of parental anecdotes and techniques. Its motto is "Progress not Perfection." Presented in five parts, it incorporates "recent personality development research." Part 1 describes the temperament and reactions of a spirited child coupled with parent-child interactions. Part 2 offers advice for dealing with the child who is extraverted/introverted, intense, persistent, distractible/perceptive, and more; suggestions are given on what a spirited child needs to hear, how to teach them to cope, and what to do if parents react to situations much as their child does. Part 3 focuses on life with a spirited child (bedtime, mealtime, getting dressed); ways to plan for success are given. Part 4 suggests ways to help the spirited child socialize with others (holidays, vacations, school) and Part 5 is the author's closure.

Evaluation:

Parents of a spirited child will find dozens of kindred spirits within this book. Written in a positive, no blame, no shame fashion, this guide not only reassures parents that they are not alone, but offers them the confidence they need so they can effect changes in their interactions with their child. The author successfully intersperses parent stories and solutions throughout, while offering succinct tips to summarize her own suggestions. Stories focus more on older school-aged children, but no doubt many parents of a younger "strong-willed" child will see similarities as they take root. As stated in her epilogue, Kurcinka believes that "spirited kids are like roses—they need special care. And sometimes you have to get past the thorns to truly enjoy their beauty." Offering wisdom and compassion from other parents, along with sound practical advice, this much-needed guide focuses on how to view spirited children's reactions in terms of strengths rather than weaknesses. Not a guide intended for every parent, this one, however, can offer all parents some alternatives to dealing with a child's behavior and reactions.

Where To Find/Buy:

Bookstores and libraries.

Overall Rating
★★★
Parent stories, author's experience, & research given to offer parents positive support

Design, Ease Of Use
★★★
Detailed but difficult to read table of contents; bold chapter subheadings; index

I–4 Stars; N/R = Not Rated

Media Type:
Print

Price:
$13.00

Principal Subject:
Growth & Learning

Age Group:
All Ages (0–5)

ISBN:
0060923288

Edition Reviewed:
1991

Publisher:
HarperPerennial
(HarperCollins)

Author/Editor:
Mary Sheedy Kurcinka, M.A.

About The Author:
(From Cover Notes)
Kurcinka has 15 years of experience as a directory of Minnesota's Early Childhood Family Education programs and she is the founder of their "Spirited Child" workshops. She is also a licensed teacher and a parent educator.

Overall Rating
★★
Offers email discussion forums for parents of special children; real info lacking though

Design, Ease Of Use
★★
Site is easily navigated and organized well, but discussion forums need organization

1–4 Stars; N/R = Not Rated

Media Type:
Internet

Principal Subject:
Growth & Learning

Age Group:
All Ages (0–5)

OUR-KIDS
Devoted To Raising Special Kids With Special Needs

Description:

The principal function of this site is to offer support to parents, caregivers, and others who work with children with physical and/or mental delays and disabilities. Developed in 1993 by a mother of a child with Angleman Syndrome, this website consists of 600+ people representing children of various diagnoses from developmental delays to cerebral palsy, to rare genetic disorders, and more; 29 countries are currently represented on their list. The site's "Email Netiquette Guide" offers advice on the best ways to access the ongoing email discussions between Our-Kids members; you can access all or a portion of the messages. A recommended book list is given for parents and kids along with a brief synopsis of each resource. Families with children that have special needs can also publish their child's picture and post their family's homepage inviting email responses from others. The "Our-Kids File Archives" contains inspirational writings from others, health care information, ways to cope and support others, and more.

Evaluation:

This site does not provide developmental, psychosocial, or cognitive information about children with special needs. What it does provide parents of special needs children is a place where they can chat and look for support, advice. It is a busy site; a recent visit found 70+ posted messages. The drawback to this website is that, although it is well-organized, its discussion forums are rambling and titles vague (e.g. "Alex's eating"). Since the site's stated function is to invite discussions between parents, positive future changes to it might well include the addition of subject headings, e.g. "Eating/Diets," "Traveling," etc. Message posters, then, could link to the appropriate headings rather than creating a long disjointed list of titles. Aside from parental input, the site offers an extensive recommended book list.

Where To Find/Buy:

On the Internet at the URL: http://rdz.stjohns.edu/library/support/our-kids/.

PARENTING YOUNG CHILDREN
Systematic Training For Effective Parenting Of Children Under Six

 Best Resource For:
Overview of young children's growth and development

 Recommended For:
Growth & Learning

Description:

This 138 page guidebook is based on the "consistent, positive, and democratic approach" of the STEP program (Systematic Training for Effective Parenting). This book focuses on children from birth to six years of age. There are seven chapters. Chapters 1 and 2 discuss a young child's development and behavior. Building self-esteem is covered in Chapter 3. Chapter 4 includes information on listening and talking to young children. Chapter 5 outlines ways to teach cooperation. Chapters 6 and 7 offer advice on discipline and young children's social and emotional development, respectively. Each chapter is followed by an "Encouragement Step" (a sidebar of advice), a section called "This Week" (an insight exercise), and a "Points to Remember" page (summation of the chapter). The chapters end with a "Just For You" page. This offers suggestions for parents to help them in their parenting role; examples include how to ease stress, communication between adults, prioritizing, and more.

Evaluation:

Filled with a whimsical array of black and white photographs, highlighted sidebars, cartoons, and "advice" charts, this resource is a wonderful first resource for beginning parents. This book covers the whole gamut of being a parent—long-term parenting goals; how young children think, feel, and act; skills to increase one's enjoyment as a parent; and ways for the parent to support himself/herself as a person. Skills to develop a child's self-esteem and confidence are included along with effective ways to teach cooperation and discipline. The book's positive and democratic approach to parenting is illustrated throughout via bulleted and numbered blocks of advice. Supplying possible dialogues to have with one's child help to model ways to effectively communicate. Based on the knowledge of experts, professionals, and other parents, this guide is a worthwhile "partner" for establishing healthy patterns of belief and behavior in a young child.

Where To Find/Buy:

Bookstores and libraries, or order direct by calling 1-800-328-2560.

Overall Rating
★★★★
Great for beginning parents, it focuses on a consistent, positive, and democratic approach

Design, Ease Of Use
★★★
Colored blocks of information helpful; highlighted tips given; layout can be distracting

I–4 Stars; N/R = Not Rated

Media Type:
Print

Price:
$15.95

Principal Subject:
Growth & Learning

Age Group:
All Ages (0–5)

ISBN:
0679777970

Edition Reviewed:
1997

Publisher:
American Guidance Service

Author/Editor:
Don Dinkmeyer, Sr., Gary D. McKay, James S. Dinkmeyer, Don Dinkmeyer, Jr., and Joyce L. McKay

About The Author:
(From Cover Notes)
The authors have also previously written other parenting guidebooks for parenting teenagers, raising responsible children, assisting marriage partners, and training teachers.

Overall Rating
★★★★
Very thorough with an impressive wealth of knowledge from experts and parents

Design, Ease Of Use
★★★
Easy navigation with comprehensive index; no photos or illustrations

1–4 Stars; N/R = Not Rated

Media Type:
Print

Price:
$14.00

Principal Subject:
Growth & Learning

Age Group:
Preschoolers (3–5)

ISBN:
0345365976

Edition Reviewed:
1988

Publisher:
Ballantine Books

Author/Editor:
Ellen Galinsky and Judy David

About The Author:
(From Cover Notes)
Galinsky is co-president of the Families and Work Institute in New York City, and recently elected president of the National Association for the Education of Young Children. David is a research Associate on the Work and Family Life Studies Project at Bank Street College.

PRESCHOOL YEARS (THE)
Family Strategies That Work—From Experts And Parents

 Best Resource For:
Overview of preschoolers' growth and development

 Recommended For:
Growth & Learning

Description:

This guidebook offers advice on the subjects of discipline, learning routines, daycare, work and family life, preschool, and other topics associated with preschoolers. The aim of this book is to "help parents through the predictably rough spots of parenthood by . . . offering practical solutions." The information within the book is based on seminars conducted by the author in which she surveyed parents of young children ages two to five for questions they wanted answers to. These questions were then posed to parents and "experts," solutions were formed, and 300+ parents were interviewed to gather "their successful strategies." There are 8 chapters within this 504 page book. Each chapter contains questions "most frequently asked by parents," solutions, and additional child development research. Parental anecdotes and techniques are interspersed throughout. The "Notes" section (37 pages) is divided by chapter referencing each entry. A 17 page index is included.

Evaluation:

This well-written, highly organized, focused reference will be of particular benefit to parents and caregivers. Although intimidating at first due to its small text and textbook-like presentation, once one becomes familiar with its organization, it reads well. Combining parents' advice and strategies along with experts' research makes this book novel. What works for one child does not necessarily work for another and this combined effort helps reach all parents. This family strategies approach is meaningful and sincere. The writing style flows easily and guides the reader through logical progressions to the solutions. Grayed-out sections within some chapters offer "viewpoints," information from experts based on current research. The "Notes" section is meticulously referenced. The book's uniqueness lies in offering the reader facts and suggestions from different viewpoints and allowing parents to form their own conclusions based upon their child's personality. This book is a not-to-be-missed, but a must-have.

Where To Find/Buy:

Bookstores and libraries.

SESAME STREET PARENTS

 Best Resource For:
Internet website focusing on preschoolers' growth and development

 Recommended For:
Growth & Learning

Description:

Children's Television Workshop (CTW), host of the TV show "Sesame Street," offers 7 options at their homepage. "Activities" highlights arts/crafts, computers, holidays, rainy days, and more. "Behavior and Discipline" is divided into 3 age ranges (0–2, 2–5, 6–11) with narratives on anger, sleeping, toilet training, empathy, and more. "Child Development" uses a similar format divided by age (1–12 years), gender, speech, etc. Inclusion, giftedness, preschool, learning disabilities, and other topics can be found within "Education." "Family & Community" features 23 subtopics such as siblings, working parents, moving, etc. Timesavers (charts, lists, and forms) are given in "Health & Safety" along with information on dental concerns, diseases, home treatment, and more. Various children's products are rated in "Reviews and Products" (audio, books, software, toys, etc.). A discussion room and email contact with CTW's consultants (a child development specialist, a pediatrician, and reviewers) are also available.

Evaluation:

This site offers a variety of information which is easily accessed. The way it is organized with subtopic headings (for example: "Time Out Tactics" under "Behavior and Discipline") makes it a breeze to explore. Specific areas include activities, behavior/discipline, child development, education, and reviews/products. Especially helpful are the activities and articles dealing with preschool ("Education"). "Family & Community," however, was quite disappointing. Hopefully future improvements will offer tips on learning what people do in the community, helping others, etc. The product reviews are useful, the criteria well-laid out, and practical advice offered (recommended ages, potential problems, etc.). The discussion forum needs revamping. The visitor needs to scroll through the whole list of titles to find others to chat with; fortunately the list isn't long. The information and tips here, then, are useful; the chats and contact with others are few.

Where To Find/Buy:

On the Internet at the URL: http://www.ctw.org/parents/.

Internet URL:

http://www.ctw.org/parents/

Overall Rating
★★★★
Great info on topics from activities to behavior, and more; little arena for discussions

Design, Ease Of Use
★★★
Well-organized (subtopics, headings), good graphics; "discussion" needs better layout

1–4 Stars; N/R = Not Rated

Media Type:
Internet

Principal Subject:
Growth & Learning

Age Group:
Preschoolers (3–5)

Publisher:
Children's Television Workshop (CTW)

Overall Rating
★★
Presents author's philosophy more than fact; disappointing compared to an earlier book

Design, Ease Of Use
★★
Good index, but a vague table of contents and chapter subheadings

1–4 Stars; N/R = Not Rated

Media Type:
Print

Price:
$10.95

Principal Subject:
Growth & Learning

Age Group:
All Ages (0–5)

ISBN:
0452268648

Edition Reviewed:
1996

Publisher:
Plume (Dutton Signet/Penguin Books USA)

Author/Editor:
Marianne Neifert, M.D.

About The Author:
(From Cover Notes)
Neifert is a pediatrician and associate clinical professor of pediatrics at the University of Colorado Health Sciences Center, as well as the mother of five children. She is a frequent lecturer and writes a column for *Parenting* and *Baby Talk* magazines.

DR. MOM'S PARENTING GUIDE
Commonsense Guidance For The Life Of Your Child

Description:
Written for those parents who feel "underprepared for parenthood and disillusioned with the on-the-job training approach to raising children," this 336 page guide offers Neifert's personal and professional childrearing knowledge and philosophies. Divided into 10 chapters, the book begins by highlighting the pressures parents of today face along with how to cope with "The Myth of the Superparent" and how to enhance a child's self-esteem. Four chapters focus on specific challenges to parenting such as raising siblings, behavior and discipline, instilling values, and the impact of divorce on children. One chapter offers suggestions for "enriching your family life" by preserving and creating family traditions, and through including a pet into your household. Neifert's husband penned a chapter and discusses "the stress of parenthood" and ways to manage it. The final chapter focuses on the "emotional roller coaster" of parenting and discusses issues such as disappointment, loss, unmet expectations, extreme adversity, and more. An appendix provides a script for a relaxation technique and an 18 page index concludes the book.

Evaluation:
A satisfied reader familiar with Marianne Neifert's earlier book, *Dr. Mom*, will be disappointed with this resource. Her views expounded here make for good discussions, if parents are simply looking for arenas to develop their own parenting philosophy. But one won't find specifics here to help in dealing with sibling squabbles, misbehavior, or other challenges. An exception to this critique is the chapter entitled "You and Your Child's Self-Esteem." Many books have been written on the subject and the term has been thrown around without much direct advice; Neifert, however, manages to sum up the essential points here in easily digested chunks. Parents should peruse this one at the bookstore. If they like Dr. Mom's writing style and tone, then they need to check into her earlier book before spending time and money on this one.

Where To Find/Buy:
Bookstores and libraries.

GETTING TO KNOW YOUR ONE-YEAR-OLD

Description:

This book is the first in the "Magical Years" series of three. Within this book there are ten chapters and a "Conclusion." There is no index. The first chapter highlights what a parent might expect developmentally from their one-year-old. Chapters 2 and 3 address physical growth and intellectual development. Language and social development follow in Chapters 4 and 5, and emotional development is the focus of Chapter 6. Discipline, the importance of daily routines, and nutrition are the subjects of Chapters 7, 8, and 9. Chapter 10 provides information on baby-proofing and keeping a one-year-old out of harm's way. The conclusion is a reflection of the first year as well as a look ahead. At the beginning of each chapter there is a situational narrative setting the stage for the topic discussed. A question and answer section concludes each chapter. "Time Capsules" recap the developmental milestones within each chapter providing general guidelines for different stages of growth in a progressive manner.

Evaluation:

This 216 page resource offers good general information on a one-year-old's development up to the second year of their life. Questions about walking expectations, discipline, daily routines, nighttime wakings, and nutrition and weight are just some of the topics addressed in this guide. Unfortunately, much of the information is presented in short, concise blocks leaving the reader begging for more complete details. Parents may find themselves having to plow through some situational content before they reach their desired subject. Some of the chapters, however, do offer additional reading materials that help to complement the chapter's related topic. The "How to Help" sections also help make up for the rather brief explanations. We suggest parents use the authors' bulleted tips and advice within each chapter for quick reference. While not a well-organized text, parents might find this book helpful as a companion to a more comprehensive text.

Where To Find/Buy:

Bookstores and libraries, or order direct from Publishers Book and Audio Mailing Service, P. O. Box 120159, Staten Island, NY 10312-0004.

Overall Rating
★★
Snippets of information touching on the major development stages from 13 to 24 months

Design, Ease Of Use
★
An index would help to find specific information more easily

1–4 Stars; N/R = Not Rated

Media Type:
Print

Price:
$4.99

Principal Subject:
Growth & Learning

Age Group:
Toddlers (1–3)

ISBN:
0312954182

Edition Reviewed:
1995

Publisher:
Skylight Press (St. Martin's Press)

Author/Editor:
Janet Poland and Judi Craig, Ph.D., consulting editor

About The Author:
(From Cover Notes)
Poland, writer and former newspaper editor, graduated from Grinnell College, and has a graduate degree in political science from the University of Wisconsin. Craig is a clinical psychologist with more than 27 years experience counseling parents and children.

Overall Rating
★★
Adequate information;
content shallow at times

Design, Ease Of Use
★
An index would have greatly
helped a rather broad list of
titles in the table of contents

1–4 Stars; N/R = Not Rated

Media Type:
Print

Price:
$4.99

Principal Subject:
Growth & Learning

Age Group:
Preschoolers (3–5)

ISBN:
0312956274

Edition Reviewed:
1995

Publisher:
Skylight Press (St. Martin's
Press)

Author/Editor:
Janet Poland and Judi Craig,
Ph.D. consulting editor

About The Author:
(From Cover Notes)
Poland, writer and former
newspaper editor, graduated
from Grinnell College, and
has a graduate degree in
political science from the
University of Wisconsin.
Craig is a clinical psychologist
with more than 27 years
experience counseling parents
and children.

MAKING FRIENDS WITH YOUR THREE-YEAR-OLD

Description:
This 216 page guide contains 10 chapters. Chapter 1's introduction
highlights "universal themes" of what to expect from a three year old.
Chapter 2 addresses a three year old's physical development explaining
both gross and fine motor skills, as well as suggested appropriate toys.
Chapters 3 and 4 focus on thinking skills, imagination, cognitive
development, and language. Chapters 5, 6, and 7 discuss social
development, preschool considerations, and emotional well-being.
The final chapters, Chapters 8, 9, and 10, deal with discipline, a
three year old's daily routine, and how to keep a three-year-old child
safe. A situational narrative introduces each chapter, bulleted list
of developmental skills follows, and a question and answer section
concludes each chapter. Chapters also include a "Time Capsules"
section noting the changes in development of a three year old at 36,
42, and 48 month intervals. "How to Help" blocks within each chapter
highlight ways parents can aid their child's growth. There is no index.

Evaluation:
This guide is one of three in the "Magical Years" series. It contains
brief information on such issues as preparing a three-year-old to read,
developing friendships, avoiding problem behavior, possible ways of
determining handedness, dealing with childhood stuttering, and more.
The book may be best read cover to cover; an index would have added
value to this book's organization by offering a much needed backup to
the table of contents. This guide does a good job of offering advice and
suggestions in a bulleted-style format, but parents should be prepared
to wade through some fluff before they actually reach information on
their specific topic. Highlights of this resource include: a brief list of
suggested books parents can read-aloud to their child, the "How to
Help" sections, and the chapter on safety (how to childproof, what to
know about household poisons, water safety). Not an end-all, this book
is a good starter for basic, general information on understanding a
three-year-old.

Where To Find/Buy:
Bookstores and libraries, or order direct from Publishers Book and
Audio Mailing Service, P. O. Box 120159, Staten Island, NY
10312-0004.

MY PRESCHOOLER
Ready For New Adventures—Ages Three To Five

Description:

This 9-chapter, 215 page book includes information on a child's physical, social, and language development, their separation/ "individuation," behavior/discipline, and their spiritual growth from age three to five. Various parenting methods are included along with a final chapter offering advice on how to accept imperfection (for "Single Parents and Others"). No index is included, but each chapter includes subheadings to inform the reader of the material covered in that chapter. Some chapters include an introductory anecdote followed by the author's advice and inspirational quotes are sprinkled throughout the book. Information is given about children's growth and changes, obesity, sleep habits, and toilet training. Sexual individualization, respect and values are also addressed. A safety section includes instructions on fire, water, and motor vehicle safety. Tables are provided throughout the book such as how play activities relate to later skills, a discipline/consequence chart, and more.

Evaluation:

The intent of this book is well-intentioned, but parents searching for in-depth information will most likely be disappointed. The book is unique in that the author has tried to explain the world from a young child's point of view to help the reader/parent understand the emotional and psychological needs of a child. He extends his points by outlining ways to provide for their spiritual and social development as well. A strong Christian theme runs throughout the book. The principal problem with this book is that it reads less like a text and more like a story, a story with no specific details, climax, or satisfying ending. It tends to wander, although the bold subheadings within each chapter help make it user-friendly, with easy to understand passages. The table of contents lists the main topics within each chapter but an index would have also been useful. This resource may provide a start for those seeking advice on helping their child develop, but other resources are available which are more comprehensive.

Where To Find/Buy:

Bookstores and libraries. Educational resources and other books in the Minirth Meier New Life Clinic Series are available by calling toll free: 1-800-NEW-LIFE.

Overall Rating
★★
Less informative than other sources; hard to access specifics due to its rambling nature

Design, Ease Of Use
★
Wanders; short vignettes could use more information; no index, no graphics

1–4 Stars; N/R = Not Rated

Media Type:
Print

Price:
$10.99

Principal Subject:
Growth & Learning

Age Group:
Preschoolers (3–5)

ISBN:
0785283463

Edition Reviewed:
1994

Publisher:
Thomas Nelson Publishers

Author/Editor:
Dr. Paul Warren

About The Author:
(From Cover Notes)
Paul Warren, MD, is a behavioral pediatrician and adolescent medicine specialist. He serves as medical director of the Child and Adolescent Division and the Adolescent Day Program of the Minirth Meier New Life Clinic in Richardson, Texas.

Overall Rating
★★
Brief, basic information given; best used as a refresher by busy already informed parents

Design, Ease Of Use
★
Navigation frustrating at times; no index, broad table of contents' titles

1–4 Stars; N/R = Not Rated

Media Type:
Print

Price:
$4.99

Principal Subject:
Growth & Learning

Age Group:
Toddlers (1–3)

ISBN:
0312955820

Edition Reviewed:
1995

Publisher:
Skylight Press (St. Martin's Press)

Author/Editor:
Janet Poland and Judi Craig, Ph.D., consulting editor

About The Author:
(From Cover Notes)
Poland, writer and former newspaper editor, graduated from Grinnell College, and has a graduate degree in political science from the University of Wisconsin. Craig is a clinical psychologist with more than 27 years experience counseling parents and children.

SURVIVING YOUR TWO-YEAR OLD

Description:

There are ten chapters in this resource focusing on what to expect developmentally from a child when they reach 30 to 36 months of age. Chapters discussed within the book include information on physical growth along with intellectual, language, emotional, and social development. Also provided are suggestions on how to set limits, the importance of daily routines, food and nutrition, and tips and advice on safety (in the house, around water, outdoors, and toys). At the beginning of each chapter there is a situational narrative setting the stage for the topic discussed. A general preview is also given that highlights the major points of the topic to be addressed. Within each chapter there are "How to Help" sections, as well as a concluding "Time Capsule" section which provides an overview of the material presented. Additionally, each chapter has a concluding question and answer section which provides situational problems and options for a variety of solutions. There is no index.

Evaluation:

One of three in the "Magical Years" series, this 212 page book attempts to address issues such as how to encourage creativity, when to correct your child's language use, how to cope with disobedience, and when to teach reading and writing. This resource provides good elementary information with some hands-on techniques. While the topics addressed are all important, unfortunately the author fails to do justice to the issues by not providing enough detail. The bulleted "How to Help" sections and the "Time Capsules" sections are both highlights of the book and best used by busy parents who need a quick refresher on any given subject matter. A cross-referenced index should have been included since the table of contents provides rather broad and vague titles. For general bare bones basics about a two-year-old's development, this book will do; but parents seeking a more comprehensive text will want to use this guide only as an informational companion.

Where To Find/Buy:

Bookstores and libraries, or order direct from Publishers Book and Audio Mailing Service, P. O. Box 120159, Staten Island, NY 10312-0004.

FATHER'S ALMANAC (THE)

Best Resource For:
Guide for new dads adjusting to fatherhood

Recommended For:
Parent-To-Parent Advice & Forums

Description:

Published originally in 1980 to invoke an argument for "involved fatherhood," this revision notes changes in the role fathers play nowadays. This 391 page book is separated into 12 chapters, about 30 pages each. Chapter topics focus on: pregnancy and childbirth, baby care, fathers' jobs, family issues (working, stay-at-home, divorce, siblings, etc.), "providing" (childcare, safety, insurance, fix-it, etc.), daily events (baths, bedtime, reading, etc.), outings and special events, teaching and discipline, learning and playing with kids (games, activities), working with kids ("handyman's helper," cooking, etc.), and "keeping a record" (photographing, videotaping, etc.). The table of contents lists major subtopics within chapters and bold headings are used for further divisions. The author has included his own black line illustrations throughout along with photographs of fathers with their children to introduce each chapter. A 16 page index completes the book along with a reference section to further reading.

Evaluation:

What a perfect addition to the family library! Sullivan offers fathers the chance to see themselves as more than "babysitters," more than a "breadwinner," more than a stand-in for mom. By presenting common hurdles and problems that fathers face and offering bite-size tidbits of advice to help fathers deal with those problems, the author has accomplished what he set out to do: instill confidence in fathers so they will be and stay involved. From instructions for how to make a teepee to how to deal with absences due to business trips, this guide offers succinct and well-constructed tips for making fatherhood an enjoyable experience. The author's illustrations are charming, but not sickeningly cute. The only area that is treated lightly concerns that of child development. Fathers will need other resources to supplement this topic. Focused on the questions, needs, and abilities of fathers, mothers, however, will also benefit from its content. This resource deserves a real place of honor within the family home.

Where To Find/Buy:

Bookstores and libraries.

Overall Rating
★★★★
Will instill confidence in fathers to help them define their roles within the family

Design, Ease Of Use
★★★★
Succinct; detailed table of contents, subheadings within chapters; whimsical drawings

1–4 Stars; N/R = Not Rated

Media Type:
Print

Price:
$17.95

Principal Subject:
Parent-To-Parent Advice & Forums

Age Group:
All Ages (0–5)

ISBN:
0385426259

Edition Reviewed:
2nd (1992)

Publisher:
Main Street Books (Doubleday/Bantam Doubleday Dell)

Author/Editor:
S. Adams Sullivan

About The Author:
(From Cover Notes)
Sullivan, a writer, illustrator, and artist, works at home allowing him to spend long hours with his children, sharing projects and pleasures, many of which found their way into this book. He is also the author of *The Quality Time Almanac*.

★★★★

Overall Rating
★★★★
Excellent advice with updated information that reflects current attitudes & knowledge

Design, Ease Of Use
★★★★
Detailed table of contents introduces a clearly written, bulleted, and highlighted text

1–4 Stars; N/R = Not Rated

Price:
$8.00

Principal Subject:
Parent-To-Parent Advice & Forums

Age Group:
All Ages (0–5)

ISBN:
0671792059

Edition Reviewed:
3rd (1992)

Publisher:
Meadowbrook Press
(Simon & Schuster)

Author/Editor:
Vicki Lansky

About The Author:
(From Cover Notes)
Vicki Lansky has authored over 25 books, and is well-known for her column in "Family Circle" magazine and "Sesame Street Parents' Guide Magazine." She has also appeared on national TV shows like "Donahue," "Oprah," and "Today."

PRACTICAL PARENTING TIPS
Over 1,500 Helpful Hints For The First Five Years

 Best Resource For:
Advice from other parents to new parents

 Recommended For:
Parent-To-Parent Advice & Forums

Description:

This 186 page resource, in its third edition, is separated into eight major sections. The first section, "New Baby Care," includes information on such topics as Cesarean deliveries, what to do if your baby cries, diapering, and working moms. The second section focuses on the "basics" in caring for your child. Some topics that are discussed here include feeding, clothing, and sleeping issues for babies, toddlers, and young children. Section 3 deals with hygiene and health. Cleanliness, dental care, first aid, encouraging good habits, illnesses, and toilet training are a few of the topics addressed. Section 4 focuses on childproofing and safety. Section 5 offers advice and suggestions on manners, tantrums, sibling rivalry, kicking habits, fears, and developing self-esteem. Family heritage and traveling with family are addressed in sections 6 and 7. The final section, 8, includes seasonal fun for both inside and outdoors, arts and crafts, encouraging reading, and preparing a child for school. An index is also provided.

Evaluation:

This book is more a rescue guide than simply a guide with helpful hints. With over 1,500 ideas for making a parent's life easier, here is a cure-all for everything from how to remove gum from hair to advice such as draping a towel over the top of the bathroom door to keep your child from locking himself inside! This guide covers a wide variety of topics in a progressive and logical manner. Included in these hints are the best shared experiences, recipes, and tips from parents, all meant to make life easier. Bold subheadings and bulleted sections make this resource easy and quick to use. The author uses a comfortable, relaxed writing style while offering a variety of suggestions from which parents may choose. Comical illustrations add to the book's humor. The book is unique in that the author has taken care to make sure that new ideas (400) have been incorporated in this revised edition and that former material updated to accommodate current lifestyles and parenting information. Parents will find this book is worth buying.

Where To Find/Buy:

Bookstores and libraries, or order direct by calling 1-800-2232 or (612) 930-1100. FAX orders may be placed by calling (612) 930-1940.

THE YEAR AFTER CHILDBIRTH
Surviving And Enjoying The First Year Of Motherhood

Best Resource For:

Guide for new moms adjusting to motherhood

Recommended For:

Parent-To-Parent Advice & Forums

Description:

The Year After Childbirth is 302 pages long and divided into fourteen chapters. The book begins with an introductory overview of the challenges and changes a woman can expect to face in the coming year. Then each chapter takes a different aspect of a woman's experience and expands on it. The topics included are: how your body changes with childbirth, learning to enjoy your body again, movement and exercises, understanding the strains and possible damage to the pelvic floor, bladder and vagina and what to do about it, breastfeeding, nutrition, depression in mothers, recognizing the personality of your child, the development of father's feelings, changes to your identity and relationships, and information on resuming your sex life. The final chapter is titled "Coming up for Air" and focuses on what a new mother can do to care for herself amid the stresses of caring for another. This book includes a glossary of terms, reference notes, a list of "helpful organizations," and an index. This book is intended to be a practical tool for the potentially stressful first year of parenthood.

Evaluation:

This book is a must read for any first-time mother. Up-to-date and concise, it is also insightful and compassionate. Beginning with information from what is normal bleeding and what is not, to the physical maladies that linger after labor, this book offers complete support with clear advice of what a woman can do to help herself. Detailed information on such things as: the pelvic-floor muscles; how to avoid surgeon-recommended "repairs;" problems inherent with episiotomies; and other information concerning why one may not want particular medical treatments. Other issues of motherhood, including depression and its causes, are also given thorough and up-to-date treatment. This work also contains a beautiful chapter on fatherhood. In short, the book addresses many more challenges than are reviewed here; and each is easily referenced, well-illustrated and practical. A lovely book to look at as well as to read, this one will sit on the nightstand and be well-thumbed.

Where To Find/Buy:

Bookstores and libraries.

★★★★

Overall Rating
★★★★
A beautiful, useful and compassionate book for surviving your first year as a mother

Design, Ease Of Use
★★★★
Clear color illustrations; highlighted inserts useful for self-help tips

1–4 Stars; N/R = Not Rated

Media Type:
Print

Price:
$13

Principal Subject:
Parent-To-Parent Advice & Forums

Age Group:
Infants (0–1)

ISBN:
0684825201

Edition Reviewed:
1994

Publisher:
Charles Scribner's Sons

Author/Editor:
Sheila Kitzinger

About The Author:
(From Cover Notes)
Sheila Kitzinger is the author of twenty-two books—including the bestselling *The Complete Book of Pregnancy and Childbirth*. She has an international reputation as a social anthropologist, researcher, and women's advocate on pregnancy.

Overall Rating
★★★★
Traces decline of the multi-child household, along w/ practicalities of raising onlies

Design, Ease Of Use
★★★
Must be read cover to cover, but easily read; detailed table of contents; no index

1–4 Stars; N/R = Not Rated

Media Type:
Print

Price:
$12.95

Principal Subject:
Parent-To-Parent Advice & Forums

Age Group:
All Ages (0–5)

ISBN:
0385249640

Edition Reviewed:
1990

Publisher:
Main Street Books (Doubleday/Bantam Doubleday Dell)

Author/Editor:
Susan Newman

About The Author:
(From Cover Notes)
Newman is a contributing editor to Working Parents and Mothers Today magazines, and writes regularly for national magazines on parenting and related topics. She is also the author of three highly acclaimed books for children and teenagers.

PARENTING AN ONLY CHILD
The Joys And Challenges Of Raising Your One And Only

Recommended For:
Parent-To-Parent Advice & Forums

Description:
Three parts and 12 chapters comprise this 239 page resource focusing on the needs of only children and their parents. Part One—"Considering the Only Child"—traces circumstances that currently lead to "the trend toward one." The other three chapters in this part debunk the myths associated with being an only child, describe the decisions and dilemmas "threesomes" face, and offer suggestions for how to be a single parent of an only child. Part Two presents advice for how to parent an only child beginning with "working attitudes" (moderation, not focusing on oneness, etc.), and then offering specific behaviors, expectations, and how to involve onlies with others. Part Three supports a families' decision to not have additional children with advice on how to deal with challenges from grandparents, other families, your spouse, and your only child. Also discussed are "future issues" such as wills, guardianship, developing support systems, and more. The book concludes with summary advice and quotes from only children.

Evaluation:
Based upon input from over 200 people who discussed the merits and drawbacks of raising or being a single child, this resource does an excellent job of supporting those families who are "threesomes." In particular, parents will find Chapter Two ("debunking the myths") not only helpful as parents defend their choice, but also reassuring that they made the right decision. By giving parents concrete advice as found in Chapters 5 through 8, parents can also look toward relieving the anxieties that often stem from these myths. This resource is not based on "numbers or statistics" but the author admits that "opinions and emotions are plentiful." The only families we found not represented in this guide were those who had little other choice than to have one. Much of the author's discussion focused on those families who, for personal, work-related, or lifestyle issues, chose to have only one child. Supportive, informative, and reassuring, this resource will prove useful to parents who face the decision of whether or not to expand their "threesome" family.

Where To Find/Buy:
Bookstores and libraries.

TRAITS OF A HEALTHY FAMILY
Fifteen Traits Commonly Found In Healthy Families By Those Who Work With Them

 Recommended For:
Parent-To-Parent Advice & Forums

Description:

This resource, winner of the Christopher Award for affirmation of the highest values of the human spirit, focuses on the regeneration of enduring family values. It contains 322 pages, 14 chapters, and describes the 15 major traits of a healthy family. These traits are based upon results from surveys (56 items) returned from 551 professionals in five fields (education, church, health, family counseling, and voluntary organizations) in which they were to choose 15 traits they considered to be evidence of a healthy family. The author's purpose was twofold: to give parents positive criteria from which to evaluate themselves, and to force institutions to scrutinize their policies as to whether they encourage or cripple those family strengths. Some of these 15 traits include effective communication, trust, respect, a sense of play and humor, balanced interactions with one another, a sense of right and wrong, family rituals and traditions, shared religion, respect of personal privacy, services to the community, and more. A chapter-by-chapter notes section, an additional resource list, and a comprehensive index conclude the book.

Evaluation:

This is a positive and upbeat book focusing on what's good about families. The author spent 18 months researching the subject and has presented it in a well-written, thought-provoking format. Her intent was to counteract the negative focus used in looking at the problems of today's family and instead aims to look at family strengths. She, however, warns about families' tendencies to compare themselves with the "legendary perfect family" and suggests instead that these 15 traits should be used as an "invitation to . . . focus upon their own family's health by becoming aware of . . . and studying the hallmarks of these traits." Parents will find the material well-supported by research and professionals alike, and useful in a "self-help" context. First person experiences, as well as shared letters and surveys, help convey and identify aspired family traits as a way for families to scrutinize their own policies and behaviors. While not necessarily easily read, it is an inspiring resource meant to be read cover-to-cover. This is an interesting, useful resource that will be well worth family's time.

Where To Find/Buy:

Bookstores, libraries, or order direct by calling 1-800-733-3000.

Overall Rating
★★★★
Supportive, useful as a measuring stick for the family to identify its positive qualities

Design, Ease Of Use
★★★
Explicit table of contents; tiny print, but good headings and use of bullets, quotes, etc.

1–4 Stars; N/R = Not Rated

Media Type:
Print

Price:
$5.99

Principal Subject:
Parent-To-Parent Advice & Forums

Age Group:
All Ages (0–5)

ISBN:
0345317505

Edition Reviewed:
1983

Publisher:
Ballantine Books (Random House)

Author/Editor:
Dolores Curran

About The Author:
(From Cover Notes)
Dolores Curran is an educator, noted columnist, international lecturer, family specialist, widely read writer and parent. She has a weekly syndicated column, "Talks with Parents" and has received two honorary doctorates. She resides in Colorado.

Overall Rating
★★★★
Advice from a seasoned traveler on how to parent a child while on the road with them

Design, Ease Of Use
★★
Humorous and engaging, but numerous subheadings within chapters halt navigation

1–4 Stars; N/R = Not Rated

Media Type:
Print

Price:
$14.95

Principal Subject:
Parent-To-Parent Advice & Forums

Age Group:
All Ages (0–5)

ISBN:
0028617320

Edition Reviewed:
1997

Publisher:
Alpha Books (Macmillan General Reference/Simon and Schuster Macmillan)

Author/Editor:
Ericka Lutz

About The Author:
(From Cover Notes)
Lutz writes fiction and non-fiction and travels extensively with her daughter, now four years old. Her writings have been published in books, magazines, and periodicals nationwide including *Parents' Press, Chicago Baby,* and the anthology, "Child of Mine."

BABY MANEUVERS

Recommended For:
Parent-To-Parent Advice & Forums

Description:
The author, a veteran traveler prior to being a parent, aims to provide reassurance and information to parents about the logistics of toting supplies and traveling anywhere with young children. Fourteen chapters make up this 224 page guide which is divided into three main parts to gradually ease parents into maneuvering around with their child—The Crawling Maneuvers (chapters 2–4), The Walking Maneuvers (chapters 5–10), and Advanced Baby Maneuvers (chapters 11–14). Chapter topics include dealing with: bodily functions on the road (breastfeeding, diapers, etc.), eating out, day trips (errands, grocery store, zoo, etc.), types of travel (by foot, car, boat, train, bus), what to pack in a day pack, air travel, types of vacation lodgings, outdoor adventures, traveling alone with a child, work travel with a baby, and overseas travel. Each chapter begins with bulleted points that summarize what will be covered. A page-by-page listing of the book's contents is included in the table of contents. Two appendices (odds and ends, resources) and an index complete the book. Lutz's tips are included throughout in colored block insets.

Evaluation:
No other book deals quite as thoroughly with this subject as this one, almost exhaustively, does. Whether parents are beginning "baby maneuvers" or already feel confident with baby on outings, they will be sure to find advice in this book that they've never come across before. The author's tone is very friendly; her humor is delightful and sure to receive a knowing glance from her audience—"the supermarket can be fun, or a trip through a chamber of horrors." A principal problem with this book, however, is that it is often difficult for the reader to maneuver through its content. Each chapter is broken into too many subheadings causing one to oftentimes become confused and/or exhausted. All that aside, this guide would make an unusual baby shower gift or perhaps a wonderful read prior to a family's first vacation together.

Where To Find/Buy:
Bookstores and libraries.

PARENTSPLACE
An iVillage Community

 Recommended For:
Parent-To-Parent Advice & Forums

Description:

The goals of ParentsPlace.com are to offer support, dialog, shopping, and more as they operate under the belief that "parents are the best resource for other parents in the adventure of child-rearing." Main features at their site include reading rooms, general chat topics, a list of daily special events, and bulletin boards. Also available daily are feature articles under the headings of multimedia reviews, nutrition, family, Webdoc, and more. The Reading Rooms offer both articles on specific topics (parenting multiples, single parenting, etc.) and a Q & A segment with various parenting professionals (a doctor, lactation consultant, marriage/family expert, nutritionist, preschool teacher, dentist, and more). Chat and bulletin board topics range from pregnancy through childhood, teens, and into adulthood; the topics of household, childcare, food, etc. are also given. Recipes are an additional feature while another offers various activities ("fun and educational") and reading lists for children from birth to 12th grade.

Evaluation:

Once one figures out this site's navigation, it's a one-stop website at its finest. Want to chat? Stay awhile, because they offer more topics than most (20+ during a recent visit with an average of 15 subtopics under each). If you're looking for an "expert's advice," this site certainly targets what most parents are searching for; each section also includes a search feature to locate previously asked Q & As. Although the site's creators specify that they do have a "liberal editorial bent, favoring environmental products, breastfeeding, and many other 'so called' liberal things," they also state that they aim to have open discussions of issues. The activities listed included recipes for homemade art materials along with open-ended art projects. Parental reviews of children's literature, products, software, movies, etc. are useful as well as the science activities (6–12 year olds). By combining objective information from "experts" with the subjective contributions from parents, this site does a fine job of addressing parents' needs. Your visit will be time well spent.

Where To Find/Buy:

On the Internet at the URL: http://www.parentsplace.com.

Internet URL:

http://www.parentsplace.com

Overall Rating
★★★★
One-stop website combining objective information with subjective advice from parents

Design, Ease Of Use
★★
Confusing navigation, lack of graphics but topics are well-highlighted and demarked

1–4 Stars; N/R = Not Rated

Media Type:
Internet

Principal Subject:
Parent-To-Parent Advice & Forums

Age Group:
All Ages (0–5)

Overall Rating
★★★
Excellent site for ways to nurture yourself, but fewer topics for nurturing your child

Design, Ease Of Use
★★★★
Graphics and layout are stimulating; very easily navigated and includes a "floorplan"

1–4 Stars; N/R = Not Rated

Media Type:
Internet

Principal Subject:
Parent-To-Parent Advice & Forums

Age Group:
All Ages (0–5)

CYBERMOM DOT COM
A Home On The Net For Moms With Modems

 Recommended For:
Parent-To-Parent Advice & Forums

Description:

Developed by a husband-and-wife team with advertising backgrounds, this site's homepage lists eight "rooms." Topics for parents of young children can be found in the following rooms: The Study, The Family Room, The Kitchen, and The Playroom. Within The Study you'll find advice from the site's "Work @Home Editor" including segments on starting a home business, getting clients, using the net to find work, etc. Also provided in this section is the "Day Care File," a provider's perspective on parent-childcare provider relationships. The Family Room currently offers costume ideas from other CyberMoms along with a 4-part series of Walt Disney World as seen through "The CyberMom's eyes." Recipes and organizational tips are offered in The Kitchen. A mom-to-mom chat forum is accessed through The Playroom with a breakdown of 10 topics given (behavior, discipline, development, child care, etc.). Other areas deal with gardening, relationships, politics, health, entertainment, and more.

Evaluation:

This site's scope is extensive, its graphics and tone are fun and upbeat, and its expanding. Future plans include a live chat forum for CyberMoms (with Issue 25.0). Women visiting CyberMom's site will feel treated like a whole person and not just as a mom. This site will greatly appeal to your personal side whether you want to get gardening advice, swap recipes, find suggestions for handling time with your spouse, or vent your opinion on events in the news. Information given for parenting concerns, however, is average in both its depth and breadth. You won't find any parenting philosophies, and you won't find an expert panel hosting questions, answers, or a topic of the week. Moms are the experts here making this site engaging and realistic. The downside, of course, is that this site's content relies heavily on its audience's contributions leaving it without an overall sense of direction. If you're looking for ways to nurture yourself, stay awhile in this site's rooms. If you're looking for ways to nurture your child, keep traveling.

Where To Find/Buy:

http://www.TheCyberMom.com/.

Internet URL:

http://www.TheCyberMom.com/

KEYS TO BECOMING A FATHER

 Recommended For:
Parent-To-Parent Advice & Forums

Description:

The stated theme of this book is that, as more fathers are becoming involved in child care, the father's relationship with his child is different than a mother's (but equally important). Sears' guide addresses the concerns that fathers face as they take on new roles with their children. Sears shares "uniquely male nurturing tips" that he himself has learned through fathering eight children. There are 36 "Keys" in this 152 page book, all of which are listed in the table of contents; these topics usually are covered in 2–3 pages. Topics include the following: fathering during pregnancy, fathering with a newborn, how to handle a fussy baby, relationships with your wife, how to juggle career and parenthood, helping your son or daughter develop healthy masculinity or femininity, being a single father, playing with your baby (3 months intervals to one year), disciplining your baby/child (increments from birth), and fathering older children (1–3 years old, 3–6 years old, 6–11 years old, teenager). A question and answer section is supplied at the end of the book listing 10 questions posed from fathers and Sears' responses.

Evaluation:

This book is not simply for fathers. Mothers, by reading this book, can get a better idea how (and why) fathers respond differently to their children. Sears speaks quite candidly about mistakes he has made, revelations he has gleaned, and the great joys and satisfactions he has received from his experiences as a father. No doubt any father will appreciate Sears' candor and feel supported without being babied—no psycho-babble here. The book's short, concise "Keys," although not written in great depth, offer just enough for busy fathers who might be reluctant to sit down and read a book on parenting. Although some of Sears' suggestions, such as working at home, easing back on work demands, etc., may not work with many fathers' careers, he does offer many thoughts on how to juggle fatherhood and careers; these tips are useful for working mothers too. His section on being a single father, however, seems weak; also, tips on how to be a "house husband/father" are missing. Hopefully these areas will be strengthened in future editions.

Where To Find/Buy:

Bookstores and libraries.

Overall Rating
★★★
Sound bites of advice offering 36 tips on concerns new dads may have

Design, Ease Of Use
★★★★
All topics—"Keys"—listed in table of contents; short, concise text for busy dads

1–4 Stars; N/R = Not Rated

Media Type:
Print

Price:
$6.95

Principal Subject:
Parent-To-Parent Advice & Forums

Age Group:
All Ages (0–5)

ISBN:
0812045416

Edition Reviewed:
1991

Publisher:
Barron's Educational Series

Author/Editor:
William Sears, M.D.

About The Author:
(From Cover Notes)
Sears, "one of America's most renowned pediatricians," has been in practice for 20 years and authored 10 books. Currently, he's a clinical assistant professor of pediatrics at USC School of Medicine.

Overall Rating
★★★
An insightful guide to ways mothers can bond with their infants

Design, Ease Of Use
★★★
Quite readable and concise

1–4 Stars; N/R = Not Rated

Media Type:
Print

Price:
$7.95

Principal Subject:
Parent-To-Parent Advice & Forums

Age Group:
Infants (0–1)

ISBN:
1558320695

Edition Reviewed:
1995

Publisher:
Harvard Common Press

Author/Editor:
Martha Sears, R.N., with William Sears, M.D.

About The Author:
(From Cover Notes)
Martha Sears, R.N., is a certified childbirth educator, breastfeeding consultant, and labor support expert. Together with her husband, William Sears, M.D., a pediatrician, they have authored several books on parenting, including *The Birth Book* and *The Baby Book*.

25 THINGS EVERY NEW MOTHER SHOULD KNOW

Description:

Written by two experts in the field of parenting and child care, this slim guide seeks to encompass the key elements of motherhood for first-time mothers. With conciseness as its goal, this book does not cover the practicalities of baby care, but chooses to focus on the transition into motherhood and effective parenting. The authors speak from both professional and personal experience as the parents of eight children in writing this book. The book's foundation is what the authors call "attachment parenting," which "includes closeness right from birth, responding sensitively to cries, babywearing, sharing sleep, and breastfeeding." It is the authors' belief that such parenting leads to the greatest closeness between mother and child as well as healthy, stable children. There are 25 separate sections to this book, each of which focuses on a separate parenting issue, such as how to respond to the baby's crying, breast/bottle-feeding, how to address baby's needs during the day and during the night, making the decision to stay home with the baby, learning to trust intuition and become the best "expert" on the baby's care, and more.

Evaluation:

For mothers without much time to wade through the sheer volume of baby books out there, this little volume includes much sage advice about mothering. It wisely leaves the practicalities to other books in order to focus exclusively on the elements of successful mothering. This book represents a shift in parenting styles away from a model of strict, authoritarian parenting towards a style of parenting that believes a mother can interpret and respond to a baby's needs without fear of "spoiling" or "ruining" the child. The authors believe the closest attachment of an infant to her mother occurs through exclusive breastfeeding, immediately responding to a baby's cries, sharing sleeping arrangements in the early months, and being a full-time mother. Even if these ideas feel conflicting for some, this book can enrich every mother's perspective without dominating her own style of mothering.

Where To Find/Buy:

Bookstores and libraries.

MOMS ONLINE (AOL)
A Home For Moms In Cyberspace

Description:

Found on AOL using the Keyword: Moms Online. Ten options are available at Moms Online's "virtual community of mothers working collaboratively to create a friendly site for Moms in cyberspace." "Chat" and "Message Boards" offer forums for moms to discuss parenting issues. The "Daily Alex" is a running "chronicle about raising a two-year-old baby boy and being a working Mom"; each day additional journal entries are posted. "Daily Sphinx" is a daily game of 3 questions related to maternal trivia. At "Hot Tips," you'll find contributions from other moms on various subjects ranging from choosing a pediatrician to limiting TV-time. Every week a mom is highlighted in "Mom of the Week" along with her perspectives on raising children. "Merion's Reality Check" is a chance to read advice from Merion, a checker at the local grocery store; you may also ask her questions but are advised to "be prepared for any answer." "Ma'Zine Essay" is an essay written by a mom giving her perspectives on life and motherhood. A free weekly online newsletter is available along with links to other parenting sites.

Evaluation:

This community's strength lies in its use of chat rooms, journals, and personal narratives from moms. Trust is placed in moms as experts, a refreshing stance for moms who often feel defeated, overly-advised, or powerless. Moms are invited to chat with one another, discuss issues, offer "hot tips," submit articles, nominate moms for "Mom of the Week," ask questions, and offer feedback making this an inviting place to air frustrations and their celebrations. What you won't get here are hard facts or objective information. Instead, we recommend this website on the basis of its novelty. Reading the ongoing saga of life with a 2 year old (you can catch up on entries you've missed) and how one family works through its problems makes this website come alive. It no doubt will strike a chord with many families out there. Many of the articles are tongue-in-cheek, offering you a look at the lighter side of raising children and being in a family. Parents know that levity can help get you through the day. If you need a lift, grab your coffee, put your feet up, and check out this site every so often.

Where To Find/Buy:

Found on AOL using the Keyword: Moms Online. Also found on the Internet at the URL: http://www.momsonline.com/.

Overall Rating
★★★
An active community of moms, with lots of useful information on having children

Design, Ease Of Use
★★★
Novel use of journaling & essays by moms; chat rooms work well

1–4 Stars; N/R = Not Rated

Media Type:
Online Service

Principal Subject:
Parent-To-Parent Advice & Forums

Age Group:
All Ages (0–5)

Overall Rating
★★★
An active community of moms, with lots of useful information on having children

Design, Ease Of Use
★★★
Novel use of journaling & essays by moms; chat rooms work well

1–4 Stars; N/R = Not Rated

Media Type:
Internet

Principal Subject:
Parent-To-Parent Advice & Forums

Age Group:
All Ages (0–5)

MOMS ONLINE (Internet)
A Home For Moms In Cyberspace

Description:

Ten options are available at Moms Online's homepage, "a virtual community of mothers working collaboratively to create a friendly site for Moms in cyberspace." "Chat" and "Message Boards" offer forums for moms to discuss parenting issues. The "Daily Alex" is a running "chronicle about raising a two-year-old baby boy and being a working Mom"; each day additional journal entries are posted. "Daily Sphinx" is a daily game of 3 questions related to maternal trivia. "Hot Tips" consists of contributions from moms on various subjects ranging from choosing a pediatrician to limiting TV-time. Every week a mom is highlighted in "Mom of the Week," along with her perspectives on raising children, her strengths and weaknesses, etc. "Merion's Reality Check" is a chance to read advice from Merion, a checker at the local grocery store. The visitor to this site may ask her questions but "be prepared for any answer." "Ma'Zine Essay" is an essay written by a mom giving her perspectives on life and motherhood. A free weekly online newsletter is available along with links to other parenting sites.

Evaluation:

This website's strength lies in its different format, namely in its use of journals and personal narratives from moms. Trust is placed in moms as experts, a refreshing stance for moms who often feel defeated, overly-advised, or powerless. Moms are invited to chat with one another, discuss issues, offer "hot tips," submit articles, nominate moms for "Mom of the Week," ask questions, and offer feedback to the site making this an inviting place to air their frustrations and voice their celebrations. Reading the ongoing saga of life with a 2 year old (one can catch up on missed entries) and how one family works through its problems, makes this website come alive and can only strike a cord with many families. Many of the articles are tongue-in-cheek, offering a look at the lighter side of raising children and being in a family—a levity that can make the day more pleasant in the life of parenting a two year old. What one will not find here are hard facts or objective information. But, for all the reasons previously listed, it can be a friendly, fun and supportive home for Moms in cyberspace.

Where To Find/Buy:

On the Internet at the URL: http://www.momsonline.com/.

Internet URL:

http://www.momsonline.com/

THE JOY OF FATHERHOOD
The First Twelve Months

Description:

Written "by a man for men," this 228 page book aims to provide new fathers with information on the possible emotions, thoughts, and behaviors that they may experience. With the exception of the first chapter which deals with labor, delivery, and the postpartum period, the book includes twelve other chapters divided month-by-month for a baby's life from birth to 12 months of age. The author uses a consistent format for each of these chapters with subheadings highlighting: what's new with baby, "focus," what's new with mom, what's new with dad, "being there for your baby," and growing together (a one paragraph summary of the chapter's important points). Icons are used in the margins to mark each of these sections. The focus sections contain how-to instructions, questions and answers, clinical information, and advice on topics that concern new fathers, such as colic, getting in shape, anger management, how to maintain relationships with friends, and more. Each chapter includes a Q & A segment and various tips are offered in the margins. An appendix gives information about common childhood ailments.

Evaluation:

The consistent format works well here making it a breeze for busy days to find information. New fathers will also appreciate the focus sections as they wrestle with practical concerns such as safety issues, saving money for baby, and other topics. The author also does a great job of summing up a baby's development in one paragraph packages that can be easily digested. Cartoon strips are interspersed throughout allowing humor to be interjected within the scope of the chapter's topic. Especially appealing about this resource is its effort to present the varying emotions new mothers and new fathers may experience along with ways to make those emotions a bonding experience rather than a divisive one. However, there are two problems with this book: the icons the author uses (amateur, distracting, and cluttered) and the lack of how-to pictures or photographs to make some of the childcare tasks a bit easier. Overall, however, fathers confused about their new roles will appreciate this author's welcome tips and concise answers to their questions.

Where To Find/Buy:

Bookstores, libraries, or order direct by calling (916) 632-4400 or contacting Prima Publishing at P. O. Box 1260, Rocklin, CA 95677.

Overall Rating
★★★
Good succinct advice and info for men wrestling with emotional aspects of fatherhood

Design, Ease Of Use
★★
Consistent chapter format, but icons are annoying; photographs would be a nice addition

1–4 Stars; N/R = Not Rated

Media Type:
Print

Price:
$15.00

Principal Subject:
Parent-To-Parent Advice & Forums

Age Group:
Infants (0–1)

ISBN:
0761504524

Edition Reviewed:
1997

Publisher:
Prima Publishing

Author/Editor:
Marcus Jacob Goldman, M.D.

About The Author:
(From Cover Notes)
Goldman trained in general psychiatry at Harvard Medical School where he also completed the Gaughan Fellowship in forensic psychiatry. He has taught psychiatry and behavioral health at Harvard and currently practices geriatric psychiatry.

Overall Rating
★★
Fun treatment of old wives' tales using fact (and opinion); good for shower present

Design, Ease Of Use
★★★
Layout and design attractive

1–4 Stars; N/R = Not Rated

Media Type:
Print

Price:
$9.95

Principal Subject:
Parent-To-Parent Advice & Forums

Age Group:
Infants (0–1)

ISBN:
0811802426

Edition Reviewed:
1993

Publisher:
Chronicle Books

Author/Editor:
Colleen Davis Gardephe & Steve Ettlinger

About The Author:
(From Cover Notes)
Gardephe is a writer and editor specializing in parenting topics. Her articles have appeared in many magazines (*Woman's Day, Parenting, American Baby, Healthy Kids*). Ettlinger is an author specializing in popular reference books.

DON'T PICK UP THE BABY OR YOU'LL SPOIL THE CHILD
And Other Old Wives' Tales About Pregnancy And Parenting

Description:

As mentioned in the foreword, the advice expectant mothers are given is well-meant, but certain sayings have passed from generation to generation and can "mislead a woman at a time when she is trying to be . . . careful about everything she does." This book is intended for those times when "everyone starts telling you what to do . . . what to expect . . . spewing out old superstitions and homespun wisdom with the certainty of a prophet." This little (7" x 7") 95 page book is broken into two parts that list myths and sayings about pregnancy and parenting. Each part is further divided into common threads. Part 1—about pregnancy—includes myths about determining your baby's sex, labor and delivery, health or looks of the mother and baby-to-be, and "myths that need no response" ("If you conceived in the morning, you'll have a boy"). The second part—about parenting—includes myths about feeding, sleeping, discipline, development, breast-feeding, bottle-feeding, and more. Each "old wives' tale" is highlighted and then a paragraph follows which debunks, explains, or extends the myth using input from the authors and a "panel of physicians."

Evaluation:

Exaggerations and superstitions abound in this little book. It's fun and it's easy to read; its format is friendly and its illustrations lend an informal, sweet touch. Much of the authors' advice accompanying the "old wives' tales" is sound, based upon facts. Some, however, is based on opinion with little basis in facts, e.g. "around seven months, however, babies can start to manipulate their parents." New parents need to be careful using this little book as a source of real information to help get through pregnancy or to obtain suggestions about parenting. Rather, it should be used in a fun way by a newly pregnant couple or passed around at a baby shower or given to those who constantly offer well-intended, but misinformed, advice. On the other hand, if a couple were to use this as their principal reference point, they would have a source that does have some solid facts, but also contains opinions that taint its solidarity. And if they heed ALL the advice contained within, they will find themselves swimming in yet another sea of tales.

Where To Find/Buy:

Bookstores and libraries.

BABYNET

Description:

Twenty five category selections can be made at the homepage of this website. Several options revolve around baby products, stores, and manufacturers; alphabetical lists are given with contact information (phone, address). Another option contains an extensive list of product recall notices. You can make birth announcements and greeting cards or participate in games and contests. Recipes and baby shower ideas are provided, along with rhymes and songs to sing to your baby. To interact with other parents or parents-to-be, you may use BabyNet's chat rooms or "bulletin board" forums; topics for the bulletin board include parenting forums (10 choices), "expectant clubs" (choose the month you're due), and labor & pregnancy issues (2 choices). "Tender Loving Care" offers information on the following: "Prenatal Care" (pregnancy, Chinese birth chart, midwifery, etc.), "Newborn Care" (breastfeeding, why baby cries), "Toddler Care" (potty training, ear infections, etc.), "Help For Parents" (product recalls, safety issues), and more. Other options here include a petition to airlines to make them more child-friendly, some children's books, and more.

Evaluation:

This site contains a little bit of everything but not a lot of anything. It is true that most of its 25 options give you some light-hearted material which tired parents certainly will enjoy; one can come here to chat, make a card, print out a recipe or two, even enter a contest and maybe come out a winner. But it offers little more than that. The information packed into "Tender Loving Care" is cumbersome, very dry with little to no graphics given to help one digest the information; most of the pregnancy information comes from a singular source: the March of Dimes. Products, stores and manufacturers can be a boon to parents looking for a given product but lacking the time to find it. Unfortunately, some necessary ingredients are missing from these categories, namely pictures, prices, or links to the stores or manufacturers. What's the point of knowing that Fisher Price has a bathtub if there is not a picture or a comparison of its price to that of other bathtubs or a link/email to the manufacturer and/or to a local store? For all these reasons, the parent's precious time will be spent more wisely at other sites.

Where To Find/Buy:

On the Internet at the URL: http://www.thebabynet.com/.

Internet URL:

http://www.thebabynet.com/

Overall Rating
★★
Good for a chat, making a card, getting a recipe; information is dry and uninteresting

Design, Ease Of Use
★★
Categories are vague at times, no site map available; graphics slow down navigation

1–4 Stars; N/R = Not Rated

Media Type:
Internet

Principal Subject:
Parent-To-Parent Advice & Forums

Age Group:
Infants & Toddlers (0–3)

Overall Rating
★★
Good for feedback from others; panel of experts & articles are worth a visit

Design, Ease Of Use
★★
Site map must be used to avoid confusion

1–4 Stars; N/R = Not Rated

Media Type:
Internet

Principal Subject:
Parent-To-Parent Advice & Forums

Age Group:
All Ages (0–5)

PARENTHOODWEB

Description:

Various options are available at this website's homepage. You can access spotlighted topical questions, a poll to express your opinion on one given subject, "facts and figures" (news abstracts), and the latest product recall notices; all of these involve child-related issues. Also available are birth announcements, greeting cards, and links to other parenting sites. Areas specifically focused on parenting concerns are "Pregnancy Corner," "Ask the Pros," "Your Turn," "Surveys," "Library," "Bookstore," and "Member Board" (a place to chat). The visitor to this site can offer her/his opinion on pregnancy and parenting issues at "Your Turn" and tell other parents "everything the experts forgot to mention" at "Surveys." Articles focusing on pregnancy and labor are grouped at "Pregnancy Corner" while the "Library" hosts articles focusing on childcare and parenting issues; many articles are linked to other websites. Additional resources are listed at the "Bookstore;" a weekly newsletter is available through email. "Ask the Pros" allows you to either ask questions of experts (their bios are given) or read their responses to others' questions.

Evaluation:

Much of this site offers parents chances to be heard and to hear others; this will certainly fulfill a need for parents at home looking for others' feedback. Less of this site is centered on disseminating information. Information from "Pregnancy Corner" amounts to half a page reprinted from The March of Dimes Birth Defects Foundation with headings of "Your Baby," "Your Body," and "Prenatal Care Guide"—pretty skimpy compared to other sites. Other alternatives are to "Ask the Pros" or check out their "Library." Both of these are excellent. The former consists of nineteen experts ranging from midwives, pediatricians and Ob/Gyns, to fitness educators, counselors, breastfeeding consultants, etc. The "Library" allows one to select articles of one's choice. This site is not the best one in cyberspace, but it's certainly worth a visit if nothing more than for the advice gained in "Ask the Pros."

Where To Find/Buy:

On the Internet at the URL: http://www.parenthoodweb.com/.

Internet URL:

http://www.parenthoodweb.com/

A CURE FOR THE GROWLY BUGS
And Other Tried-And-True Tips For Moms

Description:

Compiled by the author for MOPS, (Mothers of Preschoolers), this 109 page book is a collection of "advice, tips, and tidbits" for parents of young children. MOPS is an organization for mothers to share their concerns, explore areas of creativity, and learn ways to prepare for the responsibilities of family and community. This book is divided into 11 chapters. At the beginning of each chapter is a short story which sets the stage for the activities, games, and ideas which follow. There is advice such as giving time warnings—"Five minutes until bath time"—and safety tips, like teaching your child to "stand on the yellow parking line or 'safety spot'" while you load the car. Material lists for doing household chores, easy-to-mix "recipes" for making homemade baby wipes, window washing solution, and more are also included. One of the chapters, "Doings with Dad," offers suggestions for how dads can interact with toddlers—"take one child out to breakfast each Saturday." Related resources are also listed at the end of the book.

Evaluation:

MOPS has managed to compile a wealth of "snippets," without overpowering the reader, in a handy pocket-size guidebook. Although it's based on Christian principles, it doesn't come across as overbearing or preachy. In it the reader finds things to do with toddlers on road trips, improving a child's character, striving for consistency in parenting, and suggestions for mom's timeouts, (catnaps, spending guiltless time with friends, ways to take care of herself, etc.). Advice on soothing remedies for when one's child has the chicken pox and methods for pain-free splinter removal are events everyone will appreciate help with. The book, however, doesn't have an index, which makes searching for specific subjects difficult, especially since the chapter titles are rather vague—"Keeping House," "In the Kitchen." Also, the book itself is disorganized and the reader needs to wade through it to find desired information.

Where To Find/Buy:

Bookstores and libraries, or contact MOPS International at (303) 733-5353 or toll free at 1-800-929-1287.

Overall Rating
★★
Useful hodgepodge of advice from making memories to playtime to housecleaning

Design, Ease Of Use
★
Without an index or a descriptive table of contents, you will most likely get lost

1–4 Stars; N/R = Not Rated

Media Type:
Print

Price:
$6.99

Principal Subject:
Parent-To-Parent Advice & Forums

Age Group:
All Ages (0–5)

ISBN:
0310211352

Edition Reviewed:
1997

Publisher:
Zondervan Publishing House (HarperCollins Publishers)

Author/Editor:
Mary Beth Lagerborg

About The Author:
(From Cover Notes)
Mary Beth Lagerborg is publishing coordinator for MOPS (Mothers of Preschoolers) International. She has also coauthored other books. She and her husband have three sons.

Overall Rating
★★
One person's reflections on how to parent presented in a day-to-day format

Design, Ease Of Use
★
Rambling format (no day-to-day continuity of topic); no index or table of contents

1–4 Stars; N/R = Not Rated

Media Type:
Print

Price:
$14.95

Principal Subject:
Parent-To-Parent Advice & Forums

Age Group:
All Ages (0–5)

ISBN:
0836204999

Edition Reviewed:
1997

Publisher:
Andrews and McMeel (Universal Press Syndicate)

Author/Editor:
John Rosemond

About The Author:
(From Cover Notes)
John Rosemond is a family psychologist and director of the Center for Affirmative Parenting (CAP) in Gastonia, North Carolina. CAP is a national organization whose purpose is to provide families with advice and guidance in the raising of their children.

BECAUSE I SAID SO!
366 Insightful And Thought-Provoking Reflections On Parenting And Family Life

Description:
Rosemond, the director of the Center for Affirmative Parenting (North Carolina), has reprinted in this book 366 excerpts from his various books, newspaper columns, and magazine articles plus some new writings. Each reflection contained in this 368 page book is dated so the reader can begin at any point. Rosemond's intent is to "give parents daily doses of food for thought concerning children . . . that will hopefully help readers become . . . more grounded in . . . common sense concerning children and their upbringing." Using his autocratic family as an example in which the parents are "benevolent dictators," Rosemond expands upon his ideas of what's best for children. He insists that parents can encourage children to ask questions, but parents must make the final decisions, and offer restrictions in order to protect and guide children. He believes that "properly administered spankings can be . . . of inestimable value in the rearing of certain children." Topics range from the parents' role to the children's role, and more.

Evaluation:
As evidenced by his introduction, Rosemond has a decidedly defensive posture when describing his parenting philosophy. Referring to mental health professionals as "the more helplessly humor-challenged of the bunch," he then proceeds to explain how American families have gotten off-track because of them in terms of their child rearing principles. The rest of his book then contains his advice on how to get back on-track. With a format and tone similar to one of his other written cries for attention, this book at least contains more detail in the daily entries. Whereas Rosemond's *Daily Guide to Parenting* was far too succinct to really benefit those who agree with his parenting style, this guide is much more explanatory. Rosemond's philosophy is neither scientifically based nor research based but instead loosely based on Scripture (he rarely cites specific passages) and his own personal experience. Not for everyone, this book would only be wholly appreciated by those parents with like parenting styles.

Where To Find/Buy:
Bookstores and libraries.

FATHERS & BABIES
How Babies Grow And What They Need From You, From Birth To 18 Months

Description:

This 1993 step-by-step manual aims to "teach both practical skills and child development theory." It includes five major sections with a preceding introduction. Chapter One includes information and advice on newborns: feeding, how to handle and soothe an infant, bathing, changing diapers, and more are covered. Chapter Two discusses child care for infants 1 to 6 months. Sleeping and eating idiosyncrasies, discipline, dressing, bathing, some developmental milestones, and other topics are contained in this section. Chapters Three, Four, and Five cover similar topics of infant care but in a progressive age-specific format from 6 to 9 months, 9 to 12 months, and 12 to 18 months of age, respectively. Additional information and advice is provided on the following topics: beginning walking, shyness, first words, safety and childproofing, how to keep your patience, toilet training, activities to do with your child, infant toys, birthday parties, recipes, and more. There is no index.

Evaluation:

This is a well-intentioned guide targeting an audience (fathers) who might appreciate concise information. However, much more depth could have been added to this resource without sacrificing brevity. Lightly touching on just the very basics, this book gives fathers a sampling of what its like to be a primary care provider. The problem is that, in so doing, it sometimes delivers the message to the reader in dumb-downed fashion—"If your baby likes to poke, watch out for your eyes." Other examples include how to determine when a child is able to sit so that the father no longer needs to prop them up or how to change a baby at someone else's house. The author does provide some helpful advice and information, such as offering baby a toy to play with while changing their diaper, ways to babyproof the home, and fun activities and games. The book is written in a humorous vein, with extensive use of black and white line illustrations. Worth the read? Other resources serve fathers' needs better. Use them instead.

Where To Find/Buy:
Bookstores and libraries.

Overall Rating
★★
Too concise and hodgepodge—fathers are capable of assimilating more in-depth info

Design, Ease Of Use
★
Index would have contributed immensely; no detailed help from table of contents

1–4 Stars; N/R = Not Rated

Media Type:
Print

Price:
$12.50

Principal Subject:
Parent-To-Parent Advice & Forums

Age Group:
Infants & Toddlers (0–3)

ISBN:
0060969083

Edition Reviewed:
1993

Publisher:
HarperPerennial (HarperCollins)

Author/Editor:
Jean Marzollo

About The Author:
(From Cover Notes)
Jean Marzollo graduated from the University of Connecticut and the Harvard Graduate School of Education. She previously has written parenting articles for such magazines as Scholastic's *Let's Find Out*, *Parents Magazine*, *Family Circle*, and *Working Mother*.

Overall Rating

★

Offers only email connections for stay-at-home, attachment parenting moms and dads

Design, Ease Of Use

★

Once you're connected, you're barraged with email; email offers no clues as to topics

1–4 Stars; N/R = Not Rated

Media Type:
Internet

Principal Subject:
Parent-To-Parent Advice & Forums

Age Group:
Infants (0–1)

ATTACHMENT & BONDING

Description:

This website states that it is a "support and information forum for full time moms or dads parenting in ways that promote attachment between parent and child." Their homepage lists topics that are open for discussion: gentle pregnancy & birth, breastfeeding, delaying solids, extended breastfeeding, child-led weaning, family bed, baby-wearing, and more. Topics not supported are also listed such as: forced weaning, sleep training, spanking, etc. The site states that it does not endorse any particular medical approach, but instead supports attachment and bonding. Members subscribing to the SAH-AP (stay-at-home—attached parent) list are invited to voice concerns, ask questions, and share the joys of being a stay-at-home parent. The method of subscribing is explained at the site along with a description of what one will receive.

Evaluation:

As an experiment, one of the reviewers for this book subscribed to this website's list. She immediately began receiving an endless stream of emails (over 300!) before she got off the list. Email "conversations" ranged from "what do you look like?" to "do swings in parks promote detachment?" to "what do I bring for treats to my La Leche League meeting?" In our effort to remove ourselves from their mailing list, she contacted the webmaster/creator at the email address given if "you have any questions or problems." After several weeks, she still had not been contacted by the webmaster/creator. If one wants to eavesdrop or partake in casual conversation with other stay-at-home parents, there are other parenting sites that support attachment parenting and offer more directed/moderated forums.

Where To Find/Buy:

On the Internet at the URL: http://www.kjsl.com/sah-ap.

Internet URL:

http://www.kjsl.com/sah-ap

DAILY GUIDE TO PARENTING

Description:

Rosemond offers 365 "nuggets of . . . parenting wisdom" within the confines of a 4" x 5 1/2" spiral bound flip book. Each page is dated for use throughout a year and includes one of Rosemond's opinions on a myriad of subjects. It is intended to be used for inspiration and thought-provoking, so parents can "stay the course through the inevitable ups and downs of parenthood." Advice sometimes flows from one day to the next along a given subject. Topics Rosemond expounds upon include: the child's place in the family ("Children show respect for parents by obeying them"), the parents' role ("Children need a lot of supervision, but not a lot of attention;" "Limit your child's inclusion in adult activities, and limit your involvement in your child's activities"), discipline ("It's possible to spank a child properly and have it accomplish something . . . lots of parents make a sorry mess of it"), and more. There are no illustrations, no index, and no table of contents.

Evaluation:

Rosemond converts will enjoy getting their memories refreshed on a daily basis as they flip to yet another one of his pearls of wisdom. But parents looking for tried-and-true methods and concrete examples will definitely need to look elsewhere. At times his messages even contradict each other leaving the reader wondering if his belief system is as firmly founded as he would lead us to believe. For example, he states (July 30) that: "The young child must be convinced of his parents' ability to provide for and protect him under any and all circumstances." Then on the flip-side (June 3), he states that "When parents make a child's life into a bowl of cherries, the child will almost certainly, as an adult, be forever in the pits." If parents want opinions, they need to look to other sources that are more consistent.

Where To Find/Buy:

Bookstores and libraries.

Overall Rating
★

Just one man's opinions; parents will certainly get the feeling he thinks highly of them

Design, Ease Of Use
★

Can't refer back to a "nugget"; helpful if organized in themes w/ an overall content page

1–4 Stars; N/R = Not Rated

Media Type:
Print

Price:
$8.50

Principal Subject:
Parent-To-Parent Advice & Forums

Age Group:
All Ages (0–5)

ISBN:
1882835441

Edition Reviewed:
1994

Publisher:
Thoughtful Books/Sta-Kris

Author/Editor:
John Rosemond

About The Author:
(From Cover Notes)
Rosemond, a family psychologist, is director of the Center for Affirmative Parenting, a national parent resource center offering seminars and educational materials to those who work with families. He also has a nationally-syndicated parenting column.

Overall Rating
★
This site lacks substance and direction

Design, Ease Of Use
★
Must register to use site's features; articles in newsletter can't be fully accessed

1–4 Stars; N/R = Not Rated

Media Type:
Internet

Principal Subject:
Parent-To-Parent Advice & Forums

Age Group:
All Ages (0–5)

MOMMY TIMES (THE)
Dedicated To Preserving The Sanity Of Moms Everywhere

Description:
The Mommy Times website, also billed as "The Mom to Mom Support Community on the Web," established itself first as a publication in 1992 and as a website in 1995. Registration is required to access the site's features which include the following: "Mommye-mail," "Mommy-to-Mommy," back issues of "The Mommy Times," "plus many more features to come." The site hosts articles, questions, and answers "written for moms by moms . . . everything from birth experiences to preparing your child for his/her first day of school and many topics in between." Through "Mommy-mail," moms may quickly post messages to one another. "Mommy-to-Mommy" offers a chance for moms to create new topics, post a question and read others' responses, or read archives of past questions and answers. Past issues of "The Mommy Times" may be accessed either through their website (from the October/November 1996 issue forward) or purchased for $2.00 each for issues from January 1993 through May 1996 (the magazine was in printed format at that time). The current online issue of "The Mommy Times" (August/September 1997) includes 15 articles.

Evaluation:
Many websites have developed to support the needs of busy moms who want to communicate with others in a convenient manner with no time constraints. This site, however, lacks substance, has no direction, and is more frustrating than it is supportive. Question and answer forums are inviting, but without a helpful structure. For example, if one wants to read others' concerns and feedback regarding bedtime rituals, she needs to scroll through endless pages of posted topic headings to find the appropriate ones. What would be extremely helpful here is some categorization, e.g. "Bedtime Rituals." Also, if a mother wants to respond to a question or topic posted in the "Mommy-to-Mommy" archive, she must create a topic in the new section (since the archive is closed to responses), recap the question, and then add her response. When this site was visited, the 15 articles of the current issue of "The Mommy Times" could not be accessed— only 2 articles were fully available. Does this mean the issue is still being developed or is this a problem at the site? Busy moms could well be spending their precious time elsewhere.

Where To Find/Buy:
On the Internet at the URL: http://www.mommytimes.com/momnet.htm.

Internet URL:
http://www.mommytimes.com/momnet.htm

TERRIBLE ANGEL
Surviving The First Five Years Of Motherhood

Description:

This 98 page non-fiction book is the story of a mother and her experiences in the first five years of raising her child. The book traces the phases of the author's relationship with her daughter. There are 10 chapters, followed by a list of references. Some of the references include works by M. Scott Peck, T. Berry Brazelton, Abraham Maslow, and Betty Friedan, to name a few. The resources are frequently quoted as supportive passages to the author's topics. "Terrible Angel" weaves a Christian theme throughout. Other chapters illustrate this through their titles: "Creation," "Incarnation," "The Questions of Job," "The Sins of the Mother," and "Exodus." The book's intended audience are new mothers emerging from a conventional lifestyle, perhaps previously as a professional, and now placed into a motherhood role.

Evaluation:

Patricia Hart Clifford's book about her metamorphosis into the role of motherhood discusses various aspects of how having a child can disturb a woman's professional life, "upsetting the family balance and cluttering the house with cribs, playpens and disposable diapers." It is about the "uprooting" of her "conventional life" to raise her newborn daughter. The book's main focus is on the author's coping abilities. It is a somewhat depressing book in that the author discusses all of the "sacrifices" and "stress" she has had to deal as the result of having to make changes to accommodate the needs of her baby. She talks little of the small joys of parenthood. The author admits her limitations. She doesn't know what to expect from children, but accepts the fact that her child forces her to see what she must change about herself. But largely, the book carries a "woe-is-me" theme. The book is predominately "I-centered." Look for this in the "Never mind" section of your bookstore.

Where To Find/Buy:

Bookstores and libraries.

Overall Rating
★

An autobiographical nonfiction book written by a whiny parent

Design, Ease Of Use
★

Written in a story format; no index is included; chapter titles are extremely vague

1–4 Stars; N/R = Not Rated

Media Type:
Print

Price:
$5.95

Principal Subject:
Parent-To-Parent Advice & Forums

Age Group:
All Ages (0–5)

ISBN:
0809131927

Edition Reviewed:
1990

Publisher:
Paulist Press

Author/Editor:
Patricia Hart Clifford

About The Author:
(From Cover Notes)
Patricia Hart Clifford is an author and a mother.

★★★★

Overall Rating
★★★★
Outstandingly comprehensive and illustrative, a must-have for any new parents

Design, Ease Of Use
★★★★
Companion booklet lists all "chapter" subtopics; real-life demos; concise and interesting

1–4 Stars; N/R = Not Rated

Media Type:
Videotape

Price:
$39.98

Principal Subject:
Gaining An Overview: All-Inclusive

Age Group:
Infants (0–1)

Edition Reviewed:
1987

Publisher:
Vida Health Communications

BABY BASICS (Videotape)
The Complete Video Guide For New And Expectant Parents

 Best Resource For:
Videotape focusing on infants' care and development

Recommended For:
Gaining An Overview: All-Inclusive

Description:

Focusing on the care and development of newborns and infants, this 110 minute videotape is divided into eight "chapters" with an accompanying booklet listing all subtopics. Combining professional advice and sample footage of four new families, this videotape takes parents through their newborn's life from birth onward. Chapters One and Two discuss "the newborn at birth" along with postpartum care of the mother. Chapter Three describes the newborn and new parents' first days at home with details about emotional adaptations, changes in the newborn, reflexes, development, signs of overstimulation, sleep states, and swaddling. "Daily Care" is the topic in Chapter Four with information about bathing, diapering, dressing, circumcision and umbilical care, and more. Chapter Five includes breastfeeding how-tos (positions, problems, expression, storage) and bottlefeeding information. Chapter Six focuses on "Health and Safety" with information on check-ups, immunizations, illnesses, and more. Chapter Seven discusses babies' cries and sleep patterns, while Chapter Eight describes babies' growth and development.

Evaluation:

The price tag is not exactly cheap, but this is the closest new parents will get to having a visual owners' manual to baby care. In fact, it will be like having a pediatrician/mother/close friend on hand offering the best advice and information every step of the way as new parents struggle "on the job." The footage is excellent with real life demonstrations in every case. The companion booklet is very well-thought out suggesting that parents start their VCR counter on "0," view the tape, and then record the counter number next to each subtopic listed in the booklet. This will make for quick easy access for busy new parents who haven't the time to scan through the tape's two hours looking for the information they need. The advice is up-to-date and compiled from health care professionals, child development specialists, educators, and parents. The segment on breastfeeding in particular was outstanding offering advice and support for a subject that most often is learned visually but not often presented in that form. This video is a must whether as a gift for new parents, the focus of a parent education class, or to help train a child care provider.

Where To Find/Buy:

Bookstores, libraries, videotape dealers, or order direct by calling 1-800-524-1013.

BABY BOOK (THE)

Everything You Need To Know About Your Baby—From Birth To Age Two

 Best Resource For:
Guide to infants' care and development

 Recommended For:
Gaining An Overview: All-Inclusive

Description:

Pediatric specialists and parents of 8, Sears and his wife present their parenting philosophy as it relates to the practice of raising children in this 689 page, 28 chapter book. Detailing their parenting style—"attachment parenting"—in chapter 1, Sears uses this as a foundation for the remainder of the book. You will find 5 parts to this book focusing on topics for parents of newborns through age 2. These 5 parts deal with "Baby-Care Basics" (giving birth through the early weeks); "Infant Feeding and Nutrition" (breastfeeding, bottlefeeding, solid foods, toddler feeding); "Contemporary Parenting" ("babywearing," nighttime parenting, parenting the "fussy or colicky baby," working outside your home); "Infant Development and Behavior" (0–6 months, 6–12 months, the second year, toddler behaviors, toilet training); and "Keeping Your Baby Safe and Healthy" (baby-proofing, checkups, immunizations, medicines, self-help home care, lifesaving procedures, and first aid). Personal anecdotes from their own children as well as patients are used by the authors for illustration purposes throughout the text.

Evaluation:

A conscientious new parent has zillions of nagging questions, e.g. "should I let my baby cry or should I pick her up?" Also, "should I let the baby sleep with me or should I make him sleep alone?" Also, "should I breastfeed my baby or bottlefeed?" Different experts answer these questions in different way, for there are several schools of thought and differing philosophies about raising a child. William Sears M.D. and Martha Sears R.N. have become well known for their approach of "attachment parenting." Attachment parenting uses five "tools" to "get connected to your baby." These tools include connecting early with one's baby, reading and responding to her/his cues, breastfeeding, "wearing" the baby, and sharing sleep with one's baby. This book, then, is for those who believe that a baby who forms a strong attachment to their caretakers (trusting them to fulfill all his or her emotional, social and physical needs) will feel secure and self-confident—traits that foster independence. Whether one buys into Sears' parenting style or not, their medical advice and behavioral descriptions are universally useful, particularly their section on how to handle a colicky baby. However, some of their medical information (immunizations in particular) needs to be updated.

Where To Find/Buy:

Bookstores and libraries.

Overall Rating
★★★★
The "bible" for those who enjoy a philosophy of non-authoritarian parenting

Design, Ease Of Use
★★★★
Anecdotes interspersed throughout; table of contents lists subtopics; extensive index

1–4 Stars; N/R = Not Rated

Media Type:
Print

Price:
$21.95

Principal Subject:
Gaining An Overview: All-Inclusive

Age Group:
Infants & Toddlers (0–3)

ISBN:
0316779059

Edition Reviewed:
1993

Publisher:
Little, Brown and Company

Author/Editor:
William Sears, M.D. & Martha Sears, R.N.

About The Author:
(From Cover Notes)
Sears, "one of America's most renowned pediatricians," has been in practice for 20 years and authored 10 books. Currently, he's a clinical assistant professor of pediatrics at USC School of Medicine. His wife is a childbirth educator, registered nurse, & breastfeeding consultant.

★★★★

Overall Rating
★★★★
Insightful and practical guide to help parents develop their own parenting philosophy

Design, Ease Of Use
★★★★
Intimidating at first due to its wealth of information but it drives like an automatic car

1–4 Stars; N/R = Not Rated

Media Type:
Print

Price:
$20.00

Principal Subject:
Gaining An Overview: All-Inclusive

Age Group:
All Ages (0–5)

ISBN:
0553067508

Edition Reviewed:
1997

Publisher:
Broadway Books (Bantam Doubleday Dell)

Author/Editor:
Laura Davis and Janis Keyser

About The Author:
(From Cover Notes)
Laura Davis is the mother of a preschooler and stepmother of a teenager. She has written three previous books. Janis Keyser is a parenting educator and program director. She has conducted workshops and facilitated parenting classes for 20 years.

BECOMING THE PARENT YOU WANT TO BE
A Sourcebook Of Strategies For The First Five Years

 Recommended For:
Gaining An Overview: All-Inclusive

Description:
There are six parts to this guidebook. Part One contains 9 chapters which detail the 9 principles that lay down the authors' parenting foundation. Developing a vision, cultivating optimism, learning to value struggle, and teaching children to feel safe are 4 examples of these 9 principles. Part Two deals with children's feelings. Four chapters offer information on how to respond to crying, tantrums, fears, helping your child deal with separation, and more. Part Three focuses on children's bodies: healthy eating, toilet training, sexual explorations, and sleep. Part Four contains 4 chapters dealing with difficult behavior, such as testing limits and negotiating conflicts. Part Five's 5 chapters speak to social learning and play, and Part Six discusses issues inherent to family relationships. Subjects such as building strong sibling relationships, and parenting with a partner are addressed. Highlighted sections throughout the book offer additional insights on the subtopics. An 11 page index follows the final chapter.

Evaluation:
Simply stated, this is a superb guidebook. It answers questions all parents have as well as those they've been afraid to ask or haven't even thought of yet. The authors have done an extraordinary job of taking a straightforward approach in helping parents become all they can be. This practical resource speaks respectfully to all types of families—stepparents, single parents, foster parents, gay and lesbian parents, and others. The book is inspiring and enlightening—a confident source that will afford parents in-depth suggestions and reliable advice. This reference also demonstrates a wide range of solutions to problems that arise in the raising of babies, toddlers and preschoolers; often these tips are given with compassion, humor, and warmth. Parents will feel at ease discovering their own parenting philosophy while incorporating new strategies from this 426 page guidebook. The place for this reference is in every home where there are small children.

Where To Find/Buy:
Bookstores and libraries.

CARING FOR YOUR BABY AND YOUNG CHILD
Birth To Age 5

Best Resource For:
Guide to young children's care and development

Recommended For:
Gaining An Overview: All-Inclusive

Description:

This 670 page reference book contains advice from the American Academy of Pediatrics and is broken into two parts. The first part contains advice on basic care from infancy through age five, along with guidelines and milestones for physical, emotional, social, and cognitive growth. Early chapters address such issues as: preparing for a new baby, birth and the moments after (in a hospital), basic infant care, and the basics of feeding a baby. In Chapters 5–12, advice is grouped by age and stage, i.e. newborn, the first month, one month through three months, four months to seven months, eight months to twelve months, the second year, the third year, the fourth, and the fifth year. Each of these groupings address growth and development, basic care, family, health watch, safety check, immunizations, and more. A chapter each is devoted to how to keep your child safe and how deal with part-time childcare issues. The second part of the book, with "guide words" at the top of the page, is a thorough medical reference guide for child-related topics (behavior, eyes, skin, etc.). A great many illustrations, information boxes, and tables are given.

Evaluation:

The American Academy of Pediatrics sponsored this book with contributions from 70+ "pediatric specialists and a six-member AAP editorial review board," making it a baseline standard for child care and pediatric medical information in America today. Beautifully illustrated and nicely designed for readability, this book has all the touches that publishers use to make a book easy to look at and digest. Where other books take a question and answer approach to providing information, this book lines up its topics and hands out advice in a straightforward and authoritative manner. In this way, it covers the same information as similar books on this topic, but seems to do it in a much more readable and inviting way. If one is making a choice on a first year baby book, this may well be **the** book.

Where To Find/Buy:
Bookstores and libraries.

Overall Rating
★★★★
Comprehensive guide to children's physical, emotional, social and cognitive growth

Design, Ease Of Use
★★★★
Clear, concise, well-illustrated, and direct

1–4 Stars; N/R = Not Rated

Media Type:
Print

Price:
$17.95

Principal Subject:
Gaining An Overview: All-Inclusive

Age Group:
All Ages (0–5)

ISBN:
0553371843

Edition Reviewed:
2nd (1993)

Publisher:
Bantam Books

Author/Editor:
Steven P. Shelov, M.D., F.A.A.P.

About The Author:
(From Cover Notes)
The Feeling Fine Programs and the American Academy of Pediatrics, an organization of 45,000 pediatricians dedicated to the health, safety, and well-being of infants, children, adolescents, and young adults, developed this book as the first of a three part series.

Overall Rating
★★★★
One of the best all-inclusive guides for parents of infants, toddlers, and preschoolers

Design, Ease Of Use
★★★★
500+ color photographs, drawings, graphs, & charts; color coding makes for easy access

1–4 Stars; N/R = Not Rated

Media Type:
Print

Price:
$29.95

Principal Subject:
Gaining An Overview: All-Inclusive

Age Group:
All Ages (0–5)

ISBN:
1564588505

Edition Reviewed:
1995

Publisher:
Dorling Kindersley (Carroll & Brown Limited)

Author/Editor:
Miriam Stoppard, M.D.

About The Author:
(From Cover Notes)
Miriam Stoppard, M.D., is the author of many bestselling books on pregnancy and childcare.

COMPLETE BABY AND CHILD CARE

Recommended For:
Gaining An Overview: All-Inclusive

Description:

This 352 page reference contains six major chapters. Chapter 1 contains behavior and health information about newborn babies. The second chapter deals with a child's everyday care including their environment, feeding, dressing, bathing, crying/comforting, and sleeping. Children's development (physical, speech and language, and mental), teeth, vision, hearing, and social behavior are a few of the topics in Chapter 3.
The fourth chapter focuses on family life and discusses such topics as organization, separation and divorce, and multiple births. Children with special needs are addressed in Chapter 5, and the final chapter contains information about medicine and health care. Each topic is separated into four age groups (young baby, older baby, toddler, and preschool child), with color-coded bands given to access key information for each gender and age group. Illustrations and photographs guide parents through suggested routines. The book includes a first aid section, contact info for organizations, and an index.

Evaluation:

The word for this book is simply, "WOW!" Case studies, tips, extensive illustrations, and graphs are just the tip of the iceberg in describing this very well-presented guide. The book has made every effort to touch all aspects of child care, and has done an excellent job. The information is intelligent, with in-depth advice on topics as diverse as bathing a baby, to coping with disorders such as epilepsy and dyslexia. Special panels on the side of the page highlight and explain the differences in caring for and the differences in development between boys and girls in many areas. Case studies provide new insights, while medical facts help answer common parental questions. New parents will find Dr. Stoppard's commonsense approach informing, reassuring, and inspiring. This guide's index includes boldly highlighted topics along with related subtopics for easy access. In short, this is a wonderful book, thoughtfully constructed, offering valuable information in a sensitive, compassionate, while professional, manner.

Where To Find/Buy:

Bookstores and libraries.

FAMILY.COM
Disney.Com

Best Resource For:
Internet website focusing on young children's care and development

Recommended For:
Gaining An Overview: All-Inclusive

Description:

Coordinated with Disney, this site boasts an "online parenting service that offers comprehensive, high-quality information and a supportive community for raising children." Eleven options are available at their homepage, six of which are pertinent to parenting interests. Parents may customize their searches via drop-down lists of topics and age ranges (from birth on up). Within "Activities," search criteria includes activities for indoors, outdoors, crafts, parties, holiday, and more. Narrative descriptions are given. A reprinted book (Bennetts' *365 TV-Free Activities*) is also available here. Topics (17) listed under "Education" include articles dealing with preschool, public and private school, and more. "Food" lists a group of recipes for children to use (Kids' Cooking). Choices (15) included in the drop-down list within "Parenting" range from behavior, development, and discipline to eating, childcare, and siblings. A Q & A segment is offered here with advice from the "Experts" (Leach, Schmitt, Faull, and the Prices). The "Boards" lists forums for parent discussions and future plans include an "Chat" segment.

Evaluation:

Unusual to this site are the vast number of customized searches that can be done and the reprints from respected authorities' books making this website a must for all parents' visits. Whether parents require a check-off list for evaluating preschools, need support for their parenting decisions, or want a quick activity for their three year old for a snowy day, they will find their needs met here. The site is easily navigated, concise, and visually appealing. Parents looking for others to share ideas and tips will find the "Boards" to be the most well-organized of any website. Topics (8) are arranged under the same headings as the site's homepage with multiple subtopics found under each and age ranges can be specified. A novel feature to this segment is that visitors can specify that they want to read postings from either a year ago or just the most recent ones. This saves busy parents from wasted time and effort responding to chats that are no longer current. This is a highly recommended site for all parents.

Where To Find/Buy:
On the Internet at the URL: http://family.com.

Internet URL:
http://family.com

Overall Rating
★★★★
Comprehensive site hosting "expert" advice, customized searches, active "Boards"

Design, Ease Of Use
★★★★
Easily navigated, extremely well-organized for speedy access; book reprinted online

1–4 Stars; N/R = Not Rated

Media Type:
Internet

Principal Subject:
Gaining An Overview: All-Inclusive

Age Group:
All Ages (0–5)

★★★★

Overall Rating
★★★★
An informative look at how important quality care is on a child's brain development

Design, Ease Of Use
★★★★
Well-laid out CD-ROM; visually appealing and slick presentation; easy navigation

1–4 Stars; N/R = Not Rated

Media Type:
CD-ROM

Price:
Free

Principal Subject:
Gaining An Overview: All-Inclusive

Age Group:
Infants & Toddlers (0–3)

Edition Reviewed:
1997

Publisher:
The Reiner Foundation (Families & Work Institute/ IBM)

I AM YOUR CHILD (CD-ROM)
The First Three Years Last Forever

 Best Resource For:
CD-ROM focusing on infants' care and development

 Recommended For:
Gaining An Overview: All-Inclusive

Description:

This national public awareness campaign (funded by The Reiner Foundation, IBM, Families and Work Institute, and others) aims to make early childhood development a top priority based upon new research regarding brain development. Four options are available on their CD-ROM. "Brain Facts" highlight how undeveloped a child's brain is at birth. As the brain develops, the child's experiences and attachments within the first 3 years directly impact his emotional development, learning abilities, and how he functions later. Parents' "most pressing questions" and responses from "experts" are listed under "Parent Questions." "Ages & Stages" detail child development from prenatal to age three with "top experts" (Brazelton, Bowman, Koop, Perry) offering their child development advice and insight via downloadable QuickTime movie clips. Also given are ten "Key Guidelines" that summarize the experts' advice. A list of summarized resources and references is also available. An index is also provided.

Evaluation:

Opportunities exist every day to contribute to the healthy development of a baby or child's brain through experiences, affection, and other ways, and this CD-ROM reinforces this message. With recent attention focused on the plight of our nation's children and the lack of quality childcare, this campaign is timely. This CD-ROM offers "ten guidelines that can help parents and other caregivers raise healthy, happy children and confident, competent learners." The guidelines aren't novel ("talk, read, and sing to your child," "use discipline as an opportunity to teach," etc.). But, coupling them with the latest in brain research gives parents rationale for giving and demanding quality care for their child especially during those important first three years. This CD-ROM takes its position seriously; there are no "chats," humor, or a lighthanded look at parenting. It's free (with a $5.00 shipping and handling fee) and quantities are limited. Those seriously interested in children's welfare will be enlightened.

Where To Find/Buy:

Contact the I Am Your Child Campaign by calling (202) 338-4385, by FAX at (202) 338-2334, or through the mail at 1010 Wisconsin Ave., NW, Suite 800, Washington, D.C. 20007. There is a $5.00 shipping and handling fee.

Internet URL:

http://www.iamyourchild.org/

I AM YOUR CHILD (Internet)

 Best Resource For:
Internet website focusing on infants' care and development

 Recommended For:
Gaining An Overview: All-Inclusive

Description:

Founded by Rob Reiner, Michele Singer Reiner, and others, this national "public awareness and engagement campaign to make early childhood development a top priority for our nation" offers 8 options at their website. "Key Issues" and "Brain Facts" highlight how undeveloped a child's brain is at birth. As the brain develops, the child's experiences and attachments within the first 3 years directly impact his emotional development, learning abilities, and how he functions later. Parents' "most pressing questions" and responses from "experts" are listed under "Parent Questions." "Ages & Stages" detail child development from prenatal to age three and "top experts" (Brazelton, Bowman, Koop, Perry) offer their child development advice and insight via downloadable QuickTime movie clips. A list of summarized resources is also available. For those interested in campaigning on behalf of children, two options offer information on this site's campaign along with ways for communities to promote the cause.

Evaluation:

With recent attention focused on the plight of our nation's children and the lack of quality childcare, this campaign is timely. If you're a working parent with a child in daycare, you won't be guilt-tripped here. This site offers "ten guidelines that can help parents and other caregivers raise healthy, happy children and confident, competent learners." The guidelines aren't novel ("talk, read, and sing to your child," "use discipline as an opportunity to teach," etc.). But, coupling them with the latest in brain research gives parents rationale for giving and demanding quality care for their child especially during those first three years. Opportunities exist every day to contribute to the healthy development of a child's brain through experiences, affection, and other ways, and this site reinforces this message. You won't find chats here, you won't find humor or a light-handed look at parenting. This site takes its position seriously. Those seriously interested in the welfare of children should visit and become informed too.

Where To Find/Buy:

On the Internet at the URL: http://www.iamyourchild.org/.

Internet URL:

http://www.iamyourchild.org/

Overall Rating
★★★★
An informative look at how important quality care is on a child's brain development

Design, Ease Of Use
★★★★
Well-laid out site; downloadable QuickTime movie clips require lots of hard disk space

1–4 Stars; N/R = Not Rated

Media Type:
Internet

Principal Subject:
Gaining An Overview: All-Inclusive

Age Group:
Infants & Toddlers (0–3)

Overall Rating
★★★★
An informative look at how important quality care is on a child's brain development

Design, Ease Of Use
★★★★
Good balance between scientific /research jargon and how-tos; engrossing footage

1–4 Stars; N/R = Not Rated

Media Type:
Videotape

Price:
Free

Principal Subject:
Gaining An Overview: All-Inclusive

Age Group:
Infants & Toddlers (0–3)

Edition Reviewed:
1997

Publisher:
The Reiner Foundation (New Screen Concepts)

I AM YOUR CHILD (Videotape)
The First Years Last Forever

Recommended For:
Gaining An Overview: All-Inclusive

Description:

Developed through the financial support of Johnson & Johnson and presented by The Reiner Foundation, this video focuses on how the experiences of a child's first three years can affect their brain development. Child professionals (Brazelton, Koop, Bowman, Siegel, Perry) discuss how parents can have a profound effect on a baby's ability to think, move, feel, communicate, and more based upon their interactions with their baby and child. Coupling footage of parental interactions with new research in brain development, this approximately 30 minute video is divided into seven segments: Bonding and Attachment, Communication, Health and Nutrition, Discipline, Self-Esteem, Child Care, and Self-Awareness. These child development specialists recommend parents: respond to a baby (touch, sing, read, tune in to their cries and nonverbal language), get good prenatal care and child health care, offer predictable boundaries and limits, value the child, find quality childcare, and more. The video highlights the parental-child connection as the most important because "with the right start, you can stay in touch for the rest of their lives."

Evaluation:

With recent attention focused on the plight of our nation's children and the lack of quality childcare, this video arising from the "I Am Your Child" campaign is timely. This video and its accompanying website offer guidelines for parents and caregivers to raise healthy, happy children and confident, competent learners. The guidelines aren't novel ("talk, read, and sing to your child," "use discipline as an opportunity to teach," etc.). But, coupling them with the latest in brain research gives parents rationale for giving and demanding quality care for their child especially during those first three years. Although there are no "chats," humor, or a lighthanded look at parenting, this video would be excellent for parent education classes for prospective parents. It's free (with a $5.00 shipping and handling fee) and quantities are limited. Opportunities exist daily to contribute to the healthy development of a child's brain through experiences, affection, and other ways, and this video reinforces this message.

Where To Find/Buy:

Contact the I Am Your Child Campaign by calling (202) 338-4385, by FAX at (202) 338-2334, or through the mail at 1010 Wisconsin Ave., NW, Suite 800, Washington, D.C. 20007. There is a $5.00 shipping and handling fee.

Internet URL:

http://www.iamyourchild.org/

PORTABLE PEDIATRICIAN FOR PARENTS (THE)

 Recommended For:
Gaining An Overview: All-Inclusive

Description:

Reflecting recommendations from professional organizations (American Academy of Pediatrics, American Academy of Pediatric Dentistry, etc.) and child development researchers (Burton L. White, Erik Erickson, Jean Piaget, etc.), this 502 page resource offers a month-to-month guide to children's physical and behavioral development from birth to 5 years of age. Part I encompasses most of the book and discusses "The Well Child." The 11 chapters within this part focus on a given age range; topics that are discussed within each chapter include: a narrative description of the age group, separation issues, setting limits, health and illness, day to day issues (developmental milestones, sleep, growth, teeth, feeding and nutrition, activities, etc.), "windows of opportunity," and more. Part II focuses on "frightening behaviors" (fever, inconsolable crying, etc.), first aid, and bodily ailments. Part III offers six essays from a pediatric's point of view. Part IV offers pediatric "Handouts" designed to alleviate disagreements between parents, relatives, and caregivers. Part V is a glossary of medical terms. A 17 page index is also provided.

Evaluation:

By using her background as a pediatrician coupled with studies by well-known child development researchers, Dr. Laura Walther Nathanson allows parents to see growth and changes from the child's point of view. She then strongly encourages parents to view their child's pediatrician as a team player who should be interested in informing, but not advising, parents. With her experience of over "100,000 office visits and more than twice as many phone calls," she is able to give detailed, age appropriate information regarding medical and developmental questions. And, if the reader is still in doubt, she encourages them to seek professional advice. This resource, then, is a most unusual book— parents won't find many better resources available that offer a variety of professionals' advice and suggestions in one neat affordable package.

Where To Find/Buy:

Bookstores and libraries.

Overall Rating
★★★★
This complete guide includes advice from child development experts & professionals

Design, Ease Of Use
★★★★
Side tabs for each age group; extensive index; reader friendly

I–4 Stars; N/R = Not Rated

Media Type:
Print

Price:
$20.00

Principal Subject:
Gaining An Overview:
All-Inclusive

Age Group:
All Ages (0–5)

ISBN:
0062731769

Edition Reviewed:
1994

Publisher:
HarperPerennial
(HarperCollins)

Author/Editor:
Laura Walther Nathanson,
M.D., FAAP

About The Author:
(From Cover Notes)
Nathanson, M.D., is board Certified in Pediatrics and Peri-Neonatology. She earned her B.A. from Harvard and her M.D. from Tufts Medical School. She has handled over 100,000 office visits, more than twice as many phone calls, and says she still hears something new.

Overall Rating
★★★★
A superb, answer-all resource to your child from 13 months to 36 months

Design, Ease Of Use
★★★★
Thoughtfully laced out and comprehensive; 2 column narrative and Q & A format

1–4 Stars; N/R = Not Rated

Media Type:
Print

Price:
$15.95

Principal Subject:
Gaining An Overview:
All-Inclusive

Age Group:
Toddlers (1–3)

ISBN:
0894809946

Edition Reviewed:
1996

Publisher:
Workman Publishing

Author/Editor:
Arlene Eisenberg, Heidi E. Murkoff, Sandee E. Hathaway, B.S.N..

About The Author:
(From Cover Notes)
Arlene Eisenberg, Heidi E. Murkoff, and Sandee E. Hathaway have co-authored three previous books on child care.

WHAT TO EXPECT THE TODDLER YEARS

Best Resource For:
Guide to toddlers' care and development

Recommended For:
Gaining An Overview: All-Inclusive

Description:

Beginning with the 13th month, and progressing through the 36th month of a child's life, this four part guidebook contains over 900 pages of information for parents of toddlers. Part 1 has sixteen chapters that offer advice and suggestions on topics such as child development, setting limits, communicating with your child, encouraging imagination, and more. Each chapter has four subtitles—"What Your Toddler May Be Doing Now," "What You May Be Concerned About," "What It's Important to Know," and "What It's Important For Your Toddler to Know." Part 2 covers the care of a toddler, addressing such issues as nutrition, health concerns, toilet learning, and the special needs child. Part 3 defines the toddler interaction within the family including siblings and childcare. Part 4 includes common home remedies, height and weight charts, and "Best-odds Recipes," to name a few references. Descriptive diagrams and tips are interspersed throughout the manual. There is an extensive 19 page index.

Evaluation:

What a great reference! This guide has information on nearly every phase of a child, age 1 to 3 years of age and then some. It is well written, easy-to-use, and has a comfortable, user-friendly format. The information is impartial and thorough. This is truly an all-inclusive guide, even addressing cholesterol levels in children. The table of contents is extensive and progressive: there is information on caregivers and siblings; on treating toddler injuries; keeping worrying in perspective; and more. This book's valuable advice will take a parent through their child's adolescent years as well with such advice as poison control, preventing the spread of illnesses, appendicitis warnings, and herbal remedies. This book's forte definitely lies in preparing parents to understand the needs, behavior, and development of their children while offering hundreds of suggestions on their care, guidance, and management. This a priceless "find."

Where To Find/Buy:

Bookstores and libraries.

PARENT SOUP
An iVillage Community

 Recommended For:
Gaining An Overview: All-Inclusive

Description:

The Parent Soup website bills itself as "the neighborhood favorite kitchen table—the coffee is great and the conversation is better. . . . community is something you can see and feel." The navigation bar at the top of each page offers a chat room, discussion groups (60 different topics), a parenting library with articles from pregnancy through the teen years, listings of baby names, and more. The Department Menu at the bottom of each page includes: "Our Community," "Parents' Picks," "Answers Now," "Online Guide," and "Chill Out." Members can post announcements, photos, ask for advice, etc. in "Our Community." "Parents' Picks" includes other parents' opinions about various items such as baby products, travel, books, websites, etc. Six parenting experts are available at "Answers Now"; you select the area that best addresses your concern, send your question via their email, the "expert" will answer 10 questions a week, but you have the option to browse previously asked questions and answers. "Online Guide" contains about 100 linked parenting sites. "Chill Out" offers you relaxation tips, weekly horoscopes, and more.

Evaluation:

This site is exactly what it bills itself: friendly and informal, yet supportive and informational. Parents need a wide variety of information, and this site addresses those needs. One can participate in live chat (their free software must be downloaded), get more formally involved in discussion groups, brag about family or connect with other members. Parent Soup also supplies you with a search facility to help locate a possible friend in the "Soup family" either by name, location, or parenting issue (disabilities, divorce, adoption, ADD/ADHD, etc.). On the flip side, there is information on topics too numerous to mention. The parenting library hosts thousands of articles. Searches can be conducted via words the user supplies or through the site's index of subjects and subtopics. Although the expert panel is rather narrow compared to other websites, one should still find that that panel suits the purpose. If not, there is the parenting library or the "Online Guide" for other sources. There is a village feel to this site and its visitors will not be disappointed.

Where To Find/Buy:

On the Internet at the URL: http://www.parentsoup.com/.

Internet URL:

http://www.parentsoup.com/

Overall Rating
★★★★
One-stop-shopping for pregnancy/parenting info, chats/discussions, and expert advice

Design, Ease Of Use
★★★
Once you understand the site's structure, navigation is a breeze

1–4 Stars; N/R = Not Rated

Media Type:
Internet

Principal Subject:
Gaining An Overview: All-Inclusive

Age Group:
All Ages (0–5)

★★★★

Overall Rating
★★★★
An indispensable guide to caring for newborns and children through age five

Design, Ease Of Use
★★★
Compact print difficult to read; consistent format; numerous color photos and charts

I–4 Stars; N/R = Not Rated

Media Type:
Print

Price:
$20.00

Principal Subject:
Gaining An Overview: All-Inclusive

Age Group:
All Ages (0–5)

ISBN:
0375700005

Edition Reviewed:
3rd (1997)

Publisher:
Alfred A. Knopf (Random House)

Author/Editor:
Penelope Leach

About The Author:
(From Cover Notes)
Leach, with a Ph.D. in psychology, is a Fellow of the British Psychological Society and a founding member of the UK branch of the World Association for Infant Mental Health. She is a leading authority and advocate in the field of child development and care.

YOUR BABY & CHILD
From Birth To Age Five

 Recommended For:
Gaining An Overview: All-Inclusive

Description:
This third revised edition of Leach's book incorporates the "latest research and thinking on child development and learning, and reflects the realities of today's . . . new approaches to parenting." Leach is also known for her TV series under the same title—"Your Baby & Child." This 559 page resource is divided up into five sections which include information on newborns, babies in their first six months, older babies (from six months to one year), toddlers (one year to two and a half), and young children (from two and a half to five years). Each section includes characteristics for each age group, such as feeding/eating and growing, teeth and teething, everyday care, excreting, sleeping, and crying and comforting. Some sections also contain material on the senses, muscles, eyesight and hearing, listening and speaking skills, and playing and learning/thinking skills. The book is written in a text format with italic side bar headings, full color illustrations, charts, and highlighted question and answer sections. An index concludes the book.

Evaluation:
If parents want a book that offers all or most of the answers and that covers nearly every aspect of childcare in terms of a baby's development, they should choose this one. This resource provides parents and caregivers with the information they need to truly understand and enhance their child's growth. Different to this version is the absence of a medical section. Instead, it has been replaced by tinted text sections offering parent's point of views on various subjects. While not necessarily reflecting the author's opinion, these opinions are interesting and may open up debate issues as parents strengthen their beliefs—for example, "any toddler who bites . . . should be bitten . . . back." New questions have been added along with notes on hazards and safety guidelines. This book's advice is neither biased nor contrived; it is well-researched and based on a sound professional foundation. Truly, this is a wonderful all-inclusive guide which will benefit parents and their child.

Where To Find/Buy:
Bookstores and libraries.

COMPLETE IDIOT'S GUIDE TO PARENTING A PRESCHOOLER (THE)

Description:

This book's intent is to present parents with an "operator's manual" offering information about children's developmental stages along with warnings about potential parenting challenges and discussions about parenting issues. Divided into four parts and 26 chapters, this 345 page book includes two table of contents (one, at a glance; the other, a detailed listing), a 15 page index, and an appendix of parenting resources. Parts are divided by age ranges—the early toddler (13–24 months), "the terrific, terrible twos" (25–36 months), the three-year-old, and the four-year-old. Each part has various chapters that address parental challenges during that stage along with discussions of children's physical, mental, and emotional development, health and safety issues, and more. Summaries of what is discussed in each chapter is given both at the beginning and end of each chapter. Also provided throughout are icons highlighting parenting anecdotes, tips, safety warnings, myths, and observations.

Evaluation:

Busy parents wishing succinct answers in a well-organized format will find this book warrants their time and attention. It's extremely reader-friendly, offering basic development information and tips, advice, and reassurances for parents as they grow with their child. Parents will find the book very well laid-out with bold headings, inset colored blocks of suggestions, and an extensively cross-referenced index. Additionally, including two table of contents makes information readily accessible with major topics presented in the "Contents at a Glance" and page-by-page details listed in the second table of contents. Many areas, however, are treated lightly—discipline, sibling relations, toilet training, and activities to do with children to name a few. In trying to cover (almost) too much ground, this resource has a tendency to include generalizations in many areas while spending considerable more time in some. Other resources focus more on a child's developmental and behavioral changes. Parents interested in more in-depth coverage in these areas need to check into other all-inclusive resources instead.

Where To Find/Buy:

Bookstores and libraries.

Overall Rating
★★★
Good basic coverage of all childhood and parenting topics presented in a succinct manner

Design, Ease Of Use
★★★★
Very well-organized with 2 table of contents, extensive index, icons of various tips, etc.

1–4 Stars; N/R = Not Rated

Media Type:
Print

Price:
$16.95

Principal Subject:
Gaining An Overview: All-Inclusive

Age Group:
Toddlers & Preschoolers (1–5)

ISBN:
0028617339

Edition Reviewed:
1997

Publisher:
Alpha Books (Macmillan General Reference/Simon and Schuster Macmillan)

Author/Editor:
Keith Boyd, M.D., and Kevin Osborn

About The Author:
(From Cover Notes)
Boyd is the directory of the combined Pediatrics and Medicine Residency Program at the Rush-Presbyterian-St. Luke's Medical Center in Chicago. He is the father of three sons. Osborn, author of 36+ books for both adults and children, is the father of three children.

★★★

Overall Rating
★★★
Addresses preschool parental concerns/questions in a concise, straightforward manner

Design, Ease Of Use
★★★★
Chapters organized by topic to find specific solutions; each chapter has a summary

1–4 Stars; N/R = Not Rated

Media Type:
Print

Price:
$12.95

Principal Subject:
Gaining An Overview: All-Inclusive

Age Group:
Preschoolers (3–5)

ISBN:
0609801635

Edition Reviewed:
1997

Publisher:
Three Rivers Press (Crown Publishers/Random House)

Author/Editor:
Dr. Sylvia Rimm

About The Author:
(From Cover Notes)
Dr. Rimm is a clinical professor at Case Western Reserve University School of Medicine. She is also the Director of the Family Achievement Clinic at MetroHealth Medical Center in Cleveland, Ohio. She also appears monthly on NBC's *Today* show with her own series.

RAISING PRESCHOOLERS
Parenting For Today

Description:

The author has accumulated much of the suggestions in this 224 page guidebook through her clinical work with preschoolers and their families; she also hosts a syndicated newspaper column and appears monthly on NBC's *Today* show with her series "Raising Kids in the '90s." This resource for parents, caregivers, grandparents, and educators contains 25 chapters beginning with information on how to plan a preschooler's day and ending with how to develop a unique parenting style. Other chapters offer recommendations on social/emotional learning, discipline, finding a good daycare, introducing a new sibling, and temper tantrums. The remaining chapters focus on fears, traveling with a preschooler, nontraditional families, kindergarten, grandparents, and food and fitness. Each chapter includes related subtopics, some of which are introduced by a sample parental question, followed by supportive data. Rimm's "Summary Advice" is offered at the end of each chapter to highlight important points.

Evaluation:

This book can be used as a companion to the NBC *Today* videotape, "Raising Preschoolers: Parenting for Today" offering parents and caregivers a complete guide to helping a preschool child "start down the road to an achieving, happy life." From new research, Dr. Rimm provides clear, workable advice for parents and caregivers. The book centers on enriching a child's environment, teaching social skills, dealing with a child's fears, finding good day care, and preparing for kindergarten. The table of contents is succinct and reasonable. The index is comprehensive. An intermittent question and answer format is unique and stimulating offering parents the comfort and knowledge that others have similar concerns. The "Summary Advice" in each chapter provides parents with a useful easy recap to return to in case they need a refresher course at a later date. This is a wonderful concise reference book for parents and caregivers searching for succinct answers to a broad spectrum of early childhood development issues.

Where To Find/Buy:

Bookstores and libraries.

WHAT EVERY BABY KNOWS

Recommended For:
Gaining An Overview: All-Inclusive

Description:

This resource takes the reader through the lives of five families. The book is divided into five major sections, each of which reflect the family histories and then delve into each family's core. Part I is about the Cotton family (who have twins) with information concerning their quiet child/active child, a section about sibling rivalry, and discipline within this family. Part II focuses on the Mazza family, their separation and divorce, and the sleep problems they have had with their child. Part III is about the Considine family, questions they have about their child's crying, the feelings of their middle child, and concerns about a non-walking child. Part IV follows the Sheehan-Weber family with issues involving early learning, stressful situations, and self-esteem. The final section, Part V, is about the Schwartz family, their new baby, and their expectations. Part VI outlines the family systems theory underlying the work of Brazelton's Child Development Unit and the link between the five families in this book and the "brand of behavioral pediatrics" developed in the Unit's program.

Evaluation:

This book contains some very valuable, timeless information. It is a well-written book, with clear, concise information set in a question-answer format making it a very enjoyable reading experience. The content is thorough and does a fine job of yielding to the old textbook-type format without being aloof. Parents are given the rare opportunity of following five families through their parenting struggles, enabling the reader to more closely identify and relate to specific questions they may share with the sample families. Brazelton provides sensitive answers with appropriate developmental background information. He carefully dissects each family's issues and concerns, then allows the reader to share in his follow-up when he revisits them and sees "where they are now." There are many black and white photographs throughout this resource which help to illustrate the subject matter; content is well-supported by research with a clear bibliography and index concluding the guide. Add this book to your family library for professional advice on parenting with a personal flavor.

Where To Find/Buy:

Bookstores and libraries.

Overall Rating
★★★
Unique approach; although written some time ago, basic information still prevails

Design, Ease Of Use
★★★★
Clear and concise; question-answer format makes for untiring reading; consistent format

1–4 Stars; N/R = Not Rated

Media Type:
Print

Price:
$11.00

Principal Subject:
Gaining An Overview: All-Inclusive

Age Group:
Infants & Toddlers (0–3)

ISBN:
0345344553

Edition Reviewed:
1987

Publisher:
Ballantine Books (Random House)

Author/Editor:
T. Berry Brazelton, M.D.

About The Author:
(From Cover Notes)
Dr. Brazelton, one of the most-renowned pediatricians, is a Professor of Pediatrics at Harvard Medical School, as well as chief of the Child Development Unit at Boston Children's Hospital. He is also a political advocate for families and has a TV show.

★★★

Overall Rating
★★★
A humorous look into parent survival techniques for living with a preschooler

Design, Ease Of Use
★★★
Lots of chapter divisions adds some confusion; but recovers with complete index

1–4 Stars; N/R = Not Rated

Media Type:
Print

Price:
$13.95

Principal Subject:
Gaining An Overview: All-Inclusive

Age Group:
Preschoolers (3–5)

ISBN:
1577490452

Edition Reviewed:
1997

Publisher:
Fairview Press

Author/Editor:
Mark Yeager

About The Author:
(From Cover Notes)
Mark Yeager is an anesthesiologist. He has written this handbook for parents drawing on the preschool experiences from his three children. He lives in Lebanon, New Hampshire.

BREAKFAST IS ONLY THE BEGINNING
A Fun-Filled, Practical Guide To Keeping Up With Your Preschooler

Description:

This 210 page guidebook takes you through a day in the life of a preschooler. It begins with breakfast, continues through dressing, toileting, lunch, nap, dinner, and finishes with bedtime. A short introduction is followed by 14 chapters. Each chapter focuses on a given daily event and is broken into either "Levels" and/or "Steps" depending upon the subject matter. Levels illustrate the various "parent-child interaction levels" or "parent survival techniques" the author recommends for various procedures—Level III being "anything that makes a parent feel guilty. " Steps detail sequential tasks. For example, in Chapter 4, "Bathroom Adventures," you are lead through Steps 1, 2 and 3—"The Decision," "The Journey," and "The Event"; Levels I, II, and III are provided for handling any toileting issues that arise. The final chapter, "Surviving," offers parents techniques for managing time, redefining expectations, exercising, and reconnecting with your partner to help maintain favorable relations.

Evaluation:

This handbook affords a humorous insight into a preschooler's (and his or her parents') daily routine. The author takes you on a moment-to-moment adventure, giving you valuable tips, rules, principles, and sources on how to help you survive the preschool years. The driving force behind this book is the author's wonderful humor woven throughout the book. For example, a glossary lists words describing ideas and activities with special meanings any preschool parent can relate to; the author's definition of a bad day is: "a regrettable experience that occurs when parents have a long day at the same time they're in a bad mood." The writing style is upbeat and easy to read. The book is not a serious parenting guide. As the author states, "This book is more like a Field Guide to Tactical Maneuvers" than it is a parenting book. As such, it is an insightful, comical approach to help parents enjoy the little things with their preschooler and to give them a smile along with those "tactical maneuvers."

Where To Find/Buy:

Bookstores and libraries. For a current catalog of Fairview Press titles, visit their website at www.press.fairview.org, or call toll-free: 1-800-544-8207.

DR. SPOCK'S BABY AND CHILD CARE
The One Essential Parenting Book

Description:

Dr. Spock and Dr. Rothenberg together have created a sixth edition of the well-known *Dr. Spock Baby and Child Care Book*. This 832 page book is written in short numbered sections of about a page each. Each numbered entry covers a single aspect of child care. Sections are grouped into subject categories such as: the role of the parents, equipment and clothing, medical and nursing care, infant feeding, breastfeeding, bottlefeeding, daily care, problems of infancy, managing young children, age related issues (from birth to adolescence), child development, illness, special situations, and many more subjects. Although information is provided from the perspective of the authors, two persons with documented authority and experience on the subject, it is written in a first person format. The clear intent of this book is to provide factual and supportive information for first-time parents so they can handle the huge learning curve they need to climb in order to become well-informed parents.

Evaluation:

Spock's reassuring voice may be just the one a new parent needs to hear in order to claim some personal control over a new and occasionally anxious situation. Parents face a world offering various opinions on what a parent should or should not do, what is good and what is not good for the child. This book attempts to provide a balanced perspective in a positive and succinct way. The scope of this book is massive; every possible topic appears to be touched on at least briefly. The style of writing is authoritative, yet done in a gentle and inviting manner, allowing the reader to reflect on all possible options and not feel that it must be done "the Dr. Spock way." For the most part, the book's organization is clear and easily referenced. While not the kind of book one sits down to read straight through, each section is written in an interesting and factual way. Some sections definitely need updating due to latest findings (SIDS, immunizations, etc.); other sections reflect the author's opinion (sometimes inconsistent with current scientific fact), but generally the book seems fresh and relevant whether your child is six days or six years old.

Where To Find/Buy:

Bookstores and libraries.

Overall Rating
★★★
Comprehensive, balanced, supportive; needs updating re: SIDS, immunizations, etc.

Design, Ease Of Use
★★★
Easy to read, easy to reference; unclear as to why sections are numbered

1–4 Stars; N/R = Not Rated

Media Type:
Print

Price:
$7.99

Principal Subject:
Gaining An Overview: All-Inclusive

Age Group:
All Ages (0–5)

ISBN:
0671760602

Edition Reviewed:
6th (1992)

Publisher:
Pocket Books (Simon & Schuster)

Author/Editor:
Benjamin Spock, M.D., and Michael B. Rothenberg, M.D.

About The Author:
(From Cover Notes)
Benjamin Spock, M.D., practiced pediatrics in New York City from 1933 to 1947. Then he became a medical teacher and researcher. Michael B. Rothenberg, M.D., is a pediatrician and child psychiatrist who had combined these two fields in his work since 1957.

Overall Rating
★★★
Addresses parental concerns
in an intelligent style

Design, Ease Of Use
★★★
Three-part contents make for
easy reference; photographs
would help break up the text

1–4 Stars; N/R = Not Rated

Media Type:
Print

Price:
$5.95

Principal Subject:
Gaining An Overview:
All-Inclusive

Age Group:
Preschoolers (3–5)

ISBN:
0812014170

Edition Reviewed:
1995

Publisher:
Barron's Educational Series

Author/Editor:
Susan E. Gottlieb, M.D.

About The Author:
(From Cover Notes)
Susan E. Gottlieb is a
pediatrician, affiliated with the
Brooklyn Hospital Center,
New York University School
of Medicine.

KEYS TO PARENTING YOUR THREE-YEAR-OLD

Description:

This guide offers 186 pages of information and advice on parenting three year old children. Separated into 3 parts, the book discusses motor and language skills, emotional development, behavioral issues, and more. Part One focuses on a child's "inner world." Chapters include gross and fine motor development, language development, fears, the active child, the shy child, the 3-year-old checkup, and more. Part Two discusses child and family interactions. Some of this section's chapters include relationships, siblings, and dealing with difficult subjects such as birth and death. The final section, Part Three, concerns 3 year olds and their community. Choosing a preschool, birthday parties, and the differences between people are a few of the issues addressed. Each chapter begins with a half page narrative of a 3 year old to illustrate the chapter's focus. Parents will also find a question and answer section (5 pages), a glossary, additional resources (activity books, videos, audiotapes, and books), and a 3 page index.

Evaluation:

This Parent's Choice Honors guidebook is a well-written resource designed to provide a comprehensive view of a three year old. The book's focus is on the individual child's social, emotional and motor development, their family life, and their emergence into their community. This helps to not only understand the child but their position in a small group (the family) and a larger context (their community). The introduction does a fine job of validating these three major sections. The introductory paragraphs help to highlight the supporting text found in each chapter. This not only helps to focus parents on the issue but creates a bridge for them while reading through the chapter. The author, a pediatrician, aptly intersperses supportive tables and charts throughout the book. Preceding a concise, comprehensive index are lists of resources. If you have a toddler coming into their threes, this guidebook definitely warrants your attention.

Where To Find/Buy:

Bookstores and libraries.

KIDSOURCE ONLINE

Description:

This online community, created by a group of parents with varied backgrounds, aims to find "the best of the healthcare and education information . . . and deliver it . . . in new and innovative ways. . . ." General options on their homepage offer various articles under the headings of "Education," "Health," "Recreation," "Parenting," "Guide to Best Software," and "New Products." Specific options address four given age groups—newborns, toddlers, preschoolers, and K–12. Within these categories are subtopic headings such as safety, learning, growth and development, health & medicine, toys & recreation, and more. Also listed within these categories are online forums specific to each age grouping. Most of the articles within this website are ranked using a 5 star system with 5 stars being "best, in depth and most helpful overall." A list of articles is then presented along with a brief synopsis of the article's contents along with its rating; generally articles average 2–3 pages.

Evaluation:

This well-organized site hosts unusual contributors—the U.S. Department of Education, child-related organizations (child abuse consortia, etc.) and associations (learning disabilities), and others. The articles' succinct nature, positive tone, and friendly voice can be easily handled by any busy parent. Rating the articles presents yet another convenient way to ease up on the plethora of articles that face a parent interested in getting some new information and advice. Graphics are absent from the site intentionally, say the creators, because "most of (their) visiting parents do not have time to wait for extensive graphics to download"; they will upgrade their design as parents upgrade their systems. The general discussion forums are well-organized and titled. Unfortunately, the age specific forums were cumbersome, simply consisting of a running list of titles (57 under "toddlers"); subject groupings would be more helpful. This site is a good informational site; other sites need to be used for conversation.

Where To Find/Buy:

On the Internet at the URL: http://www.kidsource.com/.

Internet URL:

http://www.kidsource.com/

Overall Rating
★★★
Unusual contributors, succinct articles make research an easy and interesting task

Design, Ease Of Use
★★★
Graphics are absent; articles are cross-referenced & rated according to a 5 star system

1–4 Stars; N/R = Not Rated

Media Type:
Internet

Principal Subject:
Gaining An Overview: All-Inclusive

Age Group:
All Ages (0–5)

★★★

Overall Rating
★★★
Author's approach presents facts, disputes myths, so parents can be decision-makers

Design, Ease Of Use
★★
Vague table of contents; good headings within book; book's size & weight cumbersome

1–4 Stars; N/R = Not Rated

Media Type:
Print

Price:
$6.99

Principal Subject:
Gaining An Overview: All-Inclusive

Age Group:
All Ages (0–5)

ISBN:
0451163117

Edition Reviewed:
1986

Publisher:
Signet (Dutton Signet/Penguin Books)

Author/Editor:
Marianne Egeland Neifert, M.D., with Anne Price and Nancy Dana

About The Author:
(From Cover Notes)
Neifert is an award-winning pediatrician, professor of pediatrics, and mother of five children.

DR. MOM
A Guide To Baby And Child Care

Description:
Neifert coined the name "Dr. Mom" because she believes strongly in "the importance of nurturing new parents, in order to bring to blossom their long-term competency." Her 529 page book is divided into 17 chapters. The first three focus on preparation for parenthood from making the decision to giving birth to outfitting the nursery. Chapters 4–6 center on newborn and infant care. Children's development (birth to age five) is discussed in Chapter 7. Chapter 9 offers 10 pages of information on "toilet learning." Chapter 8—"The Challenge of Parenting" addresses discipline choices, while Chapter 10 focuses on understanding various behaviors (tantrums, biting, pacifiers, etc.). The next 3 chapters offer information on caring for a sick child, dealing with illnesses and disorders (80 pages), and what to do in an emergency. The pros, the cons, and feedback on "contemporary concerns" (sexual abuse, kidnapping, the family bed, breastfeeding in public, etc.) are presented in Chapter 14. The last three chapters deal with parenting styles and family strategies (nonsexist, working parents, single families, divorce, etc.).

Evaluation:
Neifert does a fine job of commingling her personal experiences as the mother of five with her professional aspiration to nurture new parents by "acknowledging their good intentions and sound intuition . . . supplying them with factual information . . . (so that they can) meet their children's needs. . . ." Throughout her book, she grants parents the privilege of making their own decisions on parenting issues. Some resources do a better job dealing with topics such as toilet training/learning, discipline, and behavior. Neifert's book does a better job at examining the various sides of "hot" issues today such as the family bed, nursing in public places, and more. Some information is outdated due to the book's copyright so, as always, parents should check with their baby's doctor before making certain decisions. The book's size is awkward; hopefully future editions will be a larger format with fewer pages making it easier to hold and read. The section on illnesses/disorders is well-done and comparable to that found in better resources. Not recommended for use on its own, this book would be a welcome companion to another more inclusive resource.

Where To Find/Buy:
Bookstores, libraries, or order direct by contacting Penguin USA at P. O. Box 999, Dept. #17109, Bergenfield, NJ 07621.

NATIONAL PARENTING CENTER (THE)

Description:

Programmed and hosted by ParentsPlace.com this website was founded in July 1989 to provide "sound advice and information so that (parents) may successfully navigate the challenges of parenting in the 1990s." Features at their homepage include articles, a mall, chat facilities, and a daily feature. Articles, presented through the "ParenTalk Newsletter," are written by their panel of 9 parenting authorities (bios include a psychologist, pediatrician, parenting authors, and more). Information is grouped by the following categories: pregnancy, newborns, infancy, toddler, preschool, preteens, and adolescence; various subcategories are then presented along with the respective author. Articles typically range from 1/2 a page to 1 page in length. "Chat" leads you to ParentsPlace.com's discussion rooms with 20+ topics at our visit. TNPC's "Mall/Shopping Center" houses their award-winning products from their Seal of Approval program which are organized by age groups and can be purchased online (nonsecure).

Evaluation:

Visitors to this site will be initially impressed by the discussion forums available here. The topics are more numerous than most other sites, they're clearly labeled for access, and the participants are active. At the "Mall," the lists of toys, books, music, furniture, and other child-related products are, of course, limited to those that were tested by their volunteers. It would be helpful to know what products overall were evaluated, i.e. is a particular product not a "quality" product or has it simply not been tested by the judges (parents)? The articles were adequate but just that and nothing more. The advice given is succinct albeit a bit too brief to be of any real help to a struggling parent, e.g. helpful hints for "Terrible Twos" invite the parent to remember the author's given 5 rules to "escape toddlerhood in one piece." Such directions are rather negative and simplistic. Also, there were no Q & A-type segment available to look for further information. Other sites provide more in-depth follow-through and situational help than this one does.

Where To Find/Buy:

On the Internet at the URL: http://www.tnpc.com/ or by calling 1-800-753-6667.

Internet URL:

http://www.tnpc.com/

Overall Rating
★★
Information and advice from "authorities" rather succinct; shopping and chats good

Design, Ease Of Use
★★★★
Good graphics in their "mall," easily navigated, well-organized headings

1–4 Stars; N/R = Not Rated

Media Type:
Internet

Principal Subject:
Gaining An Overview: All-Inclusive

Age Group:
All Ages (0–5)

Overall Rating
★★
Good resource for pinpointing basic issues involved with raising a beginning toddler

Design, Ease Of Use
★★★
Well-orchestrated layout with bulleted highlights; no photos or illustrations

1–4 Stars; N/R = Not Rated

Media Type:
Print

Price:
$5.95

Principal Subject:
Gaining An Overview: All-Inclusive

Age Group:
Toddlers (1–3)

ISBN:
0812047729

Edition Reviewed:
1992

Publisher:
Barron's

Author/Editor:
Meg Zweiback, R.N., M.P.H., C.P.N.P.

About The Author:
(From Cover Notes)
Meg Zweiback is a pediatric nurse practitioner and an associate clinical professor at the University of California in San Francisco.

KEYS TO PARENTING YOUR ONE-YEAR-OLD

Description:

This 154 page resource, one in Barron's Parenting Keys series, focuses on questions and answers for parents of one-year-old children. The table of contents is divided into three parts. Included is information on growth, developmental differences in personality, and common behavior issues. Part 1 discusses how one-year-olds grow and change. Part 2 includes highlights temperamental style with topics such as adaptability, attention span, sensitivity, and more. Part 3 addresses toddler behavior with three subsections. Section 1 deals with family interactions. Some issues in this section include tantrums, separating from parents, and clinging to parents. Section 2 deals with getting along with others; sharing, biting, and choosing childcare are included. Section 3 discusses a one-year-old's habits with topics such as drinking from a bottle, breastfeeding, head banging, and more. A question and answer section, glossary of terms, and a list of suggested resources and readings are also included.

Evaluation:

This is a great resource for parents anxious to learn about the changes their child will experience as they learn to communicate, adapt to new situations, and grow in the first year of their life. The book is easy to follow with a simple table of contents and a reliable index. Some of the issues specific to one-year-olds include toilet training readiness, sensitivity, tantrums, and "loveys." Intelligently interpreted, this guide addresses some of the more popular parenting questions, such as "How can I break her of the bottle habit?" There are 10 questions included from parents which the author, a pediatric nurse practitioner, answers authoritatively, but with compassion. The suggested reading and resources section is an added bonus. Although the information is worthy, parents will most likely want more advice and depth in certain areas. Look elsewhere for a more comprehensive resource to take home and study.

Where To Find/Buy:

Bookstores and libraries.

KEYS TO PARENTING YOUR TWO-YEAR-OLD

Description:

This 166 page book is one in a series of guidebooks offering advice on parenting preschoolers, specifically, two-year-olds. The contents is separated into three parts. Part One discusses how two-year-olds develop and change. Becoming independent, language development, feeding, sleep, toilet training, and discipline are some of the subtopics. Part Two focuses on the variety of two year olds' temperament. Their ability to adapt, their moods, attention span, distractibility, and sensitivity are some of the issues explained. The final section, Part Three, focuses on "Behavior and Misbehavior"; areas highlighted include temper tantrums, communication, social development, siblings and other children, anger and aggression, and demand for attention. Following Part Three is a dedicated question and answer section. The 10 questions range from dealing with picky eaters to time out to television usage. A list of suggested reading and materials is also provided along with a glossary of seven terms and an index.

Evaluation:

This reference strives to help parents of two-year-olds cope with raising their child in an often demanding modern time where parents often have little outside support. The author embraces the positive aspects of living with a two-year-old by dispelling the myth of the "terrible twos" and explaining their personalities so parents will better understand how to "enjoy the challenges." She offers parents suggestions on how to set realistic expectations and advice on how to cope with potential behavior problems. Helpful keys are provided in Part One describing a toddler's development and how it affects his/her behavior in his daily activities—sleeping, feeding, toileting, and discipline. This book has a comfortable layout with an easy-to-read style. The information is worthy, but leaves one with a sense of wanting more advice and depth on the subject matter. Parents need to look elsewhere for a more comprehensive resource to take home and study.

Where To Find/Buy:

Bookstores and libraries.

Overall Rating
★★
Basic no-nonsense approach to understanding a two-year-old's development and growth

Design, Ease Of Use
★★★
Detailed table of contents and index useful; no graphics to break up the text's monotony

1–4 Stars; N/R = Not Rated

Media Type:
Print

Price:
$6.95

Principal Subject:
Gaining An Overview: All-Inclusive

Age Group:
Toddlers (1–3)

ISBN:
0812014162

Edition Reviewed:
1993

Publisher:
Barron's Educational Series

Author/Editor:
Meg Zweiback, R.N., M.P.H., C.P.N.P.

About The Author:
(From Cover Notes)
Meg Zweiback is Associate Clinical Professor at the University of California, San Francisco's Department of Family Health Care Nursing.

Overall Rating
★★
Good overall discussion of child development, needs more depth and updating on care

Design, Ease Of Use
★★★
Although it reads much like a textbook, parents will gain easy access to subject matter

1–4 Stars; N/R = Not Rated

Media Type:
Print

Price:
$15.95

Principal Subject:
Gaining An Overview: All-Inclusive

Age Group:
Infants (0–1)

ISBN:
0399518045

Edition Reviewed:
2nd (1993)

Publisher:
Perigee Books (Berkeley Publishing)

Author/Editor:
Theresa Caplan

About The Author:
(From Cover Notes)
Theresa Caplan is carrying on the vision of Frank Caplan, Founder of the Princeton Center for Infancy and Early Childhood who authored the first edition of this book. She is currently Director of the Center.

THE FIRST TWELVE MONTHS OF LIFE
Your Baby's Growth Month By Month

Description:
Using a month-by-month format, this 302 page reference provides information on an infant's development from birth to twelve months. There are fourteen "Chapters." The first two offer general information for parents on Caesarean birth and the newborn (basic senses, feeding and sleeping patterns, breastfeeding/bottlefeeding, and more). The next three chapters address the infant's first three months including postpartum blues, depression, colic, baby's schedule, early learning, sensory-motor abilities, vocal and visual stimulation, immunizations, and more. Chapter Six highlights infants' fourth month and their visual powers, exercising baby, introducing solid foods, etc. The remaining eight chapters address specific milestones that appear monthly in an infant's development. Some of these include separation anxiety, language, motion, obedience, independence, and walking to name a few. A book list for parents is included as well as a 10 page index.

Evaluation:
This reference is a good choice for following an infant's developmental progression on a month-to-month basis during their first year of growth. Although this guide reads much like a textbook for a child development course, its consistent format and style help make it more easily read and less forbidding. The author provides monthly growth charts, numerous black and white photographs, and uses a two-column format throughout. She also supplies an overview at the introduction of each chapter that succinctly captures the main elements of that stage in an infant's growth. Infant development is fully addressed, albeit in a rather dense fashion with few subheadings to break up the text. Many areas of baby care, however, need updating, namely the advice concerning breastfeeding and sleeping positions. Much of the material is supported by such notables as Dr. T. Berry Brazelton and Dr. Mary D. Ainsworth. However, with the 1993 copyright date, this guide might best be used as a supplemental companion to a more current in-depth resource that discusses baby care and child development.

Where To Find/Buy:
Bookstores and libraries.

WHAT TO EXPECT THE FIRST YEAR
The Comprehensive Guide That Clearly Explains Everything Parents Need To Know About The First Year With A New Baby

Description:

What to Expect the First Year is arranged in a textbook-like fashion. The Table of Contents illustrates the details to be found in this 671 page book, with an outline type format on what is to be found within. Part One addresses the infant's first year. The facts on such topics as bottle vs. breastfeeding, along with recommended equipment for either, is coupled with the emotional concerns of impending parenthood. Each chapter covers issues for each month of the baby's life. What the baby may be doing, what to expect from the monthly checkup, feeding issues, normal parental concerns for this stage, and "what it's important to know" are included. Part Two—"Of Special Concern"—addresses special interest areas (summer clothing and winter concerns), common baby illnesses, first aid, adoption, and more. Supportive information is also provided on babies with problems, including references on the most common birth disorders. The last five chapters in this part deal with emotional and lifestyle adjustments. Part Three is a collection of recipes and common home remedies as well as a table on common childhood illnesses.

Evaluation:

Reading this book is like reading a user friendly encyclopedia. Throughout, it sounds like advice from an experienced mother/nurse down the street who can be counted on to know exactly what to expect from the baby at whatever stage of his/her development and how to do whatever needs to be done. It's light on illustrations, but made readable by frequent sub-heading breaks in the two-column text which insert questions and answers on child care issues. One example of this is the question on vegetarian diet, with a parent questioning whether a strict vegetarian diet provides enough nutrition. The answers are given in bulleted paragraphs, each with a different possible solution to the question depending on the age of the infant. This approach is used throughout the book. As a general reference this book is comprehensive; its information is mainstream with a friendly supportive tone and generous safety and medical tips.

Where To Find/Buy:

Bookstores and libraries.

Overall Rating
★★
A massive amount of information conveyed in a question and answer format

Design, Ease Of Use
★★★
Easy to reference, easy to read

1–4 Stars; N/R = Not Rated

Media Type:
Print

Price:
$22.00

Principal Subject:
Gaining An Overview: All-Inclusive

Age Group:
Infants (0–1)

ISBN:
1563058766

Edition Reviewed:
2nd (1996)

Publisher:
Workman Publishing

Author/Editor:
Arlene Eisenberg, Heidi E. Murkoff, Sandee E. Hathaway, B.S.N.

About The Author:
(From Cover Notes)
Arlene Eisenberg, Heidi E. Murkoff, and Sandee E. Hathaway, B.S.N. are the authors of the bestselling "What To Expect" series.

Overall Rating
★★
Advice and support with a light, often humorous touch

Design, Ease Of Use
★★
No table of contents, roughly listed chronologically; index helps; easy Q & A format

1–4 Stars; N/R = Not Rated

Media Type:
Print

Price:
$14.00

Principal Subject:
Gaining An Overview: All-Inclusive

Age Group:
Infants (0–1)

ISBN:
1575660555

Edition Reviewed:
1996

Publisher:
Kensington Books

Author/Editor:
Bud Zukow, M.D. and Nancy Sayles Kaneshiro

About The Author:
(From Cover Notes)
Zukow is Chairman Emeritus of the Dept. of Pediatrics at Encino/Tarzana Regional Medical Center in Tarzana, CA., where he is also in private practice. He is the author of a previous book on parenting. Kaneshiro is the mother of Ian, a patient of Dr. Zukow's.

BABY: AN OWNER'S MANUAL

Description:

This book was written by an experienced pediatrician, and a first-time mother. This book consists of "some fast answers to questions we know you're going to ask, addressing the issues that are common to virtually all new parents." It is intended to be used as a source of quick, accessible information, easy "to grab in the middle of the night." Although there is no table of contents, questions and answers are arranged in roughly chronological groupings, from taking the baby home from the hospital to bottle- and breast-feeding, setting up a feeding schedule, diaper rash, colic, and crying spells. The book progresses to questions dealing with choosing a day care, weight gain, teething, starting on solid foods, fevers and colds, child proofing your house, discipline, and maintaining balance in your own life.

Evaluation:

This pediatrician takes a decidedly and unapologetically old-fashioned approach to baby-rearing. The advice given is sensible, succinct, and often humorous, obviously drawing on his experience in answering questions of anxious mothers ("Question: Can his umbilical cord come untied? Answer: I have this vision of an umbilical cord coming untied and a baby flying around the room backward, deflating like a balloon . . ."). Dr. Zukow, a self-described "parent advocate," believes that parents who "get back into their routines as quickly as possible are generally rewarded with more easy-going and independent kids as they grow." Thus, parents will find advice about setting up feeding schedules, getting your baby to sleep through the night, and so forth. Also stressed is the parents' right to make choices, unpressured by current trends (such as deciding whether to use bottle or breastfeed). Altogether, this resource will be helpful to those who subscribe to Zukow's parenting style.

Where To Find/Buy:

Bookstores and libraries.

PAMPERS PARENTING INSTITUTE
Expert Advice For Caring Parents

Description:

This site is also dubbed "Total Baby Care: Newborn to Toddler." Their homepage focuses on six areas: "House Call," "Well Baby," "Healthy Baby Skin," "Pampers Diapers," "This Month. . . ," and "AAP." T. Berry Brazelton, a pediatrician, offers advice, encouragement, and information about your child's development in "House Call." You may select your baby's age (newborn, 3 wks., 6 wks., etc., to 3 yrs.) and interest area (feeding, sleeping, communication, cognitive, motor skills, etc.). "Well Baby" includes a "comprehensive encyclopedia of child care information" provided by Suzanne Dixon, M.D., a pediatrician.; various ages again can be selected along with various interest areas. Caring for your baby's skin "from cord care to rashes and sunburn" is the focus of "Healthy Baby Skin," written by Alfred Lane, M.D., a pediatric dermatologist. Diapering and product info is included in "Pampers Diapers" while "AAP" describes the aims of the American Academy of Pediatrics. "This Month" features a parenting topic of the month; this month's topic deals with traveling with your baby, past topics are also available.

Evaluation:

For those who enjoy T. Berry Brazelton and his perspectives, this site will likely be disappointing. The information included within his segment is droll and barely covers the subject matter. His advice reads like "sound bites," lacking the usual warmth and compassion evidenced by "What Every Baby Knows," his television program. The segment "Healthy Baby Skin" is even less inviting. It initially looks appealing: the site asks the visitor to select the child's age and choose an interest area; information is displayed and can then be browsed or printed. A redeeming facet of this site is the information included within "Well Baby;" the developmental information here is well laid out and can be easily read in a sitting.

Where To Find/Buy:

On the Internet at the URL: http://www.totalbabycare.com/.

Internet URL:

http://www.totalbabycare.com/

Overall Rating
★★
Information dry but adequate; Brazelton fans will most likely be disappointed here

Design, Ease Of Use
★★
Navigation design just average

1–4 Stars; N/R = Not Rated

Media Type:
Internet

Principal Subject:
Gaining An Overview: All-Inclusive

Age Group:
Infants & Toddlers (0–3)

Publisher:
Procter & Gamble

Overall Rating
★★
Access to abundant info, other online parents on selected topics, and "experts"

Design, Ease Of Use
★★
Most info is buried deep, but fairly well-categorized; graphics slow down the process

1–4 Stars; N/R = Not Rated

Media Type:
Internet

Principal Subject:
Gaining An Overview: All-Inclusive

Age Group:
All Ages (0–5)

Publisher:
Time Warner Cable Programming (ParentTime LLC)

PARENTTIME

Description:
Access to this site's features starts with selecting a child's age; choices range from your pregnancy trimester and then monthly through 11 months, then yearly from age 1–18. "Features" and "Departments" are the same for any age group. "Features" includes various articles, e.g. travel with your kids, sun safety, 10 things you never thought you'd say to your child, etc. "Departments" featured numerous articles and sub-articles focusing on a child's growth & health concerns, issues for parents, choosing toys, books, etc. for one's child, and more. Three articles, "selected for you" based upon the age of one's child, amount to the main difference between age group selections. A recent search for information about two year olds at this site yielded articles written by Sears, Dr. Benjamin Spock, and Maura Rhodes of *PARENTING*. A chat room is available along with "Parent Time Live!" that "put(s) you in touch with people in the know who care about nurturing your youngsters" ("Nursing Moms Online" and Dr. Bill & Martha Sears were scheduled). Their weekly electronic newsletter is also available for free and is received through email.

Evaluation:
The user of this site will find a wealth of information here to answer most of his/her questions and concerns. And that information focuses on one's child from the moment they are conceived until they are of legal age. Some parents will enjoy the chat room, others will find the online live forum fun. But one needs patience and time because most of the information is buried deep within the "Departments." Unfortunately, this section, although useful, isn't organized by age categories; one needs to weed out what's not wanted and hunt for what is. "Ask An Expert," read frequently asked Q & A's, experts' perspectives on topical parenting issues—these are other features of this site which should not be missed. Even though this website's database of articles largely comes from *PARENTING* magazine, the reader will generally get an array of opinion to help her/him weigh alternatives for various parenting issues (largely due to their online experts and contributors). And so, a visit here is definitely worth one's time.

Where To Find/Buy:
On the Internet at the URL: http://www.pathfinder.com/ParentTime/Welcome/.

Internet URL:
http://www.pathfinder.com/ParentTime/Welcome/

EVERYDAY PARENTING
The First Five Years

Description:

This ten chapter book includes the following issues: dependency; sleeping; eating; independence; setting limits; children's thinking; fear and imagination; toys, play, and socializing; being nice; and caretakers and preschools. There is no index, but instead the subtopics are listed in the table of contents under the 10 chapter topics. This 267 page book is based upon the author's newspaper column on child rearing and its aim is to answer the questions that parents most often asked her. Within each chapter there are approximately 6 to 12 subtopics, some in a question and answer format, such as, "Why Is My Child Afraid of Santa Claus?" Other topics include questions about spanking, falls and accidents, taking a child to the dentist, and how to know when a child is ready for kindergarten. Over 90 questions are addressed in the book. This book does not offer parents a "comprehensive look at theory" but instead is designed to "offer practical advice on the specific issues of child rearing."

Evaluation:

By answering common questions parents ask about raising children, this book is a somewhat useful and practical guide for parents. It offers a basic understanding of a child's social, intellectual, and emotional needs but in a limited sense. It is not comprehensive and takes a rather relaxed and random approach. An index would have been beneficial to this guide. This way parents, interested in "practical advice" on a given topic, could more easily locate the information especially if it is included in several chapters. The articles deal generally with children from infancy to five years of age. The book, by grouping this wide age range and not breaking the topics up by age group, makes it less desirable and less usable. For example, in selecting a caretaker, the needs of parents of infants will be different from those of preschoolers but the information is not easily differentiated. Such broad blanket suggestions may well confuse parents who are seeking more age-specific advice. This is a lukewarm reference; parents can do better.

Where To Find/Buy:

Bookstores and libraries, or order direct by calling 1-800-253-6476.

Overall Rating
★★
Good information, but it's tough to wade through the material to get to the specifics

Design, Ease Of Use
★
Desperately needs an index to cross-reference a clumsy table of contents

1–4 Stars; N/R = Not Rated

Media Type:
Print

Price:
$7.95

Principal Subject:
Gaining An Overview: All-Inclusive

Age Group:
All Ages (0–5)

ISBN:
0140133453

Edition Reviewed:
1990

Publisher:
Penguin Books

Author/Editor:
Robin Goldstein with Janet Gallant

About The Author:
(From Cover Notes)
Robin Goldstein, M.A., is a parenting consultant and educator. She has taught college courses on child development and helps preschools plan and improve their programs. She writes a newspaper column on child rearing.

Overall Rating
★★
Good for basic information, but outdated in some areas; there are other better resources

Design, Ease Of Use
★

Author provides no index so readers are forced to read it cover-to-cover; small print

1–4 Stars; N/R = Not Rated

Media Type:
Print

Price:
$6.99

Principal Subject:
Gaining An Overview: All-Inclusive

Age Group:
All Ages (0–5)

ISBN:
0451156250

Edition Reviewed:
1970

Publisher:
Signet (Penguin Group/ Penguin USA)

Author/Editor:
Dr. Fitzhugh Dodson

About The Author:
(From Cover Notes)
Fitzhugh Dodson, Ph.D. has more than twenty years of professional work, both as a psychologist and an educator. He has appeared on TV and radio show, and lectures throughout the U.S. Dodson is an honors graduate of John Hopkins and Yale universities.

HOW TO PARENT
The Indispensable Guide To Your Child's Formative Years

Description:

This book is composed of 14 chapters in 444 pages. Chapter 1 begins with information on mothers: their feelings, adjustments to being a mom, and a description of children's early stages of development. Chapter 2 takes the reader into the world of infants, from birth to twelve months of age, and is divided into three month segments. General information on toddlers can be found in Chapter 3, while chapters 4 and 5 further explore this stage in terms of a child's "first adolescence." Here the author discusses topics such as feelings, temper tantrums, toilet training, play, and more. Chapters 6 and 7 address the preschool years with topics such as impulses, peers, sexuality, choosing preschools and kindergarten, and more. Chapters 8 and 9 focus on discipline. Violence and its influence in the media and children's toys can be found in Chapter 10. The remaining chapters, 11–13 discuss ways parents can teach their child (language, reading, math, etc.) and how to select toys and books for children. A summary of the guide's major points is included in Chapter 14. There is no index; the author states, it was "meant to be read as a unified whole."

Evaluation:

The author has purposefully not included an index. His intention is that if readers can't look up specific topics, they will then need to read the entire guide and will gain a better understanding of the whole development process. This is not, however, convenient or user-friendly for those who have read the whole book and are trying to relocate information. Much useful information is given, but some information is bent towards the author's strong opinion. This is evidenced especially in his advice regarding breastfeeding and teaching preschoolers; the author believes there is no scientific evidence that breastfeeding is better physically for the baby than bottlefeeding; he also believes children should be taught some skills (math, reading, etc.) before their school years begin. Some strong sweeping generalizations are included, such as "the new mother's whole life now seems to revolve around this little baby . . . and frankly she resents this." Since the book's 1970 copyright date, more current information about parenting has come to light. Unless parents know what to weed out, they would be best advised to look for more updated material.

Where To Find/Buy:

Bookstore, libraries, or order direct by contacting Penguin USA at P. O. Box 999, Dept. #17109, Bergenfield, New Jersey 07621, or by calling 1-800-253-6476.

PARENTING OF BABIES AND TODDLERS
Your Mining Co. Guide

Description:

An at-home mother with a personal history as a "survivor of child abuse" studied child development, psychology, and other areas to better understand "the abusive methods of parenting." She then developed this site to offer support and information on the issues facing parents of toddlers and babies. The homepage offers "Net Links" on various topics (25) such as: baby's crying, breastfeeding, childcare issues, guiding behavior, language, newborn care, potty training, sibling rivalry, temper tantrums, and more. Each topic is a compilation of other resources' highlights (mainly print references), or a connection to other websites, or both; a one sentence summary of each resource is provided so parents will know the gist of what is included. The site's homepage also includes articles "In The Spotlight" consisting of the creator/author's newest features; separate tips on consistent guidance, delayed speech, midlife fathers, and more were given on our visit. A chat room, bulletin boards, and a newsletter are also provided.

Evaluation:

Once parents get to the information offered at this site, they'll find that the site does an acceptable job of presenting the major points concerning most parenting issues. But that is the hang-up. Navigation seems relatively easy at first within this site, but many parents will quickly become lost. Future plans for including an overall site map on the homepage will help parents better navigate this site. Also, the source of the information at times is unclear and the visitor can only be confused at times regarding what he/she is reading: is it the creator's opinion, recaps from other sites, or references to other printed resources? This needs to be made more clear. Also, the online newsletter is too concise and scattered to be of much relevance to parents. Parents need to check out more solid resources.

Where To Find/Buy:

On the Internet at the URL: http://babyparenting.miningco.com.

Internet URL:

http://babyparenting.miningco.com

Overall Rating
★★
Summary information from other references, websites; unclear as to the source at times

Design, Ease Of Use
★
Easy to get lost, needs a site map with descriptions; concise information is rather dry

1–4 Stars; N/R = Not Rated

Media Type:
Internet

Principal Subject:
Gaining An Overview: All-Inclusive

Age Group:
Infants & Toddlers (0–3)

Overall Rating
★★
Baby Grams offer good monthly descriptions about baby & child; other info mediocre

Design, Ease Of Use
★
Navigation frustrating at times

1–4 Stars; N/R = Not Rated

Media Type:
Internet

Principal Subject:
Gaining An Overview:
All-Inclusive

Age Group:
Infants & Toddlers (0–3)

Author/Editor:
Tori Kropp

About The Author:
(From Cover Notes)
Kropp, a registered nurse for 13 years, is president and founder of PillowTalk, providing prenatal and postnatal education to "25% of pregnant families" in the San Francisco Bay area. She is the "Dear Abby" of pregnancy in the San Francisco Bay area.

STORKSITE
The Premier Pregnancy & New Parenting Website

Description:
StorkSite's goal is to "provide emotional and informational support in an interactive, community-based environment." The visitor must register to gain access to the site's free features which include: The Front Porch, the Stork Site Library, The Storkzine, and The Picket Fence. The Front Porch offers you a personal due date ticker, suggested baby names, email notices, and access to a reference library, chat rooms, Baby Grams, and more. Baby Grams are one page monthly descriptions of a baby's growth and development from 1 month (during pregnancy) to about 2 years (after birth). The Storkzine, their online magazine, offers various articles (typically one page) on pregnancy, childbirth, and the first year; current articles dealt with a teen mom's story, literacy and young children, genetic roots of osteoporosis, and more. "Ask Tori R.N." is a Q & A forum for pregnancy and childbirth issues. Users can access a glossary, name database, medical references, and more through The Stork Site Library. The Picket Fence, "the heart and soul of Stork Site's community," offers chat rooms, "Best Friends Forums," and more.

Evaluation:
The most valuable aspect of this site is the information provided in the Baby Grams. It's ample, interestingly written and usually age-appropriate; however in many cases, the user is unable to access Baby Grams on older children (just under 2 years old). Reference materials available through both The Storkzine and The Stork Site Library may be useful for some. Many of these references, however, are either too wieldy (medical abstracts) or too brief to be relevant to young parents' needs. The Picket Fence may provide some emotional support; the Q & A forum provides interesting feedback but it's one person's viewpoint, not a team that might offer you varying points of view to consider. On the other hand, if a parent has time to spare, reading Baby Grams would be quite informative. Otherwise, look elsewhere for more user-friendly info.

Where To Find/Buy:
On the Internet at the URL: http://www. storksite.com/.

Internet URL:
http://www. storksite.com/

ALL ABOUT KIDS

Description:

Featuring articles that are taken from the pages of the "All About Kids Parent Newsletter," (locally representative of the Greater Cincinnati area), this website offers the following options at their homepage: Articles, Forum, Editorial, Calendar, Community, Market, Kids Show, and Bookstore. The last five options consist of a regional calendar of events, links to other parenting sites, a list of All About Kids' supporters/advertisers, information about Cincinnati's August 1997 Kids Show, and a list of recommended books that can be purchased online. Within the "Articles" section, you will find a table of contents with various subjects from choosing a childbirth method to managing motherhood to dealing with parent conferences; articles typically range from 1–7 pages in length. "Forum" presents interactive discussions between readers; many articles are also linked to these forums to encourage discussions about the article's topic. The publisher includes his "Editorial" opinion in the last option.

Evaluation:

Disorganization and lack of direction plague this site. Articles can only be accessed in a rambling list of headlines. Although the information contained within the articles was interesting and informative, busy parents will most likely get irritated at the random nature of the table of contents. For example, an article on getting baby to sleep is followed by an article on Cincinnati's private schools followed by surfing the Internet. The Forums follow a similar structure. An attractive novelty of this site is its offering an article and then inviting readers to comment on the article's contents via an open forum discussion. However, these forums suffer from a similar malady as found in Articles—a running list of contributors' titles which often give no clue to the contents of the forum ("HELP ME!!!," "Yelling," etc.). Although forum input is divided into general discussion classifications and age breakdowns, the list at some point will become unwieldy ("Terrible Twos" contained 29 dialogues at our visit). Want to know "all about kids"? Try elsewhere.

Where To Find/Buy:

On the Internet at the URL: http://www2.aak.com/aak/.

Internet URL:

http://www2.aak.com/aak/

Overall Rating

★

Information is useful for some but most likely can be found elsewhere with better ease

Design, Ease Of Use

★

Rambling list of titles for both articles and discussion topics; no site map to guide you

1–4 Stars; N/R = Not Rated

Media Type:
Internet

Principal Subject:
Gaining An Overview: All-Inclusive

Age Group:
All Ages (0–5)

Overall Rating

★

This site lacks interest and purpose

Design, Ease Of Use

★

Amateurish layout is distracting, as are the typos; no graphics except for the logo

1–4 Stars; N/R = Not Rated

Media Type:
Internet

Principal Subject:
Gaining An Overview:
All-Inclusive

Age Group:
Infants (0–1)

BABY AND CHILD PLACE (THE)
Where Parents Can Go To Find Everything They Want To Help Care For Their Children

Description:

Various options are presented at this site's homepage. Pertinent topics are entitled: "Passionate About Parenting," "On the Fire," "Net Nurse," "Your Section: Parents' Articles and Comments," along with online baby pictures you may view or you can submit your own baby's picture. "Passionate About Parenting" is a new feature to this site in which an author writes weekly on a given topic, e.g. "Quality and Quantity," a half page of advice to parents about giving time to their child, written by the editor/publisher of *Nurturing Magazine*. "On the Fire" offers one the chance to submit questions and responses, or read responses to questions already posed to the site; currently 7 questions are listed. "Net Nurse" consists of advice about common everyday questions one might have concerning one's child, e.g. "What is that stuff in my baby's eyes?" written by a nurse with a disclaimer to seek medical attention if symptoms arise. "Your Section . . ." includes advice and suggestions by parents on various subjects ranging from eating dinner to discipline to teething.

Evaluation:

Due to its amateurish layout and content, visitors to this site will spend far too much time figuring out where they're going and what they're reading than it's worth. Even if the site improves its design in the future, there isn't much content to help hold it together. It desperately needs direction, purpose, and an underlying premise. Parents want sincere answers, not pat responses (on how to have "A healthy, happy and active baby": "while your baby is asleep for about 3–4 hours, you have all this time for yourself . . ."). Parents want helpful advice, not cliches ("One of the most important ways to be a good parent is to be there . . ."). In summary, parents need to spend their precious time with other resources.

Where To Find/Buy:

On the Internet at the URL: http://www.babyplace.com/.

Internet URL:

http://www.babyplace.com/

BABY BAG
The In-Site To Parenting: Prenatal To Preschool

Description:

The creators of this website have divided it into two separate parts—"Our Departments" and "Interactive." Within the first part, you may select from various options ranging from pregnancy information to parenting tips. Articles included about pregnancy ranged from birth stories, baby shower games, and baby shopping lists to overcoming fertility, exercise, and doulas. Information returned generally amounted to several pages of dense text (sometimes tempered with graphics) written by a variety of professionals; for "overcoming infertility," 5 pages were provided by a writer for the FDA Consumer. Within the site's "Interactive" segment are various means for parents to communicate with one another. Bulletin boards are provided and are organized into a general category with 8 specific categories ("parents over 30," "single parents," "feeding," etc.). Birth announcements, birth stories, shopping opportunities, and more are also provided. Within this segment, you may also "Ask the Professional" (a pharmacist, a childbirth educator, a midwife, a home base employment specialist).

Evaluation:

Parents-to-be and new parents want information and advice and this site attempts to address those needs. However, the problem we found with this site lies in its randomness. For example, you won't find general information under the category "Pregnancy" just a list focusing on specific concerns ("ultrasound videos for entertainment"; "umbilical cord blood . . .", etc.); this may or may not meet your needs. Information returned from this list wasn't written for the site's audience—parents—but instead are simply research articles. Most parenting websites offer chat rooms and bulletin boards. At first glance, we were thrilled to note that this site's bulletin board segment was sub-categorized making it easier for parents to find each other. But the conversational summaries given were vague and difficult to decipher, once again signaling the unrefined nature of this site. The range of "professionals" was an interesting choice; too bad a pediatrician wasn't also included. The information found here is adequate, the bulletin boards are active. We recommend, however, that you try on other sites before you set your sights on this one.

Where To Find/Buy:

On the Internet at the URL: http://www.babybag.com/.

Internet URL:

http://www.babybag.com/

Overall Rating
★
Includes info about specific concerns of pregnancy, childbirth, etc.

Design, Ease Of Use
★
Site design, bulletin board forums are random; information not written for its audience

1–4 Stars; N/R = Not Rated

Media Type:
Internet

Principal Subject:
Gaining An Overview: All-Inclusive

Age Group:
All Ages (0–5)

Overall Rating

★

A variety of info is available but not easily accessed

Design, Ease Of Use

★

No information can be clearly printed, graphics are absent, discussion groups inactive

1–4 Stars; N/R = Not Rated

Media Type:
Internet

Principal Subject:
Gaining An Overview: All-Inclusive

Age Group:
All Ages (0–5)

DAILY PARENT

Description:

Consisting of articles distributed by various writers and professionals of Scripps Howard News Service, this site offers 4 options at their homepage: "Shop," "Boards," "Write," and "Topic Finder." Their sister site, Internet Baby, is accessed through the "Shop" option giving one information on various baby supplies and equipment, their prices, etc. Seven parenting forums are available through the "Boards" including "the expectant parent," "new parents," "working parents," and more; the subtopic "informed parents" here includes discussion groups for newborns, the first year, toddlers, school-age children, and so on up to adult children. "Write" allows one to send email to the site. The site's most recent articles are headlined on the homepage with their suggestion to use the "Topic Finder" to view their "complete collection of parenting and family features." This feature accesses a drop-down alphabetical list of 118+ topics from allergies to working parents with accompanying articles about selected subjects.

Evaluation:

The visitor to this site can only be amazed when accessing its lengthy topic list. The information offered in the articles provides good, direct advice along with examples of real-life situations and suggested ways of using that advice. But that's where the excitement ends. First of all the drop-down list of topics is cumbersome and awkward. It needs to be better organized into smaller distinct categories ("Health Concerns," "Discipline Problems," etc.). But the main problem is that no information uncovered here can be printed. Also, the discussion forums also seem nicely laid-out at first glance, but upon further research one discovers that the chats are relatively inactive compared to other sites. In short, this site's problem can be summed up with one word: disorganized. One can certainly find clearer routes to wanted information at other sites.

Where To Find/Buy:

On the Internet at the URL: http://www.dailyparent.com/.

Internet URL:

http://www.dailyparent.com/

MADELEINE'S WORLD
A Child's Journey From Birth To Age Three

Description:

The author, a father of two daughters, has written this biography to record the growth of his daughter, Madeleine, as she progress from being an infant to a three year old. Divided into three parts with numerous chapters within each, he uses humor, observation, and developmental information to chart his daughter's developmental milestones. This 262 page novel also includes a bibliography list of "Madeleine's Books." No table of contents or index are included.

Evaluation:

Novel approach, yes, but easily read, not necessarily. This novel is written in three parts and one might assume each part pertains to one year of Madeleine's development, but this isn't so. It would have been perhaps mundane, but more useful, to have chapters that pertained to each month of a child's life. Even though children develop at different rates, this would have improved the reader's ability to hunt for a particular phase. Certainly entertaining at times, Hall's style is overly doting and precious as he writes about his daughter's motives. His writing aptly expresses the wonderment he senses from his daughter as she learns about the world around her. He also sprinkles developmental information within the confines of this journalistic work. This is a cute way to introduce parents to how children develop, but unfortunately a bit too cute at times, giving the reader the sense that the author is too close to his subject to be impartial. This one is not great for a quick or seasoned view of infant and child development, but good for parents who are looking for a model on how to record their own child's development.

Where To Find/Buy:

Bookstores and libraries.

Overall Rating
★
Author uses the medium of a novel to record his daughter's growth from infancy to age 3

Design, Ease Of Use
★
No way to reference this novel; chapters related to child's age would have been helpful

---

1–4 Stars; N/R = Not Rated

Media Type:
Print

Price:
$20.00

Principal Subject:
Gaining An Overview: All-Inclusive

Age Group:
Infants & Toddlers (0–3)

ISBN:
0395870593

Edition Reviewed:
1997

Publisher:
Houghton Mifflin

Author/Editor:
Brian Hall

About The Author:
(From Cover Notes)
Hall has written two novels, two nonfiction books, and articles for various magazines. He lives in upstate New York with his wife and two daughters.

INDEXES

TITLE INDEX

AUTHOR INDEX

PUBLISHER INDEX

SUBJECT INDEX
1–4 Stars (4 = Best), N/R = Not Rated

Growth & Learning: Behavior & Discipline

Growth & Learning: Sibling Relationships

Growth & Learning: Toilet Training

Growth & Learning: Age-Appropriate Activities

Growth & Learning: Choosing A Preschool

Growth & Learning: Special Circumstances

Growth & Learning: All-Inclusive

Parent-To-Parent Advice & Forums

Gaining An Overview: All-Inclusive

AGE GROUP INDEX

MEDIA INDEX

Internet

CD-ROM

Online Service

Videotape

Audiotape

APPENDICES

VI

SUPPORT ORGANIZATIONS & OTHER RESOURCES

Many of the resources we've reviewed include contact information on support groups, associations, and other organizations. On the pages that follow, we've listed a number of these organizations, grouped by the principal focus of their work, using subject classifications we've used for this guidebook. You'll find that many of these organizations can further refer you to other local, regional, or national organizations that may offer you additional benefits or aspects of support that meet your needs.

The support groups, associations, and other organizations which follow are listed alphabetically within the following groups:

Care

American Council Of Nanny Schools
(517) 686-9417

American Podiatric Medical Association
Publishes brochure on caring for children's feet
9312 Old Georgetown Rd.
Bethesda, MD 20814
(800) FOOTCARE

Association For The Care Of Children's Health
7910 Woodmont Ave., Suite 300
Bethesda, MD 20814
(301) 654-6549

Association Of Sleep Disorders Center (The)
P. O. Box 2604
Del Mar, CA 92014
(619) 755-6556

Asthma & Allergy Foundation—Consumer Information Line
1125 15th Street NW, Suite 502
Washington, D.C. 20005
(800) 7-ASTHMA

Au Pair Care
1 Post Street, Suite 700
San Francisco, CA 94104
OR:
17 Neperan Rd.
Tarrytown-on-Hudson, NY 10591
(800) 428-7247

Au Pair In America
102 Greenwich Ave.
Greenwich, Connecticut 06830
(800) 727-2437

Au Pair Programme USA
36 South State, Suite 3000
Salt Lake City, UT 84111
(801) 727-2437

Careteam
Through a program called Fragile, they offer pediatric specialty
home nursing for high-risk infants and children
(800) 275-7513

Child Care Action Campaign
330 Seventh Ave., 17th Floor
New York, NY 10001
(212) 239-0138

Child Care Aware
(800) 424-2246

Consumer Product Safety Commission
Establishes and monitors safety standards for children's products;
provides safety information and lists of recalled products
Publication Request
Washington, D.C. 20207
(800) 638-CPSC
http://www.cpsc.gov

Cystic Fibrosis Foundation
6931 Arlington Rd., #200
Bethesda, MD 20814
(800) FIGHT-CF
http://www.cff.org

Epilepsy Foundation Of America
4351 Garden City Drive
Landover, MD 20785
(800) 332-1000
http://www.efa.org

Euraupair
250 N. Coast Hwy.
Laguna Beach, CA 92651
(800) 333-3804

Intensive Caring Unlimited
910 Bent Lane
Philadelphia, PA 19118
(215) 233-6994

International Lactation Consultants Association (ILCA)
201 Brown Ave.
Evanston, IL 60202-3601
(708) 260-8874

International Nanny Association (The)
900 Haddon Ave., Suite 438
Collingswood, NJ 08108
(609) 858-0808

Juvenile Diabetes Association
  432 Park Avenue South
  New York, NY 10016
  (800) 223-1138
  http://wwwjdfcure.com

La Leche League
  9616 Minneapolis Ave.
  P. O. Box 1209
  Franklin Park, IL 60131-8209
  (312) 455-7730

National Alliance For Breastfeeding Advocacy
  Office Of Educational Services
  254 Conant Road
  Weston, MA 02193
  (617) 893-3553
  MarshaLact@aol.com

National Association for Family Child Care (NAFCC)
  NAFCC Accreditation
  P. O. Box 161489
  Fort Worth, TX 76161

National Association Of Child Care Resources And Referral
  Agencies
  2116 Campus Drive SE
  Rochester, MN 55904
  (507) 287-2020, (202) 393-5501

National Child Care Information Center
  243 Church Street NW, 2nd floor
  Vienna, VA 22180
  (800) 616-2242

National Safe Kids Campaign (The)
  Provides publications on child safety and childproofing
  111 Michigan Avenue NW
  Washington, D.C. 20010
  (202) 662-0600
  http://www.safekids.org

National Sleep Foundation
  122 S. Robertson Blvd., #201
  Los Angeles, CA 90048
  (213) 288-0466

Nursing Mother's Council
2509 NE Thompson
Portland, OR 97212
(503) 293-0661, (415) 591-6688

Sickle Cell Disease Association Of America
200 Corporate Point, Suite 495
Culver City, CA 90230
(800) 421-8453

Trustline Registry
(800) 822-8490

Women's Bureau
United States Department of Labor
Women's Bureau Clearing House
Box EX
200 Constitution Ave. NW
Washington, D.C. 20210
(800) 827-5335

World Learning/Au Pair/Homestay USA
1015 15th Street NW, Suite 750
Washington, D.C. 20005
(202) 408-5380

Growth & Learning

American Reading Council (The)
45 John Street, Suite 811
New York, NY 10038

Association For Childhood Education International
11501 Georgia Ave., Suite 312
Wheaton, MD 20902
(800) 423-3563, (301) 942-2443

Association of Waldorf Schools of North America
3911 Bannister Rd.
Fair Oaks, CA 95628
(916) 961-0927

Center For Parent Education (The)
2 day institute presented by Dr. Burton White that provides a
grounding in "sound child development understanding."
55 Chapel Street
Newton, Massachusetts 02160

Children And Adults With Attention Deficit Disorder (CHADD)
    499 NW 70th Ave., Suite 308
    Plantation, FL 33317
    (800) 233-4050, (305) 587-3700, (954) 587-3700
    http://www.chadd.org/

Learning Disabilities Association Of America
    4156 Library Rd.
    Pittsburgh, PA 15234
    (412) 341-1515

National Academy Of Early Childhood Programs
    1834 Connecticut Ave. NW
    Washington, D.C. 20009

National Center For Learning Disabilities (NCLD)
    381 Park Avenue, Suite 1420
    New York, NY 10016
    (212) 454-7510

Orton Dyslexia Society
    Chester Building, Suite 382
    8600 LaSalle Rd.
    Baltimore, MD 21286-2044
    (410) 296-0232
    http://ODS.org

Parent Cooperative Preschools International
    P. O. Box 90410
    Indianapolis, IN 46290-0410
    (317) 849-0992

Parent-To-Parent Advice & Forums

Depression After Delivery
    P. O. Box 1282
    Morrisville, PA 19067
    (215) 295-3994

Family Resources Coalition
    200 South Michigan, Suite 1520
    Chicago, IL 60604
    (312) 341-9361

Miss Mom/Mr. Mom
    535 Oliver Street
    Moab, UT 84532
    (801) 259-5090

MOPS International
P. O. Box 102200
Denver, CO 80250-2200
(800) 929-1287, (303) 733-5353, (888) 910-MOPS
info@MOPS.org
http://www.mops.org

Mothers At Home
8310-A Old Courthouse Rd.
Vienna, VA 22182
(800) 783-4666, (703) 827-5903

Mothers' Home Business Network
P. O. Box 423
East Meadow, NY 11554
(516) 997-7394

Parents Helping Parents
535 Race Street, Suite 140
San Jose, CA 95126
(408) 288-5010

Parents Without Partners (PWP)
8807 Colesville Rd.
Silver Spring, MD 20910
(800) 637-7974, (301) 588-9354

Single Mothers By Choice
P. O. Box 1642, Gracie Square Station
New York, NY 10028
(212) 988-0993

Women On Their Own
P. O. Box 1026
Willingboro, NJ 08046
(609) 871-1499

All-Inclusive

Adoptive Parent Association Of America (APAA)
P. O. Box 53
Sun City, CA 92586
OR:
P.O. Box 20726
Riverside, CA 92516

American Academy Of Pediatrics
   141 Northwest Point Blvd.
   P. O. Box 927
   Elk Grove Village, IL 60009-0927
   (800) 433-9016
   http://www.aap.org

American Red Cross
   431 18th Street NW
   Washington, D.C. 20006
   (202) 737-8300
   http://www.redcross.org

Birth To Three And Beyond
   3411 Willamette Street
   Eugene, OR 97405
   (503) 484-4401

Center For Study Of Multiple Birth
   339 East Superior Street
   Chicago, IL 60611
   (312) 266-9093

Child Welfare League Of America, Inc.
   440 First St. NW, Suite 310
   Washington, D.C. 20001-2085
   (202) 638-2952

ERIC Clearinghouse On Elementary And Early Childhood Education
   51 Gerty Drive
   Champaign, IL 61820-7469
   (800) 583-4135, (217) 333-1386
   ERICEECE@UIUC.edu

International Twins Association (ITA)
   6898 Channel Rd.
   Minneapolis, MN 55432
   (612) 571-3022, (612) 517-8910

National Association For The Education Of Young Children
   (NAEYC)
   1509 16th St. NW
   Washington, D.C. 20036-1826
   (800) 424-2460

National Organization Of Adolescent Pregnancy And Parenting
4421A East-West Highway
Bethesda, MD 20814
(301) 913-0378

National Organization Of Mothers Of Twins Clubs
5402 Amberwood Lane
Rockville, MD 20853

National Organization Of Single Mothers
P. O. Box 68
Midland, NC 28107-0068
(704) 888-KIDS

Parents Of Premature And High-Risk Infants, International
c/o National Self-Help Clearinghouse
24 West 43 Street, Room 620
New York, NY 10036
(212) 642-2944

Triplet Connection
P. O. Box 99571
Stockton, CA 95209
(209) 474-0885

Twin Services/Twinline
P. O. Box 10066
Berkeley, CA 94709
(510) 524-0863

Special Circumstances

American Academy Of Child And Adolescent Psychiatry
3615 Wisconsin Ave. NW
Washington, DC 20016-3007
(800) 333-7636, (202) 966-7300
http://www.aacap.org

American Psychiatric Association
(202) 682-6069

American Psychological Association
(202) 336-5700

Anxiety Disorders Association Of America
6000 Executive Blvd., #513
Rockville, MD 20852
(301) 231-9350

Childhelp, U.S.A. (also known as National Child Abuse Hotline)
(800) 422-4453

Council For Children With Behavioral Disorders
A division of Council for Exceptional Children.
1920 Association Dr.
Reston, VA 22091-1589
(703) 620-3660

Council For Exceptional Children
1920 Association Dr.
Reston, VA 22091-1589
(703) 620-3660

Federation For Children With Special Needs
95 Berkley Street, Suite 104
Boston, MA 02116
(617) 482-2915

Federation Of Families For Children's Mental Health
1021 Prince Street
Alexandria, VA 22314-2971
(703) 684-7710
http://www.ffcmh.org/

NAMI-Children And Adolescent Network
(703) 524-7600

National Alliance For The Mentally Ill (NAMI)
(800) 950-NAMI

National Center On Child Abuse And Neglect (The)
Department of Health and Human Services
P. O. Box 1182
Washington, DC 20013
(202) 245-0586

National Child Abuse Hotline
(800) 4-A-CHILD

National Committee For Prevention Of Child Abuse (The)
Prevent Child Abuse
P. O. Box 2866
Chicago, IL 60690
(312) 663-3520

National Council On Child Abuse And Family Violence
1155 Connecticut Ave. NW, Suite 400
Washington, D.C. 20036
(202) 429-6695, (800) 222-2000

National Depressive And Manic Depressive Association (NDMDA)
(800) 82N-DMDA

National Depressive And Manic-Depressive Association
730 N. Franklin St., Suite 501
Chicago, IL 60610-3526
(800) 826-3632, (312) 642-0049

National Institute Of Mental Health
Depression Awareness Campaign
(800) 421-4211

National Mental Health Association
1021 Prince Street
Alexandria, VA 22314-2971
(800) 969-NMHA, (703) 684-7722

Parents Anonymous Hotline
520 S. Lafayette Park, #316
Los Angeles, CA 90057
OR:
6733 S. Sepulveda, Suite 270
Los Angeles, CA 90045
(800) 421-0353

RESOURCE PATHWAYS, INC.

For every important issue we face in our lives, there are resources available to us that offer suggestions and help. Unfortunately, we don't always know where to find these sources of information. Often, we don't know very much about their quality, value, or relevance. In addition, we often don't know much about the issue we've encountered, and as a result don't really know where to begin our learning process.

Resource Pathways guidebooks help those doing research on important decisions or facing a challenging life-event by helping them find the information they need to understand the issues they face and make necessary decisions with confidence. Every guidebook we publish includes these important values:

- We review and rate **virtually all quality resources** available in any media (print, the Internet, CD-ROMs, software, and more).

- We define and **explain the different issues** that are typically encountered in dealing with each subject, and **classify each resource** we review according to its primary focus.

- We make a reasoned judgment about the quality of each resource, give it a **rating**, and decide whether or not a resource should be **recommended**. We select only the best as "Recommended" (roughly 1 in 4).

- We provide information on **where to buy or how to access** each resource, including ISBN numbers for print media and URL "addresses" for Internet websites.

- We publish a **new edition of each guidebook annually**, with updated reviews and recommendations.

Those who turn to Resource Pathways guidebooks will be able to locate the resource they need, saving time, money, and frustration as they research decisions and events having an important impact on their lives.

ABOUT THE EDITOR

Julie Soto, M.S., is a Parent Educator, a Family Life specialist, and mother of two grown children. Julie's career includes twenty years of experience in teaching parenting classes, teaching child development to college students, training professionals in the field of family support, designing parenting curriculum, and developing programs for families with young children. Since 1989, she has been Director of Parent Education at Bellevue Community College. Julie has presented parenting seminars locally in Washington and throughout the United States, with a recent focus on the subject of new brain research and its application to the first three years of a child's life. She is currently a member of the Family Resource Coalition of America, a member of the National Association for the Education of Young Children, a charter member of the Northwest Parent Education Network, and a member of the task force working on the new National Parent Education Network Organization. Her past professional appointments included Board member of the Family Resource Coalition of Washington State and President of the Organization for Parent Education in Washington Community and Technical Colleges. Julie is committed to empowering all families with the understanding that parenting is one of the most important jobs that one can have.

ORDER FORM

Order by phone: (800) 247-6553

Order by fax: (419) 281-6883

Order by mail: Complete order form and mail to:
Bookmasters, PO Box 388 (Dept. ITP), Ashland, OH 44805

Please send me:

Divorce: The Best Resources To Help You Survive
(ISBN 0-9653424-2-5)   _____ copies at $24.95 = _____

Having Children: The Best Resources To Help You Prepare
(ISBN 0-9653424-3-3)   _____ copies at $24.95 = _____

College Choice & Admissions: The Best Resources To Help You Get In
(ISBN 0-9653424-4-1)   _____ copies at $24.95 = _____

College Financial Aid: The Best Resources To Help You Find The Money
(ISBN 0-9653424-5-X)   _____ copies at $24.95 = _____

Anxiety & Depression: The Best Resources To Help You Cope
(ISBN 0-9653424-6-8)   _____ copies at $24.95 = _____

Graduate School: The Best Resources To Help You Choose, Get In, & Pay
(ISBN 0-9653424-7-6)   _____ copies at $24.95 = _____

Infants, Toddlers, & Preschoolers: The Best Resources To Help You Parent
(ISBN 0-9653424-8-4)   _____ copies at $24.95 = _____

($3.95 for first copy; $1.00 per copy for additional copies)   Shipping & Handling = _____

Total = _____

Payment enclosed   ☐ Check (Make payable to Resource Pathways)

Charge my credit card   ☐ Visa   ☐ MasterCard   ☐ AMEX

Account Number _____ Exp Date _____

Signature _____

Name (please print) _____

Organization _____ Title _____

Address _____

City _____ State _____ Zip _____

Resource Pathways, Inc.

c/o Bookmasters

P.O. Box 388 (Dept. ITP)

Ashland, OH 44805